Total Commitment

Total Commitment

Yosef Almogi

Translated from the Hebrew by Ted Gorelick

A Herzl Press Publication

New York • Cornwall Books • London

Cornwall Books
4 Cornwall Drive
East Brunswick, NJ 08816

Cornwall Books
27 Chancery Lane
London WC2A 1NF, England

Cornwall Books
Toronto M5E 1A7, Canada

Herzl Press
515 Park Avenue
New York, New York 10022

Library of Congress Cataloging in Publication Data

Almogi, Yosef.
  Total commitment.

  Translation of: Be-'ovi ha-ḳorah.
  Includes index.
  1. Almogi, Yosef. 2. Statesmen—Israel—Biography.
3. Israel—Politics and government. 4. Haifa (Isfael)—
Politics and government. 5. Labor and laboring classes—
Israel—Haifa. I. Title.
DS126.6.A493A3213   956.94'04'0924   81-70146
ISBN 0-8453-4749-7   AACR2

Printed in the United States of America

Contents

Foreword

Israel will never know a generation similar to that which Yosef Almogi portrays in these pages. In a few decades the Jewish people passed through its deepest anguish and achieved its highest goal. The European holocaust and the rise of an independent State of Israel are the two extremities of an emotional journey more dramatic and vivid than any that our nation has ever traversed. The land and the people are small in material dimensions, but they loom large in the general human experience, and they engage the mind and conscience of mankind with a particular intensity.

Yosef Almogi has followed this drama from a central vantage point. The Israeli Labor movement began its career on the margin of Jewish history, growing from humble beginnings to a commanding rule. It created social forms and human textures of startling originality and showed a rare talent for solving difficulties by the exercise of a passionate force of will. In a single generation the world passed from a situation in which the existence of an independent State of Israel seemed inconceivable to one that seemed inconceivable without it.

One of the components of this arduous enterprise was a group of men unlike the normal mold of political leaders. Pioneering Zionism established a brilliant gallery of spokesmen and thinkers who knew how to unite ideas with action and to translate freedom into creative growth. With these leaders, and especially with David Ben-Gurion, Yosef Almogi lived and worked in intimate partnership. As a Labor leader feared for his tenacity and perseverance, he led the workers of the port city of Haifa to a position of strength and pride that has remained fundamentally intact to this day. As the secretary of a ruling party, he became a force, sometimes for revolt, but usually for conciliation, in a society striving for cohesion in an epoch of war and turmoil.

As a cabinet minister under four prime minsters, he participated in decisions with grave bearing on issues of peace and war, of security and national recuperation. He was always an "organization man," seeking to influence events not so much by publicized individual thrusts as by the gentle but solid power of dynamic teamwork. In managing the municipal affairs of a growing city or the relations of Israel with its Jewish kinsmen abroad, he displayed an essentially ecumenical temperament. He sought compromise, harmony, reconciliation, unity, and mutual forbearance. These have not been the dominant qualities of the Jewish people in its turbulent history, and Israel has reason to be grateful to those who transcended its conflicts and diversities by constant reference to unifying human principles.

Yosef Almogi tells the story of his struggles much as he lived them—with energy, conviction, and patience, but without rancor or prejudice. The reader will feel the storm and tension behind the serene rhythm of his narrative. Almogi does not obtrude his own personality with excessive zeal, and he therefore gives us a clear vision of his field of action. With all its difficulties and imperfections, Israel emerges from his portrayal as an affirmative expression of human and social values—a continuing hope nourished by continuing achievement.

ABBA EBAN

Total Commitment

1
Zionism: Early Bee in My Bonnet

In July 1960 I was appointed to lead a Knesset delegation to the British Parliament. Our group was made up of representatives of the leading political parties in the Israeli legislature. We were accompanied by Knesset Secretary Moshe Rosetti who, before coming to Israel from England had been parliamentary agent on behalf of the Jewish Agency (the representative body of the Jewish Community in Palestine to the British Mandatory government).

After a ceremonious reception by our British colleagues, we had the opportunity to observe the mother of parliaments in session. As I watched the proceedings in the House of Commons, I could hardly help being deeply impressed by the orderly way in which British parliamentarians went about the job. The speeches were brief and to the point and were spoken without benefit of notes. The questions put to the speakers were of a kind to promote exchanges of views between members of Parliament and ministers of state.

We were taken on a tour of a number of provincial towns, after which there was to be a formal leave-taking. A farewell party was arranged for us at the speaker's table in Parliament. Protocol required that we wear formal evening clothes—a variety of costume unlikely, in those days, to have made its way into the wardrobe of any self-respecting member of the Knesset, where an ordinary suit and tie were rarely seen even on festive occasions and short-sleeved shirts with collars open at the neck were the accepted mode of dress. This simplicity of dress among members of Knesset reflected the Labor Zionist ideal of working-class egalitarianism—a spirit that dominated the history of modern Jewish Palestine and the early years of the State of Israel. All of which is to say that none of the delegation had packed a tuxedo! It was a near certainty that none of our company had ever owned one. But the wonderfully energetic Mr. Rosetti came to our rescue and provided each of us with rented evening clothes. And to top it all, he even managed to find time in his busy schedule to prepare a pretty parting speech in English for me.

So, dressed to the nines and feeling sheepish in our black suits, we went out for our last engagement in England.

We entered a hall that to us, accustomed to the severity of Israeli architecture, seemed incomparably elegant, with its rich antique furnishings made lustrous in the candlelight. Never had we seen such pomp. And the illustrious company that received us was in every way a match for the setting. Among the guests were my old friend Lord Herbert Morrison and Lord Herbert Samuel—respectively, the co-author of the Morrison-Grady Plan and the first British high commissioner of Palistine. Lord Samuel was then about ninety, but still fit and intellectually as sharp as ever. He was still, as in the old days, very much interested in everything connected with Israel.

At the end of the dinner, after the Speaker of Parliament and Lord Morrison had had their say, it was my turn to speak. In an access of self-confidence inspired by the friendliness shown to our delegation throughout the evening, I decided to chance a few impromptu words of my own before reading from the prepared text. I put aside for a moment the speech Mr. Rosetti had composed for me and begged leave to tell a short autobiographical anecdote before giving my formal address. It went something like this:

> In a remote provincial town in Poland, about four decades ago, there lived a Jewish lad named Yosef Krelenboim, who dreamed of the establishment of a Jewish state. And then the extraordinary news reached him that a Jew had been made high commissioner of Palestine. The boy's imagination took wing, and he knew no rest until he himself was able to reach the Promised Land, there to work its soil and keep it from harm and defend it from its enemies. And now, here, seated at my left, is the very man who was that high commissioner; and beside him the same Jewish boy from Poland, who today appears before you as a representative of the Jewish parliament of an independent State of Israel.

The applause at the end of my introduction was gratifyingly enthusiastic. I then read the text of my prepared speech. When the evening came to a close, the aged Lord Samuel approached me and thanked me warmly for what I had said. He was visibly moved.

For myself, I had been wholly sincere and unpremeditated in what I said. Seeing Herbert Samuel at the leave-taking banquet I could not help remembering the day in 1920 when my father came home and told us the news of the appointment of a Jewish high commissioner in Eretz Israel—the Land of Israel. He told us how the high commissioner had gone on foot to the Old City of Jerusalem to take part in Sabbath prayer at the venerable Hurbah Synagogue, how he had been honored by being called up to read the blessings before and after the lesson from the Prophets, and how he had chanted the portion from Isaiah, "Comfort ye, comfort ye my people, saith your God." I still recall the thrill I felt hearing my father tell the story. From then on I knew that I was a Zionist, that I had to go to Eretz Israel and help build a home for my people.

Some years later another event in Eretz Israel exerted a decisive influence on me. Toward the end of 1928, when I was eighteen or so, I joined a group of young people from Labor Zionist youth movements who were taking part in a

Zionist pioneer-training program. The aim of such training programs—collectively called *hakhshara* ("preparation") in Hebrew—was to prepare young Jews for settlement in Israel. Jewish young men and women, most of whom had never worked with their hands, were trained for manual labor in the factory and on the farm in anticipation of the kind of work they would be called on to do in Palestine. But *hakhshara* was more than merely a job-training program: it addressed itself to the whole person and aimed at nothing less than the creation of a Zionist pioneer-laborer type—a *halutz*. Through it young candidates for settlement in Eretz Israel were molded, morally no less than practically, for living and working in a collective community; they were taught the principles of Zionist ideology and the history and geography of the Holy Land. Just as important, they were taught to use their ancient national tongue, Hebrew, as a medium of routine communication for the first time since biblical days, rather than to reserve it only for prayer.

Joining the program was the first practical step I had taken toward settling in Israel. Some months after I had joined, the Arab anti-Jewish riots of 1929 broke out in Palestine.

News of the riots stunned us all. The details were horrifying. Forty-five Jews were killed and wounded in the Upper Galilee town of Safed, long the seat of Jewish religious learning; sixty-eight men, women, and children were butchered in Hebron in the Judean hills, most of them members of the town's old religious community, whose origins in Hebron went back many hundreds of years.

For me there was one small bright spot in the whole dark business, one consolation, however slight. The Hagana, the Jewish underground defense organization in Palestine, had hurled itself into action to defend Jewish homes and communities against the fury of the rioters. Jews had organized themselves before in their own defense in the Diaspora; they had even done so recently and with notable success in Russia. But this was different—the Hagana was the beginning of a national army. Jews had banded together in an armed military body to defend themselves *on their own soil.*

I had nurtured the ambition to live in Eretz Israel for years, and by joining the training program I had put myself on the road to realizing my goal. The events of 1929 settled matters for me once and for all: I would leave for the land of my fathers at the first opportunity.

One memory of violence haunts me from the country of my birth—my fight with the Russian. It happened while I was on the training program. I was nineteen, tall, and seemingly robust, although I was actually much weaker physically than I looked. My *hakhshara* group was working at a sawmill in a small town near the Russian border. It was hard work, and we had stiff competition on the job from émigré Russian workers, "Whites" who had fled from Communist Russia. They were burly men, used to hard manual labor, and confirmed anti-Semites.

One morning I found myself face to face with one of the Russians: he was huge, and his eyes were bloodshot from drink. He demanded that I turn over to him the cart I was using to haul lumber to the mill. Without the cart I couldn't work, so I refused. He leered wickedly and then, without warning, brought his great paw of a hand down hard on the nape of my neck.

I struck back immediately, hitting him full in the face with my fist. No sooner had he reeled back than his friends came running to the rescue. Fists began to fly as a brawl broke out between Russians and Jews. These were Jews of a kind the Russians had never before encountered—Jews who were unafraid, who would defend their honor at all cost.

The crack of a rifle shot fired by the foreman (who, incidentally, was Jewish, as was the mill owner) brought the melee to an abrupt end. But I was singled out as a troublemaker, and under the pretext of wanting to avoid further incidents of violence, the management asked me to leave. I refused and insisted on my right to remain on the job with my comrades. My stubbornness paid off, and I was allowed to stay on.

As I've said, I was a Zionist well before I began training to become a *halutz*. On this subject I knew my mind before I had even reached my teens. Like many Jewish youngsters in my home town, I had devoured the works of the great founders and theoreticians of Labor Zionism: Ber Borochov, Chaim Zhitlovsky, and Nachman Syrkin. All of them spoke of the anomaly of Jewish life in the Diaspora; each insisted on the necessity of righting the inverted Jewish socioeconomic pyramid, to make it stand firmly on its base rather than allow it to remain precariously poised on its apex. Instead of remaining a nation of merchants and shopkeepers, Jews must contrive—so they argued and we believed—to become a nation of laborers and farmers capable of building their future in their own land. As a result I and my contemporaries began to dream of a Jewish state in which we would live as a free people, rather than as a persecuted or, at best, tolerated minority amid the Gentiles. We realized that giving as good as we got when attacked by our persecutors was not enough. Jews had already learned that they could do that and that this worked as far as it went. But what was needed was a fundamental and permanent resolution to the problem.

My opinion was strengthened by living examples. One of my own relatives, the late Meir Hoffman (d. 1978), a founding member of Kibbutz Shefayim, was a special source of inspiration to me. "Meytshe," as he was affectionately known among family and friends, had just come home after completing his studies in Russia. He immediately made his mark by breathing new life into the Zionist movement in Hrubieszów. The overwhelming majority of our town's population was Jewish—seven thousand out of a total of eleven thousand residents. So that Hrubieszów contained a considerable reservoir of potential Zionists—a situation Meytsche was quick to exploit in behalf of the cause. He established a local branch of the socialist Zionist youth movement Dror (also called *Freiheit,* in Yiddish). It had been founded in Russia before the World War I, had gone underground after the Bolsheviks took power, and had finally moved its headquarters to Poland.

A remarkable person, Meytshe was easy to admire. I suppose he was also dear to me because he was related to me through my mother, who had died when I was very young. The Hoffmans, my mother's kin, were a large family with excellent Zionist credentials, and they were decimated by the Germans during the occupation of Poland in World War II. Among the survivors were those who, like Meytshe, came to Palestine as pioneers before the outbreak of the war.

Another part of the family, who had left earlier, had settled in the United States, and some had gone on to Canada. In recent years their children have started coming to Israel to settle, and I hope to see the elder Hoffmans in Israel soon, too. It would round out perfectly the Zionist odyssey of one Jewish family.

When Meytshe set about establishing a branch of Dror in Hrubieszów, the movement was engaged in a bitter ideological battle within the Jewish community. The battle occurred on two fronts simultaneously. On one side were the Communists and their ally on this one issue, the radical left-wing Jewish nationalist labor party called Bund, which was anti-Zionist and had as its slogan "Nationhood without Statehood." On the other side was Agudat Israel, the organization of ultra-Orthodox Jews who, on strictly religious grounds, were utterly opposed to political Zionism.

I was fourteen when I joined Dror, and very soon I was one of our branch's most active members. Dror shared the goal of all Zionists—to establish a Jewish homeland in Palestine—but it was also a Labor Zionist movement concerned with the social character that a Jewish entity should have. Simply put, it wished to build an egalitarian, socialist society in Zion, and it therefore took a strong populist line. It worked among poor Jewish youth, whom it sought to enlist in its ranks. One of my own special activities in the movement was to teach reading and writing to the children of underprivileged Jewish families in Hrubieszów.

By now I had committed myself wholly to the pioneering ideal of manual labor, and I felt strongly enough about it to want to put my values into immediate practice. And so, in the company of my friend Abraham Ziegel (later director of the Absorption Department of the Jewish Agency in Israel), I approached the Municipal Department of Road Construction in Hrubieszów to ask if they would take us on as laborers. I think we were both a little surprised when they actually hired us. But *surprise* is a weak word to describe the effect that seeing us paving roads alongside Gentile laborers had on the Jews of Hrubieszów—or on our families! Our parents couldn't bear either the sight or the thought of it, and they quickly arranged things at the municipality so that we would be fired. And, to be frank, neither of us was sorry; paving roads was not easy.

My father gave me no encouragement in my Zionist activities, not to speak of my plans to pull up stakes and leave for Palestine. He was a pious Jew, a Hasid, and a devoted follower of the Belzer rebbe. He believed that the redemption of the Jewish people was a matter to be left for God to accomplish in His own good time—by the coming of the Messiah. So there was just no point in mankind precipitously anticipating divine providence. Better for me, he thought, to stop dreaming about making deserts bloom in a far-off wild country and stay home where I belonged helping my brother Jacob tend the family store, a cloth and sewing accessory shop from which the family drew a respectable income. The shop was located in the town marketplace, and it positively hummed with customers. It did so well, in fact, that in time my father was able to open a second shop in Wladimir, some sixty miles distant from Hrubieszów, and leave the first store to be managed by my elder brother and my sister Rachel.

My mother had died when I was four years old, and my father did not remarry until I left home for Israel. He carried the whole burden of my upbringing alone, and he made certain that I had a strictly Orthodox upbringing. When I reached the age of four, Father, following the custom of Hasidic Jews when a male child comes of school age, wrapped me in a prayer shawl and brought me to the *heder*—the traditional Jewish religious elementary school. Still—and in this he deviated somewhat from the pattern of most very Orthodox parents—he saw to it that I also received a secular education. But by the time I was fourteen and had fulfilled the reqirements of the law of compulsory education in Poland, my schooling was over. Everything I have learned since then I learned on my own.

On my own I read hungrily, ravenously—in Yiddish, in Polish, and, later, in Hebrew. I devoured every book that came my way, along with political pamphlets (how they flourished in that period!) of all the parties active in the Jewish community: the Bund, the Communists, and the Zionists. I read them all. And as I read, I grew intellectually more confident in my beliefs, and was not above letting my opponents have a sharp rejoinder even when they were my elders and deserving of respect.

I remember one such occasion. Father asked me to accompany him to a neighboring town to welcome the rebbe of Belz on his arrival in our district, and to please father, I agreed to go. The reception took place on a Saturday evening, after the service marking the end of the Sabbath, and the rebbe's disciples crowded into one of the small vestry rooms of the synagogue to wish him a "good week." There, too, were *klezmers*, musicians playing a medley of cheerful tunes. The gathering was warming up, and I was standing next to my father when the rebbe's wife appeared. As she threaded her way among the guests, greeting them, her eyes lighted on me. She gave my cheek an affectionate pinch, and with a kindly twinkle asked: "And where are your *peyes*, child?" She was referring to my missing side-curls, whose absence was an unmistakable breach of Orthodox Jewish custom. Father blushed in embarrassment.

But I, self-confident as only a young man preening himself on his intellectual superiority can be, had my answer ready, although it was only a catchphrase I had picked up from one of the political pamphlets I had been reading: "Better a Jew and no *peyes* than *peyes* and no Jew!" I said defiantly. The rebbetzn took my rejoinder in stride and, far from becoming angry, even appeared to agree with a small reservation, that I had a point. "Child, you're right," she said," but *peyes* wouldn't hurt."

My father was greatly relieved that the episode had ended without a scandal.

As time passed, my estrangement from the life I knew in Hrubieszów, from my home town itself, kept growing. All my thoughts, all my hopes, were bent toward one and only one goal—Eretz Israel.

My feelings were shared by everyone in the *hakhshara* group. And when news of the Arab riots came, we acted. We called a meeting and decided, then and there, to schedule our immigration for an earlier date than had been planned. No! there would be no delay. We would demand our certificates for immediate immigration to Palestine!

I returned to Hrubieszów to get ready for the journey.

My father was greatly opposed to my going. He tried very hard to dissuade me. But when he saw that I wouldn't be moved and that my decision was final, he generously offered to finance the trip.

Some of my friends were less fortunate—poorer would be a better word. They couldn't scrape together the money to go. We decided to send one of the group to go around to the neighboring towns and raise the funds for our passage. I was chosen because it was felt that it would be more appropriate for someone who was himself not in need to do the asking.

I traveled from one Jewish community to another, called meetings of the local Jews, and convinced them to contribute money for my poorer comrades.

At these gatherings I met Jews who had already been to Palestine and, unable to stand up to the harsh conditions there, had returned to Poland. *Yordim* is what they would have been called had they left Israel in more recent times. The word is very old in Hebrew and comes from the Bible. It means literally "those who go down": one descended, "went down," into Egypt and went "up" to the Land of Israel. In the main, these expressions had to do with the topography of the area and with direction—like "downtown" and "uptown" in English today. But in Jewish tradition the words took on a definite moral connotation, and to leave Eretz Israel came to mean a spiritual descent, a "going down" from holy ground. In a way the same meaning has attached itself to the expression as used in modern Israel, where *yordim* is more than the neutral term used to describe those who leave the country; it implies, in addition, "deserters."

In all events, I found that these *yordim* were suffering from feelings of guilt for not having stuck it out. It was perhaps the reason for their being so helpful in assisting me to raise the money for our own "going up" to the Land of Israel.

Returning to Hrubieszów one day from an out-of-town fund-raising meeting, I found one of my close friends from the movement waiting for me at the train station.

"Listen, Yoske," he said, "we've got a problem. It looks like you've got to get married!" He handed me a telegram. It read: "YOSEF,—REPORT BACK IM-MEDIATELY TO BIALYSTOCK TO MARRY AVIVA. FAMILY WAITING. IF NOT GIRL IN TROUBLE." It was signed by the secretary of my *hakhshara* group.

My friend gave me time to take in the contents. Then he added: "Oh, and by the way, your sister-in-law's worried! She says for me to get you down to my place so we can all sit down and figure out how to get you out of this mess."

He was laughing by now. We were both laughing, I as much from relief as from the humor of the situation. My poor, sweet, innocent sister-in-law had never heard of that well-established institution among pioneer candidates, the fictitious marriage. She was worrying about a shotgun wedding when all that was involved was one last routine assignment from the movement before I left for Palestine.

The movement had its ways of getting around the restrictions being set by the British on Jewish immigration to Palestine. One was to exploit a loophole in the law: marriages were arranged between young men who had certificates for entry to Palestine and young women who lacked them, thereby qualifying the girls to settle in the country as wives of immigrants. The couples underwent formal divorces immediately on arrival and went their separate ways. In my case, even the fictitious marriage was canceled, and when I went to Palestine, it was as a bachelor.

At last, in January 1930, the great moment arrived. All the Zionist parties active in Hrubieszów got together for a farewell party in the town cinema. There were speeches in our honor, and I spoke in the name of my group and thanked particularly those who had worked to bring Zionism to Hrubieszów. The following day, when we arrived at the railway station—nine very excited young men— many of the Jews of Hrubieszów were gathered there to see us off. My brother Jacob was there too, and when I boarded the train, he joined me and rode along with me to the next town, Zamoscz, a journey lasting an hour and a half.

As we rode together Jacob offered me a rather large sum of money, just in case I would have to come back from Palestine and needed to buy a ticket. "You're just not strong enough to rough it out there, Yossele," he said kindly. I knew my brother was being genuinely solicitous for my well-being, and I loved him all the more for it. But I couldn't accept the money. It would have been like admitting defeat before I even started.

The train was bound for Warsaw; this was the first leg of our journey. We rode until morning the next day, and throughout that day and night we kept our spirits up singing songs of Zion—some of them old and looking back with yearning, others new and filled with hope.

The singing helped ease the pain of leaving. I knew I would never return to Hrubieszów, and I had a premonition that I would not see my family or friends ever again.

In 1933, my brother Jacob was getting ready to come with his family to Palestine. As he was making preparations to leave Poland, the Polish government put a ban on taking assets out of the country, and he canceled his plans. Neither he nor any of his family survived the Holocaust.

At daybreak we pulled into Warsaw.

I became acquainted there with a whole crowd of eager young pioneers, all of them waiting for their immigration certificates. I also met some of the leaders of the Zionist youth movements active in Poland. One of them was Pinhas Koslowsky—the man who, under the hebraized name Sapir, would one day be Israel's finance minister. But even in those days in Warsaw he had already found his calling: by the time I first met him, he was already headquarters treasurer of Hehalutz, the youth organization affiliated with the General Federation of Labor of Eretz Israel, known as the Histadrut. Already in his salad days, he was a dynamic fellow who was liked by everyone.

At the end of January we traveled by rail to the Italian port of Trieste. There were now sixty young pioneers in the group that boarded the Greek vessel *Helena,* bound for Palestine.

A week later we were riding at anchor off the coast of Eretz Israel and looking out at the ancient port of Jaffa.

2
Kibbutz and Hagana

We came ashore and were welcomed by agents of the Kibbutz Meuhad organization of collective settlements. They took us first to Tel Aviv, for a short breather, and then on to the place that was to be our new home, a recently established kibbutz called Hakovesh, "The Conqueror." The implied conquest was of the land in Kfar Saba.

I was in no doubt at all then that my place was in a kibbutz—a collective-farm settlement. It seemed to me the perfect embodiment of Labor Zionist ideals. Nor had I the least hesitation about which of the three movements in the country— Hever Hakvutzot, Kibbutz Artzi or Kibbutz Meuhad—I should be a part of. It had to be the Kibbutz Meuhad ("Unitd Kibbutz"), the association of kibbutz settlements affiliated with the moderate Socialist-Zionist Mapai Workers' Party.

Of the three movements, the Kibbutz Meuhad was the most dynamic and the best prepared for the great task that lay ahead for Zionism. The Meuhad was just as committed as the others to social and economic collectivism, but it was more broadly based than its sister organizations. Its understanding of the importance of mass immigration in the Zionist enterprise had led it to make the establishment of large settlements and their rapid expansion a corner stone of its policy. So it seemed clear to me that the Kibbutz Meuhad was capable of providing the kind of social and economic framework in which the masses of indigent young idealists now streaming into Palestine could hope to realize their dream of creating an egalitarian, socialist Jewish state.

When we arrived at Kibbutz Hakovesh we were given time to rest up and settle in. Then we were assigned jobs.

I was assigned to work on a citrus plantation near Tel Mond. There I was handed a formidable-looking broad-bladed hoe that goes by the Arabic name of *turiya*. The *turiya* is not one of your ordinary, light gardener's hoes, but a stout, heavy, multipurpose agricultural tool used for actual tilling—serious digging and furrowing. In Palestine, where farming was still largely done by hand, the *turiya* was the farm worker's principal tool, and a murderous it was, too, on the back and shoulders and on the heart.

All the same, we young pioneers took to working with it with an enthusiasm born of our agrarian idealism and regard for labor. We even had our own pet Hebrew name for it, *kinor* the "fiddle" because the back-and-forth movements involved in working with it reminded us of the sawing motions a violinist makes with the bow.

I went to work with a will. I just had to succeed; for wasn't manual labor what the Zionist revolution was all about? Besides, it was the one way a member of a collective settlement earned the privilege of his membership.

Getting used to the work was difficult for me. It took almost everything I had. I tried my utmost to conceal the toll the back-breaking work was taking on me. I summoned every ounce of physical and mental reserves I possessed. Just living together with the members of my commune—being with them—gave me much of the emotional strength I needed to persevere, and working under the appraising eyes of the other plantation laborers also stiffened my will to succeed.

I made it. The citrus groves became my natural element. I spent the summers harrowing the ground between the long lines of citrus trees, weeding, hollowing out the soil around the tree trunks and watering the trees. In the winter, I carried the hulking crates of harvested fruit to the carpenter's shop and then lugged them over to the warehouse.

One searing summer's day, as I was "fiddling" with my *turiya* among the citrus trees, I looked up to see the plantation work boss watching me. He was on horseback and wearing one of those tropical pith helmets with the broad brims that colonial Europeans used to wear. He asked me my name and when I had arrived in Palestine. When I told him, he asked, "And how long do you expect you'll last as a plantation hand?"

I didn't quite get his drift and immediately sailed into a set speech. I declaimed about "the joy of labor," "putting the reverse pyramid on its base," "building the homeland," and so on. All the while Joseph Berger, the work boss, sat at his ease in the saddle and indulgently looked on as I harangued him. When I wound down at last, he said gently, "Well, son, you'd better slow down a bit in that case and save your strength, because it looks like you've got plenty of work waiting for you."

I ignored his advice and went back to fiddling up a storm. In a short time I had the reputation of a first-class hand. The plantation owners in Kfar Saba who hired kibbutzniks to work in their groves began insisting on my being included in their work gangs.

I met Pinhas Sapir again. He was working in the plantations at Kfar Saba too, but not as a member of a kibbutz. I also became close to Joseph Bancover, who was then one of the leaders of Kibbutz Hakovesh. My friendship with him, too, was to last many years.

Neither of them was exactly a paragon of labor. They spent most of their time in the groves talking politics, and if their *turiyas* ever swung into action, it was only when they raised them to make a point. I would just keep on working and in a short time leave them far behind, still deep in their discussion.

In Kfar Saba I also became acquainted with Moshe Droyan, who was a planter well known throughout the country. He was a fruit packer as well, and in those days a fruit packer was a man of considerable status in the plantation community. His pay was high by the standards of the time, and among agricultural workers fruit packers were part of the labor aristocracy. It was a coveted job, and fruit packers were generally the sons of the plantation owners. In any case Droyan had taken a shine to me because of my work, and he initiated me into the secrets of the trade by teaching me how to select, wrap and crate fruit.

After six months of plantation work, I was elected to the Kibbutz secretariat, the governing body of the kibbutz. At about the same time I joined the Hagana. Evenings, after putting in a full day's hard work, I underwent Hagana training. After a short while, I was accepted into the Hagana noncommissioned-officer course. I was the youngest trainee in the course and had the distinction, as well, of being the group's "greenhorn," just off the boat.

I can still remember my NCO training. We were taught to handle a mind-boggling variety of weapons of diverse provenance. The Hagana arsenal was unhomogeneous to say the least and consisted of every conceivable make of hand weapon, each of which had to be mastered. The lack of weapons uniformity enormously complicated the job of the Hagana both in training its men and, operationally, in the field, but it was a situation dictated by the conditions of purchasing arms. The Hagana simply had to use whatever gun or grenade came to hand.

There were rifles in a great variety of makes, although we used sticks in field exercises. There were three pistols: the Steier, Parabellum, and Mauser. At the end of the course, we had to be able to break each kind of weapon down and put it together again blindfolded. We also learned how to handle the clumsy but effective German machine gun, the "Schwartzlose."

There were also two types of hand grenade. One was produced in the Hagana's secret workshops; the other was an English make we learned to fire from grenade-launchers attached to the rifle. This last was our "light artillery." For the "heavy stuff" we relied on a two-inch mortar, another weapon of home manufacture.

All in all things were going along smoothly, and I was pleased. Then I hit my first snag. The Kibbutz Meuhad was asking for volunteers to work at Sodom, the site of one of the notorious Cities of the Plain upon which God had rained fire and brimstone. It was now the location of a promising new enterprise for the extraction of potash from the Dead Sea. The kibbutzniks were asked to lend a hand to the young men already on the job there.

Nothing suited me better. I rushed to put my name down on the list of candidates. I was thirsty for new experiences, and I felt I could do with seeing a bit of the country after being cooped up in so small and tame a corner of it for so long.

Nothing at a kibbutz is decided without the agreement of all the members, and this includes whether a volunteer, even for the most noble undertaking, should be allowed to go. So before the elections that were to decide who would go to Sodom, I made the rounds of my comrades, asking for their support. I got many promises and thought I was a shoo-in. I was in for a shock.

On the day of the election an overwhelming majority of the members voted against my being sent. I had expected to get the vote of at least those friends who shared a table with me in the kibbutz mess (it was called the "rabbi's table" because of all of the good cheer and loud singing that went on there at meal-times, which made everyone think of Saturday night dinners among Orthodox Jews). But not one of my boon companions voted for me.

Their reason was that I was such a good worker that the kibbutz just couldn't do without me, not even for a short time.

Eventually the kibbutz did let me go as a volunteer, not to the Dead Sea, but somewhere just as good, if not better—the Upper Galilee. This was the northern frontier of Zionist pioneering, the march land of Jewish settlement in Eretz Israel. I was put down for Kfar Giladi and Tel Hai, names that were already legend in the short history of modern Jewish Palestine. The kibbutz sent a girl with me, Shifra Weinblat, whom I would soon marry. Together we set up house in Tel Hai.

Tel Hai! To a Zionist the very name evokes images like those once conjured up in the imaginations of Americans when the Alamo was mentioned or in the minds of Englishmen when they heard tell of the "thin red line." It was in defense of this tiny settlement that Joseph Trumpeldor, the revolutionary genius of pioneer Labor Zionism, fell on the eleventh day of the Jewish month of Adar (March) 1920 while leading a handful of Galileen Jews against the on-slaught of the Arab army sent by Damascas to conquer northern Palestine. The Battle of Tel Hai was inseparably bound up with the beginnings of the widescale organization of Jewish self-defense in Eretz Israel. To this day, Israelis com-memorate the event by annual pilgrimages to the settlement.

Kfar Giladi has the distinction of being among the earliest kibbutz settlements, and there I met some of the original settlers of Tel Hai. These were the people who had actually fought at Trumpeldor's side. I had already heard and read so much about these people, and I had come to know their stories by heart when I was still in Poland. They were the men and women of the Second Aliyah, the pre–World War I wave of Jewish immigrants who were part of the heroic dawn of Zionist settlement in Palestine.

I came to know the men—Nahum Hurewitz, Eliezer Kraol, and Kayleh Giladi—who had been in on the making of the organization of settlement guards called Hashomer ("The Watchman"), which led to the creation of the Hagana. Meeting them I recalled those wonderfully romantic photographs of Hashomer sentinels that were circulated in Europe when I was a boy: manly, bearded figures in Circassian costume, on horseback; woolly astrakhan hats askew, chests criss-crossed by bandoliers, long rifles cradled in their arms. It was a boy's dream come true.

I became close with the tall and courtly Eliezer Kraol; his son and I worked together at planting. I drew close as well to Gideon ("Geda") Shochat, the son of Israel Shochat, yet another founder and leader of Hashomer. And I remember the lovely evenings at Kfar Giladi—the hallooing bark of jackals, the soothing whisper of the waterfall nearby, the cool and crystal air, Saturday nights in the barn.

A few months later I returned to the kibbutz. Shifra did not come with me; she had gone to study at the Women's Agricultural School in Nahalal, in the Jezreel Valley.

Back at Hakovesh, I became involved in the political life of the kibbutz and of Kfar Saba. At meetings of the Histadrut—the General Federation of Labor—in Kfar Saba, younger members were beginning to play a prominent role. Among them were Pinhas Sapir and Reuben Shari (Shreibman); both would soon be holding important posts in the World Zionist Organization.

Those were the early days of the Mapai Workers' Party. It had come into existence only in 1930 as a result of a merger between the moderate left Zionist-Socialist party Ahdut Avoda ("United Labor") and Hapoel Hatzair ("The Young Worker"), a non-Marxist labor party. Seen from the perspective of today, the ideological differences that had been keeping the two groups apart, despite a decade of cooperation in founding and running the Histadrut, seem utterly trifling.

Near Hakovesh, in Magdiel, there was a kibbutz group belonging to the Marxist Hashomer Hatzair movement. Its leader was Aaron Cohen, the noted arabist and founder of Kibbutz Shaar Haamakim. Aaron Cohen never failed to leave the impress of his extraordinary mind and personality on the meetings of the Histadrut in Kfar Saba.

The atmosphere at these meetings was always charged with ideological tension. I remember particularly the meeting at which the great Zionist labor leader from Hapoel Hatzair and chief of the Political Department of the Jewish Agency, Dr. Chaim Arlosoroff, spoke. The gathering was at Magdiel and marked the May 1 labor holiday of 1932. That was only one year before Dr. Arlosoroff was shot dead as he strolled on the Tel Aviv seaside. The murder was believed at the time to be the work of right-wing Zionist-Revisionist gunmen, although the case against the suspects did not hold up in court.

Arlosoroff was the keynote speaker. His matter-of-fact speaking style contrasted starkly with the dramatic and emotionally laden kind of rhetoric we had grown accustomed to at political gatherings; in its own way it was impressive, but it was what he was saying that impressed me particularly. He talked of the grim fate that threatened German Jews in the event of a Nazi takeover in Germany. It didn't take long for Arlosoroff's forebodings to be confirmed.

After returning to the kibbutz, we all sat down to a May Day feast of potato pancakes, a special holiday treat. At the end of the meal, we all showed unmistakable signs of food poisoning—vomiting and violent stomach cramps. An older woman kibbutznik, who had come to us as a volunteer, died as a result. The cook had inadvertently put laundry powder into the pancake mix. A mistake that might have ended up as a kibbutz joke—once we had recuperated from our bellyaches—had, instead, resulted in tragedy. This occurred because of our innocence of the day-to-day routines of running a household. We were, many of us, the spoilt children of middle-class homes who had never had to do household chores. Then, too, we did not regard the domestic arts as coming under the heading of dignified labor. It was an attitude that was silly, but generally harmless. This time, however, we had paid dearly for it.

After a while I again began to feel the urge to get out into the world and experience something more than just what the kibbutz had to offer. I wanted to get away from being confined to a closed group, to be on my own for a change—to try the "solitary life," as we kibbutzniks called it. Others at the kibbutz—some of the boys I knew from back home—felt the same way.

It wasn't that being in the commune was bad. On the whole I liked the kibbutz way of life, and I wasn't eager to make money or accumulate private property. And I rather enjoyed the hard work. However, one thing at the kibbutz did bother me, very much. The principle of egalitarianism, the one principle that should have been inviolate at a commune, was being bent—and more than once to my disadvantage.

First, there had been the episode of the vote rejecting my candidacy for work at Sodom. And now there was the matter of the tractor. When the kibbutz received its first tractor, which was to be used to prepare the ground for the permanent site of our settlement at Ramat Hakovesh, I put in for the job of tractor driver. Once again a vote was taken at the kibbutz, and again my candidacy was rejected. And the grounds? "Yosef is so good with the *turiya* it would be a pity to waste him on a tractor, which, as everyone knows, doesn't require much effort to operate."

I had had it! The vote on the tractor had made a doubter of me. I saw that the harder and more devotedly I labored at the kibbutz the less chance I had of being given the kind of work which would interest me and from which I could learn. This wasn't reward for outstanding work, it was punishment—or, to put a fine point on it, exploitation of the better workers.

I Leave the Kibbutz

My mind was made up. I and three other members from my home town announced our intention to leave. Our decision came at a bad time for the Kibbutz. It was planting season, and I was an expert at transplanting saplings. The kibbutz secretary, Zalman Alperovitz, asked me to stay on for another couple of months so I could teach the technique to other members of Hakovesh. I agreed, and when the time came to leave, Zalman and I parted in friendship.

So we left—four young men without means. The first few months we lived together and worked in the citrus plantations in Kfar Saba. And then we all went our separate ways.

I decided to stay on in Kfar Saba, and I soon found myself in the middle of a labor struggle that engulfed all of Palestine and had vast political significance for the future of organized Jewish labor in the country. Laor relations between planters and farm workers had been satisfactory all along, but they soured suddenly after a group of Zeev Jabotinsky's followers showed up. These were members of the right-wing Zionist-Revisionist Party.

Jabotinsky had founded his party on ultra-nationalist grounds in opposition to the World Zionist Organization, then under the leadership of Dr. Chaim Weizmann. In time the Zionist-Revisionists turned to social and economic questions as well, favoring private interests and taking a militant position against organized labor. And now, after the publication of Jabotinsky's article "Yes, Smash Them!"

inciting his followers against the Histadrut, the Revisionists set out to destroy the Histadrut.

The result was that a Pandora's box of perils was opened, threatening not only the Jewish workingman in Palestine but the viability of the Jewish community there as a whole.

The Histadrut's Labor Exchange began to be bypassed by employers. As workers were hired in increasing numbers without the mediation of the Labor Exchange, a breach was opened through which cheap Arab labor poured in, displacing Jewish workingmen, especially in the citrus groves. At Kfar Saba the situation came to a head. The Jewish workers were up in arms.

We Histadrut men organized pickets around the groves to prevent Arab laborers from entering. I had to make certain that my involvement in these activities should not be too evident. Locally, I was one of the key men in the Hagana, and it wouldn't do to put the British on the scent of what was going on in the area. My being connected with both clandestine Jewish defense and the labor struggle was not unusual, however. The Hagana was closely affiliated with the Histadrut.

It was a long and hard struggle, and at issue were the very principles of Labor Zionism. The attack on the Labor Exchange, the guarantor of fair work distribution, was bad enough, but an even more serious issue was at stake than wage scales or organized labor. Nothing less than the social and ethical character of Jewish Palestine was involved. Labor Zionists were just as keenly concerned with the kind of Jewish society that should be established in Eretz Israel as with the need of creating one. Apart from the importance of creating a Jewish homeland, no principle was more fundamental to the theory and practice of Labor Zionism than the idea of Jewish labor. It lay at the heart of the Labor Zionist Ideal.

As a policy, it meant that Jewish enterprises in Palestine should employ Jewish workingmen. The policy had been devised not against Arabs, but for Jews. It aimed at creating a normally structured Jewish society based on a balanced economy. This could only be one built by Jews, Jews alone—not administered by Jews and built by Arabs. Labor Zionists were intent on preventing Eretz Israel from becoming like South Africa. It would have spelled doom for the Zionist undertaking, which was about the establishment of a Jewish national homeland and not a colonial outpost where a handful of Jewish planters and entrepreneurs would grow fat on cheap native labor.

The main arena of the struggle was the Jewish-owned citrus plantations; there the problem of the displacement of Jewish labor was most acute. The plantation owners argued that Arab laborers were more efficient and did the job for less money than Jews. They were adamant. No one, they said, was going to force them to pay Jewish workers to just hang around the plantation. The workers, too, dug in their heels.

The Mandatory government supported the planters and set all its agencies into motion to force an end to the strike. The British police went into action, breaking up strike demonstrations and jailing workers. The leaderships of the Histadrut and the Mapai party alerted the entire Jewish public in Palestine to the issues.

The battle was on, and Kfar Saba was one of the major fronts. Some of the most prominent figures in Eretz Israel arrived to help man the picket lines. Ben-Gurion and Berl Katznelson, men who had been instrumental in forming the Histadrut, came to Kfar Saba to stand with the strikers at the gates to the citrus groves. The great pioneers of modern Hebrew poetry, Chaim Nahman Bialik and Shaul Tchernichovsky, were there, too. They all came to make one important point to the whole country: Jewish labor was a fundamental, moral, Zionist imperative, and its defense was a duty all Zionists owed to their ideals.

My contribution to all this was helping to organize picketers from among the local farm workers and kibbutz members.

The strike was a long-drawn-out affair that lasted until the Arab riots began again in 1936. It was in fact the 1936–39 "Arab Revolt" (as it was styled by the British) that put an end to the hiring of Arab labor by Jewish employers.

Once again Kfar Saba became a front, this time in a shooting war. Now it was up to the Hagana to defend Jewish interests in Palestine.

The Hagana had been founded in 1920. At first it took the form of units organized by each Jewish community separately. When the Arab pogroms of 1929 took place—the very ones that had made me decide on immediate immigration to Palestine—it was recognized that an adequate defense of Jewish communities could not depend on the initiative of individual settlements. The scale of Arab violence was just too great. Communities then pooled their resources and Hagana organization became regional. Under the impact of the 1936–39 Arab Revolt, which released its armies of guerrillas against the Jews of Palestine, the Hagana became a countrywide underground army, recruiting most of the young Jews in Eretz Israel.

I had been an active member of the Hagana for some time in Kfar Saba, and with the new outbreak of violence, I found myself appointed the Hagana's commanding officer in Kfar Saba. My biggest headache was getting money for arms, and my worst bugbears on this account at the meetings of the Hagana headquarters in Kfar Saba were Grandpa Beilin, a resplendidly bearded old gentleman hailing from Russia, and my good friend Pinhas Sapir.

Whenever I would ask for a budget for guns, Beilin would insist that buying rifles and revolvers was only a waste of good money. What we really should do, he suggested, was to make up a batch of those homemade grenades and distribute them to the men; then if the attackers came up to our positions, all the boys had to do was shy a couple of the bombs at the rascals, and that would finish them. When I objected about the absurdity of Beilin's concept of military tactics, Sapir would chime in, saying, "Far be it from me to deny the fact that Yoske Krelenboim [meaning me] is a fine officer, but he doesn't know the meaning of money. . . ."

One night I invited Sapir out for a tour of inspection of Hagana emplacements in a plantation bordering on the Arab part of Kfar Saba. As we approached the position commanded by Arieh Klaper (Arieh Nir, who would later be commissioner of prisons in Israel), we heard the sound of gunfire coming from the Arab side. I knew we were out of range and in no particular danger, but I ordered Sapir to hit the ground and crawl with me to Kalper's emplacement, so we could take cover behind the sandbags. As the shots continued to crackle from the Arab side—the firing was still a long way off—I shouted to the men hold their fire until the enemy got close enough for a sure hit. "Remember, boys, every shell costs 2 mil" (just about the price of a glass of soda water), I added, making sure Sapir heard me. Sapir smiled knowingly and called me a "cheeky bastard," but I never heard him say another word about keeping expenses down.

My home was a frequent meeting place of Hagana commanders. Some of the participants in the staff consultations there were Hagana chiefs from national headquarters: Eliyahu Golomb, Dov Hoz, and Yosef Avidar. My wife, Shifra, did more than just pass around the refreshments during the meetings: she was an expert communications officer and maintained headquarters' contact with the men in the line.

Kfar Saba was a representative community of Jewish Palestine, and the ideological allegiances of its population ran the gamut of political views then current in the country. Like everywhere else in Eretz Israel, political loyalties often shifted as people groped for solutions to the problems of Jewish national self-determination.

Among the people I became especially friendly with were the Strelitz (Kalai) brothers, three splendid boys, each of whom was an important figure in the community. One of them was secretary of the local council, and another, Hanokh, was very active in the Hagana. Hanokh left the organization with a group of members who seceded in 1937 in protest against the Hagana's purely defensive strategy, and formed an independent armed underground movement under the aegis of the Zionist-Revisionist Party. The group was called the Irgun Zvaï Leumi (IZL) or National Military Organization, becoming known abroad simply as "The Irgun" and acquiring an international reputation under Menahem Begin's leadership. Hanokh became district commander of the Irgun in Tel Aviv.

Another Kfar Saba man who became known in the country was Tzvi Rosenblat, one of the Revisionist youths who was charged with the murder of Dr. Chaim Arlosoroff and later acquitted. If memory serves, it was I who trained Rosenblat to handle weapons.

Then there was Yehoshua Cohen. He became one of the heads of Lohamei Herut Yisrael (LHY)—Fighters for the Freedom of Israel—the "Stern Gang" as it became called internationally. This group broke with the Irgun when it called a truce in its war on the British Mandatory government at the outbreak of World War II. It became notorious for its advocacy of terrorist attacks against individuals. As for Yehoshua Cohen, he eventually became a member of David Ben-Gurion's kibbutz, Sde Boker, and one of Ben-Gurion's most constant and devoted friends.

During the period of the 1936–39 Arab riots and afterward, the Hagana's relations with armed Jewish extremist groups of the Right grew increasingly strained. The situation at Kfar Saba during the Arab Revolt came near to exploding when a group of men from the Irgun stole thirty rifles from the Hagana's arms cache there. Only the timely intercession of some of Kfar Saba's good citizens averted an armed clash that would have torn Kfar Saba apart, and echoed throughout the country.

3
Hapoel

On a winter's day in 1936, Yitzhak Ben-Aharon, then secretary of Tel Aviv's Labor Council, regional headquarters of the Histadrut, asked me to come down from Kfar Saba for a meeting at his office. I arrived to find Yosef Avidor and Shaul Avigur from Hagana High Command there for the meeting.

I was told that the Plugot Hapoel or "Worker Squads"—the Histadrut-sponsored association of youth sports clubs—would be expanding their operations in Tel Aviv, where they had only recently been activated. I was asked if I would mind coming to Tel Aviv for a few months and organizing the Squads.

That the Histadrut and the Hagana were represented on such a high level at this meeting indicated that I was not being asked to become the Labor federation's temporary director of sports in Tel Aviv. Plugot Hapoel was only nominally a young people's sports organization; its real function was to provide the Histadrut and the Hagana with reserve manpower for tasks vital to Jewish organized labor and defense. It was thought that my Histadrut and Hagana background, in combination with my status as a veteran member of Plugot Hapoel and its current executive head in the Sharon District, qualified me for the job of running the organization in Tel Aviv.

Then, too, the memory of the performance I had put on shortly before, at a Plugot Hapoel gathering, still lingered in the minds of the higher-ups in the Labor Zionist movement. I had led a company of Hagana officers from the Sharon District through a set of precision drill exercises; it was quite a show and was hugely enjoyed by the crowd. I decided I would take on the assignment, and Yosef Avidar explained at length what it would entail.

The Hapoel squads had been established by the Histadrut to serve as its defense force when tensions were mounting between organized labor and its opponents on the Right in the Jewish community in Palestine after the murder of Arlosoroff in the summer of 1933. The specific threat to labor came from groups that had been recruited from the Betar youth movement of the Zionist-Revisionist Party; and it began after Zeev Jabotinsky had taken publicly to advocate destroying the power of the Histadrut and breaking what he called the federation's "monopoly" over organized labor. The sight of the brown shirts being worn by Betar members raised unpleasant associations in the minds of many who were then following with alarm the rise to power of the extreme Right in Europe.

Labor's position was stated with explicit clarity in a meeting at Mapai head-quarters in 1934 by David Ben-Gurion, who was then secretary-general of the Histadrut:

> In this war against those assailing the Histadrut, none of the means that have been used by the labor movement either abroad or here at home are adequate. . . . We are being confronted by a force that will stop at no means in order to destroy the labor movement. . . .
> If that force of several hundred is not confronted by a well-disciplined force of several hundred of our own, then I do not believe that the strength of our membership, though it number in the thousands, will protect us on the day the fury is unleashed. . . . In our war with Betar it is impossible to rely merely upon moral preachment; we must confront them with an organized force of our own.

This is the background of the establishment of the Hapoel squads. They had been created to guard the meetings of the Histadrut and to defend Jewish labor, but they also became an instrument to implement the national goals of the organized Jewish community in Eretz Israel under the leadership of the labor movement. They helped protect the products of Eretz Israel so that nascent Jewish industry in Palestine had a chance to develop and thrive, they assisted the Hagana in bringing illegal Jewish immigrants past British blockades and in establishing new settlements; and they became a training ground for Hagana recruits.

I made the move from Kfar Saba to Tel Aviv and threw myself into the work of organizing the Hapoel groups, most of whose members we recruited from the youth movements and the trade unions. We began training them in exercises whose real purpose, military drill, was kept secret from British authorities by being disguised as part of a physical-fitness program. They were trained in close-order drill, crossing obstacle courses, quarterstaff fencing, close-quarter combat, and the use of small arms and grenades. We also tried to prepare them ideologically for the tasks that lay before them. We held group discussions about the struggle of democracy against its enemy on the Right that raged in the world outside; about the Schutzbund, the Austrian Social Democratic Party's defense organization, which was locked in desperate battle with the armed bands of the fascistic Heimwehr; and about the civil war in Spain, where the Republic was fighting for its life against a fascist insurgent army. This was the broad context of our attempts to understand the political struggles of Jewish Palestine and the functions and tasks of the Histadrut.

At the end of six months I felt that I had completed my assignment, and I asked to be relieved so I could return to Kfar Saba and be with my wife and my baby boy Yoram, who had just been born. The executive committee of Hapoel decided I be offered a choice of either remaining for another tour of duty in Tel Aviv or going to Haifa for three months, to help organize the Hapoel there. Kfar Saba, it seems, was out.

There was nothing I could, or would, do. This was the movement's verdict *(Din Ha-tuna)*, which in those days carried a moral force for Labor Zionists that swept away all personal considerations. It needed no coercive machinery for enforcement, but relied entirely on the devotion of movement members to the cause.

My choice was Haifa; it seemed to me the shortest route back to Kfar Saba. I was homesick. But I had another, more prosaic reason for wanting to get back. The family allowance I was receiving—which was determined by family size, according to the wage scales established by the Histadrut—was a bit thin, and I thought I could do far better in making ends meet if I went back and took up my work in the building trade once more.

Putting together the Hapoel groups in Haifa turned out to be a much easier job than in Tel Aviv. All I had to do was train two groups of instructors. They were a first-class group and managed on their own to set up Hapoel units at their places of work. During my work in Haifa I made the acquaintance of Yaakov Dori, then Hagana commander of the Haifa District and, later, first chief of staff of the Israel Defense Force (IDF).

Our membership increased rapidly. By the beginning of 1938, there were one thousand members, and in a short while our number had grown to eighteen hundred. On Jerusalem Street we put up a temporary two-story structure out of which the activities of our groups were directed. We were beginning to draw the attention of men in the upper echelons of the labor movement: Dov Hoz, Eliyahu Golomb, Zalman Aran, Zeev Sharef, and Yitzhak Sadeh began taking an interest in our doings. The Hapoel groups were becoming a real power in Haifa and a manpower pool of some importance to the Hagana. District Commander Dori was already demanding that the Hagana order me to remain in Haifa, and from time to time I found myself having to take evasive action to get out from under the pressure he was having put on me.

As a general rule, the Hapoel groups in Haifa were not involved in the struggles then rife between Right and Left political parties in the country. Another battle was raging in Palestine with an enemy that made no distinction among Zionist ideologies and regarded all Jews as fair game.

It was the height of the 1936–39 Arab riots, and the strain was beginning to show on settlements in the north, which were having problems maintaining their security. We decided to recruit volunteers from our ranks for guard duty in the northern communities, and we soon had four hundred signed up and ready to be posted.

Our men also took part in "Operation Stockade and Tower" *(Homa Umigdal)*— the campaign undertaken to establish border settlements with stockades and watchtowers, which were put up overnight under Hagana direction in defiance of British restrictions on Jewish settlement in the area and which were designed for defense against attack by Arab guerrilla bands.

The first job of this kind that we undertook was the establishment in March of 1938 of Kibbutz Hanita, which was the first Jewish settlement in the Western Galilee, near Lebanon. Several hundred of our lads left Haifa under Hagana convoy in the morning. By the end of the day, they had succeeded in pushing a road through to the site, hauling up the building materials and putting up the walls, tower, barracks, and all. Then, at the request of the settlers, a part of the crew remained behind at Hanita for a week.

Our links with the Hagana grew closer, and Hanita became the site of a special training program for instructors of Hapoel groups. The course was run by Moshe Carmel, a Hagana commander. When the British imposed a curfew, bringing activities to a standstill, Hgana command would have Hapoel squads carry out liaison work and participate in Hagana operations.

When the civil authorities of the Jewish community decided to flout the curfew, they would also use our men, who, at a word, would be out to rouse the population of Haifa for whatever undertaking was on at that moment. Sometime in April 1939, we received word that the British were getting ready to turn back a boatload of Jewish immigrants from the port of Haifa. The civil agencies of the community gave the order for a general strike and street demonstrations. Immediately Hapoel squads were on the street calling the people of Haifa out to demonstrate.

Tension in the city ran high. I received instructions from Hagana Intelligence, Shai, not to return home for a few nights because I might be slated for arrest. Abba Khoushi had been called down by the commander of British forces in Haifa and warned against using violent tactics.

The English general told Khoushi that, if it were up to him, he would not be driving Jews away from the shores of Palestine and that the British would be needing them soon enough in the war against Germany. But orders were orders. Then he added:

> Look here, I'm ready to remove all of my men and the British police from Hadar HaCarmel, and you can demonstrate there to your heart's content. I don't care in the least if those Blue Shirts of yours [the Hapoel groups] take over the streets—but for chrissake, man, *don't* come down to the harbor! If you do, it'll be a bloody three-way war between Arabs, British, and Jews!

In fact, a group of Revisionists—students from Haifa's technical college, the Technion—did attempt to lead some of the demonstrators down to the lower city, but members of Hapoel blocked their path and so averted what would have been a very violent episode.

4

Service in the British Army

When World War II broke out on September 1, 1939, I was shaken. I found no peace of mind. My routine of activity suddenly seemed trivial and terribly irrelevant. I waited for our leadership to call upon us to get into the war against the Nazis. And when Ben-Gurion proclaimed that we would fight Hitler as though there were no White Paper (the British White Paper of 1939 severely restricting Jewish immigration to Palestine for five years) and that we would fight the White Paper as though there were no Hitler, I felt he was talking good sense. For all that, I had no doubt about the order of priorities so far as I was concerned: as a Jew, one living in the Jewish homeland, my first duty was to join the war against the greatest evil our people had ever had to face.

In the early months of the war the British were in bad straits. Clearly, this was not going to be a short war, and the British were making a supreme effort to draw on the reservoir of able-bodied men throughout the British Empire for the long, hard pull ahead. The pool of men Jewish Palestine had to offer was very small, but it had the advantages of good quality and a high proportion of fit young men, whom the British were anxious to utilize.

Nevertheless, they refrained from approaching the Jewish Agency in the matter, lest it be thought they were retreating from the anti-Zionist policies they had just put into effect. To get around their predicament, they contacted individuals in the Jewish community to ask help in recruiting Jews with needed skills for service in the British armed forces. This measure was without success. Each time they were referred to the one representative recognized by the organized Jewish community in Palestine—the Jewish Agency.

Not to be outmaneuvered, the British took another tack. On the October 12, 1939, there appeared in the Hebrew press a notice of the British command announcing that Palestinian citizens would henceforth be admitted into the service branches of the British army—the supplies and medical corps and the Royal Engineers. The advertisement had an effect, and close to seven hundred young Jewish men enlisted in foreign units, even foregoing badges that would identify their nationality. Many enlisted because they thirsted for revenge against the

Germans, but not a few joined up because they were poor or out of jobs or just looking for adventure. They were to have a hard time of it in the army.

Next, the British created mixed units of Arabs and Jews lumped together under the heading Auxiliary Military Pioneer Corps (AMPC), whose duties would be to dig trenches and build fortifications along the front. Again, the British succeeded in attracting men to join up: some 450 Jews—most of them new arrivals in Eretz Israel, who had managed to get out from under the Nazi boot—enlisted in the first such unit, along with 250 Arabs. Both commissioned officers and sergeants were all British. The Jews in the AMPC found themselves in double difficulty: under pressure from their British officers, and from Arabs in the ranks.

The Jewish leadership in Palestine regarded enlistment in the AMPC with something less than enthusiasm. First, there was the matter of the men being deprived of any insignia identifying their nationality; then there was the fact that this was a detachment only of "hewers of wood and drawers of water"—coolies— and it did not bring the Jewish community of Eretz Israel a whit closer to its goal of joining in the war against the Nazi and Fascist foe under its own colors as an independent military unit.

I tensely followed the developments and waited impatiently for the moment to come when I could enlist. I knew I had to get into the war, but I was not going to let myself be swallowed up as an alien of unspecified nationality in some English company or be just another native in a colonial labor brigade.

At last, early in 1940, the moment came. The British secretary of war had announced the formation of companies of Palestinian Jews which would be attached to British brigades and would gradually come under the command of the Jewish volunteers who had enlisted in them. It was an important advance in the campaign of the Jews of Eretz Israel to establish an independent corps of their own. The Jewish Agency published a special proclamation announcing the victory and calling for volunteers to join the units, which would be serving in Israel and neighboring countries.

I decided I was going to be with the first group that volunteered. I could not agree with the line taken by those who were opposed to having Palestinian Jews enlist in the British armed services, and were arguing that it was, in effect, an agreement to drain the Jewish community in Eretz Israel of its young fighting men. To me it seemed that the whole of our survival in Eretz Israel depended on defeating Hitler and that we owed it to ourselves to put every ounce of strength we could deliver behind the Allied war effort. In addition, joining the British army would give us a boost in establishing a well-trained armed force of our own for our struggle with the Arabs, which was sure to resume, full scale, once the war was over. After our service with the AMPC, we would become the pioneers of such a force. This was why we kept demanding that the corps be classified as a fighting unit.

Ideologically, I had no doubts, but my decision to enlist put me in great difficulties in my private life. It meant I would have to leave my wife and baby to fend for themselves for who knew how long—perhaps I would never even return home. Or, if I did make it home, God only knew in what condition. Financially, all my wife could expect in my absence was the pitiful allowance the army disbursed to the families of servicemen.

But my wife Shifra knew me well enough to see that if I did not join up I would have no peace of mind. She understood what difficulties lay ahead of her, but she nevertheless agreed that I had to follow where my conscience led me, and she supported me in my decision.

Strong opposition to my enlistment came from another source—the Haifa leadership and, in particular, the people on the Labor Council, with Abba Khoushi at their head. With sympathy running high for enlistment throughout Jewish Palestine and the enthusiastic support the project had from the Jewish Agency, the attitude in Haifa was exceptional. But the men in Haifa were adamant. The work I was doing in the city was too important, they claimed, for them to consider doing without me. When their importunities to me fell on deaf ears, they turned to Moshe Shertok (later Sharett, Israel's prime minister) on the executive of the Jewish Agency—the man who oversaw the recruitment of volunteers—and demanded that he forbid me from joining up! Shertok would do no such thing. He himself had a young assistant in his office by the name of Yeshurun Shiff (later a senior officer in the Israel police), who had been doing vital work and had just volunteered, and Shertok was not going to stand in his way. "Besides," Shertok summed up, "if the volunteers to the British army include such men as Yitzhak Ben-Aharon and Joseph Bancover and others holding senior commands in the Hagana, I cannot make myself an obstacle to Krelenboim's enlisting."

In July, Hagana Commander in Chief Israel Galili instructed Ben-Aharon, Bancover and me that we would be the representatives of the Hagana—*Sokhnutniks* as we came popularly to be called in the British army. I was appointed coordinator of Hagana "secret command." The evening before our departure we were invited by Histadrut Secretary-General Yosef Shprintzak to the Executive Building, where we took emotional leave of him.

Our unit was made up of forty volunteers. When we reached camp the following day, I lined up the men in a column and, giving the order in Hebrew, marched them to command barracks. When the officer in charge of new recruits, a British colonel, came out to receive us, I handed over to him the command of our men, using Hebrew again. Harry Beilin, who was the Jewish Agency's liaison man with the British army, translated. The colonel, in turn passed us over to a British sergeant, under whose commands, rapped out in pure English, we pounded toward the first station on the way to our transformation into soldiers in His Imperial Majesty's Army. We were issued uniforms of the Pioneer Corps, and having got into them, we stood back and gaped at one another in utter amazement. The white suspenders were a particular difficulty until we could figure out how to get them over our shoulders properly so we could keep our trousers up.

After we were carefully instructed how to wear our caps and badges, polish our brass buttons until they gleamed, shine our boots till we could see ourselves in them, and wrap our puttees so they ended exactly two fingers' breadth beneath the kneecap, we were finally allowed to do some soldiering.

The drill exercises caused us no special difficulty; we had already had basic training in the Hagana. Many of us already knew the procedures and military etiquette of the British army, which we thought comical, but we kept our opinions of them strictly to ourselves. We were a good unit and well disciplined, and unlike many of the other recruits none of our group ever lost a Saturday leave. We easily learned to use the rifle (an art we had already mastered in the Hagana), the bayonet (here was something new), and the entrenching shovel; we were taught to put on the gas mask and to do a proper close-order drill in full gear.

We were quartered together in a large barracks—one of those still standing on the hills at Tsrifin. Every morning we rushed out for parade—clean shaven, perfectly appointed, and raring to go. Our English officers loved us.

Saturdays I regularly traveled to Kfar Saba, to which my wife and son had returned so they could be closer to Sarafand. During my leaves, friends brought me up to date on developments in Palestine.

At the end of basic training, everyone in our group received corporal's stripes—this at the intercession of Dov Hoz and Moshe Shertok, who had asked the British authorities to grant us officer's rank. They had intended for us to receive the rank of sergeant, but the English weren't prepared to go quite so far. Once we each received a unit to command, they promised, we would be made sergeants; but for the time being corporal would have to do. It was, in any case, a very respectable rank.

Yitzhak Ben-Aharon and some of the others from our group were sent to officers' training. Dov Hoz told me that I was up for the course too, but that first I would have to learn English. All the same, the English CO of Pioneer Battalion 606, to which I had been posted, gave me his word that by April 1941 I would be made an officer without having to go through the course. In the interim, I received the rank of company sergeant in the battalion; my main job was to get the unit ready to leave for Egypt. Pioneer Battalion 605, where another part of the *Sokhnutnik* group was serving, was already stationed somewhere along the Nile.

Egypt, Cyrenaica, Greece

We were granted a few days' furlough in December 1940, and then we boarded the train for Egypt. When we finally reached Camp Mina, on the desert sands near the pyramids, we set up house under field conditions and got to know the staff of battalion HQ. We set about trying to convince the English major, the CO of 606, to treat us like a unit of the line and got him to meet us halfway. He arranged things so we could do weapons training and battle drill.

We also wrangled permission to put up our own blue-and-white standard at the camp gate. In Cairo, which was not far off, we managed to find a pole and a flag, and then, standing in full-dress parade, next to the Union Jack we raised the Star of David. As our national colors rose so did the morale of our men. We watched with undisguised pride when non-Jewish units would pass in columns along the road opposite the entrance to our camp and salute our flag.

During our stay at Camp Mina, we contacted the Jewish community in Cairo. Joseph Bancover and I paid the chief rabbi a visit and met the community leaders. The men attended services at the synagogue, and the congregation arranged a reception for us to which we brought the British officers from battalion headquarters.

Our sojourn near Cairo was short. In a few weeks we were transferred to a military camp in the vicinity of Alexandria. There we made contact once more with the local Jewish community; among them there were some who had been to Palestine in the 1920s and 1930s. They were overjoyed to have the chance to speak Hebrew again.

In those days the Jews in Egypt felt quite secure and enjoyed a large degree of freedom. Not a few of the young in the community were undergoing training for settlement in Palestine. They were also experiencing great exhilaration at British advances in the Western Desert and the retreat of the Italian Army, but the reverses in that theater came soon enough.

In the meantime we, too, got the opportunity to take part in the British offensive. In the beginning of 1941 we were sent to the front in the Western Desert, near the Libyan border. Battalion 605 of the Pioneer Corps was already encamped there, after having been in the action that deprived the Italians of what was then called Cyrenaica. On our way we passed thousands of Italian POWs, looking very wretched as they were being sped toward Egypt. But, as we discovered, the war was not over yet!

When we reached Marsa Matruh, we came under attack by Italian aircraft, and got our first taste of what it meant to be under air bombardment. We had no antiaircraft guns, and all we could do was dig ourselves into the sand and hope for the best. We were lucky the Italian airmen had consistently rotten aim and never scored a hit. The desert was our worst enemy. Our tents couldn't hold up in the frequent desert sandstorms, and we were always having to get them up again. Being isolated in the middle of nowhere was infinitely harder on us than laying down the roadbed, which we found to be relatively easy work.

In the spring of 1941, my turn came at last for home leave. After what seemed an unending journey, the train pulled into the station at Lod (Lydda), where my wife and young son waited for me on the platform. It was a thrilling homecoming.

During my leave I met some of the people from the Histadrut and Hapoel in Haifa, who reported that enlistment in town had not gotten off to a flying start. I spoke at demonstrations of Haifa volunteers, organized to urge the public to join up. I brought greetings from our boys at the desert front, and told them that every new recruit from Eretz Israel increased our chances by that much to form a Jewish combat regiment that could wear its own insignia and fly its own colors in the British army.

I was invited to participate in a meeting of the Executive of the Jewish Agency in Jerusalem and reported there on the situation of the men in the Western Desert. Moshe Shertok, Yitzhak Grinboim, and Reuben Barkat (who headed our Soldiers' Welfare Committee and later became Speaker of the Knesset) followed attentively what I had to say and made note of our problems.

After only several days, I took leave of my family to begin the journey back to my unit. We were depressed: we had the feeling that this time our separation was going to last a very long time. Little Yoram, who hadn't reached his fourth birthday yet, wouldn't let go of me. The whole way back to Marsa Matruh I couldn't stop thinking about them.

It took me little time to get back into army routine. Days were spent working in the blistering desert heat, fighting only the sandstorms and choking on the dust. In the evening it was down to the sergeants' club, where Bancover and I stood drinks for the other ten sergeants in the Battalion. From time to time we were invited to the officers' mess. These occasions served to improve my English and my head for whiskey, the drinking of which became indispensable after a while, although I could never even aspire to the gargantuan capacity of the Englishmen.

Our time in the desert also drew to a close. The battalion returned to Alexandria, there to be put on the Australian destroyer *Perth* bound for Piraeus in Greece. Our not being English stood us to advantage with the Australians, who showed us special favor on board. When we reached the thronging port city we met up with Jewish soldiers from Palestine serving with other units, and we exchanged experiences and news with them. There, too, Yitzhak Ben-Aharon joined us. He had finished officers' training and had earned the rank of second lieutenant.

The battalion was put to work unloading guns and cargo at the harbor and getting equipment and supplies into good order and stowed away ashore. Whenever a consignment included whiskey or rum or tinned delicacies of any sort, the temptation was just too much for the boys. I soon found that ordinary disciplinary measures got me nowhere in stopping the pilferage. The hankering after food and drink was just too great. So I decided to "socialize" the thieving. I called my men together and put it to them, in the strongest terms, that henceforth I would not permit more than one man, a larcenist of proved and conspicuous merit, to steal in the whole unit's behalf; the loot would be distributed fair and square among all the men. The soldiers agreed to the system, and after that our platoon had all others on the dock beaten, hands down, at the job of getting the freight off the ships.

The Greeks treated us kindly, although their circumstances were hard. Their economy was in shambles, their currency worthless. The streets were filled with hundreds of wounded and crippled victims of the Italian invasion of October 1940.

There was also a fifth column of Nazi sympathizers at work propagandizing for the Germans. They added to the troubles of the Jewish community, which had become desperately impoverished. We tried to help the Jews as much as we could, but what we had to give them did not go very far. When Passover eve neared we decided to invite them to our holiday seder, but the celebration never took place.

A few days before—on April 6, 1941—the Germans joined their Italian allies to invade Greece once more. The Luftwaffe bombed Athens and Piraeus—and our camp. Between raids, we continued to unload supplies and munitions for the

British troops, who were now reeling from the blitz the Germans had mounted from Yugoslavia and Bulgaria.

A German bomb scored a direct hit on a giant fuel-storage tank. It burst thunderously into flames, the burning fuel flowing into the sea and setting a nearby ship afire. The water around it was an inferno, and we on shore could hear the terrible screams of the men on board. There was no way we could reach them. Then we saw a ship hit a mine: it was tossed into the air, and it broke up before coming down. Our men and the Australians who were watching with us dived into the sea to pull out survivors.

Last Days of Greece

Things went from bad to worse. One morning orders came down from Brigade Command for two platoons led by an officer and two sergeants to secure a section of road along which Allied troops were withdrawing. There were reports that German commandos had been dropped behind our lines to cut off our retreat. Yitzhak Ben-Aharon asked for volunteers, and I and Sergeant Loebl (Professor Yehoshua Arieli of the Hebrew University) came forward. I asked my men for volunteers. To a man, the entire platoon stepped forward.

Joseph Bancover tried to dissuade us from taking the assignment. After all, this was a service corps, not a unit of the line. I disagreed. We could not demand to be treated as fighting men and then refuse to go out when there was fighting to be done. Bancover was unimpressed and warned that if the crunch came, the British wouldn't think twice about abandoning us, despite our having volunteered.

We set out in a convoy of military vans to Kalamata, where there was an arms depot we were supposed to guard. On the way we came under attack by German Stukas. They hurtled down on us repeatedly, strafing mercilessly each time. The air was filled with the banshee screams from the sirens of the diving aircraft and the chatter of their guns. Even the battle-tried Australians and New Zealanders wre finding the experience unsettling.

We took warning from the assault, and from then on we moved only by night. With lights out we made our way gingerly along bad roads until reaching a small port city where a British ship evacuating troops was riding anchor. We asked to be taken on board, but were turned down and forced to go on to Kalamata. The Germans had advanced at a terrific pace: in two weeks they had become masters of Greece. Kalamata was the major point of embarkation out of which Allied armed forces were being evacuated to Crete and other safe harbors.

On reaching the outskirts of Kalamata, we got down from our trucks and continued on foot in two columns, along both sides of the coastal road. Sorties of enemy dive-bombers were now swooping down and raking us with their machine guns with appalling frequency.

During one such attack I threw myself down for cover next to a low stone wall at the edge of the road. Another soldier, a Cypriot, took cover on the other side. He was shrieking in terror, and his hysterical yammering—on top of the earsplitting screams of the Stukas overhead—became too much for me. I ran for a grove of medlars nearby. When the planes had gone, I picked some fruit from the trees and pushed them into my haversack.

Back on the road, I made out Ben-Aharon with a group of soldiers standing some way off. I saw that they were agitated, and I walked toward them. When they saw me they broke into cheers and slapped me on the back. Then I found out what it was all about. They had found a corpse riddled beyond recognition at the fence where I had taken cover. When I was missing at the head count, they assumed I was the dead man. But seeing me now stuffing myself with fruit, they could have no doubt that I was still very much alive and kicking. The dead soldier was the Cypriot.

We remained in the vicinity of Kalamata. Every evening we went down to the harbor in the hope that our turn for evacuation had come. There was unrelieved pandemonium. In the dark, under unremitting bombardment, a disorderly mob of panicked men jostled and swore as they were pushed aside by columns of fighting units that were being taken on the ships.

One evening, while enemy shells dropped around us, Ben-Aharon and I took rapid stock. Both of us were pulling everything we had in writing or that was printed out our pockets; all we allowed ourselves to keep were the pictures of our families.

On the April 29, German parachutists took possession of Kalamata and opened fire on the ships that were removing Allied troops. That evening a British officer formed a detachment of volunteers to attempt to recapture the town. In a valiant counterattack, they succeeded in reestablishing British control over part of the city and even took a number of the enemy prisoner. But it was too late. The battle had already been decided.

At three o'clock the next morning we were informed that the English brigadier had announced our surrender. Thousands of Allied soldiers were declared prisoners of war without even seeing their captors.

At 7:30 we had our first look at a German panzer trooper. One of the Jewish soldiers recognized him as a schoolmate who had attended the same high school in Vienna. And now there they were, jawing away in German as though they were friends. The sight was revolting. We passed the word down that all Palestinian Jews should speak only Hebrew; there was nothing to be gained from sucking up to the Germans. To raise morale I ordered my men out on parade and had a talk with them: they were to shave, stand straight, and keep up a soldierly appearance. Prisoners or not, discipline would be maintained for our own good.

On the way to the mustering point for POWs, I felt a bit envious of the British troops. They were stepping smartly and singing marching songs. We marched with them, triple file and with our backs straight, but we were sick at heart. Two of our boys had just ended their lives with their own bullets because of what they expected the Germans to do to them when it was discovered they were Jews. When I found out, I decided I would do everything I could to prevent this from happening again. We had been taken prisoner, but that did not mean we had to give up on survival.

Nevertheless, I brooded over the implications of what had happened to us.

Some of my comrades were saying that the British hadn't evacuated us because of their hostility to Jews; I thought that they had acted on the basis of the priorities imposed by conditions. There were British units as well that had not been evacuated. Still, I thought, they ought to have considered what Jews had in store for them at German hands. And then the full irony of what had happened to us came home to me. For it was exactly this eventuality that the British had pounced on when we were insisting on the right to form a combat unit: "Sorry," they said "but we can't oblige you. What if the Germans ever took you prisoner?" So here we were, noncombatant prisoners, while the British were sparing no effort to get their fighters out of harm's way!

But of this I said nothing. The main thing now was to keep a grip on myself and a level head. We would all need strong nerves for what was ahead.

5
Prisoners of War

On the way to the temporary internment station that the Germans had prepared for us in Kalamata, I began to assess things. I took the view that although we were in enemy hands our part in the war needn't be played out. We could continue our fight against the Nazis by different means. Our struggle would have to be indirect and it might be more difficult to wage, but we could still give a good account of ourselves. One thing was clear to me: we had to prove to the Germans that Jews from Palestine were prepared to defend their honor and the honor of all Jews, even if it cost us our lives. In the very worst case it would be a matter of kill and be killed: if it seemed to us the Germans were getting ready to kill us we wouldn't wait, but go for them first. In all circumstances, it was essential for us all to put on a brave show and behave in a manner that brought us honor as Jews and men. On no account must we let ourselves be humiliated.

I knew this would be difficult to achieve. Among the Jewish prisoners in our Palestinian unit—about fifteen hundred men—few, perhaps no more than 10 percent, were old settlers who knew Hebrew and had volunteered out of any real sense of commitment. The rest were a mixed group of immigrants, some mature men, some mere youngsters; some had joined for the adventure, others to get back at the Nazis. The question was whether we could succeed in imposing our authority on this unsorted lot of humanity and mold it into a coherent body ready for the struggle when called upon. I realized that our success would depend on the quality of leadership we ourselves could provide. After a few days of thinking matters through, I decided to devote myself to the task.

As we marched toward the internment station, I consulted with some of my fellow officers, and we passed three orders down the line. First, we would openly identify ourselves as Jewish soldiers from Palestine. Second, there would be no direct communication by any soldier with the enemy—all contacts with the Germans were to be through the representatives of the prisoners. Finally, only Hebrew would be used when speaking with Germans; anyone who did not know Hebrew would either be assisted by a translator or would keep his mouth shut.

We did not have long to wait before our policy was put to its first test. When we reached the site set aside for POWs in the center of Kalamata, a German officer came up and asked if any of us spoke German. No one said a word. Finally, Sergeant Loebl (Professor Arieli, that is) raised his hand. It was he whom we had appointed to act as our translator. The German ordered us to sit down and stay put. He then added matter-of-factly: "We'll make sausages out of you in Germany."

Night fell. Powerful searchlights flooded the crowded compound. We lay freezing on the ground; we had received neither food nor water. At dawn we were allowed to get up and move around. Some of the German sentries began to abuse prisoners, making no distinction between Jews and British. They ordered some of the soldiers to leave the grounds to search for food and then shot them and claimed they were trying to escape. Two of our own men were killed this way. It was on that same day—our first as prisoners of war—that we witnessed the extraordinary gallantry of the Greeks. At great risk to themselves they smuggled food to us through the barbed-wire fence which surrounded the compound, and they continued to supply us in this way for as long as we were kept in their country.

On May 2, 1941, we were taken by rail, in sealed boxcars, to the POW camp at Corinth. The train came to a halt at night a little under a mile from our destination and we were marched in a column the rest of the way. The guards were not above knocking us about a bit as we marched. The camp barracks were too small to house us all, so there were prisoners who had to bed down out-of-doors. We Palestinian Jews kept together, both indoors and out.

The next day we learned that there were about ten thousand prisoners of war interned at Corinth and that they were divided up into groups of one hundred, according to country of origin. The crowding and filth were overwhelming. Lack of space had driven many of the prisoners to dig themselves pits, which dotted the grounds of the compound. The men scuttled in and out of them like rats.

Fights broke out among the men over mere spoonfuls of soup and over the thickness of the broth. Not unexpectedly, the officers were suspected by the ranks of keeping the best of the rations for themselves. The Greeks would bring small amounts of bread and cheese and toss the food over so it fell near the wells; the hunger-maddened men threw themselves on the food and fought one another over crumbs. Seeing what was happening even to the best of us, I realized how little it took to make us lose our humanity. Later, when the stories of the behavior of Jews in German-erected ghettos and concentration camps began to come out, I recalled the conduct of the men in Corinth and wondered how anyone could expect civilians to show any more spirit than trained soldiers.

The Germans began to draw up lists of prisoners and interviewed us all. We were instructed to give them nothing but name, address, rank, and serial number—as prescribed by the Geneva Convention. We were worried that the men in our group who came from Germany would be in for it, but by keeping strictly to the orders we ourselves had issued, we managed to frustrate completely our captors' attempts to force additional information out of us.

There was a German corporal who once decided to scare us into submission. He called us all out and began to harangue us in real Nazi style about the fearful treatment being prepared for us in Germany. One of the men snapped to attention after the corporal had stopped for breath and asked if he would be allowed a question. Permission was granted and the man asked, "Is there anything worse than death?" The corporal fielded the question in straightforward Teutonic fashion and answered with a very definite "No!" At that our man said to him, "Then what the hell is all this palaver about? We're not afraid of you!" We could see the German's jaws drop. he sputtered, he boiled and then he turned on his heel and stomped off. With that it finally got through to our captors that we were unimpressed by their abuse, and they stopped threatening to have us shipped to the sausage factory.

One day SS chief Heinrich Himmler, with a large retinue of Nazi officers in train, put in an appearance at the camp. Himmler asked to see the senior man among the prisoners—a brigadier well advanced in years, who had been taken captive by the Germans once before, in the World War I. "Well," Himmler said, addressing the brigadier, "do you think the British are going to win the war this time too?" The Englishman drew himself up and answered, cool as you please, "Naturally!" "Fool!" Himmler shot back, and stalked off.

We received orders to get ready for transfer to Salonika. Commissioned officers were moved to another camp. I said good-bye to Ben-Aharon; it was the last I saw of him until the end of the war. We were crammed once more into those notorious boxcars. Part of the way we had to go on foot, since the bridges over which sections of the track ran had been bombed out. Some of our boys who knew the country and the language seized the opportunity to escape. The Germans imposed collective punishment on the men who shared vans with the escapees, but the punishment caused us no special grief. It only goaded us into gloating all the more openly to show the satisfaction we felt at having so many brave men among us.

When we reached Salonika we were put up in squalid barracks. We stayed there a month, packed like sardines and with absolutely nothing to do.

At the end of May, we were back on a train again, and we rode under heavy military guard. The cars were sealed and had been used for carrying cement. We sat bunched together, choking from the dust and feeling absolutely wretched. Then it occurred to someone that it was Friday, the eve of the Sabbath. This was no time for a Jew to be glum, and we prepared to receive the Sabbath day joyfully, as tradition bids us to do. Some of the men who had good voices sang for us; others told funny stories. The punishing journey was made bearable.

In Yugoslavia we changed trains. Civilians pushed food through the shuttered windows of our vans. The bits of bread, cheese and sausage were gifts of love from lovers of liberty.

When we arrived in Belgrade, members of the Red Cross were waiting for us at the railway station. A few prisoners were allowed to leave each boxcar to receive articles of food which, in those days, anyone would have regarded as the choicest of delicacies.

Stalag 8B

Five days later we came to a halt at Wulfsberg, but it was only a way station to our destination—Lamsdorf, a small town near Breslau in upper Silesia. After nightfall we were taken to our place of internment. It was a sprawling POW camp enclosed by barbed wire and containing enormous barracks. Each had bunks three tiers high with straw mattresses and blankets. This was Stalag 8B— in which were concentrated about thirty thousand British POWs who were being farmed out for labor throughout Silesia. At any one time there were only about five thousand actually within the compound.

Being brought here was a good sign. Our luck was holding. German command wasn't sure how we fitted into the scheme of things. We had been officially made British prisoners of war by the Wehrmacht, but we were also Jews, and everybody knew where that put us in the opinion of Third Reich headquarters at Wilhelmstrasse. The question of our treatment had become a bone of contention between the German military authorities and the Nazi party, and from time to time we got wind of the conflict. The party was accusing the army of giving us the soft treatment. But the German military had its own policies on POWs and was reluctant to give in to party pressures to differentiate among British war prisoners.

I was given a rundown on camp routine by the German corporal who was our barracks warden. He informed me that British Sergeant-Major Sharrif was POW representative at Stalag 8B and the man who looked after internal matters among prisoners in the camp. The corporal even arranged for me to meet Sergeant-Major Shariff at the barracks serving as prisoner HQ, which contained the quarters of the representatives of national groups interned at the camp: Englishmen, Canadians, Australians, New Zealanders, and now—Palestinians.

Sharrif was friendly and gave me his assurance that he would back us to the hilt if the Germans singled us out for bad treatment. He was as good as his word.

Our morale improved enormously. We had the feeling now that we were inseparably a part of a vast community of POWs, the rights of whom, without exception, were recognized under the Geneva Convention. For their part, the Germans tended to conduct themselves in accordance with Convention requirements, although they tried to bend its rules when it suited them, and there were enough cases of outright violation.

We settled into our barracks, which were located in the center of the camp, and set about organizing the routine of our lives as prisoners of war.

It was the ninth of Ab of the year 5702 according to the Jewish calendar (July 23, 1941)—*Tisha be-Av*, the day Jews fast and pray and mourn the destruction of the Temple in Jerusalem. I approached the German corporal with a request to hold public services to mark the day. To my surprise, permission was granted.

I ordered my men out on parade and had them stand before nightfall in the middle of the parade ground in full view of the other prisoners. Hundreds of Jewish POWs participated. Then I faced the men and spoke to them in Hebrew about *Tisha be-Av*, while our puzzled neighbors from the other units looked on dumbfounded. Standing on parade, except by order of the Germans, was unheard of at Stalag 8B, and odder still was the language I was using, which fell strangely on the ears of the other POWs.

I ended my talk by telling the men that I was sure that our generation would live to wipe out the memory of the destruction of the Temple and establish a Jewish state on its ancestral land. For a moment there was utter silence. Then all at once the men began to sing our anthem, *Hatikva*—lustily, exaltedly. When they had finished, applause broke out all around us from the crowd of onlookers. Then Jews serving in the other Allied armies, who had heretofore kept their identity to themselves, began calling out to us in whatever Yiddish or Hebrew words they knew, however inappropriate—*sholem aleykhem! bar mitsva! simkhes toyre!* All of this with the Nazi standard and its crooked cross waving over our heads.

It was the turning point in our lives as prisoners of war. That same evening the barracks were totally silent. You could actually feel the change coming over the men. We realized as never before that the destinies of Jews and Eretz Israel were one; and we now knew what this demanded of us morally, in our relations among ourselves and in our bearing toward the Germans.

The next day we made our first contacts with the prisoners who had revealed their Judaism at our *Tish be-Av* parade. Our group had in it not only *Sokhnutniks* and Histadrut men, but Revisionists and members of Betar. We agreed to set aside our political differences and act as a single group dedicated to one cause. Reinforcements arrived, too. A group of *Sokhnutniks* returned to Stalag 8B after having been taken to Camp Marburg, where they had undergone indescribable suffering. Chaim Glubinsky, Shlomo Sela-Slodash (who subsequently wrote a book on the internment), Chaim Beili, the Boim brothers, and the others who joined us made invaluable contributions to consolidate us and give us a sense of purpose.

One of the first tests we met, with success, had to do with our assertion of our right to receive gift parcels from the Red Cross. The parcels contained not only such choice edibles as meat, milk, sardines, chocolates, and raisins, but even cigarettes and soap, all worth their weight in gold to the POWs. Responsibility for distribution was shared by German headquarters at the camp and the POWs' representatives. Every prisoner was supposed to receive one parcel each week; but we rarely got what was due us. The Germans were not particularly eager to distribute the parcels—out of envy perhaps because they themselves had long forgotten what these delicacies tasted like), or because they wished to prevent the prisoners from having articles of value with which to bribe the guards. There was also the fact that the parcels were one of the POWs' links with the outside world, which the Germans were not especially enthusiastic to encourage.

When our group arrived at Stalag 8B, we learned that the Germans had decided that, unlike the rest of the prisoners, we were not eligible for Red Cross parcels. We lodged a protest with Sergeant-Major Sharrif, who went round to the Germans and let them know that if the Palestinians were denied parcels from the Red Cross, the British would refuse to take theirs and would demand to see the Red Cross representatives to report on the incident.

The British stood their ground, and within a week the Germans announced that we also would receive the Red Cross parcels. The solidarity the British demonstrated in our behalf and their plain decency were admirable, and we would have more occasions than this to witness these qualities in the British POWs.

The Red Cross parcels became as much a curse as a blessing. As we were taken from place to place for labor, illicit traffic in them grew until its scope was no longer tolerable. Some of our people conceived an absolute mania for trade on the civilian black market and among their fellow prisoners. These men began modestly by, say, bartering five cigarettes for one onion from a peasant and then passing it on to a prisoner for ten cigarettes. At a later stage they took to ordering fruit and vegetables in wholesale quantities from black-market agents. Finally, in flagrant contravention of the rules set by our group, they made fraternizing with the enemy a matter of routine, each of these entrepreuners cultivating his own private "reliable Goy."

The profiteering mania was undermining the orderly existence we had worked so hard to establish and maintain at camp, and its malign influence was beginning to be felt outside our set. It was no longer just a question of how it was affecting us alone, but the impression we were making on the non-Jewish POWs. Not that the Gentile prisoners were behaving better than our men, but as Jews, we were in a special position. The other prisoners were constantly exposed to Nazi propaganda against Jews, and all we had to counter it with was ourselves. Every anti-Semitic Nazi canard was being tested by our behavior. So, like it or not, in the eyes of the rest of the POWs, we Palestinians were the show window of Judaism.

We therefore decided to ban the traffic. Our tradesmen responded by calling us "kibbutzniks," and every camp in which we succeeded in imposing our ban on commerce they called a "kibbutz," which pleased the authentic kibbutz members among us not at all. We put a ban, too, on gambling and card playing when the stakes were money or articles of value—not only because these were in themselves shameful practices, but also because they often ended in quarrels which the Germans resolved by the use of force.

Once, when I was sent to the prison camp at Tarnowitz to act as representative and senior of Jewish Palestinian POWs there, a youngster called Isio (Isidore) Strogano came to me to protest the changes I was demanding in the way things were being run by the prisoners. (Isidore was the son of one of the old-time Salonika dockworkers at Haifa port).

He began by saying, "Look, Yosef, my father tried to make a man out of me and got exactly nowhere, so how far do you think you're going to get? I like to kill time at dice and cards and that sort of thing. If I feel like losing my shirt or starving, what's it to you? It's no skin off your nose."

I explained with great care why what he was doing did bother me, why it was doing us all harm, and that all the Germans were waiting for was for us to slip up so they'd have an excuse to knock us around and make us really suffer.

"So what will you do—turn us in?" he asked.

"No," I said, "but the minute this war's over and we get back, I'm going to have you up on charges before a military court for breach of discipline!"

He thought for a while and then said, "Know what? If we ever get back in one piece, I couldn't care less if I am court-martialed!"

He was stubborn, but no fool. After weeks of trying to reason with him, I managed to get him to concede I had a point, and he changed his ways. Strogano and I have been fast friends ever since.

Meanwhile, the Germans in Stalag 8B would not let us forget just what and where we were. They came down on us particularly hard during the winter months, when they took to rousing us at midnight and herding us outside for a head count while they searched the barracks. After standing out in the freezing cold for hours, we would return bone-cold to our bunks till morning, and another day of enforced idleness in which to let go of a bit more of our humanity.

Camp routine ate away at everyone, even at the strongest prisoners. Its effects on some men were disastrous. Some lost all touch with reality and would lie wallowing in their own filth; they would end up in the mental ward of the prisoners' hospital, usually for a long stay. For a time, suicides among POWs reached epidemic proportions. At nightfall, before lock up, we would often see a man walk bemusedly along the fence and suddenly leap at the wires and, in a frenzy, try to hoist himself over the top. A burst of automatic fire from the watchtower would cut him down.

But then our situation changed. The Germans realized that we would be of more use to them as cheap labor. They called for us to supply them with 150 men to work in the forest near the village of Jakobswalde, not far from Stalag 8B. Some of our men with rank opposed having NCOs included in the labor gang and cited the regulation of the Geneva Convention freeing officers from having to do work. I wouldn't hear of this and made certain to be the first to volunteer to leave with the men. Yehoshua Loebl put his name down as well. We could not abandon men who were leaving the camp, even if we were not under any legal obligation to go with them. It was our duty to look after them at their new place of internment and to see that the Germans did not violate their rights. As for the letter of the law, we could be with our men without doing any labor.

On arrival at the work site we were broken up into two groups. I was lucky. My group included some of our best—men who were only too glad to have been released from their languishment in that immense, overcrowded slough. It made things easier for me, and I got my group organized quickly; not just for work, but socially and even culturally.

We had no books or newspapers, but we got some of the men to prod their memories and the results were sometimes remarkable. We managed to produce a series of lectures on the Histadrut that lasted for the better part of a year and a half! And then there was Israel Yarkoni (today military adjutant to the president of Israel), who got together a prisoner orchestra, with himself playing first violin.

We spent long hours talking together, each of us telling the story of his life. This was group therapy in the best sense. We uncovered whole universes of Jewish experience—both suffering and hopes.

We also put out a daily news bulletin with information we picked up from the German radio and sometimes, secretly, from the BBC. It was from the BBC that

I found out that the Czechoslovak underground had killed off Heinrich Heidrich, Hitler's executioner in Czechoslovakia and one of the worst butchers the Gestapo had. I told the rest of the lads about it when we were by ourselves. One of them, in his enthusiasm over Heidrich's death, scrawled the name on the side of his bunk. It was spotted by the German sergeant on his tour of inspection, and he asked the boy why he had written that name (luckily he hadn't found out yet about Heidrich's death). I spoke up and told the sergeant that writing down the name was just a token of our interest in the leading figures in Germany. Our jailer didn't appear to be convinced, and when the news of Heidrich's assassination finally reached the Germans, he became suspicious of us. For some time after that we enforced discipline more rigorously.

We maintained the custom of putting bulletins up on the wall for a very long time, even after our depature from Jakobswalde. To mark the appearance of its five-hundredth edition on July 9, 1944, one of the men wrote the following editorial:

> I was asked to tell about the Bulletin—about its founders and those who made it what it is, and, first and foremost, about its progenitor, Sergeant Yosef Krelenboim, who was Senior among us in those days. It was he who conceived, made and planned it; he who dedicated the best of his time to maintain the cultural standard in our Compound. . . . We remember the days when the men returned from work totally exhausted, their clothes wet through with sweat and caked with filth, and before they had even given themselves a chance to catch their breath—they would be elbowing their way toward the wall on which our daily broadsheet hung.

Before we left Jakobswalde, we collected copies of all of our bulletins, journals, and other documents and placed them in a container, which we sealed. We then buried them. We hoped to get back to Jakobswalde after our liberation to salvage the material. As far as I know, the container still lies buried somewhere under the site of our camp.

6

Behind Barbed Wire

One day the German sergeant-major who was commander at the Jacobswalde compound ordered me to remain behind when the men went to work: a Wehrmacht officer was coming and wished to see me.

Early the next day the officer arrived, and I was called in to the camp commander's office. I entered and found myself facing a captain who, abruptly and without even a gesture of ceremony, addressed me: "I have come to inform you that you are to go to Tarnowitz. There are three hundred Palestinian prisoners of war there, and you will replace Sergeant Kaplan as senior."

I was taken aback. My spontaneous response was refusal. I had no wish to leave Jakobswalde. I told him that if the Germans wanted to send me back to the stalag, they were perfectly within their rights, but that they could not compel me to go anywhere else.

The captain kept his temper. He asked me in English to accompany him on a short tour of the compound. Once outside he explained that the camp at Tarnowitz was in a state of absolute chaos. Jewish POWs were working there with Poles, and they had turned the camp into a marketplace for Red Cross parcels and a cesspool! The Germans were unable to control the situation without resorting to guns. In fact they had already opened fire on prisoners in some places and found that killing a few POWs got things back to normal. As an officer at HQ for POW affairs, he did not approve of this method. And then, to my surprise, he added: "The Germans have killed quite enough Jews! If it is in my power to save your men, I see it as my duty to do so. For that reason I have not approved the proposal to use force. Instead, I have approached POW representation at Lamsdorf, and it was they who suggested I send you down."

Then, after a pause, he went on: "You must understand that I cannot permit such abandonment to filth, or the trade between prisoners and guards. There is a serious hazard in this for us, too, you know. If ever an epidemic should break out it would strike us as well."

I wasn't sure if the captain was to be trusted, so I played for time. I told him that prisoner representation was in the hands of Sergeant-Major Sharrif and that if Sharrif approached me on the matter, I would reconsider the captain's proposal. He accepted my condition, and by the time we said good-bye to one another, the strain of our meeting had become sufficiently relaxed for him to tell me about some amusing incidents from his experiences with prisoners of war. One story was about a prisoner who had cut up his trousers and resewn them into a haversack. When a German NCO reprimanded him for destroying army property, he said: "'Op it, Jerry. . . .It's not 'Itler's bloody trousers, it's Churchill's!"

That evening I told my men what had happened. They wouldn't hear of my going. I couldn't leave! Why, when the word had got out that Krelenboim was running things down here, the boys at the stalag had started queuing up so they could come. I had to stay; it was my *moral* obligation. About the only good thing to be said for my meeting with the captain was that conditions at Jakobswalde had improved since his visit. The food had improved, as had the attitude of our guards. It would make things easier for my replacement. A few days later the Germans handed me a letter signed by Sharrif instructing me to appoint a replacement and get myself down to Tarnowitz.

When I arrived at Tarnowitz I received a mixed reception. Some of the men already knew about what we had achieved at Jacobswalde and were happy I had come. There were others, though, who were unhappy because of my reputation for cracking down on business, on fraternization with the locals, and on card playing. I ignored them and immediately went to work organizing prisoner activities at Tarnowitz on the pattern we had introduced in other POW camps.

I had a club opened in one of the barracks, had it filled with books from the stalag, and outfitted it with a stage and study rooms. The latter were to be used for learning Hebrew and English, and for lectures and group discussions on subjects ranging from literature to Jewish Palestine and its problems.

We established our own court to try men who violated the rules we made. Use of the German language, and contact with German residents of the area were treated as the most serious offenses, and called for a fine of two cigarettes—a heavy penalty under the conditions of POW life.

Our prisoners' court was effective, and as time went on, it convened more rarely. The men learned that not only did virtue pay, it improved the atmosphere in the camp. Even those who had not been keen on the new regimen became more cooperative.

After a few months, we were transferred from Tarnowitz to Pieskerczim, which was also in the southwestern district of occupied Poland. The work we were assigned was the same. We distributed lengths of rail for assembly along a new railway under construction. Conditions at the new site were somewhat more congenial than at the last, and the camp commandant did not give us too much trouble. In a matter of days we were able to reestablish the social routines that had by now become customary and even came up with some improvements.

The ban we had put on trade with the local population had some unforeseen adverse side effects, not the least of which was that it reduced the flow of vegetables into the camp. The only source of fresh vegetables was the German nationals who lived in the area. To deal with the problem, we chose a few reliable men, and by giving them the "exclusive concession" for bartering the contents of our Red Cross parcels for vegetables we effectively took control of the trade in the camp. Our "concessionaires" brought the goods they had obtained to the camp, where the entire stock was distributed in equal lots to all the prisoners. The business acumen we had shown was widely admired and copied, even by British POWs in their camps.

We Meet Our Brethren

The first day we set out for work from Pieskerczim, we encountered a work gang of Jewish forced laborers. They were doing the same job as we, but were under guard by SA men—storm troopers. The state they were in shocked us. They were in rags, without shoes, their feet wrapped in newspapers; and they were evidently starved. Their faces had the look of utter wretchedness and despair; they seemed dazed as they moved along the railroad bed, dragging their feet through the winter sludge.

As soon as we returned to camp, we ran an emergency food collection. We collected bread and the food contained in our gift parcels and put some of our men to work preparing sandwiches. I went to the German sergeant-major over us—a middle-aged, even-tempered man—and asked him to have a chat with the SA commander in charge of the Jewish labor gang and to offer the man cigarettes and coffee in exchange for his turning a blind eye to our distribution of sandwiches to the forced laborers. I also asked him to arrange things with the SA officer to have thirty Jews sent to our camp every day, to replace our men on fatigue duty. Then I was able to get a request through to Sharrif at Stalag 8. I asked him to send us one of the camp doctors with a stock of medicines. Sharrif got word back to me that my request would be granted.

Looking on every day while our fellow Jews were being abused by their guards was getting to us. The inevitable finally happened. When one of the storm troopers struck a Jewish laborer on the back with the butt of his rifle, one of our men went for the German, ripped the gun out of his hand, and hit him across the back with it. All the storm troopers rushed to the spot, their rifles cocked. We were sure there was going to be a massacre.

Rescue came from an unexpected quarter—one of our own guards. They were regular army, Wehrmacht men, and generally despised the SA. The guard told the storm troopers to leave our man alone and shouted at them: "You've no authority to touch my prisoner! The Wehrmacht will decide what to do with him!"

The forced laborers were looking on with alarm. They knew what was in store for them because of the episode.

By the time our men got back to the camp we, too, were worried. We were proud enough of what our man had done, but we knew that, from the point of view of the Germans, striking a German soldier bordered on lese majesty. There was also the thought of what the beaten storm trooper was likely to do to the Jews on the work gang.

Again I applied to our camp commandant. This time his even temper gave way, and he flew into a rage. By plying him with a tin of good coffee and some first-rate English cigarettes, I managed to cool him down, and I convinced him that it would in his own best interests to keep the incident from getting out so that all of us could get back to our jobs again.

The requests we had submitted before the incident were granted, and thirty of the work gang came to our camp daily. The storm trooper who was assigned to guard them was entertained by our jailers, while we gave the laborers whatever clothing we had managed to scrape up and fed them with our choicest food. The doctor from the Stalag did his best for them with the meager means at his disposal. They were in bad shape, so bad that in many cases the doctor thought the best he could do for them was to help them along to a merciful death. I brushed this suggestion aside, and told him to do everything he could for them, even if he succeeded in saving only one.

The experience of meeting our wretched brethren had shattered us all. We alternated between anger and despair. We couldn't sleep. Often, as I passed through the barracks late at night, I would find men lying awake smoking nervously in their bunks, or hear them groan in their sleep.

Watching the men from the work gang and hearing them tell of their sufferings made us realize just how gently fate had dealt with us and how great was our privilege to have had the chance to bear arms and make war on the Nazis, if only for a short time. Many of the forced laborers who came to the camp expressed their regret at not having joined the Zionists when there was still time, at having been so innocent as to have believed they could go on living among the Gentile nations, whose hatred of Jews was now revealed in its full and terrible scope. They swore now they would take revenge and would join us in creating a Jewish state.

It did not take long for us to run out of clothing and food to give them. Somehow, I was able to come up with a convincing story that enabled me to go to Stalag 8B, where I could collect more supplies. I went to everyone, Jews and Gentiles, and they all gave. In no time I had collected cigarettes by the thousands, hundreds of food tins, a pile of soap and bundles of clothing. Then the whole lot was brought to our camp, at great risk, and distributed to the Jews of the work gang. Everyone in Stalag 8B had participated in the operation, and for a short while, the lives of our charges were made a little easier. But soon afterward they were taken away to another site, and we never saw them again.

Chief of Palestinian Jewish POWs

At about that time Shlomo Sela, one of our active members, asked me in the name of our group to return to Stalag 8B and take on the job of chief of Jewish POWs. In his book *Be-khavlei ha-shevi* ("Shackled in Captivity"), Sela writes:

Yosef Krelenboim was Senior at the labor camp in Pieskerczim—which was an exemplary camp in respect of organization, concern for one's fellows, and internal social life. We asked him to come immediately and put himself at the head of our POWs. . . . Life at the Camp underwent an enormous change with the arrival of Yosef, who was appointed Representative of Palestinian Jewish POWs at the Stalag and, after a short time, Representative of all Palestinian Jewish POWs in Germany. With his coming, highly ramified activity was initiated both within and outside the Camp. Eretz Israel became a focus of inspiration for the prisoners. . . . The assumption that a Zionist purpose could be pursued in captivity was verified.

I became a very busy man. Prisoner HQ put a room at my disposal, and from it I set in motion scores of committees for cultural activities in the camp. There, I also interviewed the men who came to me with problems. We made a special point of holding religious services on the Jewish holidays, when Jewish POWs from all over the British Empire joined us for prayer. There were Christian chaplains among the inmates of the camp who also showed an interest in our services.

My private life became increasingly submerged in my activities as prisoner representative. I had practically no time left for taking care of my personal affairs. I began to feel the need to go off by myself. I was able to do so mainly in the winter, when on particularly cold days, as the snow fell, I would make off to the library and there wrap myself in a blanket and read. I read only English, my knowledge of which had considerably improved.

In the spring reinforcements came our way from a most unlikely source. We were joined by a contingent of about 150 Palestinian Arabs. They came to us after the Germans had failed utterly in their attempt to enlist them in the Wehrmacht. These Arabs had resisted beatings and even the exhortations of Haj Amin Al-Husseini, the Mufti of Jerusalem, who had been brought especially to Berlin for that purpose by the Germans.

When they arrived at the camp they were informed that there was a Palestinian prisoner representative at the stalag to whom they could apply should they have any questions or complaints. There were some who did come to me with their problems. In one such case, four Arab lads who had been badly beaten by some English POWs during a dispute over a commercial transaction came to me. They were shaken and feared for their lives, and they asked for my protection. I took up their case and was able to see the incident through to a peaceful conclusion. Also, when I found out that the Arabs were not receiving their gift parcels, I undertook to investigate, and I wrote to the Arab Soldiers' Committee about it. Their parcels had, in fact, been sent; it was the Germans who had kept the parcels back and forwarded them instead to the military camp of the pro-German Arab unit. The Arab POWs maintained good relations with us and took part in our activities; there were some who even learned Hebrew.

Early in 1943, after their defeats in Russia, the Germans underwent a perceptible change of mood. It was reflected in the behavior of our guards, which became less harsh. Before the Easter holidays, for which the prisoners were preparing a carnival in which all the national groups were to mount exhibitions and performances representing the life and manners of their countries, the Germans asked to be permitted to photograph the event so they could send the pictures to Switzerland as proof of how well they were treating POWs. They seemed already to be preparing for the day when they would have to take their turn doing time in POW camps.

We decided to join the Easter celebrations and put on a show that would make the whole camp sit up and take notice. We would drive home our identity as Jews of Palestine and Zionists. We threw all our ingenuity into making props and costumes.

Our section of the parade was headed by a great poster with the inscription ERETZ ISRAEL in Hebrew and PALESTINE in English (this despite the opposition of some of our men to making any public display of our standard or insignias). Behind the sign were two lads costumed as a very dignified camel, which bent its long neck over the crowd and nodded greetings to the onlookers; it carried on its back two crates of Jaffa oranges. The camel was led by a Yemenite-Jew in a tarboosh, playing Eastern melodies on a reed flute.

The camel tableau was followed by a man dressed as a nurse, wearing a cap with the Star of David. This greatly surprised our audience, most of whom knew that the symbol was despised by the Germans. Behind the nurse marched two men in the uniform of the Palestinian border patrol.

The march was closed by another tableau in which a Jewish farmer led a cow being milked by his wife. We had constructed the creature out of cardboard and put in its belly a vat of milk we had concocted out of our stock of powdered milk in tins; we hooked up a rubber tube to the vat so that the farmer's wife could squeeze out jets of the real article. The milking bit was our pièce de résistance.

About twelve thousand POWs, representing all the armies of the British Empire, were strung out along the route of the carnival parade, as were the Wehrmacht officers and their wives. Ordinary German soldiers were barred from entering the camp, but we could make out crowds of them, too, peering at us through the barbed wire of the compound fence. It was undeniable—our exhibit was a hit with the POWs. We were greeted with rounds of loud applause; again and again we heard cries of "Palestine . . . Palestine!"

After the parade, we waited for the judges to decide which were the prize-winning exhibits. Each contingent had labored hard and invested much imagination. The South Africans had offered a fantastic performance of folklore in Zulu costume. The RAF had displayed an impressive model of a fighter plane. The judges, two British colonels and the German camp commandant, sat deliberating for an unconscionably long time, and then—"First prize . . . Palestine!"

The applause was overwhelming, and our boys ecstatically embraced and planted huge kisses on each other's cheeks. First prize was two thousand cigarettes, and on the spot we contributed the lot to Prisoners' Welfare. Our reputation was made.

Our purpose and achievement at the Easter Carnival was to present an image of the Jew that would counter, at least in Stalag 8B, the savage image presented by the whole machinery of Nazi propaganda to which the POWs were being continuously exposed. William Jones ("Lord Haw-Haw")—the English traitor who broadcast on German radio—had been bombarding British ears with anti-Semitic lectures of the most vicious kind, with more effect than one would have liked to believe. Receiving first prize was therefore our vindication as Jews and Zionists and acknowledgment by the whole camp that what the Nazis were saying about Jews was a lie. We felt sure that the two British judges had given us their vote because they admired us for having the guts to make a defiant display of our identity.

As for the Germans, we never let them degrade us, living or dead.

One of our men, Sergeant Yitzhak Belkin, died in the camp hospital. The Germans had not bothered to inform us of his death, and they buried him without ceremony near the fence of the military graveyard of the camp. We were in a rage when we found out; we doubted he had died a natural death. That same day we lodged a protest with the Red Cross representation in the name of Palestinian POWs.

The protest had an immediate effect. Within two days the camp command was ordered to arrange a funeral with full military honors for the deceased. For us it was a signal victory. We set about making arrangements for the ceremony. We found a white sheet and some blue cloth, out of which we put together a flag. We also procured a Union Jack and spread both over the coffin. Then we got together some of our men to form a guard of honor and drilled them in the slow march. The British put their orchestra at our disposal, and a non-Jewish British army chaplain asked permission to read from the Old Testament at the funeral. We accepted his offer gratefully. One of our own men, who was knowledgeable in these matters, was appointed rabbi for the occasion.

The funeral cortege formed with two German soldiers bearing a wreath in the van; behind them troopers formed a guard of honor. The camp orchestra and our own guard of honor followed, with me in the lead. From every part of the camp, POWs lined up on both sides of the way, and they doffed their caps in respect as the coffin passed.

To the sound of a dead march and a salvo, the procession reached the grave site. The coffin was lowered into the grave with all points of military ceremony observed. Our acting rabbi chanted the *El male-rahamim* ("God Full of Compassion") and recited the Kaddish. The German troopers stood at attention, ramrod straight.

When we returned, we arranged for a grave marker. We had the German carpenter in Lamsdorf make a Star of David, with the Hebrew initials pe and nun (*po nitman*, "Here lies buried . . ."), inscribed on it. That was how we set a proper Jewish tombstone in a Nazi cemetery.

A Killer Named Pantke

The struggle went on. We were in a fury again. The object—Feldwebel Pantke, camp commandant of Beuthen, where the youngest and strongest of our men had been sent to work in the coal mines.

The man was a fanatical Nazi; he seems to have become a party member even before Hitler seized power in Germany. Pantke had it in for the men. He reduced their food rations, worked them till they dropped, had them continually roused out of bed while their barracks were searched, and repeatedly called them out for endless and exhausting parades and roll calls.

One day he went wild. He ordered two of our men, Krausner and Eisenberg, to leave work and go back to the camp. When they turned to go, he came up behind them and shot them in the back. Krausner fell dead and Eisenberg was mortally wounded; he died a few days later in the camp hospital. The Germans announced that Feldwebel Pantke had shot them when they tried to escape.

Our prisoners' senior at Beuthen, Master-Sergeant Yaakov Friedland, reported to us and asked to return to the Stalag. I asked Sergeant-Major Sharrif to inform the Germans, in his capacity as chief prisoners' representative at Stalag 8B, that I would be replacing Friedland in Beuthen. Sharrif advised me against going and told me that my efforts there to raise morale and face down Pantke could well cost me my life. Restraint was what was called for, he said. After all, he pointed out, nearly thirty of *his* chaps, British soldiers, had been killed at one of the camps, and he had not gone and interfered. I answered him that the British Empire was vast and had a population to match, but my people were few. I was not going to let Pantke get away with murder. At last Sharrif gave in and agreed to let me go.

I was taken under guard to Beuthen, which was not far from Auschwitz, neither geographically nor morally. At Beuthen I was taken directly to my quarters, which had been prepared for me in advance, and immediately a German soldier entered to ask if I had reported to the Feldwebel. I told him I had not, adding, "I'll wait for him to ask me." In the meantime I tried to get the feel of the situation at the camp: I discovered that he treated his own men like dirt and that they hated him. *That* was going to be the card I would use.

Toward evening a guard came to announce that Pantke wanted me to report. I received the news with apparent calm, which surprised the German.

I asked, "Why do you look so surprised?"

"You don't know Pantke," he said. "He's a killer!"

I filed away the information, betook myself to Pantke's office, entered, and saluted. He was sitting behind the desk with a scowl on his red face, his tunic unbuttoned.

"Name?"

"Krelenboim."

He raised his voice: "So, you are a Jew too?"

"Indeed yes, thank God," I replied, sighing with pleasure.

Pantke brought his fist down on the desk; his face was pure crimson by now and he began to scream:

"Filthy Jew! Out!"

"Don't you yell at me!" Without realizing it, I was shouting back at him. "I'm your equal in rank. I won't turn my back on you so you can shoot me like the coward you are! You'll pay yet for your murders!" (I didn't realize it then, but it was prophecy. After the war, the man was caught, tried, and hanged.)

"Out!" He almost tore his throat out with that.

I saluted, said, "Thank you," and left.

When I returned to my quarters some of our men were waiting for me. They were tense and impatient to know what had happened. I gave them a brief account of the mutual courtesies Pantke and I had exchanged. They were amused but understandably anxious. So was I.

As we were talking a German soldier came in. He and his friends had been in the guardroom and overheard my shouting match with Pantke, and he had come on behalf of them all to wish me luck.

My confrontation with Pantke quickly became general knowledge throughout the camp. In the evening, I called together the men to warn them that our celebration was premature. We had only just begun to fight. The next stage is for us to give Pantke a taste of the "Good Soldier Schweik" treatment. We all salute him the instant he looms into view and carry punctilio in the observance of military discipline and courtesy to the point of absurdity.

On a Sunday, Pantke informed me that he would be making a tour of inspection of the barracks. As was the custom, I accompanied him. I made note of his confiscation of scissors, pencils, and other effects of the prisoners which, according to regulations, they were permitted to purchase at the German canteen in exchange for the paper certificates they received in payment for their work. I sent a detailed report of these and other of Pantke's eccentricities to Sharrif and asked him to intervene. One day three weeks later I was told to appear within the hour before a commission from Wehrmacht Intelligence, which had arrived in the camp. I assumed this was the result of Sharrif's intercession and the report sent to the Red Cross about the murder of the two men.

I testified before the commission in detail about Pantke's infractions and outright crimes: the murder, the beatings, the threats, the confiscations of personal effects not under ban (including the men's toilet paper!), and the reduction of food rations.

My testimony lasted two hours, with the members of the Commission of Inquiry cross-examining me every step of the way. At one point in the proceedings I was asked by one of the officers exactly what the nature of Pantke's threat was. I said it was to have us sent to a concentration camp The officer dismissed Pantke's threat with a wave of the hand: "Not to worry! That's no more serious than what we frighten our children with in Germany—the 'Black Man' or Chimney Sweep who's supposed to come and steal them away when they are naughty." I reminded him that our camp was not very far from Auschwitz, and there were some among us who suspected that their own parents were there.

On my testimony concerning food, one of them remarked, "Well, what can we do? After all you people don't eat *khazer!*" (He used the Yiddish word for pig, and was obviously pleased by his own wit.) I let the remark go and told him that we did eat bread and potatoes and vegetables, and that we never got enough of these.

After the hearing, the commission members asked me to go with them to inspect the camp. The POWs, who knew what was going on, played their parts well. When the inspection was over, one of the officers on the commission said to me, "It will be all right."

That night Pantke packed his bags. The next morning he was gone. The new commandant was a more reasonable sort, and the atmosphere at Beuthen became more relaxed. I parted from the men and returned to the stalag. A little later a delegation of POWs from Beuthen visited me to tell me that they had made a collection and raised several hundred pounds sterling, in promissory notes, and had asked British army authorities to instruct the contributors' banks to transfer the money *in my name* to the Jewish National Fund (JNF). All of which had been conceived by the POWs at Beuthen as a way of having me inscribed in the *Golden Book* of contributors to the land development fund of the World Zionist Organization.

I was touched and thanked the men, but told them it was too much of an honor to be paid to one man. I suggested they make a real fund drive out of it, collect contributions from the other camps as well, and send the money in a lump sum to the JNF in Palestine for a forest to be planted in the name of all the Jewish POWs in Germany.

The fund-raising drive was advertised in many of the bulletins of POW camps in Germany at the time. The following item appeared in Bulletin No. 10, dated October 18, 1944, from Camp Malpana:

> The comrades in Camp Malpana, to whom Yosef was known even before he was active at L   (to most he was not just the Sergeant and Camp Senior, but a friend, and to many a guide), have announced their intention to inscribe his name in the Golden Book of the JNF as an expression of their great esteem for all of his work in behalf of Jewish POWs, and have proposed to all of the labor camps that they join in this enterprise.
>
> Both of these actions testify to the great awakening in anticipation of our redemption, which is at hand, and to the mounting feeling for Eretz Israel; and both are being expressed through the contributions that are being made to our nation's fund for the redemption of our Land.
>
> We include the following announcement by Sergeant Yosef on the transformation of this undertaking into one for the planting of a forest in the name of the POWs. We also include the correspondence between the Initiating Committee at Malpana and our Representative.

> > To all labor camps:
> > Our fellow prisoners in Camp Malpana have decided to inscribe me in the Golden Book of the JNF, and wish to have the campaign taken up in all labor camps where Jewish POWs are interned. The great honor being done me has taken me by surprise; it has also given me the idea for a one-time fund drive on behalf of the JNF in the other camps. To this end, I have decided that the campaign should not be tied to my name, but that a campaign should be undertaken instead for the planting of a forest in the name of all Jewish prisoners in Germany.
> >
> > Friends! I appeal to you all to contribute to the planting of a copse in the name of all our fellow prisoners. By making this contribution we express our ties to Eretz Israel, even at a time when we are still deep within the land of our enemy. Even from here—within the confines of our suffering—we can take part in

the redemption of the Land of Israel. Jewish POWs! You have proved your devotion more than once; I hope that this time, too, our efforts will be crowned with success.

Yours sincerely,

(——) Yosef

L   , 10.11.44

This correspondence, of course, was highly illegal, and it was undertaken at great hazard. In the end, the results of our fund drive exceeded our expectations. When the war was finally over and we got back home, the JNF had a receipt for our contribution ready for us, accompanied by a warm note of thanks.

7

Light at the End of the Tunnel

The organization of Jewish Palestinian POWs of which I had been made head acquired great prestige within the network of POW organizations of the armed forces of the British Empire. In time we were even able to stimulate Zionist activities among Jewish prisoners of war from other countries. However, the thrust of our operations was directed mainly at our own men—to see to it that their rights were preserved, to support and guide them in maintaining their identification and involvement with the homeland and its purpose, to keep up our contact with the men although they were dispersed in seven different camps. The seven camps presented difficulties because contact between the camps was put under a strict ban by the Germans. All the same, I was able to invent pretexts to visit the other camps from time to time in order to speak with the men and give their morale an occasional boost.

Our information bulletin, which appeared with fair regularity once every ten days and was distributed among the camps, was the link binding us together. The bulletin was our medium for passing on news to the men and making known to them the problems we faced and the demands we were making. In April 1944 we established the General Association of POWs of Eretz Israel, to which I was elected chairman; the Executive Committee included Prisoners Shusterman, Shlomo Slodash, and David Wiener. On May 6, 1944 we approved our regulations in which our objectives were defined. These included:

Objectives during the period of internment: Sport, cultural activities, mutual aid, contact and advice.

Objectives for after the war: (1) Mutual aid, contact and advice. (2) To advise and represent members with pension rights about their health problems and those of their families. (3) Legal aid in all matters falling within the scope of the

Association's activities. (4) Setting the agencies of the Government and communities into motion for aid to members in need. (5) To act as an advisory body for members about to begin their own enterprise, and for members about to join an existing general enterprise. (6) Organization of activities in culture, sport, etc.

There were five paragraphs devoted to a single aim: aid to the families of those POWs who died during their internment. For this purpose, we established a memorial fund for which money was collected from our men. We also drafted the administrative regulations of the association which included a clause obligating the committee to hold its first general meeting in Eretz Israel one month after two-thirds of our POWs were demobilized.

But for all our anticipation of liberation and preparations for existence afterward, we had still to deal with the present. Our association made and maintained contact with three international bodies that were especially active on behalf of POWs: the Swiss government, which in its capacity as a "protecting power" represented the citizens of countries in a state of mutual hostility; the International Red Cross; and the Christian welfare organizaton, the Young Men's Chritian Association (YMCA).

At one meeting with the YMCA representative, I included in my list of the routine items of which we were in need—such as sports equipment and books—a request for a supply of matzoth, the unleavened bread for the Passover. It was an article of food the YMCA man had never heard of, and he asked innocently if the matzo could not be prepared in Germany. I said no, and puzzled but anxious to help, he passed our request on to the Red Cross. They too were at a loss, and knowing that no request to the British ever went unanswered, they put the matter in the competent hands of the War Office in London. Three months after Passover, we received a letter from the British War Office. Our correspondent wrote "with deep regret" that he was unable to send us the "matzes bread" we requested, but ("he was happy to report") we would shortly receive, instead— biscuits!

A more pressing matter was our linking up with the POW escape organization's secret committee, established by the British at the central POW camp. The work the committee did, with exemplary efficiency, was to gather intelligence and arrange for escape routes to England and neutral countries. It also outfitted escaping POWs with what were indispensable articles if their attempt was to succeed: a supply of properly forged documents, including false identity papers. Its operations were highly sophisticated, exceedingly complex and on an epic scale: literally thousands of POWs participated gallantly in the face of more than an ordinary degree of risk even for those who stayed behind. Success was rare. Attempts would often fail even before they were put into operation when camp security got wind of it through a stool pigeon or an intelligence agent planted among the POWs. Even when escaping prisoners managed to get out of the compound without being detected, they were more often than not caught. Then their fate depended on who had caught them. If it was the Wehrmacht, the men were returned to the camp and locked in punishment cells. Falling into the hands of the Gestapo was an entirely different matter: many of the men recaptured by them were tortured abominably or shot, or both.

When my request to have our men included in escape operations was approved, our Palestinians began taking part in escape attempts. The escapes were usually made in teams of two or three men, one of whom was ours. Some of the lads were undeterred by failure and would try again and again. One of our men was caught six times and then went on to a seventh try. This time, teamed up with an English officer, he made it to Hungary. His partner went on to England, and he remained in Budapest. There he found his parents and was working on getting them out when the Germans took over the government in Hungary. He was caught, returned to the camp, and once more thrown into a punishment cell.

In the aftermath of the failed attempt on Hitler's life of July 20, 1944, the regimen at POW camps was made palpably more severe. SS chief Heinrich Himmler and General Guderian were now determining Wehrmacht policy. Toward the end of the year, camp command at Stalag 8B underwent a change of personnel. The replacement for the elderly and, by POW camp standards, moderate commandant had been chief of German Secret Police in Breslau. It took no time at all for him to get his grip on things at the stalag. Daily searches were made in the barracks for weapons and radio receivers; they were thorough. Punishments for infractions of camp discipline were stiffened and arrests of POWs multiplied. Red Cross parcels became a thing of the past. Food rations were drastically reduced.

We took consolation in the dramatic change in the war. There were now hundreds of sorties of British and American bombers passing overhead carrying bomb payloads to targets all over Germany. Our morale lifted the moment we caught the drone of their engines and looked up to see the sky thick with them, and we took heart from the long faces of our jailors.

In January 1945 a Red Cross commission paid the stalag a visit. None of us imagined then that it would be the last. They had come to inquire about the distribution of Red Cross parcels, the supply of which had been reduced to a trickle. The Germans blamed Allied bombings for interfering with delivery.

At the request of Palestinian POW representation, two Swiss members of the Red Cross Commission met secretly with us. The chief of POW representation at Stalag 8B, Sergeant-Major Sharrif, was also present. I put to them the situation of Palestinian POWs with the war drawing to a close and expressed our fears that when the Germans retreated they would take it out on Jewish prisoners of war in particular. I asked for full backing and active assistance from the agencies of all organized POWs if we were forced to defend ourselves from an assault by the SS against us, either as a group or as individuals. I even outlined the manner of our planned defense and gave them a rundown of the steps we had already taken.

The Red Cross representatives thought it was a certainty that the Germans in retreat would have their hands full with far too many pressing matters to bother themselves about POWs. They stated their conclusion and left. We did not share their confidence. The alert was on among our men in all the interment camps.

We were resolved to defend ourselves to the limit of our abilities, whether we could count on the British or not.

Death March

Not many days later the camp's loudspeakers came to life: "All prisoners from blocks"—there followed a sequence of barracks numbers—"are to be evacuated from the stalag this afternoon." Block 4 was included in the list; it contained five hundred Palestinian prisoners of war. The loudspeakers continued: "Prisoners' representation HQ is to remain behind."

In effect, I was being told that my status as staff at prisoner HQ had just won me official sanction to abandon the men who had put me there to represent them. I was not buying it.

I called our men together and spelled out what the German order meant—a forced march in the dead of winter, in snow and freezing temperatures, to an unknown destination. Therefore, anyone who planned to hide, or make a break, had better do it now. For my part, I was joining the marchers; after four years of representing the interests of our POWs, I was not going to abandon them now when the going got rough.

At noon about four hundred of us reported to the mustering point. We each carried a small bundle of what little food we had managed to save. The Germans issued rations—one to a man. Then we moved out, forming a long, drawn-out column which, in addition to ourselves, included over two thousand British.

Two hours later we stopped for a short break. I was approached by a delegation from the British POWs with a request that I undertake to represent all the prisoners on the march. It took me by surprise. Curious: they had ten officers of their own, among them chaplains and physicians, yet they came to me. I told them they would have my answer soon.

I called my men togather. We set hunched in the snow at the roadside and I told them about the British proposal. Then I said that I had made up my mind to go on the march with them because I wanted to be with them for the duration, until we were all liberated. Now I was asking them what I should do. Before they gave me their decision, there was one thing they had to know: if I took on the job, none of them was going to use the fact of his being one of us to get special favors. The way I saw it, sink or swim, all the POWs on this march were in the same boat.

The vote was unanimous that I accept. I went to the head of the column where I got in touch with our convoy of guards—about thirty German troopers under the command of a captain.

The first night we spent at a village. Only a few hundred of us could squeeze into the storage sheds, stables, and pigpens. Most of us had to settle down outdoors for the night as best we could, hugging the walls of builidngs for shelter from the snow and the bite of the wind.

In the morning I advised the Palestinians not to stay together in a group but to break up and work themselves in among the rest of the POWs. It was a precaution. The temptation to gun down Jews could prove too great for the Germans to resist.

We moved on. Whither we had no idea, nor did our guards, apparently. Each day they received fresh instructions about our direction. We were proceeding generally westward into the heart of Germany. After a few days I had an idea of what sort of men made up the company of guards, and even found common ground with their captain. He, too, sensed the beginning of the end of the Third Reich, and he was anxious to be on good terms with us.

We dragged our feet through the deepening snow; ice formed at the corners of our mouths and round our nostrils. I did twice the distance covered by the column. In the course of a day I passed up and down the line from end to end a couple of times as I checked on the condition of the men, determined the length of our rest periods, and tried to keep spirits from flagging. Groups of prisoners, Britishers and Palestinians, kept dropping out of the column to take unscheduled rests. I urged them to rejoin the march. The important thing was to keep them from lying motionless in the snow: it would have meant certain and quick death. I remember one of our own who was angry with me and began to argue when I tried to force him back on his feet. But I wouldn't let him have his way and finally got him back in line. He walked with difficulty; his toes had already gone numb.

Our tale of days on the road mounted; there seemed to be no end to the snowfall. When we were lucky we were able to get under a roof at some roadside village; otherwise, we slept outdoors. During the whole thirty-day trek our daily ration consisted of only a single loaf of bread shared by five men. Without the little store of food we had brought along from the stalag we would never have survived.

The cold grew less bitter as we got farther west. But none of us yet dared to take off his shoes: They had become stuck to our feet and to get them off was excruciatingly painful. When we made bivouac, I would assign each of our units their place for the night, and then immediately "attach" myself to the German captain to pump him for information. He never knew much, but his mood was grim. We expected liberation any day whereas he knew the end was at hand for Germany. He and his men were as exhausted as we were and they barely kept guard over us any more. But none of us even considered running away at this point: the end of the war was already in sight.

The conduct of the men on the march was exemplary. Not only did they hold up under conditions that took them almost beyond the limits of human endurance; they were constantly finding reserves of strength to help one another and me. There was one cold night when I started out of sleep to see Fogel's face hovering over mine. "Wh-what is it, Fogel?" I remember saying still half asleep. "Yosef," he whispered, "I brought you some bread. . . ." I can still hear the sweet sound of his voice then. One of the boys told me that Fogel had singled me out for his special protection as far back as Jakobswalde and had been keeping me under his wing every day of the march, always managing to finagle a tidbit over the norm for me. There were others, as well, who showed their concern for me in a thousand little ways.

At Death's Door

One night I suddenly felt sharp stomach cramps. By morning I was barely able to get to my feet. I saw to the distribution of rations for the day (now only one loaf to every six men), and then the march was on again. The pains in my stomach were unbearable: I left the road and stretched myself out under a culvert. In a little while I saw the German captain peering in. He had noticed I was missing, and someone told him they had seen me go down to the culvert. He asked me what was wrong. I told him I was at the end of my rope and asked him to shoot me to put an end to the pain. He called over some British officers from our column to lend a hand and hailed a peasant who was passing in a wagon. The British carried me to the cart and laid me down inside. There was a doctor among them, who gave me a shot of morphine. "Take him to Beutzen—and don't get too far ahead of us!" That was the captain speaking to the man with the wagon. As the wagon moved through the line of POWs I sank into semiconsciousness, but I could hear the men talking.

An English voice: "How's Joe?"

"Dying." It was one of the officers. The word was soothing: no more pain. The wagon stopped and someone brought a stretcher. Four men carried me into a hospital. One of our German guards told the doctor on duty that they were bringing in an English sergeant suffering from acute appendicitis. The doctor ordered his medics to take me in, but when the four Englishmen who had brought me tried to follow he block their path. "If you don't trust us take him away!" he told them. The British officers approached the stretcher, then bent over me and gently said, "Pray to God. He will help."

My friends turned and left. I was taken into the ward, and a young German army doctor came over to fill in my admission form:

"Name?"

I quickly repressed the impulse to give him an English alias. "Yosef Krelenboim." I enunciated my name clearly. His eyebrows shot upward.

"Where are you from?"

"From Palestine," I said.

"Jewish?"

"Yes."

I had decided to chance it. I knew that if I gave him a false identity and died, I would be declared missing by the British, and my family would never know what had happened to me. It was too late in the day for me to be false to what I was.

The German swallowed hard. He bent over to me and whispered: "Have you any idea where you are, man?"

"Yes," I said, "a German hospital."

"Right!" He was breathing the words out in a hoarse whisper now: "A special hospital for the Waffen SS!"

I let what he said sink in. It didn't matter and what earthly difference could it make now? He lingered awhile and seemed to be trying to make up his mind about something. He said, "Do you know German?" "Yes," I answered. Then he left.

A few minutes later he was back with a colleague. The second doctor had the rank of major and wore eyeglasses. The senior began asking questions in German, which the younger man rapidly translated into English before I had a chance to answer. He was clearly trying to prevent me from speaking German and letting my accent give me away.

The medical examination was short. "So," the major said, "on the table with him!" Two nurses arrived before the words were out and began preparing me for surgery. I was lying on the table now and being asked to count:

ONE (it was 8:00 p.m.) . . . *TWO* (February 13, 1945) . . . *THREE* (Beutzen) . . . *FO* . . . (I was dying) . . .

I awoke before dawn. I was in a soft, clean bed; the room was white. It was five years since I had experienced anything like it. There were two nurses in the room. One jumped up and warned me not to touch the tube attached to my stomach; the second hurried out to fetch the doctor. He came in and told me I had peritonitis, an inflammation of the membrane lining the abdominal cavity, and that my stomach was full of pus; which was being drawn off by the tube. If I did not come down with pneumonia, I would be all right. In the meantime I was to breath normally, although doing so caused me hellish pain, I was *not* to drink water. The nurses followed the doctor's instructions to the letter. They would not give me a drop, even though I was terribly thirsty. And I received no pain killers.

The same morning I had another visitor: the same young medical officer who had admitted me and filled out the forms. He sat down at the edge of the bed. He asked me to be open with him. "Who are you, really?"

The question surprised me. I repeated what I had said to him before the operation. He then told me that there was a delegation of four French officers come to see me. French? I was stunned; I asked him to show them in.

As it turned out the British officers who had brought me in had discovered that Beutzen had a camp with French POWs who were already partially free. My friends asked the Frenchman to look after me: if I died, to see to it I had a proper military burial; if I lived, to get me whatever I asked for. And here they were, bearing gifts, even cigarettes rarer than hens' teeth and dearer than gold. I thanked them from the bottom of my heart.

I was recovering, and by the end of the week they were getting ready to release me, when the order came through to evacuate the hospital. The staff decided to have me transferred to a POW camp about twenty-six miles away. They left the tube in my stomach. The road seemed made up only of potholes, and every jolt wrought havoc on my insides. The pain was extreme. When I arrived, I was checked over by a British medical officer, who pronounced himself dissatisfied with my condition. "Your stomach is still full of pus," he said. "The stitches are going to have to come out if we're to keep that thing sterile, you know." He then added that he would have to operate without adequate sterilization since supplies were exhausted. I asked if I had a choice. He shook his head.

Three days after my improvised operation the camp was evacuated. The seriously ill were brought to the freight train. The normal complement to a car was fifty POWs; only forty of the seriously ill were packed into a car. A British officer determined who would remain standing and who would be permitted to lie down. I was still sick enough to be among the lucky ones; I lay down. After two days in transit, we reached Dresden. The train pulled into the station in the midst of a heavy bombing attack by the RAF. One of the passengers died.

We continued on to Leipzig. There was an Australian sergeant sitting beside me. He convinced me to make every effort to appear well. "If they put you into a German hospital now, you won't get out alive," he said. When we arrived we were taken into the large basement of a hospital. As we waited for the doctor to appear, the Australian, with the help of a friend, shaved me and gave me a thorough cleaning for the medical examination. When the doctor came in I rose to my feet and shot him my most fetching smile. When he asked me how I felt I told him, "First-rate!" He let me remain in the basement with the light cases.

Apparently, I *was* getting better. I started to feel hungry again. I managed to scrounge some potato peels, which I cooked. They tasted wonderful!

A few days later I was taken with a group of presumably healthy POWs to a camp of British POWs who worked at a German synthetic gasoline factory. I was the only Palestinian there and the other prisoners behaved wonderfully to me. I gradually regained my strength.

Liberation

In the spring of 1945 the Americans were advancing in Germany, and our camp came under heavy shelling. We spent most of the time in shelters. The coolness of the British then was exemplary. My admiration was tinged with envy on one particular occasion. We were in the shelter, which was covered over by earth, with trees growing on top. We suffered a direct hit, and the shell that struck the roof set the trees on fire. There was a stampede for the door, when out of the turmoil one of the British officers shouted, "Remember, we're British!" It was the magic word: Order was instantly restored, and we all filed out quietly.

On Arpil 11 our guards announced to us that they were pulling out. We were on our own. That was all there was to it—quite suddenly we were free. We were exhilarated, but we couldn't make a move for as long while, as long a the artillery barrage kept up. When the shelling finally died down, we quickly made up some white flags and went out to meet the Americans.

The first one I saw was a black GI and very tall, and his machine-gun was pointed at me. When he saw I wasn't a kraut, he came over and hugged me and pressed my hand. I hugged him back, very hard.

The Americans received us enthusiastically and heaped on us the best their field kitchens could offer. It was very good, but I was still weak and in pain. So I left my friends while they were gorging themselves and sought out one of the American medics to tell him about my condition. He was a shrewd boy and advised me that if I wanted to get home quickly I'd better not let them know that I was sick; if I complained, I would end up in a hospital in Germany and be left there for a long time. I took his advice.

Together with the rest of the former POWs, I was taken to a large army camp in Munich. There I was quickly listed among those being taken to London. But just before I boarded the plane I was checked over by an American army doctor. He spotted what was wrong with me and his face fell. As he took down my medical history, I urged him not to have me committed to a hospital. He let me go. In a few hours we had landed in London and were driven out to Newcastle. There I was admitted to a small military hospital and given a thorough medical examination. The doctor there said that my getting well was nothing short of a miracle.

As soon as I arrived in London, I wired home to let my family know I was well. I later found out that one of the newspapers in England had published an article containing interviews with former British POWs, and that my name had been brought up. It seems they praised me for my activities in the POW camp and added that I had been lost track of and was presumed dead. That news, as Mark Twain once said in similar circumstances, was greatly exaggerated.

All the Palestinian former POWs were concentrated at Newcatle, and from there we were taken all over England to be the guests of various Jewish communities.

Itzhak Ben-Aharon was among the liberated POWs. When he found out that the Mapai party had split (it happened in 1944, when a dissident faction had reconstituted the Ahdut Avoda), he announced that those among us who had left for the war as Mapai members must avoid choosing sides; we should be a factor in reestablishing party unity. When I procured my doctor's permission to participate in the party meeting, I spoke up. "God forbid," I said, "that we should become a kind of third party. When we get home, we must return to the bosom of our political family—Mapai."

It was amazing how quickly we were transformed from liberated POWs taking their ease in England back into politicized Jews from Eretz Israel. The urge to reassert our ties with the homeland was overwhelming. Scores of Palestinians who had never dreamed of becoming party members now filled the hall at Newcastle for party meetings.

Finally, in May, the good tidings came. The first ship to carry liberated POWs bound for Palestine would set sail shortly. The announcement added that the vessel would not have room for us all and that those who wished to spend a little while longer in England were free to do so. My doctors advised me to stay or wait for a ship equipped to take on the sick and wounded. I was still bandaged and feeling a bit shaky, but I ignored their advice and boarded the first ship bound for Port Said in Egypt. There I took the train to Sarafend.

En route to Sarafend the train stopped at Rehovot, where Eliahu Golomb appeared at the head of a large delegation of Jewish Palestine's leaders to welcome me home. At Sarafend, my wife and son were waiting for me. Our meeting there was unforgettable.

Friends streamed in at all hours to visit us at my father-in-law's home in Tel Aviv, where we had stopped for a few days' rest. Then, in Haifa, a large gathering was arranged in honor of my homecoming. When I rose to speak about the experiences of the war, I was in acute discomfort; my wounds had not yet healed. I also began to suffer from the psychological aftereffects of my internment. The memories of my time in captivity haunted me day and night; they robbed me of my sleep. I needed more time to free myself of the nightmare.

This was one of the reasons I decided to reject the offer of a publisher in Palestine to tell my story to a writer and have it published as a book. I was offered a good price, and I could have used the money. During my internment, my wife had been forced to sell our house in Kfar Saba, and with the help of friends had moved into a one-room flat in Haifa. I wa perfectly aware that financially, at least, I would have to start all over again. But I could not bring myself to relive my experinces as a POW in all their horrid detail, even if only in the retelling.

For the same reason I at first refused a request by Ziama Aran to appear at a meeting of the Central Committtee of the Histadrut in order to report there on the experiences of our men in the POW camps. Ziama would not be put off and spoke to Abba Khoushi, at whose intercession it was arranged that a taxi would pick me up at home and bring me down to the Central Committee meeting in Tel Aviv. All that was asked of me was that I should be present while Globinski and Ben-Aharon did the talking. By the time those two had finished, they had managed to bring up my name so many times that the chairman, Yosef Shprintzak, declared that he was unable to keep his part of our bargain and was compelled to call me to the rostrum.

I had not prepared anything, but I rose to speak. I talked for over an hour, and when I had finished I was given a succession of warm hugs by Meir Yaari, Tzvi Yehuda, and a host of others—too many. Each time I was clasped to the bosom of another well-wisher, it was all I could do to keep myself from wincing. But how could I tell them I was in pain?

Moshe Sharett closed the meeting, and the next day in the Histadrut newspaper, *Davar,* his speech was published under the title *Ka-zot od lo shamanu* ("We Never Heard Anything Like It").

8
Striking Roots in Haifa

Like many of my friends who had been demobilized, I was at loose ends and fretted with indecision during those first months after my release from the army. I had spent five years during which virtually all decisions were made for me, and now all at once I had to decide everything for myself. I had to put my life in order and settle my future.

I had army experience and a background in defense and military organization, so it was only natural I should receive offers from that direction. Over a beer in a small café opposite the old building of the Tel Aviv Executive Committee, Itzhak Sadeh—one of the leading personalities in operational Jewish defense in Palestine—asked me if I would take on national command of Hagana Infantry; he also suggested I replace Zeev Feinstein as Histadrut representative at Hagana HQ. But for all of my admiration of the job being done by the chiefs of the Hagana, and my sincere appreciation of the honor they were doing me, I could not see myself making a career of the military.

Then there was David Remez, secretary of the Histadrut, who wished to co-opt me to the Labor Federation's Executive Committee. Finally, I was being urged by Hapoel to become the organization's secretary-general. Because of my earlier association with Hapoel, I accepted the post, but after some hesitation and only for a trial period. The trial was less than successful. After a brief interval, I found that the job did not meet with my expectations.

Then I was asked to undertake a mission on behalf of the Jewish National Fund to Argentina, Uruguay, and Brazil. Getting away for a while was exactly what I needed, I thought, and I quickly accepted the offer. On my way to South America, I stopped in Paris to await my visa to Argentina. It was December 1946, and the Twenty-second Zionist Congress was in session in Basel. This was the Congress's first meeting since the start of war. Basel was close enough to Paris to enable me to participate.

The Congress is the representative asembly of all the parties in the World Zionist Organization, and it determines policy for the Zionist movement. During its deliberations that year, tempers, not unexpectedly, ran high. Dr. Weizmann was under attack for his supposed pro-British orientation and resigned the presidency, which he had held since 1935. (The post was to go vacant until 1956;) The Zionist-Revisionists were back in the fold as the Congress dealt with the problems of illegal Jewish immigration and the political and military struggle against the British Mandate.

My wife had in the meantime arrived in Paris, and we set out for a tour of Jewish refugee camps in Germany, Austria, and Czechoslovakia. The campaign to smuggle Holocaust survivors into Eretz Israel was at its height then. Thousands of homeless Jews were being taken clandestinely across European borders to staging grounds and from there to ships that attempted to run the British blockade of the coast of Palestine. The whole operation was being run out of Paris, where I renewed my acquaintance with those who stood at its head.

The Jewish Nation Fund, (JNF) on whose behalf I went to South America, is the central land and development fund of the Zionist movement. It was responsible for the purchase of land in Palestine on behalf of the whole Jewish people and for its lease to Jewish settlements in Eretz Israel. With Jewish Palestine preparing to receive vast numbers of homeless Jews from Europe, the JNF was making an all-out effort in its fund drive among Jewish communities throughout the world.

For three months I travelled among the Jewish communities of South America and addressed audiences sometimes two and three times a day. I generally spoke to them in Yiddish; my hearers were in the main Yiddish speakers, many were still tied to the culture they were born to and which the Germans had just recently nearly destroyed on its home ground in Eastern Europe. Although their sense of national identity was strongly Yiddishist, it very much took in Eretz Israel. They gave, and gave generously, but they found it hard to believe that the creation of a Jewish state in Eretz Israel was at hand. The obstacles seemed to them insurmountable.

I arrived back in Israel and had not even unpacked when I received an urgent telegram from Abraham Granott, chairman of the Board of Directors of the JNF, who proposed that I return to South America and work for the organization another three months. The telegram was tempting; this time I would be able to take along my wife and son. Unhesitatingly I turned down Dr. Granott's proposal: if I kept up this sort of thing I would become a professional broker-cum-ambassador-at-large, shuttling between Eretz Israel and the ends of the earth, with roots nowhere. I needed to settle down.

At the time I was living with my wife and child in a small one-room flat on Jerusalem Street, number 15, in Haifa—the same flat my wife had taken while I was a POW. My neighbor on the top floor was Abba Khoushi, secretary of the Haifa Labor Council; it was only natural that we should reestablish the association we enjoyed before the war. During our conversations, Khoushi laid out before me the activities of the Labor Council in all of their range and scope; he was certain that I would fit in. The idea of working with the Labor Council was attractive.

I liked Haifa very much. I'd often walk to the top of Mount Carmel to take in the view of the city, fringing like a chaplet the blue waters of the bay of Haifa.

The factory chimneys in the harbor area edged the city's delicate grace in a ring of strength. Haifa was not only touchingly beautiful, I thought, but the hub of great economic power, actual and potential with its deep-water port, refineries, and railway terminus. Haifa also contained some of the most important industrial enterprises in the country: the Nesher Cement Works, the only one of its kind in Palestine; and the headquarters of the building enterprise of the Histadrut, Solel Boneh; the Palestine Electric Corporation; the Postal Service; and Customs. . . . Haifa was without doubt already one of our vital commercial centers, and I felt sure it was destined for great things in the Jewish state that must soon arise. I was also convinced that the Labor Council would have a key role in the whole scheme.

The Labor Council's scope was not confined to trade-union activities; it comprehended municipal and national affairs of first-rank importance and contributed to the educational and cultural life of the Jewish community. One field that particularly interested me was that of economic relationships between Arab and Jewish residents in Haifa. Haifa was the center of the "Covenant of Workingmen in Eretz Israel," which gave expression to the strivings for amity and cooperation between the two peoples. This was an approach that deserved more vigorous pursuit, especially now that the Mufti's adherents were gaining ground among the Arabs of Palestine.

I made up my mind to accept Abba Khoushi's suggestion and become engaged full time in the activities of the Labor Council. Avigdor Eshet (Eisenstadt), with whom I would be working for many years to come, joined the council at the same time.

In October 1947 Abba Khoushi left for the United States on an extended fund-raising tour for the Histadrut, and I was elected to take his place in the Labor Council for the duration. Avigdor Eshet was supposed to share the burden of office and act as a restraining nfluence on me. In my short time with the Labor Council I had acquired a reputation for making rapid decisions (some called them hasty) and for being temperamental. The months Khoushi was away turned out to be stormy and not only at the Labor Council, but in the whole country.

In Room 10 (Abba Khoushi's office) at Labor House, I began to review and master the complex structure of the organization that had been put into my hands. I had to learn a great deal quickly; the Labor Council was involved in the operations of every public institution that touched on the lives of the city's Jewish and Arab populations. Chief among these was the municipality, which was under a mixed administration and served the needs of 70,000 Jews and 60,000 Arabs, according to the statistics available.

The mayor of Haifa was Shabbtai Levi, an Oriental Jew and a public servant of long standing; he was a man of liberal convictions who was affiliated with no political party. The Community council, whose backbone was the Histadrut, stood at the head of the Jewish community of Haifa. The Situational Subcommittee was another body of considerable importance in the life of the city. Its job was to deal with defense and supply and it was made up of representatives of various political parties and public bodies. Still another active public group was the

Hadar Hacarmel Committee, which oversaw the management of municipal services such as water supply. The Histadrut was represented in all these institutions. In addition, it also had taken upon itself to work among the Arab and Druze populations living in Haifa and its environs; it did this through the Histadrut-affiliated Covenant of Workingmen in Eretz Israel, which was administered by the Labor Council.

I went to work. The working day began punctually at 6:40 A.M., when the Council Secretariat met in my office. There we went over the morning papers together and exchanged news and ideas before getting down to the day's routine. In addition to handling the day-to-day affairs of the Histadrut in the Labor Council, I took Abba Khoushi's place at civilian headquarters of the Hagana; my work there put me back into contact with the future first chief of staff of Israel's army, Yaakov Dori. Chief of the Hagana civilian HQ at the time was Yaakov Lublini, and military matters were in the hands of Moshe Carmel, Hagana CO of the Northern District. Cooperation between the Histadrut and the Hagana was very close indeed: part of the Hagana's military headquarters was housed in the Haifa Labor Council's own building on Jerusalem Street, and other sections of the defense force were distributed among various Histadrut institutions throughout the city.

The City as Battlefield

On Saturday evening, November 29, 1947, I was sitting with the family around our ancient radio, avidly following the voting at the UN General Assembly on the resolution for the partition of Palestine into two independent states—one Arab and one Jewish. We were keeping count, taking down the results as they came in. Each time we heard "yes" we were exalted, and our spirits plummeted when a delegate pronounced "No" We were tense, although the results of the vote were clear enough before the final tally was officially announced—thirty three nations for, thirteen against. We were out of our seats, hugging and cheering. It was true—we had a state!

I made a dash for Beitenu, Labor Council headquarters. There would be great crowds out in front celebrating.

There assuredly were. It was only with great difficulty that I could work my way through the throng of celebrants. The café owners were handing out free drinks, and circles of dancers were whirling round in the streets; in among them there were British soldiers, warmed to the event by the wine. Hehalutz Street was mobbed by the time I got there, and it took a good deal of squeezing and pushing before I could worm my way past the doors of the Labor Council buildings. Once inside and up the stairs I spotted one of our men dragging a ship's bell onto the balcony. This was all that remained of the *Patria*—a ship used in 1940 to run immigrants past the British blockade. The *Patria* was caught, and to prevent the British from turning her back and interning her passengers, a bomb was planted on board with the intention of only crippling her. The charge was excessive and the explosion took the lives of 216 out of the 1,800 people she carried. Now her bell was being vigorously rung by the man as he bellowed, "No more *Patrias*! Free immigration! A Jewish State!" with the crowd cheering him on. David Bar-Rav-Hai, one of the most prominent political workers in the city, and I each made short speeches. There were cheers again.

The celebrations in Room 10 were at their height when a man broke in on us, shouting "They've come—the people from the mixed neighborhoods!" We headed out to the street to see what it was about. At the entrance to the building we found ourselves facing a group of families parked bag and baggage on our doorstep. They were obviously afraid. Anticipating trouble from their Arab neighbors when news of the UN vote was out, they had cleared out their homes on Hashomer and Syrkin streets down in the bay area and had come on foot all the way up the Carmel and over to the Labor Council building. It was the first place of refuge they'd thought of.

We calmed them as best we could and came to a quick decision about what to do for them. We would get in touch right now with the Community Council and the Situational Subcommittee and ask them to clear some school buildings immediately for temporary shelters. The next day, after a mass public rally held a few streets up from us at Beit Hakranot Square, where Gutl Levin, chairman of the Hadar Hacarmel Committee, David Bar-Rav-Hai, and I spoke about the significance of the Partition Resolution, we set up emergency headquarters for dealing with the evacuees, whose numbers were growing by leaps and bounds.

The Arabs mounted an assault on Jewish residents in Burj and Stanton streets and were lying in ambush along routes taken by Jewish commuters in the city. The battle was joined and growing more fierce with each passing hour. It would soon reach a decisive stage.

Clashes were taking place especially along the major arteries of communication, at points were the Arabs had the advantage of high ground: along the Haifa–Tel Aviv highway at Tira, just south of Haifa; along the roads to the Plain of Jezreel; at Lad a-Sheikh; and along the streets connecting the Upper City at Hadar Hacarmel with the bay area and the ones running from the Lower City through Wadi Rushmia to the string of suburbs north of Haifa. The Hagana met the Arab offensive with vigor, and Jewish civil organizations put themselves on an emergency footing in preparation for a long siege.

The most important challenge being faced by Labor Council was to hold on to integrated places of work, those employing both Jewish and Arab workingmen; these included the most vital of the city's enterprises and services: the refineries, the railway, the harbor, the oil companies, and the postal service. We had to see to the security of the Jewish workers and at the same time avoid creating a rift between them and the Arab laborers, who made up a very large sector of the work force. Both objectives had to be achieved or we would be forced to surrender strategic positions of incalculable value.

Every morning I went over to Industry House on Herzl Street in the Upper City to see off the workers who were waiting for buses to take them down to their places of work in the harbor. On their way they would be passing through Wadi Rushmia where they might well have to run a gauntlet of Arab ambuscades. You could feel the tension among them. They boarded the buses and sat brooding in silence. Their wives and parents lined the pavement to watch them pass, uncertain if they would see the men again.

Some of the men ran a risk only on the way to and from work; others, working in places where the majority of the workers were Arabs, lived with danger throughout the working day. Among these workers, there were also women and girls. As I watched the bus move out my prayers went with them. I tried to console the wives and mothers who were clutching with their eyes for a last glimpse as the bus drew out of sight; many were in tears. I think they were all aware we had no choice; these were the hazards imposed on us by the exigencies of the time.

The mixed places of work in Haifa were so unquestionably vital to the economy and security of the state that it never even occurred to us to abandon them—not to any of us. Indeed, as any check run on the work cards issued during those months will show, despite the daily exposure to sniping on the road to and from work and the expectation of violence on the job, absenteeism was down to the barest minimum. These statistics are a token of the extraordinary courage shown by our men, particularly when we keep in mind the relative numbers of Arabs and Jews at work in these places: as against about ten thousand Arab laborers, there were only a few hundred Jews. Moreover, when we tried to increase the number of Jewish employees at integrated places of work, we ran into trouble because of the poor working conditions and low pay. All the same, Haifa was unique in Israel for the fact that Jews and Arabs were working side by side while the war raged all round and with increasing ferocity from one day to the next.

By now the whole city had become a battlefield. Exchanges of gunfire could be heard day and night in the Lower City and along the line where Arab and Jewish neighborhoods met. There was now no let up in the sniping along major routes. We continued and even increased our activities at the places of work, holding daily briefings for the workers. At the same time, we checked security measures and recruited men for the Hagana. Nor did we neglect union matters or cultural activities and immigration. I kept goading the men at the Labor Council to maintain the pace of work; I knew that once we grew slack the efficiency of our organization would weaken and hurt the war effort.

We grew increasingly concerned about the situation at the mixed places of work. Our position was weakest in the oil refineries, which at the end of 1947 employed 1,810 Arabs, 460 Jews, and 60 British. Security there was in the hands of three distinct groups: a company of the Arab Legion under the command of an Arab officer; 30 Arab watchmen; and some British security officers taken on by the enterprise. The legionnaires were concentrated in two enclaves, where they had the job of protecting company property. As for the Arab watchmen and the British security officers, they were hardly a factor since they were distributed throughout the company grounds, which stretched over an area of miles.

Violence mounted. Jewish workers at the refineries felt themselves threatened. On December 1, 1947, the Jewish workers' representatives called on company personnel manager John Hopkins. He had served as an intelligence officer in the British navy; even now he had more to do with intelligence than with business administration. The workers' representatives told Hopkins about their anxieties over the safety of the Jewish laborers and clerks; there were so few of them compared to the great mass of Arab workingmen at the plant. They asked for changes in the security routine and suggested that Jewish watchmen replace the legionnaires or, alternatively, a British guard be set up in place of the Arab guard. Hopkins insisted that the company assumed responsibility for the security of all its employees and not just a small group of them; moreover, he did not believe that the refineries were in any danger. Still, he promised to bring up the request for consideration by the proper authorities.

Weeks went by, and our workers' representatives again applied to the plant management for a change in the security arrangements. The management replied that British army authorities were unwilling to introduce changes in existing security routine; nor did the civil authorities believe any change was necessary.

By now we were really concerned, and on December 20 we met with General Stockwell, British military commander of Haifa and the North. We asked for the Arab Legion to be removed from the refineries and withdrawn from those traffic routes in the city that were under direct Arab threat. General Stockwell, a tall man with a pronounced stoop, promised in the presence of his aide, Brigadier Rom, that he would consider our proposal. I had the feeling that Stockwell understood our problems and was ready to help. A few days later we got word that our request had been rejected.

During the last week of December a general meeting of Jewish workers at the refineries was called. Every speaker warned of the violence that would certainly erupt at any moment. The security of Jewish workers could not be placed in the hands of legionnaires or Arab watchmen, whose unreliabiity was already a matter of record elsewhere in Israel. I was present at the meeting, and as soon as it ended, I went to see the personnel manager to report the decisions taken by the workers. I also delivered an ultimatum—if the workers' demands to have the Arab guards replaced by either Jewish or British guards were not met, a strike would be called. Hopkins tried to conciliate me. The British also had guns, he said and as for the Arab legionnaires, they were, after all, under British command and would doubtless do their bit to protect the Jews should the need arise; in any case he fully intended to deal with the situation immediately.

More negotiations followed, and then the management announced that British authorities saw no possibility of removing the legionnaires from the refineries but promised that in case of a conflict, the Arab Legion would remain neutral. Moreover, the Arab watchmen would be disarmed; some would be dismissed outright and others posted as unarmed guards. And there would be the same number of Jewish guards as Arab.

I was not satisfied, and I argued that the Jewish workers still remained a minority, without any defense whatever. He asked me to keep in mind the sixty British clerks at the plant, all of whom were armed.

All the while I was meeting with the personnel manager, the Community Council was desperately arguing the same issue with the British district authorities and British Army HQ—and with as little success. By the end of December, not a single Arab watchman had been disarmed, and the legionnaires had stayed put.

Carnage at the Refineries

On the morning of December 30, 1947, a large group of Arab workmen was routinely shaping up in the area between the inner and outer gates of the plant grounds. At 10:15 a car passed by the entrance to the refineries and two hand grenades were tossed out of its windows into the crowd. The explosions killed six Arab workmen and wounded fifty. The bombers—as it later turned out—were Jews and members of IZL, the Irgun.

When the first shock of the explosions passed, the workmen began to hand the dead and wounded through the inner gate into the plant grounds, and the rest of the crowd followed; in the meantime Arabs already at work were running toward the entrance. In a short time, rumors had swelled the tale of dead to several score, and the cry for vengeance was out. Within minutes a mob of hundreds burst into company grounds, armed with iron bars, tools, or whatever came to hand. They broke up into groups and, with cries of "Let's get them!" set upon any Jew who crossed their path.

A group of about two hundred made for the workshops where nearly forty Jewish workers had barricaded themselves. The Arabs beat at the gates with hammers, tried to pry them open with crowbars and batter them down with wood beams. Then they brought a tractor and rammed it into the doors until they gave way. The Jews inside fought back, and nearly all of them were wounded. At the nearby electrical supply warehouse one of the Jewish workmen shouted that the door was electrified, and the mob retreated. At the main warehouse the Arab keeper passed out tools to the attackers. Jews who were unable to defend themselves sought refuge wherever they could find it. Two of them, with the mob at their heels, ran into the area where the legionnaires were bivouacked only to find guns leveled at them; they continued at a run in another direction and managed to save themselves.

The riot went on for more than an hour. It took the lives of thirty-nine Jews, and fifty-one were injured. Most of the British section bosses and clerks, after telephoning, or trying to telephone, the head office, left at the very beginning. Not one of them had even tried to help. Nor did the Legion raise a finger to protect the Jewish workers. Many of the Arab workmen took no part in the assault, and some even tried to defend the Jewish workers, but on the whole, they made no effort to hold back the fury of the rioters.

The company officers had received news of the riots very shortly after they had begun; a whole hour passed before the police finally arrived. When they did come, it was with only three policemen and one officer in two armored cars; it took time before reinforcements were brought up and the riot was put to an end.

The same morning I was in the harbor area. Around noon I received a telephone call from the Labor Council: something was up at the refineries and all traffic in the area had been halted. I rushed down and found the legionnaires ranged in front of the gate with their weapons cocked, letting no one in. I had to wait for the arrival of the police before I could get the details of what had happened and take action.

I found out that when the Jewish workers asked for assistance against the rioters, the managers did nothing but assure them that the police were on their way. Some English clerks saved men and helped evacuate the injured, but they were the exceptions. The British let the Arab workmen leave in Arab buses that had been brought in under British convoy; there was no attempt to ascertain which of the Arab laborers had taken part in the riot: not one was detained even for a short while for questioning. But the British did detain the ambulance with a red Star of David that had rushed over to collect the injured.

Not in our wildest dreams had we imagined that anything like this would happen. We were furious with the British for having ignored our warnings and left our men unprotected. The British countered by saying that the whole episode would never have taken place if it were not for the bomb throwing of the Irgun. Our own Situational Subcommittee had already published a denunciation of the act, but the statement insisted that the provocation in no way excused company management from its responsibility; they had been repeatedly warned but refused to meet their obligations. A Commission of Enquiry headed by the late Dr. I. Kaiserman, then chairman of the Lawyers' Association in Haifa, came to the same conclusion.

Trying to Get Back on the Job

The workers struck the refineries. They were down at the Labor Council building every day. On the day after the riot there was a meeting of workers in Beitenu. An ad hoc committee was formed to maintain contact with the Labor Council and to look after the immediate and most pressing needs of the strikers. The anger we felt was not assuaged by the Hagana's reprisal raids on the Arab villages of Lad a-Sheikh and Hawasa, during which dozens of those who had had a hand in the murders at the refineries were killed. Three of our own boys fell in the actions: Yohanan Zelinger (after whom Tel Hanan was later named) and Haim Ben-Dor (whose name is memorialized in the neighborhood of Ben-Dor), both from Yagur; and Amos Galili. The question uppermost in our minds was, What would happen at the other integrated places of work?

On January 8, British District Governor A. N. Low asked me in to discuss the refinery workers' security demands. He had received company proposals that called for the withdrawal of Arab Legion troopers from plant grounds; a British armored-car convoy for our men on their way to and from work; and the removal of suspected rioters and putting them on trial. Nothing was said concerning our demand to have Jewish watchmen posted on the grounds.

We decided to reject the management offer and stay off the job. The trauma had been too great and the proposals inadequate to meet the need. But the Jewish community was under siege, and fuel was in short supply. There was a danger that if the refineries did not get back into production we would have no gasoline. The British and Arabs had other sources, we did not.

Later that month the Hagana commander in chief informed me that the defense force's fuel reserves—indeed, those of the whole country—were running fearfully low; the situation was so bad that Ben-Gurion himself was ready to come down to a meeting of the strikers to persuade them to go back to work. I told Galili that if we began to call on Ben-Gurion to deal with every problem that developed at mixed places of work in Haifa he might as well take on the job of Labor Council secretary himself. I proposed, instead, that we renew negotiations with the management and try at the same time to convince the workers to return to the job. If we failed, then we would call Ben-Gurion.

We called another refinery workers' meeting at Labor Council Headquarters. I spent hours trying to explain to the strikers the enormous strategic importance of the refineries to the nation; the fact that they were the only ones of their kind in the entire country; that they had to be put back into operation if a normal supply of fuel was to reach the Jewish community. But the men were not about to forget the lesson they had learned from bitter experience. They set conditions for their return, and they would not retreat from them.

While the meeting was still going on, I rode out to the refineries to have a talk with the management. My way took me through Wadi Rushmia, which was at all times hazardous to pass through, but particularly so at dusk, when I went. But I was only doing what the men had to do every day. I had come to the management to discuss the changes that had to be made for a revised work agreement. We had got Zvi Berenson, legal adviser of the Histadrut and later an Israeli Supreme Court justice, to help us hammer out a new agreement.

I returned to the meeting, which went on late into the night. We examined the agreement in minutest detail, went over every clause with a fine-tooth comb. It was finally put to a vote: the overwhelming majority of the men voted to go back to work. Churchill's praise for the RAF about so many owing so much to so few seemed to me to apply to the refinery workers. They deserved the gratitude of the whole nation for their readiness to risk their lives to keep the fuel flowing. The workers who lived in the bay area were prevented from attending the meeting because of travel difficulties, but even if all of them had voted against going back to work, the decision to return would have been carried. In fact, during a second meeting I called at Kiryat Motzkin, one of the suburbs in the bay area, the result of a vote was similar to what it had been at Haifa.

January 20 the men went back to work. Because I had been one of the agreement's chief sponsors, I went along with the first shift. We were accompanied by a gratifyingly strong British military convoy. Two days later part of the Arab work force returned as well, having accepted the agreement that stipulated that Arab Supernumerary Police would be disarmed. Our own people made certain that none of the Arabs who returned to work had been involved in the riot.

Toward the end of March, the senior Jewish workmen informed us that the plant had received orders to get all processed oil still on refinery grounds out of the country; oil tankers for the purpose had just arrived in Haifa Bay. I immediately met with the manager of the refineries to let him know that no fuel was going to leave the country. We would use force, if necessary, to prevent it. I had strapped on my Parabelum pistol (for which I had a license) as a hint that I had the Hagana behind me and that the threat was serious.

The manager, who was an Englishman, seemed embarrassed; he asked me if I would be willing to go with him to meet the manager of Shell and try to convince the head office to cancel the order and save the plant and the tankers from destruction. That was precisely what I did. The next day the senior workmen got through to me with the news that the instructions had been canceled.

In April, as the date for final British withdrawal from Palestine neared, the management of the refineries received instructions to leave Israel. I met John Hopkins and reached an agreement with him: we would assume responsibility for keeping plant property and equipment safe; in return we would try to keep the Hagana from confiscating the flats on Mount Carmel that belonged to British company managers, or using their homes to house Jewish evacuees from the border neighborhoods.

At last in mid-April 1948, we found ourselves masters of the refineries. That same day I went to meet Ben-Gurion at Hagana HQ in Ramat Gan, near Tel Aviv, to bring him the news personally. I also wanted his approval for our program to keep the plant operating.

My news took Ben-Gurion utterly by surprise; he was astounded. "What kind of pull have you got with the English that they should have handed over the refineries, just like that?" he said. I told him that I had been in touch with the British not only on matters having to do with Haifa, but also about Hagana affairs, so they tended to regard me as a Jew in authority. Besides, the management was impressed by my having exact knowledge as to when they were intending to pull their oil reserves out of the country; and they also admired the way I persuaded the workers to go back to work after the massacre of December 30. Maybe it was all those things that made the British attribute to me power and authority that I did not have.

Ben-Gurion said I had nothing to regret.

I suggested that a manager be appointed to the refineries, and that we could help him keep the plant going. I brought up the name of one of the most gifted plant managers of the time—Dr. George Landau, who was manager of the Nesher Cement Works. Ben-Gurion had no objections, but one thing did bother him: he wanted everyone in an official position to answer to a Hebrew surname, which "Landau" definitely was not. Both of us were stumped, and for the moment could think of no appropriate Hebrew name for him. So Landau remained Landau.

It was only after I received Ben-Gurion's OK that I informed Dr. Landau, who accepted. Before the refineries were officially transferred to the state, Dr. Landau found himself frequently confronted by problems of a delicate nature. Sometimes, when he felt himself to be over his head, he would apply to me for help. One day the plant received a request from the Air Force for airplane fuel and pipes of a special sort, which, apparently, only the refineries had in stock. "What are we to do?" he asked. "I have absolutely no instructions about the matter." I said to him, "About the fuel—give it to them and write it down; we can do the arithmetic later. The pipes?—let the boys filch them."

I sent to the refineries units of the Army Labor Brigade, which I commanded. In a surprisingly short time, our men mastered the complex job of operating the refineries; they did it without the aid of the British experts, who had taken off without even briefing the men. By the time the state was proclaimed, our refineries were supplying all the country's essential fuel needs. Lives had been lost, but the results vindicated the decision to continue the struggle.

9
The Battle for Haifa

The massacre at the oil refineries had put a halt to Jewish labor in all plants and enterprises that had a mixed work force. Families simply refused to have the lives of their members put in jeopardy; they would not let their breadwinners go out on the job unless efficient protection was provided. The leadership of the Jewish community was not prepared to surrender vital industries and services, and these could not be retained without Jewish workers being on the job. Organized labor had to find a way of meeting both requirements: Jewish workers' presence on the job and the defense of Jewish employees in those places of work where they were under the threat of Arab rioters.

One of the danger points was the Mandatory Railway, which employed more than two thousand workers, of whom about one hundred and fifty were Jews. Most of these worked in the railway's workshops in the Kishon area to the north; a smaller number worked in the Lower City at the locomotive repair shed and the Traffic Department. Despite the war being waged by Arab irregulars on public transport and the daily and rising toll of dead and wounded on the roads, Jewish railway workers continued to show up at their places of work even though they were greatly outnumbered there by Arabs. Their dedication was remarkable. So much so, indeed, that whenever the traffic routes were sealed off because of shootings and ambushes, they would stay overnight in the nearby Jewish neighborhood so they could get to work the next day.

We were worred about them and wanted to reduce the risk they ran. We asked the railway officials to have those Jewish workers who were spread out among various departments concentrated in the Kishon workshops, and those in the Traffic Department brought to the Central Railway Station in Haifa. Our proposal was accepted.

To move things in the direction we had in mind, we tried to increase the number of Jewish personnel who would be ready to take over the running of the railway the moment the state proclaimed the takeover. The veteran workers trained the young people we recruited for the purpose. We also directed the old-timers to build up as large a concentration as they could of railway cars and locomotives on our side of the borders established by the UN partition plan. Finally, we undertook to get hold of as much of the railway workshop equipment as possible—it was worth millions in pounds sterling.

The riot at the refineries set these efforts at naught. Our railway men refused to continue on their jobs, as did the rest of the Jewish work force in places of mixed employment. After the first shock had passed, we realized that we had to make every effort to deny our enemies control of the railway system. Moreover, if the Arabs took over the railway workshops and warehouses these would become bases from which they could make war on the very heart of the Jewish community. We therefore called together the railway workers for a general meeting and spelled out our reasons for wanting them back on the job. To our immense relief, a majority voted to go back to work.

All the same, we were not about to let them start work without making certain that the risks they ran were reduced to a minimum. The memory of the bloodletting at the refineries was still fresh in our minds. We let the railway administration know that the return of our men would be conditional on the implementation of a number of security measures: the Arab guards had to be removed; security was to be in the hands of the British military; the clothing and tools of everyone entering the workshops would be searched. Members of the shop committee and Labor Council were asked to see to it that these measures were actually carried out.

We then had the Hagana arrange for firearms to be introduced and concealed in caches prepared beforehand. Our earlier failure to provide weapons and to arrange for a proper defense for our men was one error we were not going to repeat.

Among the security measures we arranged among ourselves was a permanent observation post set up on the roof of the Fenitzia factory near the Kishon railway work area. From there, Hagana spotters would keep watch on the workshops and call in help should the need arise. A special unit of the Hagana was assigned to break through the fence around the grounds and provide covering fire for our workmen in the event of an Arab assault.

As it turned out, the return of our men came just in time to prevent an Arab takeover of the railway. Arab workingmen were already systematically making off with workshop property: they were lifting spare parts, tools, and materials, and the pilferage was almost certainly organized.

The British—knowingly at times, unwittingly at others—aided the Arabs in their bid to take control of strategic points in the city. On the night of April 20, the British army cleared out of many positions they had occupied in the buffer zone between Arab and Jewish neighborhoods in Haifa, with the result that a unit of the Arab National Guard succeeded in getting hold of the administrative offices of the railway in the Houri Building. The next morning two Jewish clerks, who had made their way through streets in which battles were raging, were on their way in when they were met by a British officer who shouted to them, "Get away, quick—the Arabs are inside the building!" The men retreated. A few minutes later, when a call was put through to the offices, an Arab soldier answered the telephone. The retaking of Houri House by the Carmeli Brigade was one of the toughest battles in the liberation of Haifa.

On the evening of April 22, immediately after liberation of the city, I assigned the secretary of the Railway Shop Committee, Efraim Krisher, the task of getting the railway back into operation. Within days I was able to send good news to the People's Administration (the temporary institution of national government before the establishment of the government of Israel): "The railway in the Haifa area is in the competent hands of Jewish workers and at the service of the Jewish state about to come into existence."

We expended great effort in order to secure our position in the port of Haifa, where only about three hundred Jewish workers were employed among thousands of Arabs. The port director was British and took his orders from the railway administration; the section foremen were all Arabs, as were the private contractors, who hired thousands of seasonal Arab laborers.

As the hazard grew, the Hagana—coordinating its actions with us—sent a crack unit of the Palmah (its striking force) under the guise of dock workers into the port; the men carried concealed weapons and spread out, keeping their eyes on the Jewish workmen, ready to defend them should they be attacked. Although tension was high we decided that we had to keep the port going come what may and that we had to enlist as many Jews as we could to add to our numbers among the dockmen. At the same we arranged to get more firearms into the harbor area so that our men should not remain defenseless.

The Jewish workers employed by the oil companies (Shell, Socony-Vacuum, and the Iraqi British Petroleum Company) constituted another small and vulnerable group whose protection had to be secured. By negotiating with the companies, we were able to obtain conditions for them similar to those we succeeded in getting at the refineries.

We had quite a struggle with the administration of the NAAFI (the British equivalent of the American USO), which refused to accept our demands on security measures for its Jewish employees. Only after we wired the head office and warned them that our people would not return to work if our demands were not met did the branch in Haifa give in.

The only integrated place of employment in which we met no problems was the court and district governor's building. There the Jewish and Arab clerks met and decided unanimously to demand the replacement of British guards by Jews. The Arabs expressed their full confidence in their Jewish colleagues and informed the British that they had no need of "neutral" protectors.

Caring for Servicemen and the Homeless

An entirely different emergency had to do with the several score of families who had fled their homes in the neighborhoods abutting the Arab sections of the city and were unable to return. The Situational Subcommittee, in which the Labor Council played a major part, made a number of proposals, among them to increase community taxes and water tariffs in order to finance the temporary housing of the evacuees and cover their basic needs.

The proposals became the subject of sharp debate in the Executive Committee of the Labor Council. There were members of the executive who opposed increasing taxes because they felt that the burden would fall mainly on the workers and the poor. They proposed requisitioning rooms of large flats occupied by small families or, as a second possibility, demanding the payment of a room tax by owners of large homes. It was finally recommended that a progressive tax be introduced, based on home-occupation density, with payments in direct proportion to home size.

Meanwhile, we housed the evacuees in school buildings, summer-camp barracks, and temporary camps that we established in the Kiryat Eliyahu and Kiryat Nahum suburbs to the north of Haifa. Not even during the most difficult stages of our fight for survival were these people without a roof over their heads, and during the entire time their children continued to attend school.

Those embattled days brought with them a host of human problems that had to be dealt with if our people were to hold up as the pressures and the need for personal sacrifice mounted. There was the case of the families of unofficial Hagana recruits—several hundred men who had been sent out under Hagana command for guard duty. The Hagana was as yet in no position to maintain their families, and their situation was growing intolerable. The Labor Council took it upon itself to deal with their needs temporarily, until the problem was resolved officially and on a national scale. We established what we called a Security Fund for the families. The first infusion of money came from voluntary contributions by workmen of their overtime pay. After our men did their bit, we approached the employers and suggested to them that instead of paying time-and-a-quarter for overtime, as was then the practice, they should pay double. The employers in Haifa were amenable, and soon money was flowing into the Security Fund. Thus, our Hagana irregulars were able to take up their posts and participate in operations without leaving their families to starve. I think this may have been the first instance of having men receive their salaries while on reserve military duty, which has since become the legally sanctioned custom in Israel, where so many of our men are annually called out of their civilian jobs to serve in the reserves.

Then there was the problem of feeding our regular enlisted men. One morning Abba Khoushi's wife, Hannah (Khoushi was still in the United States, flew into my office in high indignation. "This can't go on!" she fumed. "How in Heaven's name are we supposed to cook meals and get them down to the boys on the line if we don't get a budget?" Money was the one thing we couldn't oblige her with; what we could do, though, was give her the things that the money would have bought. We converted Women Pioneer House into a field kitchen. The women from the Working Mothers' League cooked the meals and then ran the gauntlet of gunfire until they reached our emplacements on Hashomer Street, with the food still hot. The ingredients we bought on credit from Tnuva, the sales cooperative of the agricultural settlements. After we ran up a debt of two thousand liroth, Tnuva canceled our credit; the Labor Council was constrained to borrow money from the Savings and Loan Fund in exchange for a pledge to cover part of the debt, but we managed to keep Hannah's larders and her boys' stomachs full.

While the battle for Haifa raged on, illegal immigrants were being smuggled in on barely seaworthy ships past the continuing British blockade. Here too, the Labor Council lent a hand. It often organized groups of workers who boarded the ships and exchanged clothes with the passengers, who were then taken off disguised as stevedores.

The Arab Legion, administered and officered by the British, began making a dangerous nuisance of itself as the time for the British evacuation drew near. With the British turning a blind eye, legionnaires were indiscriminately firing on passersby in Haifa streets. I was in the delegation that met with British CO in Haifa, Major General Stockwell and the District Governor A. N. Low. I was with M. G. Levin and A. Friedland, the chairmen, respectively, of the Hadar Hacarmel and community committees. We lodged a vigorous protest with the official representatives of British government in Haifa. We put it to them that the Arab Legion had grown wild and was not being restrained, especially in the Lower City, in Ahuza, and at Hareiba; that police charges claiming that Jews had been the first to attack were plain lies. We demanded that the legionnaires be withdrawn immediately from all Jewish population centers. We had made our point: at a subsequent meeting two days later, Major General Stockwell informed us that the Legion would be removed from the Upper City. The legionnaires were taken away as promised and confined to the areas of Bat Galim and Nesher to the south and north of the lower part of Haifa. We had thus cut down, even if to a limited degree, the number of men under arms the enemy was able to field in the city.

A New Era Begins

In addition to my activities as acting general secretry of the Labor Council, I was also heavily engaged in the operations of Hagana HQ. "Staff" at Hagana Headquarters was made up in equal parts of representatives from what was then referred to as "the civilian camp" and from the Histadrut Labor Federation. Our "war office" was in the Café Werner in the Hadar area of Mount Carmel, where we held frequent consultations in a back room set aside for us.

At one of our regular sessions, our windows were rattled by a tremendous explosion set off by the Arabs in one of the railway carriages parked at the Central Station down in the Lower City. My long experience enabled me to keep up the appearance of utter calm. But one of our "civilians" sitting at my side was visibly shaken. It was Yaakov Lifshitz, the owner of the refrigeration warehouses in Haifa. "Don't be afraid, Lifshitz," I said soothingly, "there'll be a state just the same." Lifshitz had gone white with fright; he grabbed hold of my hand and asked with great intensity, "Do you really believe that?" "Well, let's make it a wager," I said. I said it lightly, as though I had not really meant it. But the words were out, and Lifshitz took me seriously. "What stakes?" he asked. His handsome watch caught my eye. "A watch!" "Done!" he replied, and we shook hands. The day after the state was declared, when I had completely forgotten about my wager with Lifshitz, Lifshitz had not forgotten.

But there was still time before all of that happened. It was only April—the evening of the twenty-first—and I was sitting at the headquarters of the Home Guard with Abba Khoushi (just back from the United States) and some people from the Jewish Agency. We were awaiting word from brigade HQ about the start of the offensive to liberate Haifa. All day the Hagana had been advancing to take up positions in the city as, one by one, they were abandoned by the British army and police. Some of the positions, especially those of strategic value between the Upper and Lower Cities, the British handed over to bands of Arab irregulars, who put them to immediate use as staging grounds for attack on Jewish population centers in the city.

We had a pretty good notion, too, of what British intentions and plans were— thanks to the special relationship Abba Khoushi enjoyed with Major General Stockwell. Our liaison in these contacts was Harry Beilin, the son of a rabbinic family who had immigrated to Palestine from England. He and his wife, Judith, were invaluable to us in developing our contacts with the upper echelons of the British police and army, both in Haifa and in the whole northern region of the country. The dignity and the Jewish pride with which he carried out his duties won the admiration of us all.

Under cover of darkness on the night of April 21, the Carmeli Brigade launched the campaign for control of Haifa. It was advancing in a pincer movement; one arm debouched from Wadi Rushmia in the east, the other from the west, starting at the northwestern end of the Hadar quarter on the Carmel. The information coming in reported success all along the line, with Arab forces falling back in confusion.

The next morning, while fighting was still going on, I rang up the workers at the Central Post Office on Bourj Street. This was the nerve center of Haifa and the Northern Region, and it was absolutely essential that we retained control of it: it contained not only the postal and telegraph service, but was the central telephone-communications switchboard for all Haifa. Our men there reported that the Arab employees were carrying on, and that communications within the city and with the rest of the country were in order and being closely watched by Jewish workers.

Still, Abba Khoushi and I thought we should pay the boys a visit. We made our approach from the back of the building; the rear, too, was under heavy fire, but less exposed to snipers. We first had to negotiate the concrete wall that fenced the building: It had to be taken at a running jump. Khoushi was the first to go, and as he went over and dropped down on the other side, he injured his leg seriously. I took him over to Rothschild Hospital for emergency treatment, after which he was transferred to the private clinic of Dr. Betar on Pevsner Street, where a private room was provided from which he could run things at the Labor Council.

That morning Hagana Radio in Haifa announced that Arab resistance in the city was broken and that Arab representatives were in contact with the British army's CO in Haifa and the North, Major General Stockwell, with British District Governor A. N. Low, and with Mayor Shabtai Levi. The Arabs were asking them to mediate a cessation of militry hostilities and an armistice. Stockwell contacted the Hagana commander in Haifa and asked him to draw up our conditions for a cease fire. Hagana terms for a truce were, in the main, (1) complete disarmament of the Arabs, including all weapons and military equipment, (2) withdrawal of Arab and European armed forces from Haifa and the surrender to the Hagana of all Nazis in their service, and (3) the placement of the whole city, with the exception of British security areas, under Hagana government.

At 4:00 P.M. Jewish and Arab representatives appeared for a meeting at City Hall. It was chaired by Major General Stockwell, who had that morning transmitted Hagana terms for a truce to an eleven-man Arab committee that had approached him. The Jewish side included Mordecai Maklef for the Hagana (openly, for the first time) and Mayor Shabtai Levi. Labor Council Secretary Abba Khoushi was still laid up from his injuries, so I took his place at the negotiating table.

It was a short meeting. After an opening address by Shabtai Levi, in which the mayor urged the Arabs to renew their cooperation with the Jews, which had been so fruitful in the past, the terms of the truce were read out. The Arabs listened with stoney faces, and then asked for time to think over the terms. Stockwell acceded to their request and established nine o'clock that evening as the time for the next meeting.

We hoped with with every fiber of our being that the Arabs would choose the path of cooperation, and that together we could prove to the world that Arabs and Jews could live amicably together in one city. Meanwhile, attorney Yaakov Solomon worked on translating our terms to the Arabs into Hebrew and English.

In the course of the day, the Arab representatives—led by Hajj Tahe Tahe Karman, Victor Khayat, and attorney Eliyas Koseh—were in touch with Damascus for instructions. The orders they received dashed all our hopes for an Arab-Jewish peace in an integrated Haifa. Their spokesman announced that the Arabs could not accept Hagana terms and preferred to evacuate all Arab residents from Haifa. Under the influence of their advisors in Damascus, they were confident they would return soon at the head of a victorious Arab army coming out of Syria and Lebanon. All they asked was for the British to help them to evacuate the city in peace and to leave behind a handful of their people to look after their sacred places. The attempts made by Major General Stockwell and Mayor Shabtai Levi to change their minds were to no avail.

As I watched the Arab delegation I thought they looked more sad than determined. They had not taken their decision lightly. The rout of their men at arms and our conquest of the city had taken them by surprise.

The next day Arab residents were still fleeing the city. However, at further meetings of Arab and Jewish members of the municipality, the Arabs informed their colleagues of the desire of thousands of Arab residents to remain in Haifa. The city workers sat down to consider the problem of assuring municipal services for the Arabs wishing to remain.

The Haifa Labor Council issued an emotional proclamation urging the Arabs to remain in Haifa, telling the Arab residents that life lived in the city in friendship and cooperation would benefit both peoples:

> Years upon years we have lived together in our city of Haifa in mutual understanding and sympathy. Thanks to this our City has flourished and developed to the advantage of its Jewish and Arab residents, and has furnished the rest of the cities in the country with a model. . . . Ours is a nation of Lovers of Peace! Do not fear, and do not destroy your homes! Don't bring down the catastrophies on yourselves that will follow your needless wanderings.
>
> The gates of the City—yours and ours—are open to you to work, to live, to enjoy the benefits of peace: to you and your families. . . . The Haifa Labor Council and the Histadrut urge you to remain in the City in your own best interests, and to return to your regular places of employment. We are ready to come to your assistance to help you return to the routines of a decent life, to help you obtain food, to open up employment opportunities for you. Workers! Our city of Haifa, ours in partnership, calls on you to take part in its building, advancement and development. Do not betray her, do not betray yourselves!

Our proclamation did not help. The Arabs of Haifa left, in great numbers.

Two days after the Liberation of Haifa the lights were on again in the city streets. The residents began to prepare for the Passover seder. This time, the Festival of Freedom had special meaning.

10
The Day After

The day following the liberation of Haifa our excitement reached a peak as we read the official announcement of the Hagana district commander:

> By the authority vested in me, and with the endorsement of High Command, I hereby proclaim Jewish self-government in the city of Haifa. The Jewish defense force, which has subdued the Arab foe and gained control by arms of the entire city, will constitute the sole authorized government in Haifa, until such time as there will be established in the city, by the People's Administration, a permanent civilian government.

Within a few days Ben-Gurion came for a visit, accompanied by Zeev Sharef. Ben-Gurion had a short conference with Abba Khoushi, and then he and I went in his car to inspect the Arab neighborhoods. We passed through Wadi Nisnas and Wadi Salib. They looked empty. Why did they leave? He kept repeating the question, and I tried to explain that we hadn't wanted them to leave, that Shabtai Levi asked them not to leave, that the Labor Council published a proclamation, but that Damascus. . . . Ben-Gurion hardly paid attention. He was not demanding an explanation; it was the reality that shocked him—the reality of sixty thousand refugees from Haifa, of all places, and without cause.

In the evening Ben-Gurion received the men of the Hagana and the Situational Subcommittee. After a report on the fighting that had taken place, the question of demolishing the battle-wrecked houses came up; they were getting to be a public hazard, especially in the Lower City, in the Arab marketplace opposite the train station. Ben-Gurion gave the Hagana commanders pointed instructions that the mosques in the area were not to be touched. They stand there to this day.

Another of our visitors at the time was Golda Meir. Yaakov Lublini, chief of Hagana HQ in Haifa, invited her for a tour of the Lower City. It had been badly hit during the fighting, and Golda told Lublini she had no wish to look on waste and destruction. She suggested a visit someplace where the Arabs had remained. Lublini decided on Wadi Nisnas.

Our entourage was making its way in Wadi Nisnas through Muchlis Street, when Golda stopped at a partially demolished house. The outer stairway running up the side of the wall was sound enough, and she led the way up.

When Golda—with Lublin behind her—reached the third floor landing, an old Arab woman emerged, carrying bundles of what was probably all she had salvaged from her wrecked home. When she saw Golda, she burst into tears. Golda pulled up short, and she, too, began to cry. And the two weeping women stood facing one another until Lublin began to urge Golda away.

I remember thinking what a rare thing I was seeing—the victor crying over the vanquished. I was proud of Golda.

Our immediate concerns had to do with establishing civilian rule in the city. For the agencies of civilian authority in Haifa—the mayor's office, the Community Committee, and the Situational Subcommittee—all to remain subordinate to military control was intolerable. Abba Khoushi came up with the idea of having a civilian governor appointed who would be responsible to the People's Administration. It was only natural that he should have regarded himself as the most suitable candidate for such a post.

When Golda came to Haifa a second time, I had a long talk with her about Khoushi's proposal. Golda was less than enthusiastic. "In the State of Israel there will be no governors!" was her verdict. And then she added: "The city will be run by elected municipal institutions, and when a national government is established, *it* will run the whole state." However, knowing how much Khoushi wanted to be appointed governor of Haifa, I gave it another try. By now Golda's fuse had got perilously short: the matter was closed.

On May 7 I took time out from my official duties. My wife had just given birth to our second son at Molada Hospital on the Carmel. We called him Zvi Israel— Zvi for my deceased father, and Israel for the state, which was proclaimed on the day appointed for his circumcision. Yosef Erdstein, an old-time settler from before World War I and a veteran Histadrut activist, stood godfather to Zvika and cradled him in his lap for the rite. Comrades from community institutions and from the Haifa branch of the Histadrut appeared at the celebration. The family had grown although our quarters had not: we were still living in our one-room flat and sharing a kitchen. It was getting cramped, but we were happy.

I was back on the job again. A new problem had arisen. The call-up to meet the expected Arab invasion from the north was beginning to drain many of our services and industries of their manpower. Some of these were vital, and we found ourselves on the horns of a dilemma: either essential workers would be freed from military service, or the vital enterprises they served would close down. Something had to be done, but what? The problem of how to stretch our ever-diminishing work force taxed and frustrated us at meetings lasting well into the night.

The port was particularly hard hit. Essential consumer goods, food included, was piling up on the docks and, for lack of hands, not being supplied to the nation. It was an emergency that had to be dealt with immediately. I had no choice but to go down to our largest places of employment and exact a tithe of workers from them: each would have to contribute 10 percent of its labor force to handling produce in the port. The employees of some of the factories—notably the Ata Textile plant and the Vulcan Foundries—found themselves laboring as stevedores after having done a full day's work on their regular jobs. It was at this time that my relationship with the port became firmly knit: from then on, and for a period of twelve years until 1960, hardly a day passed when I was in Haifa when I did not visit the docks.

Military Labor Brigades

Spurred by the problems brought on by the depletion of our labor resources, we hit on an unorthodox solution: a levy on men to work in vital industries. Already at the end of February I had written to Ben-Gurion, outlining our proposal for the formation of work brigades whose troops, so to speak, would be conscripted by the community institutions and put under military discipline. We thought that in the initial phase of the operation, we would create three battalions of five hundred soldier-workers each, and we even had a budget worked out.

Finally, early in May, after sending a number of memoranda and campaigning hard to put our idea across, we received the go-ahead from Ben-Gurion in a letter addressed to the Situational Subcommittee in Haifa. It read:

> In view of the urgent need, and the vital importance to our future in Israel, of securing labor at the Port in this time of emergency, you are being granted the authority to proclaim forthwith an order of compulsory mobilization of married men between the ages of 26 and 35 with one to two children for service in Labor Batallions at the Port, Railway and other enterprises having value to the Government, in accordance with the conditions set by you and confirmed by the People's Administration.
>
> With the blessings of Zion,
D. Ben-Gurion

Then began a period of working closely with Ben-Gurion. He demanded to know about every detail of the formation of the Labor Brigades, and became involved in every aspect of the operation. In the journal kept by Ben-Gurion, I find the following entry for May 19, 1948:

> I called in Krelenboim from Haifa to get an account of the levy of workers for the Port, Railway, Refineries, etc. . . . .1,170 workers have already been called up. . . .800 have been sent to the Port. This number in insufficient. They will levy 400 more for this purpose—that should do.

I remember the day well: it was the day I received my appointment as commander of Military Labor Brigades.

As usual for Ben-Gurion, the decision having been made, he immediately sat down to write out my letter of appointment and then, just as suddenly, stopped. He fixed me with with one of his withering looks and said, "No! You just can't possibly write "Krelenboim" in a letter of appointment. You must Hebraize that name—what is a krelenboim anyway?" I explained that it meant "sandalwood tree." Ben-Gurion was delighted: "Good, good! Your name is now Almogi." "Almogi" is the Hebrew equivalent for sandalwood. I had no say in the matter; Ben-Gurion wrote my new name into the letter of appointment just like that.

When I brought home the news of the change in our surname my son Yoram (then eleven) was furious. "What's going on? Doesn't anyone want to know my opinion?" he protested. I read him a short lesson on Ben-Gurion's attitude on opinions, of any kind, and summed up saying, "It's settled. Ben-Gurion has decided." Yoram was not going to be put off: "But you said we're going to have a democracy!" As usual, Yoram's logic carried the day, but the name remained.

The next day I received a letter from Ben-Gurion in which for the first time he addressed me as "Almogi." He summed up the points agreed to at our meeting on the Labor Brigades. He also settled a number of issues, among them that the salary, including family subsistence allowance, was not to exceed what was received by all men mobilized for military service. Then he added that military authority and discipline would be in force in the Labor Brigades and that no army commanders or former soldiers were to be seconded to the Brigades without special approval from the Army Manpower Branch. Much as Ben-Gurion valued the Labor Brigades he was not going to allow them to draw off trained fighting men from the army.

In my reply I was able to report that by mid-June we had managed to recruit 1,978 men in the Labor Brigades, and that a good many of them were in the 32–36 age group. I also sent him the breakdown he asked for of the numbers of men who had been posted at each place of work. As for production figures, the statistics at the docks were particularly encouraging. Port records indicated that the Labor Brigades had reached a record of freight unloading of 3.5 tons per man, as opposed to 2.6-ton average before our men came to the port. On other jobs, the reports were mixed, with the results better at some places than at others.

The Haifa experience inspired the decision to form Labor Brigades in all the larger cities in Israel. The proposal had not met with the approval of the left wing members of the Histadrut, and Mapam (United Workers' Party) raised the issue of Military Labor Brigades at a session of the Executive Committee of the Labor Federation. Levi Eshkol, then one of the chiefs of the Ministry of Defense, argued strongly in the brigades' favor. The main thrust of his argument was that the brigades would make possible the mobilization of men not called up for the armed forces who could, nevertheless, be of service to the nation. For their part, the representatives of Mapam callenged the very right of existence of a military labor brigade not under trade-union control, but at the meeting's close, the Mapam proposal for disbanding the brigades was defeated. My own contribution to the debate consisted of bringing in official data, according to which there were more than 40,000 men between the ages of 18 and 35 who were not serving in the army. The clincher, that prevailed over any possible objections, was the simple fact that putting this enormous reservoir of manpower under military regimen was the most effective means of fielding a labor force in those areas which were vital to the war effort.

A closing note on the subject of the Labor Brigades: Not only did our Labor corpsmen make their contribution to the economy during the War of Independence; they also went out on guard duty, and some even did real fighting. Labor Brigadesmen were in on the battles for the villages of Tira, near Haifa, and Igazim in the Little Triangle area in the North. They also took part in the actions east of the Sea of Galilee.

11
A First Taste of Politics

In my early period in Haifa I was hardly ever involved in political conflict. In my work on national defense and in the Labor Council, I depended on a broad national consensus which, at least in labor circles, was the ideological setting of political debate in the period before the establishment of the state.

There was a marked change, however, during the election campaign for the Constituent Assembly, which, once elected, would become Israel's Knesset and initiate parliamentary rule in the country. It dramatized the ideological gap between my own Mapai Workers' Party and the Mapam United Workers' Party, which had been recently formed by a coalition of the Left factions of Zionist Labor. The conflict between the two parties grew out of differences of orientation toward international affairs and out of different conceptions as to how events in the world at large were to be applied to the policies of organized labor in Israel and to the conduct of politics within the country.

Mapai was ideologically socialist-democratic and in this resembled socialist parties in the West; in foreign policy it favored developing friendly relations with the two great powers, both of whom had supported the establishment of the State of Israel. Mapam, on the other hand, conceived of itself as a pioneer Zionist party with a Marxist ideology and so felt that its sympathies should be with the world-revolutionist camp led by the Soviets.

One international issue in particular that polarized the two labor parties was the Marshall Plan, America's massive aid program for the recovery of Western Europe after the war. The USSR charged that it was simply another capitalist tactic for furthering American influence in Europe. In Israel, Mapam was among the opponents of the Marshall Plan. When a Marshall Plan for Israel was discussed and received support from Ben-Gurion, Mapam was in strong opposition. Mapam even opposed negotiations with the United States for a loan, the acceptance of which they believed would be a surrender to "enslaving capital."

Within the context of national politics, Mapam initiated a campaign of revolutionist sloganeering and instructed its members in the trade-union movement to act as the vanguard of the struggle against the "revisionism" of the Mapai party—this despite their being partners with Mapai in leading the Histadrut. Further, Mapam bore a grudge against Ben-Gurion for having disbanded the headquarters of Palmah—the Hagana's elite fighting force, many of whose members belonged to Mapam and its kibbutz settlements. Ben-Gurion carried out the policy that no unit of the state army could retain its own separate command, but Mapam interpreted the move as calculated to undermine the influence of their party and its kibbutzim.

Such was the political setting in which elections for the Constituent Assembly, which became the nation's First Knesset, were held. When the results were in, Mapai had won forty-six seats, and Mapam nineteen. The two parties went into negotiations to form a coalition government. After lengthy bargaining, Mapam decided it was not going to join the government after all, and when the state's first government was presented to the first parliament in our people's history, Mapam leader and member of Knesset (MK) Meir Yaari took the floor to warn against "accommodation of the government to the pressures of reaction from within, and to economic and political dictates from outside forces." On the same occasion another of Mapam's leading figures and parliamentarians, Yaakov Hazan, went on record, saying, "For us the Soviet Union is the citadel of world socialism; it is our second homeland." With this Mapam took its place in the Knesset as a Left opposition party.

In the Histadrut, however, Mapam enjoyed the best of two worlds. The Histadrut's governing bodies and constituent trade unions, like the government and Knesset, are organized on political party lines, and parties compete in internal elections. Within the Labor Federation, Mapam was still part of the ruling coalition; but at the same time the Mapam party campaigned among workingmen against the official Histadrut policy for whose formation Mapam as the majority party had largely been responsible. Mapam cells in the trade unions and at places of work became bases for the party's struggle against both the government and the Histadrut; it created action committees outside the framework of the Histadrut and organized noisy mass demonstrations—all calculated to demonstrate that unless Mapam were taken in as a partner in the government there would be peace neither in the country nor in the Histadrut.

As the conflict between Mapai and Mapam sharpened and spread, it led to confrontation within the ranks of salaried working people in the large cities, especially in Haifa.

From almost every point of view, Haifa was a unique city. After the majority of its Arab residents had left on the eve of the War of Independence, Haifa absorbed vast numbers of new immigrants; during the first three years of the existence of the state, membership in the Histadrut increased by roughly thirty thousand, making a total of about fifty thousand rank-and-file members of organized labor in the city. During the same period there was a commensurate expansion of industry and services, and new enterprises were established.

With Haifa's working population, and industry, and economy expanding at such a lively pace, little wonder that it should have become one of the major arenas of conflict between the factions of the labor movement. Both Mapai and

Mapam set up party cells within the trade unions and on the job, at the more important places of work.

A party card soon became a ticket to special favors, including obtaining a job and housing. New immigrants were quick to catch on and were soon joining the rest of the population in using the system to their own advantage. That was when the Yiddish joke began to make the rounds about the new immigrant shaping up at the Labor Exchange who, when asked by the deputy making up the work schedules to which party he belonged, pulled out the membership cards of four different parties and asked, "So which do you need?"

People's private lives also had a way of becoming entangled in interparty strife. In one such case, Ruthie, Abba Khoushi's daughter, was at the time engaged to be married to Amnon Lin, then a member of Kibbutz Mishmar Haemek. Now in addition to this being a settlement belonging to the Hashomer Hatzair faction of the Mapam, Amnon himself was the son of a veteran pioneer family that had been among the founders of Hashomer Hatzair and whose members now occupied leading positions in Mapam. Just before the wedding, which was to take place at the Kibbutz, I happened to go to visit the Khoushis. I found Abba Khoushi's wife, Hannah, in tears: Abba Khoushi was unhappy with the match and refused to be a party to the ceremony. When I discovered that all Khoushi had against the marriage was the bridegroom's party credentials, I had a heart-to-heart talk with him and convinced him to go to the wedding. For moral support, I even went with him. On the way to the wedding I tried to perk up Khoushi's spirits by telling him that from what I knew of Ruthie she was quite capable of winning Amnon Lin over to Mapai. And that's exactly what happened.

During the period of Haifa's absorption of masses of new immigrants and the attendant expansion of the city's population and economy, Mapai succeeded in gaining more than a 60 percent majority on the Haifa Labor Council, as opposed to something like 30 percent for Mapam. The solid majority we now enjoyed gave us the opportunity to determine the course of Haifa's development and to frustrate attempts to undermine our plans, though this cost us a great deal of effort.

By the early 1950s, we had good reason to know that the returns in elections to the Histadrut Convention or the Labor Council need by no means be the same as the results of the voting for workers' shop committees. In the general and nationwide Histadrut elections, the organization's entire membership took part—that is to say, members of the free professions, housewives, and even young people, in addition to salaried workers. However, the constituency of each shop committee consisted only of the workers employed at a particular plant, and there what counted most in getting votes was not so much a party platform as the personalities and rhetorical gifts of the people running.

A shop committee chosen by direct ballot by a constituency of workers at a plant can become a basic building block in creating a sound and democratic edifice for organized labor—or a power base for those whose aim is to undermine it. In essential enterprises, shop committees are in possession of very great powers which they can use to enormous effect in negotiations with employers, the government, and the Histadrut itself. They can whip up feeling among their constituencies and throw the social and economic system out of kilter, or they can restore calm, reduce the tension in disputes, and play a vital part in securing the prosperity of the society.

The closeness and the quality of relations between the Labor Councils and workers' shop committees determine the strength of the Histadrut. The closer a Labor Council secretary gets to the working public and the more he keeps in touch with it through the shop committees, the greater his control over the situation when labor disputes arise. Then he can further workers' just demands and put a restraint on demands that are not justified; at times, he can take a position that is not to the liking of central headquarters.

During this period Haifa had about five hundred places of employment; of these only about a dozen were of first-rank importance as power centers the control of which was the key to governance in the Histadrut, the municipality, and sometimes even the country as a whole. These latter included the port and all its subsidiaries, the merchant fleet, the railway, the post office, the Electric Corporation, the refineries, the Ata Textile Company, Fertilizers & Chemicals, Ltd., Vulcan Foundries, Phoenicia Glass Works, the flour mills, the municipality, and the hospitals. At the beginning of the 1950s nearly all the shop committees in these places were controlled by Mapam and Maki—the Communist party. It took us almost three years—until the end of 1952—to convince the employees that, for the sake of the country and for their own good and that of the Histadrut, they should back the Mapai-sponsored lists of shop committee candidates. We were not always successful, and there were times when the struggle was very sharp indeed.

In the spring of 1948, when the main stages of the War of Independence were over, the provisional government scheduled elections for the Constituent Assembly for January 1949, and put off elections for local government to a later date. The winning candidates of Mapai in Haifa were Abba Khoushi, David Hacohen, and David Bar-Rav-Hai. After the Constituent Assembly was declared the First Knesset, they took their seats in Israel's parliament.

12
Secretary of the Haifa Labor Council

In the beginning of 1951, after Abba Khoushi's election as mayor of Haifa, I was officially made head of the Haifa Labor Council—not just acting secretary, the position I had held since the end of 1947, but official head. Quite suddenly I found myself in a position of economic and political power, responsible for determining policy at the Labor Council when it was in the thick of both internal strife and struggles with outside forces.

The largest centers of employment in Haifa—including the port, the railway, customs, and the refineries—passed into the hands of the government, whose wage policy became a part of its general economic policy. Wage policies were hammered out in the chief institutions of the party and, once passed, had to be supported by Mapai representatives on Labor Councils and in the trade unions. The state was, in those first years of its existence, under daunting economic pressures. It had to absorb hundreds of thousands of Jewish refugees from Europe and the Middle East, to house and feed them, and to develop its industry and agriculture to keep pace with the growth in population and provide the country with an adequate economic base. It also had to maintain and equip an army capable of resisting the ongoing military threat from neighboring Arab countries. These considerations were uppermost in the minds of party representatives sitting in the government and working in the Histadrut's national organization. However, we members of Mapai in the Histadrut represented working people on the job. We had the responsibility of looking after their interests, and we were under the pressure of their demands. Demands were made not only by workers in government enterprises and services, but also by those employed in industries owned and run by the Histadrut, which ranked second only to the government as the nation's biggest employer. In Haifa, Histadrut plants and factories constituted the major sector of economy, upon which the city's working population largely depended for their livelihood. Workers at Histadrut enterprises demanded conditions better than those that prevailed in privately owned companies and in governmental places of employment, and they did so on the understandable grounds that they themselves were part of the organization that owned the places in which they worked. By the same token, the administrations of Histadrut-owned plants asked for greater productivity from employees and a greater understanding for the problems faced by management.

As Labor Council secretary, I had to determine my position on labor policies established at the national level and accept responsibility for actually applying these policies to the reality of the shop floor. I had to decide if I was primarily to represent Haifa's working public and their basic needs or represent the Histadrut Executive Committee, the party, and the government—to carry out national policy within the particular domain of my authority. It seemed to me that the relationship between the Executive Committee and the Labor Council should be one of cooperation and not one in which central headquarters dictated policy to its local agencies.

Already during the first years of the state, the foundations were laid for collective agreements that guaranteed fair wages and fringe benefits for employees in Haifa and the surrounding area. In the forefront of this achievement marched the workers of the Histadrut's own Koor Industries. Among the achievements we tallied up then were wage bonuses calculated on the basis of established work norms, the introduction of labor-management production committees, and the first inclusive Israeli pension plan for employees. These gave us a reputation for being trailblazers in the field of labor relations, and for this reason I found I had no choice but to throw myself into the thick of the economic and social controversies then raging in the institutions of the party and the Histadrut. I participated in nearly all the economic deliberations by party institutions, and at these sessions I sometimes met with sympathy and agreement and at other times with anger. I remember clashing with Golda Meir during the Seventh Mapai Party Congress in the summer of 1950. Golda took a very strong position against construction workers who, she felt, were earning exaggeratedly high wages. I was able to show that some of her data were wrong.

My positions, and what was regarded as my "cheek" in putting them forward, were not to the liking of everyone in the party executive. Some even believed that I was demanding salary increases just to make myself more popular among wage earners. For all that, it was clear to everyone that after even the stormiest debates, once a decision was reached I could be counted on to carry it out—even if it meant running counter to my own convictions in the matter.

During my term in office, I reached the conclusion that the weak point in our economy's ability to compete on the foreign market was not wages but productivity. My experience taught me that plants that were effeciently managed and had good planning and proper machinery and tools on the pattern of factories in Western Europe could hold their own, and more, against their European competitors.

I found myself repeatedly making the point to workers that the best work contract in the world and the strongest union will not guarantee the survival of their place of employment if it isn't making a profit. With employers I would argue that their business would be profitable only if they made their workers partners in their enterprises by a fair exchange of wage increases for production increases.

The Dilemma of Active Trade-Union Men

From the moment I assumed the office of Labor Council secretary, I tried hard to keep in close touch with the working people in my constituency, and especially with the workers' shop committees, with which I frequently met and consulted. I regarded the shop committees to be the bedrock of the Labor Council. They were, in addition, an inexhaustible source of recruits for active members of the Histadrut and the Mapai party.

The Haifa Labor Council was the only one in the country that was responsible for five cities and seven smaller communities. The vast area of our jurisdiction was a source of endless friction between ourselves and Histadrut headquarters, which was not at all pleased by the extent of our expansion.

Among the problems we addressed successfully was that of housing. Although thousands of immigrants who had arrived in the area of Haifa had been put under roof in special camps or in abandoned Arab neighborhoods, old settlers in need of housing had to wait for the flats being built by the Shikun Company, whose units were few and very expensive. After talking the matter over with the custodian of abandoned property, the people of the Histadrut building company, Solel Boneh, and the administrators of the Savings and Loan Fund, I found that it would be possible to build hundreds of inexpensive housing units. The project for housing veteran settlers was brought before the Executive Committee of the Labor Council and received the go-ahead, and as a result the housing problems of hundreds of families were solved.

Another of our achievements was to put up a new building for our headquarters, Beitenu, exactly on the spot where we had built the shack of the Hapoel squads years before. For this project we received financial aid from the American fund established in the name of the great CIO labor leader William Green.

Public Transportation on the Sabbath

We never lacked for battles. They were not always of our making and often came from unexpected quarters. One day, for example, I found myself confronted by a delegation from Shahar, the public transport cooperative which ran commuter services in Haifa before it merged with the nationwide Egged Transport Cooperative Society. The head of the delegation announced that, beginning Saturday next, public transportation in Haifa on the Sabbath would cease.

I regarded this as a serious change. Haifa was one of the few places in Israel in which public transportation ran on Saturdays and religious holidays. This had been true even before the establishment of Israel. It came about in part, because in the very early days the city's commuter services had been Arab. In any case, the agreement of the government with the religious parties allowed those public transportation services which had operated during Jewish religious festivals before independence to continue to do so after the establishment of the state.

There was more than the mere technicality of Haifa's legally established right to public transportation during religious holidays involved here. The city's enormous area and mountainous topography made the operation of public transportation every day in the week an absolute necessity. In addition, public commuter lines provided thousands of Haifa's residents with their only link to the city's beaches, which attracted thousands of working people on their days of rest.

Mayor Abba Khoushi was out of the country at the time; the government minister of transport was David Zvi Pinkes, a member of the Mizrahi faction of the National Religious Party. The coincidence of these two circumstances put me on my guard. I suspected the transport minister of hoping to make a bargain by which, in exchange for granting the cooperative request for an increase in profits, he could make a political gain for his party at the expense of the agreed-to religious status quo in Haifa. Much as I tried to persuade the delegation from Shahar to change their minds, they remained stubborn, determined to shut down holiday transportation. They argued that the cooperative was losing money on Saturdays and that their members wanted their weekend rest like everybody else. The last argument did not hold water because in any enterprise that had crews working in shifts, there were always Jews to be found who would even work on Yom Kippur, the Day of Atonement.

When nothing I said seemed to impress them, I warned them that if they stopped their buses from operating on Saturdays and holidays I would put a fleet of trucks on the streets to do the job they refused to do. The delegation did not think I was serious, and they were amused. But I meant what I said, and I was positive I could organize alternate public transportation. My relations with the truckers in the city were excellent. They had organized themselves on my initiative and in the context of the Histadrut when the state was founded, and I had helped them put the teamster enterprise back on its feet.

After my meeting with the Shahar delegation I called in the secretary of the teamsters. Within three days a fleet of trucks had been scrubbed clean and modified. The public had their Saturday commuter service and enjoyed the infinite satisfaction of knowing that Shahar had failed in its plot to deprive them of their holiday transportation. I also managed to persuade many employers to make use of our fleet of trucks to transport their workers to and from work. One thing I made certain of, though, was that the truckers would not raise the fare. After two months, the company gave in and renewed its service on holidays and Saturdays. They also had to accept the fact that some of the trucks continued transporting workers, and to admit two new members of our choosing into the cooperative.

I made it my business to advance cultural and educational activities. For example, I managed to lease from the custodian of abandoned property a large building in the center of the city at the top of Mount Carmel and had the structure modified so it could serve as a school for workingmen. This became the

Oranim School, which was run in partnership with the Cultural Center of the Histadrut. I also made arrangements with Haifa employers to release between twenty and thirty workers every week for studies at the school—half the period of study being on company time and half on the workers' own vacation time. In this way hundreds of workers were able to acquire some background in economics, the workings of the Histadrut, and the history and geography of their country. Many of them, inspired by the courses at the Oranim School, took up studying more seriously and went on to complete their education.

To strengthen the ties of the working public with the Labor Council, we published a weekly called *Haifa Haovedet* ("Working Haifa"), which circulated in thousands of copies. We also used radio to reach workingmen on the job. At our initiative, a half-hour program devoted to labor matters and workers' rights was broadcast by the Voice of Israel at noon. The broadcasts began in April 1954, but because of insufficient cooperation between the workers and the Voice of Israel, the show was taken off the air. However, when I became minister of labor in the late 1960s, I was able to revive the program and it is still on the air, billed as Bemiktsav Hayotser ("Creative Beat").

One day I received a letter from the poet Shin Shalom, who wrote that he wished to move from Rehovot to Haifa and was asking for help to find housing in the city. I passed his letter on to Mayor Abba Khoushi, and thus was born the idea to attract writers and artists to settle in the city of the Carmel. Our lure was to offer housing at rock-bottom prices, which we were able to do by coming to an agreement with Haifa's building contractors. After a number of writers made Haifa their home, we decided to go into publishing. The idea was to put out low-cost pocketbook editions in large numbers and distribute as many as we could at places of work. We began by publishing high-quality literature which had gone out of print, and by dint of a well-organized campaign gained about fifteen thousand subscribers for what we called the Yalkut ("Book-Bag") Library. Subscribers received one new book a month. Local shop committees subsidized part of the purchase price, so that workers paid less than one-half lira—the cost of one pack of imported cigarettes.

Our undertaking was highly praised, but it also drew fire from Am Oved, the Histadrut's publishing enterprise. They accused us of having stolen a march on them in the paperback field. Moshe Sharett, who was Am Oved's chairman, and its treasurer, Gershon Levinson, asked us to hand the whole project over to them. I was not able to withstand the pressures being brought to bear, and so I agreed to take a cooperative view of the matter. After having published fifty-one books, I made our little "business" over to Am Oved, and our books were published by their subsidiary, Sifriya La'am ("The People's Library"), which produces profits to this day.

"Book and Author Week" was another of our literary ventures by which we sought to stimulate public interest in the world of living literature. We arranged for authors and their public to meet in local neighborhoods and places of work—encounters that enhanced both sides.

Another project that enriched the social activities of Haifa's workers arose in January 1956 when I put forward a proposal at the plenary session of the Labor

Council to ask Haifa workers to volunteer for labor and guard duty in border settlements. My proposal was passed unanimously, and the volunteer program got off to a running start when public figures and members of the Haifa community of authors joined the volunteers. Some places of work in the city "adopted" the settlements to which their employees had gone, and the connection was maintained for much more than the period of a week or two that the volunteer program lasted. After a few months I was able to report to the Council plenum that the project had drawn about 11,000 volunteers and that a much as it cost us in effort, the results had made it all worthwhile. The project had brought home to the whole country that the Histadrut was more than just a trade-union federation; it was a movement based on the principle of cooperation and mutual aid on a national scale.

13
Haifa Port

Putting Jewish labor on the job at the Haifa docks and gaining control of the port for the nation was among the great achievements of the Haifa Labor Council. Since the port was first established as a military harbor in the early 1930s, the Histadrut, in close collaboration with the Jewish Agency and the other organizations of Jewish Palestine, worked hard first to gain a foothold there for Jewish workers and then to ensure its authority over what was a point of supreme strategic and economic importance in the country. In those days the port was one of the most difficult places to work. Machinery of any kind was almost unheard of, and longshoreman had nothing but their hands and backs with which to move tons of freight.

It was, without exaggeration, back-breaking labor, and even local Arab workers, who were inured to hard manual labor and very tough, buckled under strain of working the docks. The heavy season was in the winter months, when coal had to be unloaded and crates of fruit put on board. Then thousands of Arab laborers were brought down to the harbor from the mountainous Hauran district in southwest Syria. These men were famous for their extraordinary endurance at work under the most primitive conditions. A typical port scene at such times was the Haurani docker, nearly invisible under a mountain of bundles and crates on his back, negotiating his way past the glut of haphazardly piled cargo on the narrow wharves. It was a sight to daunt anybody, even members of kibbutz pioneer groups temporarily in Haifa before moving on to their settlements, who were sent by our port labor bureau to compete for work with the Haurani stevedores.

The task of establishing Jewish labor on the docks—all but impossible though it seemed—was undertaken by setting up, with the aid of the Jewish Agency, a number of contracting companies under the aegis of the Histadrut's building company Solel Boneh. In addition the Haifa Labor Council created the Port Bureau which took work under subcontract from, among others, Abu Zaid, the port's chief Arab contractor. Among the organized groups active on the docks was the private contracting company owned by Yitzhak Rokeah, the brother of

Tel Aviv Mayor Israel Rokeah. Rokeah's company later merged with the Solel Boneh port contractors and eventually took over the Port Bureau.

Abba Khoushi made an invaluable contribution to opening up Haifa Port to Jewish labor. In the early 1930s, he brought Jewish longshoremen to Haifa from the Greek port city of Salonika, where they had long formed the majority of the labor force on the docks—so much so that the whole harbor of Salonika shut down on the Jewish Sabbath. Because of their professional qualifications and seafaring tradition, the Salonikans were able to secure positions at Haifa Port with little difficulty. In this way, Abba Khoushi succeeded in introducing into the port a small group of Jewish workers capable of mastering the complex job of shipping clerk, a field at which Jews had never before tried their hand. That nucleus of Jewish labor at the harbor proved its strategic worth during the upheavals of 1946–49, and especially in the difficult days between the passage of the UN partition resolution and the liberation of Haifa, when Arab dockers tried to shut down the port in response to the Mufti's instructions. By their resource-fulness and their loyalty to the cause, a relative handful of Jewish workers kept the port open and, under the circumstances, running quite smoothly. Their presence at that critical time, when the nation was under siege, made it possible for the Jewish community in Palestine to receive essential shipments of arms, munitions, and, no less important, Jewish refugees.

During the battle for the liberation of Haifa and the subsequent flight of Arab residents from the city, the labor force at the port was drastically reduced. According to a February 1948 survey by a joint commission of the Jewish Agency and the People's Administration, there was a shortage of three thousand workers at the port. For example, as against the nearly four-hundred-man harbor se-curity force guarding the port before the liberation of Haifa, there were now only three Jewish watchmen to do the job. The commission recommended free-ing an appropriate number of young men from the draft so they could be put to work on the docks.

I went to see Ben-Gurion to put the commission's recommendation before him. When he asked where he was supposed to find three thousand men for us, I suggested that the date of mobilization of the needed number could be put off for a few months, and that they could be sent for work in essential industries for that period. Ben-Gurion pointed out that it was impossible to fill a labor shortage in one place without creating another shortage elsewhere.

The problem was more than one of numbers alone. Some twenty thousand Jews had already tried their strength at the job—and had given up. Nor was mere physical endurance all that the job of longshoreman required: it became apparent to us that a dock worker also had to be psychologically and emotionally suited to the work—something not easily come by or easily developed.

Therefore, considering how the cards were stacked against us, we had every reason to expect a sharp decline in productivity at the port. We were in for a surprise: productivity rose dramatically from one thousand tons per man per day in 1948 to five thousand tons in 1950. We—the Labor Council, Solel Boneh, and the port administration—accomplished this by training thousands of workers as longshoremen and introducing technology and organizational methods that were a little in advance of those familiar to Haurani stevedores.

The people who were the real authors of this magnificent achievement were most of them recent arrivals to the country. They had come with the wave of Jewish refugees that arrived in the period just after the creation of the state. During that time, men of every conceivable physical type, dressed in a rich variety of national costumes and speaking a babel of tongues, worked cheek by jowl. This variegated mix actually became, in an unbelievably short time, a highly efficient, organized, and disciplined work force whose accomplishments on the job exceeded every expectation.

From the time I became Labor Council secretary, I was personally involved in every aspect of the port operation, down to the smallest detail. Formally, as chief of the council, I did not have to deal with the routine details of the organization's work, which were seen to by six undersecretaries. But the port—well, that was something else again. I made it my own special portfolio, which I was loath to let out of my hands.

I estimated that another deep-water port would not be built in Israel for some years to come; until then the port of Haifa would be the sole port of entry for immigration, the only point to which foreign cargo could arrive and out of which native produce be sent abroad, and the major staging base for the defense of the coast. There would soon be fifteen thousand people employed here, of whom thousands would be on the job at any given hour in a twenty-four-hour day. They would not only set the pace of production for all the enterprises in Haifa and, as a consequence, in the whole country, but would be the first citizens of Israel encountered by immigrants and tourists. Here they would meet seamen, stevedores, and clerks who were Jews, something unprecedented in the experience of anyone coming from abroad. Here the public services of the young state would be put constantly to the test. This was our reason for being very careful about whom we chose to work at the port and for prohibiting workers in the arrival and departure center from taking tips.

Work Efficiency and Social Integration

We made many efforts to increase job efficiency at the port. We introduced work norms for loading and unloading cargo and paid wage premiums for exceeding the norms. The system proved to be to the advantage of both management and labor. Workers who were denied the possibility of wage increases above the limit established by national policy were, nevertheless, able to increase their income by increasing their productivity. The result was that the efficiency of Haifa's port became a match for any port on the Mediterranean Sea.

Concurrently, we stepped up our efforts to encourage the social and cultural integration of the port workers, who tended to segregate themselves in parochial groups according to the Jewish community they had belonged to before coming to Israel. They spoke about seventy different languages and preserved the customs and traditions of as many countries of origin. Although this helped divide them, this pattern was not without its charming aspects. I remember once after my wife and I had come home from a party given by Salonikans and had gone to bed, we were suddenly roused from our sleep, as was the rest of the neighborhood, by singing to guitar accompaniment. Two of my Salonikan friends from the port, who had been to the same party, had stationed themselves in front of the house and were serenading us with Greek songs—in the best tradition of Salonikan Jews.

I made it a custom to take part in the celebrations and festivities of workingmen and was often honored by them by being asked to stand godfather to their children. I made it a point as well to visit them when they were ill or in mourning. In my relationships with them I made certain not to make distinctions either with respect to ethnic origin or position at work. But the intimacy of my relationships with the men brought quite a few problems in train—for many are the wants of the sons of Israel. As everyone knows, a Labor Council secretary has a lot of pull, and I was constantly having requests referred to me for help in housing, assistance to family members, contributions to charities, and the like. I tried my best to see to it that no one who came to see me on an urgent request left without receiving at least some satisfaction.

I had frequent occasion to play host to individuals and delegations visiting the harbor, where their ships had docked. At the time the Port of Haifa was the Histadrut's showcase, American labor leader Walter Reuther and his wife were guests of ours; Reuther was impressed, not only by our strength, but by the utter lack of corruption on the docks.

One of the finest hours of Haifa's dockers was during the Sinai Campaign of October 1956 when the IDF, coordinating its actions with the armed forces of Britain and France on the Suez Canal, made its lightning thrust into the Sinai Peninsula in response to the Egyptian blockade of Israel's port of Eilat. The campaign was concentrated into a few days, during which ships arrived under cover of night, loaded with tanks, arms, and ammunition that had to be taken off before dawn. The enthusiasm and will with which the dockers accomplished this difficult task were an inspiration to the men visiting us on those nights—Prime Minister Ben-Gurion; the poet Nathan Alterman; Chief of Staff Moshe Dayan; and the commander of the Armored Corps, Haim Laskov.

When I moved on to other posts, far from Haifa, it was only natural I fall out of touch with the port. Still, every once in a while I would drop by for a visit to say hello to old friends and smell the sea air. As it turned out, my maintaining ties with the people and the place was kept in mind by fellow party members, who made use of my connections to help work out problems that occasionally arose at the Port.

One such occasion was during the longshoremen's strike in the winter of 1962, when I was government minister of housing and development. I was asked to go down to the port personally and use my influence with the men to get them to start loading the fruit produce for export. I went to Haifa and spent the whole night trying to resolve the dispute. At six o'clock the next morning, when I was already on my way back to Jerusalem, I heard a radio report that the dockers had decided to go back to work because of my intercession. I felt deeply gratified that the port workers had done me a good turn for old times' sake.

My pleasure was short-lived. The seven o'clock news carried an item noting that the Histadrut's Coordinating Committee had expressed shock that a minister of state should have interfered in a labor dispute. When I got back to Jerusalem, I met Ben-Gurion, who congratulated me for a job well done at the port; he hadn't heard the latest newscasts. When I told him what the Coordinating Committee was saying, he fell silent and walked back to his office.

A few hours later Meir Avizohar, then head of the Party's Information Center, came in to tell me that Ben-Gurion had appointed him to look into the matter. Not long after that, Party Secretary Reuben Barkat announced that it was the party and its ministers who had asked Yosef Almogi to use his influence to get the longshoremen to load the fruit, and that they all expressed their thanks for his contribution to resolution of the dispute. Three days later Avizohar reported to Ben-Gurion, who then advised me not to take the Coordinating Committee's deliberations too seriously: "Keep up your good relations with the dock workers," was his parting comment to me on the subject.

And I did.

Jewish Labor Committee dinner in honor of Lane Kirkland, 1973. Almogi greets Mr. Kirkland and Bayard Rustin.

During the Histadrut campaign of 1962 in the presence of Dr. Sol Stein.

During a Histadrut convention in New York City, 1953.

Walter Reuther visiting the port of Haifa, 1957.

A visit to the Israeli Navy, 1969.

George Schultz, the Nixon administration's secretary of labor, and his wife on a visit to Israel at Almogi's invitation, in the company of the American ambassador to Israel, Walworth Barbour, 1971.

With Ben-Gurion, 1958.

The Presidium of the Ninth Convention of Mapai in Israel, enjoying an anecdote Almogi told at the opening of the convention, 1960.

The first time the Israeli flag was raised, in an army camp in Egypt near Cairo, 1940. Almogi is on the extreme right with the Israelis. On the other side, the British.

The writer, David Pinski, in Almogi's office in Haifa, when Almogi was secretary of the Haifa Labor Council, 1953.

Ben-Gurion as part of the wedding party for Almogi's son, with Almogi's daughter-in-law Yuta and his wife, Shifra, 1962.

Almogi welcoming the leaders of the Socialist International Organization, among them Hugh Gaitskell of Britain, who was then prime minister; Guy Mollet, who was prime minister of France; Vandervelda, the oldest Belgian socialist; and Erich Olenauer, leader of the German socialist party. Also present are David Ben-Gurion, Golda Meir, and Moshe Sharett, 1960.

Almogi conferring with Levi Eshkol, trying to settle a problem between Eshkol and Pinhas Sapir, 1964.

After a speech at the opening of the 29th Zionist Congress, Almogi greeted by Prime Minister Begin. Also present are President Efraim Katzir, General Ariel Sharon, and Yitzhak Navon, later president of the State of Israel.

A visit to a Druze village in Daliat Carmel where Almogi was made an honorary citizen of the village, 1970.

With a part of the leadership of Conservative Jews in Israel, 1976.

Speaking for the Israel Bond Drive, 1972.

On an official visit to Rumania, Almogi is honored at a cocktail party given by Rabbi Rosen of Rumania in the presence of the chief Christian official in Rumania and a representative of the Rumanian government, 1972.

With Guy Mollet, prime minister of France, on the right. On the left is Erich Olenauer of Germany, 1960.

With Ben-Gurion and Hugh Gaitskell, 1960.

At the opening of the Brussels Conference for Russian Jews, 1976.

Meeting the Turkish governor of Istanbul (a general). This was the first official visit of an Israeli minister to Turkey.

14
The Seamen's Strike

The year 1947 marks the start of the dramtic growth of a Jewish merchant fleet. Beginning with one vessel and 104 seamen, Israel's merchant marine grew to fourteen ships and 560 seamen in 1949, and to twenty-three ships and 840 seamen in 1951. The fleet consisted mostly of ships that had been used in running Jewish refugees past the British to Palestine—old, leaky tubs with conditions on board far from answering to even the barest minimum of what would be required of them at sea. But somehow the vessels were refitted, through what small means could be made available at the time, as merchantmen, and only the fact that they flew the national colors could compensate the crews for their hardships on deck and the small financial rewards they received for their labors. Great vision, powerful conviction in the vital importance of a merchant marine to the nation's economy, and plain doggedness were required to put the enterprise on its feet both professionally and financially.

As the time approached for signing the first work contract for the merchant fleet in January 1949, a labor dispute was brewing, and feelings were running high among the men in the Seamen's Union. As acting secretary of the Haifa Labor Council, I found myself becoming increasingly involved in efforts to resolve the dispute. My attitude toward the Seamen's Union ran counter to my general convictions about the need for the Labor Council to jealously preserve its independence in dealing with the labor problems of any enterprise within its jurisdiction. It seemed to me that this policy of reserving exclusive authority to ourselves could not be applied to the seamen, who had come from and lived in all parts of the country. It was, therefore, legitimate for them to organize as a national union, for which the Trade Union Department of the Histadrut Executive Council had responsibility.

After receiving a report from the union's committee on the tangled skein of problems that made up the dispute, I suggested calling a meeting of all the representatives of seamen serving on the ships of the Zim National Navigational Line's maritime service company, Shoham, so I could get a first-hand account of the men's difficulties and demands. I had no doubt of either the committee's or its secretariat's loyalty, but I had the sense that they were insufficiently in touch with what was actually taking place on board the ships. I wanted to put myself in direct contact with the men who had to live daily with the hardships of the job.

The First Seamen's Meeting

On September 2, 1949, the seamen's meeting took place in Haifa; there were two representatives from each vessel. The picture they gave of life on board ship was appalling: crews' quarters were cramped and unventilated, their supplies inadequate, their wages bad. The situation was being especially exacerbated by the attempts of management, under pressure from the Ministry of Finance, to get out of honoring the agreement according to which a part of the seamen's wages was paid in foreign currency which was worth more than all they received in home currency. Then, too, there was the matter of the unreasonable thoroughness with which customs officers conducted their searches whenever the ships made home port; the seamen were asking customs to take a more lenient and humane view of their purchases abroad. They were also bitter about the incompetence of the company's staff on land, whom they considered ignorant about shipping and seamanship and the cause of much loss in time and effort. The workers on land belonged to an earlier generation of pioneer settlers and maintained operations ashore in strict keeping with their very high ethical standard. They had done a magnificent job of getting illegal settlers into Mandate Palestine by sea, but they were less than successful in dealing with the complex of problems involved in running a shipping company.

I had come prepared for a stormy session. I had learned in my work that sweeping the problems in labor disputes under the rug leads only to the accumulation of dust that will combust spontaneously. I therefore paid careful attention to what the seamen had to say; I even managed to derive some small pleasure from listening to these young men—most of them native-born Israeli sabras—sharply criticizing the bad conditions on the ships and taking to task the shipping administrators for their failure in labor relations. I had invited representatives of the company's management who, when their turn to speak came, didn't bother to contradict the main points in the seamen's complaints, and merely put the blame for most of the troubles on the shortage of manpower, the company's growing pains, and the lack of a seagoing tradition among Jews.

After three consecutive days of discussions I summed up the conclusions reached at the meeting: three veteran seamen, who were experienced and knowledgeable in professional matters and were seriously concerned about the men's social and wage demands, should be added to the Union Committee; a Department of Seamen's and Shipping Affairs should be added to the Histadrut Executive; and, finally, the Seamen's Union should become a national trade union.

On the Road to Confrontation

The seamen's situation continued to deteriorate. In July 1950 a second seamen's meeting took place. This time the participants represented, not each ship, but the three main branches of the profession—engine room, deck, and management. This guaranteed a representation more favorable to the seamen. The discussions were calmer than at the first meeting, and no exaggerated demands were made in anticipation of the signing of a labor contract for the years 1950–51. I suspect this was because the left-wing opposition in the union needed a little more time to clear the decks for action. This they did soon enough, and their activities took the form of sporadic strikes on board different ships and of violence undertaken by criminal elements against the union's offices. Things weren't improved either by the Finance Ministry's periodic announcements of further curtailments in the foreign-currency earnings of seamen. I tried each time to have the harshness of the measures reduced, but even when I succeeded, the damage to the credibility of work agreements had already been done.

For a whole year, strikes kept breaking out on the vessels of the merchant fleet. The issues were always different and at times quite odd: reduction in foreign-currency earnings; new wage demands; the opening of a "slop chest," a shop on board which sold goods at reduced prices to the crew; the quality of beds and mattresses; the withholding of permission for a crew to disembark at a port of call; and so on. It was a kind of relay strike, taken up by each ship in turn—first on the *Biltmore,* then on the *Galila,* then the *Komemiut,* then the *Negba,* the *Tel Aviv,* the *Zefonit,* and so on.

Nineteen fifty-one, a Knesset election year, was marked by social tensions and by a bitter political contest between Mapai and its opposition of the Left, Mapam. The latter party was intent on creating a "revolutionary" atmosphere in the country, and it showed very obvious pro-Communist inclinations in international affairs. On June 18, for example, Tel Aviv longshoremen refused to load a consignment of fruit-juice concentrate bound for South Korea; their justification was that they would not be partners to the shipping of Israeli products to the "American aggressor." For this the dockers received congratulations and support from the Israeli branch of the Communist-organized World Peace Committee.

I had good reason to believe we were heading toward a power struggle over a very different issue from the contest over control of the Seamen's Union. Loyal Mapai seamen with whom I met in connection with the establishment of party representation in the union informed me that some of the rebel leaders were in close touch with Communist trade unions in Europe. Moreover, the conduct in Israel of this group gave every indication that they intended to take over union government by the same means regularly employed by Communist parties in the West: one of the most prominently used of these was deceptive rhetoric, filled with distortions and inaccuracies of fact, which were designed to pander to the ignorant.

At end of June 1951, the crew of the *Negba* went on strike when the vessel anchored in the port of Marseille. The issue was the old one of foreign currency allotments, but this time the strikers did not limit themselves to presenting their demands to the Shoham management, they turned to the Communist-dominated French seamen's union to intercede on their behalf. Outwardly, the French seamen made it appear as if they were responding to the Israeli crew's call for support; in fact, the Frenchmen were somewhat less than anxious to help a crew striking away from its home port. In the end, the men of the *Negba* accepted the proposal made by Zim's representative in France that they return to Haifa—on the promise that no disciplinary action would be taken against them.

I maintained contact with the rebel union men. Against the advice of the union's secretary, I met with many of the men in the radical group on shipboard, at Labor Council headquarters, and even in my home: I wanted to get the feel of their mood and understand what was driving them, so that I could try to influence them not to paralyze the nation's shipping. In our face-to-face chats, these men showed greater moderation than they did at rallies, where they let their rabble-rousing rhetoric run away with them. I recall sitting with them on the roof of the house for hours on end, trying to rouse their interest in a new labor contract that should have offered a solution to a substantial portion of the problems that seemed to be bothering them. The more we talked, the more it became clear that it was not the financial aspects that interested them most. Much the opposite was true: the last thing they wanted were gains in wages and fringe benefits. This was in keeping with the well-known Communist theory that the worse socioeconomic conditions become, the more likely they are to realize their ultimate objective. In their eyes we Social-Democrat "Mapainiks," by our insistence on the exact observance of the rules of democracy, were working against the development of a revolutionary situation out of which the forces that would create the world of the future could arise.

When I had finished pointing out to them that they had no quarrel left with either the Shoham Company or the Histadrut respecting financial issues and that their demand for a national union was being realized, I asked them directly what it was they were still fighting for and against whom. Their answer was that I should get rid of the union's secretary general.

My response was that much as their ultimate goals were dear to them, the way they were going about this particular matter would achieve nothing but increased strife and contention. If they were interested in changing the union secretary, elections for the union committee were coming up soon, and the chances were better than even that they could get a man in who was more to their liking.

However, they refused to wait for the elections for two reasons: first, now that they had created a "revolutionary situation," they were not about to settle for crumbs; and second, they were not at all sure that they would do better in this committee election than they did in the last, held in May 1950, when the opposition was able to get only two of its people into office. As the rebels well knew, the Seamen's Union contained a silent sector that could go either way during the balloting.

In October 1951 elections were held for the third seamen's convention. The meeting was to be a one-time affair and was not supposed to take over the function of the elected committee. The responsible elements in the Seamen's Union, among whom Mapai party members could be counted, did not attempt to take part in the revolutionary festivities and would not put their names up for election to the convention, but waited for the Histadrut and the government to respond. Much to my regret, neither the rebels nor the Histadrut loyalists properly understood the Haifa Labor Council's real desire for compromise.

They saw our attempts to reach a settlement agreeable to all sides as a sign of weakness.

October 16 was election day, and the results showed that supporters of the Seamen's Provisional Representation, which had been appointed by the Histadrut to deal with the problems of the union until a permanent seamen's union committee was elected, had made gains. On November 4, the seamen's convention met at Seamen's House in Haifa. I made a short welcoming speech, and then announced that the Haifa Labor Council would no longer be responsible for the seamen, whose affairs would now be dealt with by the Trade Union Department of the Histadrut Executive Committee—something that had already been agreed upon. One of the secretaries reported on the respectable achievements of the Seamen's Union in the period 1948–51, but it soon became apparent that this was not what the meeting's tone-setters had in mind. I made my way out at the first opportune moment and thanked my stars I was free of the business. I hoped that with this my part in the episode had come to an end. I never imagined that very soon I would again find myself back in the middle of the same controversy.

Yeruham Meshel, who was then in the Trade Union Department of the Histadrut Executive (and later became secretary-general of the Labor Federation), learned painfully at firsthand about the methods used by the Seamen's Provisional Representation. They made their demands known to him at the opening of the convention: recognition, in violation of union rules, of the seamen's new secretariat, which was entirely made up of rebel representatives; changing the articles according to which the Union operated; the right to strike vessels while they were abroad; and putting the Seamen's Labor Exchange into the hands of the Seamen's Union.

It was obvious that Meshel could not have given his answer to such demands right there on the spot. Nevertheless, a motion was put to the vote to demand that Meshel respond immediately to these radical proposals. As was to be expected, the convention unanimously supported the motion, and Meshel, who was unused to this kind of tactics in labor disputes, grew angry and walked out of the meeting hall. After further debate, marked by a good deal of shouting and disturbance, Meshel got a twenty-four-hour period of grace (later extended to thirty-six hours) in which to return an answer to the convention.

The real nature of the dispute was now made clear both to Mordecai Namir, secretary-general of the Histadrut, and to Yeruham Meshel. It had nothing to do with legitimate labor issues, but was created by the drive to gain political control. Nevertheless, after Namir had met with the Seamen's Representation on Friday, September 11, he gave a surprisingly optimistic report of his discussion with them.

However, the representatives of the rebels reported to the seamen's convention about the "contemptuous attitude" taken by Namir toward them, saying that he had kept them waiting until he finished his conference with me. Then, after some harsh words about Namir, the rebels announced the session closed for the day, to be resumed on Sunday.

That same day, the director of the Labor Exchange in the Haifa District announced that the Seamen's Exchange was being transferred to the General

Labor Exchange. This was in direct opposition to the demand being made by the leaders of the convention, and it was then that the conventioneers made their fateful decision to announce that all seamen would leave their ships "if within twenty-four hours there is no satisfactory answer to our demands." In face-to-face talks, the rebel leaders explained that they had no quarrel with their employers—only with the Histadrut, since the men could not go to sea without labor rules, which the Histadrut was refusing to approve within twenty-four hours.

The way was now clear for the great seamen's strike, which began the following day, November 12, 1951. The seamen announced their resignation and left their ships. Not all—there were those who remained on board and continued to work, but for all intents and purposes the whole merchant fleet might just as well have been in dry dock. The revolutionaries were ecstatic, to judge from the highly inflammatory slogans they now made free with. They also put out feelers once again to the longshoremen for a united front against the "Social-Democratic softies."

15

The Big Confrontation

Two days after the seamen's mass resignation I was asked to come to Jerusalem for an emergency meeting with the secretary and the members of the Coordinating Committee of Mapai at the party's office in the Knesset. Everyone who spoke at the meeting agreed that this was a political struggle that had to be fought by political means. Histadrut Secretary Namir insisted that we could not put up with the immobilization of the nation's merchant fleet and that we had to put it back into operation immediately. The participants in the meeting concluded that since Haifa was the actual arena of the conflict, there was no choice but for me to take on the job of relaunching the fleet.

I resisted. I explained that I had just managed to free myself from the onerous responsibility of dealing with the seamen's problems, in which I had been involved for two full years, and here I was being asked again to involve myself in a struggle that could reach who knew what level of intensity. I asked my comrades to reconsider whether this job really ought to be handed to me and the Haifa Labor Council.

The meeting dragged on, and when we could not agree, we decided to ask for a meeting with Ben-Gurion. The delegation that went to meet with him included, beside myself, Mordecai Namir, secretary-general of the Histadrut; Zeev On, secretary of Hevrat Haovdim (the cooperative association responsible for running Histadrut enterprises); Reuben Barakat, director of the Political Department of the Executive Committee; and Meir Argov, secretary of the Mapai party. The delegation gave a full report to Ben-Gurion and asked him to appoint me and the Haifa Labor Council to the task of getting the fleet back into operation. I again objected and pointed out that the job required central authority and the highest backing; I explained that the problem we were facing was not in essence one of economics. So far as wage and labor conditions were concerned, I was more likely than not to be on the side of the seamen. The real issue was of political control, and it was probable that the leaders of the seamen's convention would even waive all their professional demands if that could get us to recognize as legitimate the secretariat they had chosen. Finally, I made a special point of saying that we had to bring the dispute to an end in a way which would not leave this illegal secretariat in its unrightful place and that if those present at this meeting wished to reach a compromise, they had best do it *before* the confrontation, which promised to be a rought one, rather than after.

Ben-Gurion concluded that it was the responsibility of us all to keep the nation's sea routes to the rest of the world open and in good order and that we would have to work together to achieve this task. However, it was his opinion that the specific job of getting the men on shipboard again and the merchant fleet back into operation should be mine.

I returned to Haifa in a less than cheeful mood and began to consider the steps I would take until the Coordinating Committee determined officially what its position was on the issues of the dispute. I at least knew what I personally could expect. I would be the most slandered man in the country—they would be calling me "warmonger" and "capitalist lackey." But then I said to myself, What of it? Let them call me what they want, just so long as the fleet puts out to sea again!

The battle was joined immediately. The Executive Committee of the Histadrut ruled that the seamen's strike was illegal, that it contravened the position of the Histadrut and the government and was in violation of national interests. The Executive Committee therefore announced that it was breaking off all contact with the representatives of the seamen who had turned in their resignations and that it would withdraw its recognition of the seamen's convention.

We now had the way cleared for action. Our first step was to enlist volunteers who could put the ships to sea. We put out a call in the Histadrut's name for those who had left their sea trades and asked them to volunteer for work on board the ships; The response was gratifyingly large. We also appealed to experienced ship's officers, and I opened an information campaign among the strikers themselves. A number of shipmasters volunteered their services, and some chief engineers and deckhands as well. We had men coming to us from kibbutz settlements, from the Electric Corporation, and from factories both in Haifa and outside the city. We drew up lists of volunteers, had the men clasified, and then began getting each of the ships in turn out to sea. The first vessel put to sea within a matter of days after we had got to work.

It would be appropriate here to set one story straight—a story which has made its way into history without being true. It is commonly believed that the ships were entirely manned and operated by volunteers, but without a full complement of trained and experienced mariners of all ranks on board all the ships, this would have been, if not impossible, at least a very dangerous thing to do. The truth of the matter is that nearly half of the merchant seamen returned to the ships. They had never wanted to strike in the first place, but when they saw how we had responded to the strike they had expected us to give in: All they had wanted was to avoid being victims, whoever won.

The scope of our activity and the great number of volunteers who had answered our call took the seamen's convention by surprise: The rebels had been sure that without them the fleet could not be put back in operation. At the same time the public was becoming aware that the strike was political. This impression was reinforced by the left-wing parties, the members of whose youth movements were propagandized by their instructors about the "dictatorial steps" taken by the majority in the government and the Histadrut and called on to demonstrate their opposition to the tyranny. Most of the barbs were aimed at Ben-Gurion and me. Groups of youngsters gathered near my home and shouted slogans like "Almogi out! Ben-Gurion out! Namir out!" Among those participating in the demonstration calling for Namir to leave was Namir's own nephew, who was a pupil in the maritime school and was unable to get out of joining the demonstration and taking part in the verbal assault on his uncle. My son Yoram, too, most of whose classmates were members of Mapam's youth movement Hashomer Hatzair, found himself being called names such as "capitalist lackey" at school.

Face to Face

As the organized demonstrations became rowdier (in itself a sign that the strike leaders sensed defeat on the way), we decided to call on workers to guard the Labor Council building in case demonstrators should try to force their way in. So it happened that one evening during the strike, two large groups of men had assembled in the streets of Haifa. One was made up of jobless men and their supporters—mostly former members of the Palyam (the Hagana's operational naval force) and young people who had joined them for the demonstration, the other group consisted of workers who had responded to our appeal, most of them employees of the Electric Corporation. I had purposely refrained from calling in the longshoremen; that could have led to violence, the one thing I wished to avoid. Happily there was none. After two of the seamen's representatives made speeches the demonstrators went home quietly, and things simmered down.

The fight to keep the merchant fleet in operation and to preserve the integrity of the Histadrut threw the Mapai party into a frenzy of activity. When party representatives serving in the goverment and on the Histadrut met again during the second week of December to decide what action should be taken if striking seamen carried out their threat to oppose the removal of the crew of the ship *Tel Aviv*, which was on its way to Haifa, all agreed that the strikers who were on board had to be taken off, even if by force, and replaced by volunteers. Carrying out the decision would not be easy, and there was even a legal barrier. Only the ship's owners—in this case either Zim Lines or its operating agent, Shoham—had the right to take such action. We easily got the cooperation of the company; the Mapai members of Zim's management were just as upset as we were by the disorder at sea.

On Friday, December 14, which afterward became known as "Black Friday," the *Tel Aviv* arrived in the post of Haifa, iron bars and wood clubs bristling behind her gunwales. The men had barricaded themselves on deck. When the crew would not answer the police summons to disembark peaceably, the police threw up ladders on the vessel's side to board her. Skirmishes broke out between the boarding party and the crew. Striking seamen ashore were trying to break into the port and were stopped by longshoremen massed to meet them. Here and there down the line fights broke out between the two groups, but they never developed into pitched battles. After a struggle, the strikers on board the *Tel Aviv* ended their resistance.

Formally, the strike went on for another ten days, but after Black Friday tension definitely decreased. On December 21, after the intercession of various groups who acted as arbitrators in the dispute—among others, ship's captains and the heads of the Histadrut—the seamen called a meeting at which they accepted the Histadrut organizing committee's decisions:

1. The seamen's convention would respond to the call of the Histadrut and the Knesset to end the strike; At the same time, the Histadrut would announce the return to work of all seamen.

2. The organizing committee would recommend to the Executive Committee that the Histadrut Labor Council meet immediately to consider all the organizational problems of the Seamen's Union.

3. No measures would be taken to punish the seamen who took part in the strike and handed in their resignations, nor would any be taken against the members of the seamen's convention.

I felt no pleasure when the strike came to an end. There is nothing pleasant about having to break a strike, even if it was the wildest experienced by the state up until that time. I was pained at having been forced to undertake a struggle with young and decent men whose only fault was that they had let themselves be carried away by their own foolishness and misled by unprincipled people. Throughout the dispute, I never had the slightest doubt that getting the ships that flew the colors of Israel underway again had both saved the nation's merchant navy and preserved the integrity of the Histadrut. My regret was only that it was I who was Haifa's Labor Council secretary when the seamen's strike took place.

Recently I found support for the views I held then, and still hold, about the issues involved in the seamen's strike in the memoirs of the late Levi Kantor, *Le-lo maso panim* ("Without Prejudice"), published by Yahad Press in 1977. Levi had been union chief in the Mapam party at the time of the strike, and as such was not only personally involved in the events but one of the moving spirits; he had been sent, together with Eliezer Preminger, by his party to manage the dispute on behalf of the seamen. He writes:

"The 'Black Friday' of Israel's merchant fleet must remain stamped in the memories of all those who hold the existence of Israel dear. The violent seamen's strike was a *tangible* threat to the survival of the young State of Israel, and first and foremost—a threat to *democratic* government in the State of Israel" [italics in original].

There is nothing I can add to Levi Kantor's words. He testified to the character of the events from his own personal experience and revealed things that were clear to us throughout the whole period of the strike.

16
The Histadrut

The seamen's strike was at an end. After two years in which the merchant fleet nearly foundered in the troubled public waters whipped up by opposition on the right and left wings, the sea was calm once again. The Histadrut General Federation of Labor emerged with its unity intact. Moreover, as a result of the prolonged period of labor tranquillity that followed, and the augmented efforts to restore and improve the whole complex of labor relations between the shipping companies, the merchant mariners, and the Histadrut, the revivified industry was able to enjoy a period of physical growth and economic prosperity.

With the end of the strike, I was free to take up my routine work once more on the Labor Council. There were new challenges to be met. The seamen's strike, and the tensions in industrial relations and sharp political conflict among working-mens' parties which arose on a national scale as a result of it, had raised to the surface the problem of the nature, structure, and role of the Histadrut. The tens of thousands of new Israelis who had been absorbed into the country's labor force only since the foundatin of the state experienced real difficulty in understanding the special character of the Histadrut—especially when they attempted to do so by comparing it with workers' organizations in their countries of origin. It was the source of misunderstanding not only by the mass of working people who were represented by the Histadrut in labor negotiations, but by many who belonged to the organization's cooperative societies, social agencies, cultural services, and administrative bodies. The opposition parties added to the public's confusion by representing the Histadrut as a giant economic conglomerate profiting from the labor of the workingman. Failure to understand the real nature of the Histadrut was in part what exacerbated relations between the Labor Federation's administrative bodies and various shop committees, with the result that we often found ourselves on the brink of crisis within our own ranks.

We therefore undertook a major information campaign to teach our rank-and file membership about the nature, purposes, and operations of the Histadrut. We called rallies and meetings and organized courses and discussion groups for workers at their jobs. At the same time we worked for the introduction of

industrial democracy in the plants. We wanted to create an atmosphere of cooperation that would encourage the formation of a partnership between management and labor in each enterprise and to give workers a sense that their place of
work was a home and that to the degree that the household prospered, so would
they. The Histadrut succeeded in introducing worker participation in management in Histadrut-owned enterprises—an achievement which not only helped to
prevent labor unrest, but got employees more directly involved in the development of their plants.

In my own talks with shop committees I would explain that the Histadrut was
unique among labor organizations in the special nature and breadth of its commitment and by the degree of its unity. Trade unions in other countries were
formed to fight for a more equitable distribution of the national wealth; they
operated in the context of well-established states, economies, nationalities, and
cultures. The Histadrut, in contrast, came into being as a result of a vision of
reuniting as a modern nation a people that had been dispersed and atomized
into a myriad of seperate ethnic, communal, and tribal groups. Under the special
circumstances that prevailed in Israel, the "national cake," so to speak, with
whose fair apportionment the trade-union movement in Israel was concerned,
still awaited baking. The commitment of the Histadrut was, therefore, to the
combined task of watching over the interests of labor and working for the
achievement of broad national goals. The Histadrut General Federation of
Labor had to be more than the representative of trade unionism; it became
directly involved in creating a productive economy, extending the area of land
being settled, ensuring cooperation among the sectors of the economy, developing social services, diffusing the use of the Hebrew language among a
polyglot population, laying the foundations of a homogeneous culture, and
educating the nation's young.

The primary purpose of Histadrut enterprises—which include kibbutz and
cooperative settlements organized under the aegis of the Agricultural Center
and such commercial or national undertakings as the agricultural cooperative
marketing society Tnuva, the Bank Hapoalim (Workers' Bank), the cooperative
wholesale society Hamashbir, the housing company Shikun Ovdim (Workers'
Housing), Hassneh Insurance Company, the Kupat Holim sick fund and health
insurance plan, the Hapoel sports organization, and the Noar Oved (Working
Youth) youth movement—is to serve the essential goals of Zionism and the state.
The same purpose accounts for the labor federation's direct involvement in
security and defense, immigration, running refugees past the British blockade
during the Mandatory period, land settlement, and education.

The protection of working people's interests is, then, only one aspect of a vast
complex of activities undertaken by the Histadrut. Even that particular responsibility has implications broader than merely looking out for workers' salaries and
fringe benefits; for these cannot be divorced from the economic, social, and even
cultural policies of the state and the government.

Earnings, as I used to explain, are only one factor, and not necessarily the
most important one, determining living standards and well-being. To improve
wages and social benefits, workers must have at their disposal a strong organiza-

tion—one they can mobilize in time of need to defend themselves against being exploited and to guarantee a fair return for themselves. The most advantageous work contract is not worth the paper it was written on in a period of precipitous decline of productivity and export: such a state of affairs must inevitably lead to mass layoffs.

The uniqueness of the General Federation of Labor resides in the inclusiveness of its view of the essential interests of working people. The Histadrut's outlook is at once broad in scope and long-term, taking in the general interests of the nation as a whole. Its prescription for a fair standard of living is always coordinated with the levels of productivity and profit in the national economy—a policy of utmost importance to an economy whose foundations are being laid and which finds itself in the full swing of development.

There is certainly a marked difference in the attitude's taken by workers engaged in productive labor and those in the services toward the question of the apportionment of economic benefits: the first are obliged to take into the account the balance between production and profit, whereas the second tend to regard the public budget as an inexhaustible resource whose deficits can always be covered either by the increase of charges to the public or by the receipt of outside loans. As a consequence, it frequently occurs that in periods when the industrial sector is relatively free of labor disputes, the services continue to be plagued by them. This is the kind of situation the Histadrut has found unacceptable.

The Histadrut's broad commitment is what accounts for its extraordinary unity. It stands out among trade-union organizations throughout the world because it includes all categories of working people, from sanitation workers to members of the free professions. Moreover, all its members, rather than paying their membership fees to their own particular trade union, which in turn participates in the budget of the trade-union federation on the basis of the size of its membership, pay directly into the Histadrut's treasury. These funds are then redistributed according to needs determined by general policy. This has made the Histadrut an economic instrument of great potential. It is without precedent or parallel in the labor movement anywhere in the world. It is this aspect of the Histadrut which caused David Remez to remark, when he was secretary-general of the Labor Federation, that although the Employers' Association of Israel was a poor organization of rich members, the Histadrut was a rich organization of poor members. The membership-funding policy of the Histadrut has enabled it to undertake vast economic and industrial projects that have returned enormous benefits to the organization's entire membership and enriched the nation as a whole. It might therefore be of value at this point to recount some of the Histadrut's major industrial undertakings.

Koor Industries & Crafts, Israel's largest industrial corporation, was started in 1940. At about that time, Solel Boneh, the Histadrut's building and public-works company, acquired the Phoenicia drawn sheet-glass factory when it was closed down and its machinery about to be sold to the Egyptians. Solel Boneh then bought up the Vulcan Foundries when that company, too, was being closed down. To these were added the factories of Hamgaper Rubber Goods, which had started by retreading old automobile tires; the Harssa Works for the production of sanitary ceramics; and Vulcan Batteries. These plants all became part of Koor Industries, which officially came into being in 1944.

The employees of the Phoenicia glass factory and the Vulcan Foundries were mostly experienced construction workers whose average age was forty and who wanted steady work at a permanent place of employment. The majority had come to Israel in the late 1920s and during the 1930s. They were men who had been active in the service of the Jewish community before the establishment of the state and had from their youth enthusiastically taken up work in industry. Many of them had gone through periods of unemployment. They were now ambitious for their plants to succeed. These men were joined by recent immigrants, for many of whom this was the first encounter with productive labor.

Great difficulties were experienced by the employees of the Phoenicia glass plant. For them the manufacture of glass was something entirely new, and it took many months of hard work before they succeeded in producing their first plate of glass. Nor was it any easier getting Vulcan Foundries back on its feet. Solel Boneh had to make a considerable investment to expand the plant. In the end, the foundries proved their worth. It was certainly a good thing for the future of Israel that Vulcan was in the right hands at the outbreak of the War of Independence, when the foundries were able to supply the Hagana with all the cast iron it needed without having to take account of the cost.

That all four of the firms were located in the harbor area was of great help in consolidating their employees. The geographical concentration of the plants made it natural for Koor's first managing board to choose Vulcan, for the location of its headquarters.

The workers at these plants, in addition to getting their factories into operation, made significant social contributions to Haifa and the country as a whole. Once during the Mandate period, when a Palmah unit broke into the Atlit internment camp, where illegal Jewish immigrants were being held by the British, and released the inmates so they could be smuggled into Kibbutz Beit Oren on Mount Carmel, workers from the plants responded to the call of Jewish leadership and went up to the Carmel forests to mix with the immigrants and so frustrate the efforts of the British police to identify the escapees. During the War of Independence, when Rushmia Bridge was constantly under Arab fire, the factories arranged to have work crews brought to and from the plants in armored vehicles. It is to the credit of the employees that work was never interrupted because of Arab attacks on the routes of access to the factories.

Koor continued to establish and acquire new factories. We of the Labor Council, in turn, supported both the Koor management in its development and expansion and the employees in their efforts to improve labor conditions. Without the people of Koor, the development of the great complex of heavy industry that stretches from Haifa to Acre and the establishment there of "Steel City" would have been inconceivable. It was the rare combination of vision and professional know-how that built Koor Industries, which has by now acquired an international reputation. The thousands of workers employed by Koor work under decent labor conditions; they are the mainstay of the company and the guarantors of its continuing development.

The concentration of Histadrut industries in Haifa brought many blessings: it added to the city's power in the country and to the Histadrut's strength in Haifa. But it brought problems as well. The managements and workers of the plants would stubbornly cling to opposing positions, which they defended on the same grounds. The workers demanded better working conditions and management demanded greater productivity, and both justified their demands by arguing that the factory belonged to the Histadrut. I was in no doubt that the resolution to the problem lay in establishing real collaboration between management and labor. Both locally and in the country at large, conditions had to be created that would give workers a sense that they were an integral part of their plant and that, as it prospered and its productive capacities increased, so did the profits, from which—once they were redistributed according to agreed and fixed criteria—the workers would benefit as well. It was fortunate for us that both sides eventually gave up their infantile tug of war. The Histadrut is now stable, with its workers active partners in the management of its enterprises. Labor disputes have been reduced with the workers' deepening sense of partnership and increasing participation in the processes of production.

In the port of Haifa, there was once a cooperative of veteran dock workers who came originally from Salonika and specialized in unloading wheat cargoes. When a ship carrying a bulk cargo of wheat arrived, the cooperative would hire hundreds of workers who had to stuff the wheat into sacks by hand—a job which not only involved exhausting labor and high cost, but delayed ships at port.

Then one day Dr. Reuben Hecht, a man from a well-established family who had a strong national consciousness, came to see me. He explained that he had received permission to build a modern grain elevator near the port. I immediately told him that we were ready to give him all the help he needed, but that the cooperative and the workers who would lose their jobs because of the project would have to be compensated. It was only natural that the dock workers were not happy about the introduction of an up-to-date port silo that would raise the efficiency of unloading grain to a degree they could not hope to compete with. All the same, I rejected the arguments of the cooperative and gave my full support to the establishment of what became the Dagon Silo of Haifa. Another important enterprise had made Haifa its home. Labor relations at the Dagon Silo are exemplary. And as for Dr. Hecht, besides managing the Silo, he is active as well in the arts, publishing, and public life. Most recently he was appointed an adviser to the prime minister.

17
Member of the Knesset

During the national elections for the Constituent Assembly in January 1949, I was sixty-second on the Mapai party list of candidates. Forty-six Mapai candidates were elected to the assembly, so that I was among those who only made it as far as the threshold of the nation's first legislature.

At the time of the election campaign for the Second Knesset, in 1951, I was party chief of election headquarters in Haifa. The city's branch of Mapai asked for me to be placed on the party list in a position that would give me a realistic chance for a seat in the Knesset. Just before the party's Central Headquarters was to meet in order to confirm the list of candidates, I was invited to talk with the Appointments Committee, which was meeting in Ben-Gurion's home in Tel Aviv: in addition to the "Old Man," the committee members included Moshe Sharett and Pinhas Lavon.

When I came in with Sharett (whom I had driven down from Haifa with painstaking care, since I was a new driver), I found Ben-Gurion deep in conversation with Lavon. Ben-Gurion began to explain to me the problem that was facing the Appointments Committee: the committee wanted to put me in a realistic place on the party list, but that would be difficult without doing the same for Eliezer Shechter and Moshe Baram, who were secretaries of the Tel Aviv and Jerusalem labor councils, respectively. Both Sharett and Lavon assured me that even had the Haifa branch of the party not asked, they would have wished to see me in the national legislature, were it not that this would be unfair to my colleagues in Tel Aviv and Jerusalem.

Quite likely all three were expecting a sharp discussion with me and a hard fight with the Haifa branch of Mapai, which could well have forced them to include me on the list. They must have been relieved when I announced that I understood their problem and that the last thing I wished was to make things more difficult for them. If I couldn't be included, so be it, I told them. I thought it no great tragedy if I were not a member of Second Knesset.

From the looks on their faces I could see that my attitude had taken them completely by surprise. The conversation then turned to the Histadrut, Haifa,

136

and the political battles that lay ahead. We parted amicably, and I returned home in a reflective state of mind, but not feeling especially disappointed.

Four years later, when elections were held for the Third Knesset, the Histadrut, and the municipality, I refused to manage the election campaign in Haifa. At a meeting in Abba Khoushi's home I announced that the time had come for a change in personnel; after eight long years of activity on the Labor Council and participation in so many battles on its behalf, including the struggle during the seamen's strike, I wanted a rest and an opportunity to study. Only if I received a guarantee—in writing—that I would be free, to do as I wanted, would I agree to take on this last assignment.

After nearly two hours of discussion Mordecai Namir was able to come up with a compromise—that I should enter the Knesset and during my four-year term as MK hand over my job on the Labor Council to one of the other secretaries; and if before my term was up I succeeded in finding a replacement, I could resign my seat in the Knesset and take a holiday. Then, just to be on the safe side, Arieh Bahir added that the proposal had to be approved by Ben-Gurion, who had just returned from temporary political retirement at Kibbutz Sdeh Boker in the Negev to take over the Ministry of Defense in the government of Moshe Sharett and to take part in the election campaign.

The following day I was invited by Ben-Gurion to his home in Tel Aviv. I found him dressed in uniform and in the mood to talk. He spoke to me for close to an hour about the situation in the country and made the point that we were only at the beginning of the process of becoming an advanced nation.

He agreed to the decision that had been reached the day before in Haifa, and promised to come to the city to help us in the election campaign. Mapai Central Headquarters also approved the Haifa decision, and in August 1955, I was sworn in as an MK in the Third Knesset.

My Upper and Lower Houses

My Knesset membership, which was to last for twenty-two successive years, brought about a significant change in my life. My many acquaintances tended to regard my joining the legislature as a significant step forward in my political career, and congratulations poured in from all sides. There were, however, some in the party who claimed that I got into the Knesset because of pressures that were brought to bear through the workers at the port and in Haifa's factories. None of those who wished me well or ill ever imagined that I was not really enthusiastic over my election or that I had little expectation of feeling at home or finding satisfaction in the nation's parliament. Only a very few, who were really close to me, knew that I thought of my term in the Knesset as only an interim period between my service on the Labor Council and an extended period of rest and study, which I was impatiently looking forward to. Nor was I just dreaming: I had studied the matter and discovered that it was possible for me to go to America in an official capacity for a period of two or three years, during which time I would be able to fulfill my duties of explaining Israel to the Jewish public in the evenings and devote the day to study. All I needed was the agreement of the party to release me from my duties in the Haifa Labor Council. Hence, being in the Knesset was, to me, something I was obligated to go through to get to do what I really wanted.

My fellow parliamentarians received me with a sense of puzzled curiosity. My public image was of an aggressive, tough trade-union leader accustomed to dealing with stevedores and porters. What was a man like that doing in the Knesset? As for the MKs of my own party, for some reason I seemed to inspire in them feelings of envy and competitiveness.

I quickly entered into the swing of things. Monday afternoon I would arrive at the Knesset and remain in Jerusalem until Wednesday afternoon. I spent as much of my time as I could at Knesset sessions and in committee meetings. In my free time I sat in the Knesset library where I soon made myself at home. When I was not needed for meetings or appearances in the legislature, I did a great deal of reading. I was often asked by my colleagues to "let down my hair" and join them for a film in one of the Jerusalem theaters, but I never took them up on their invitations; I felt I had more important things to do.

For close to four years I drove by myself from Haifa to Jerusalem every Monday, and back to Haifa every Wednesday. The Haifa Labor Council had put an old Chrysler at my disposal—a reliable workhorse of a car carrying a license plate with the numerals 2222; it was a number easily remembered, which made the car familiar to a lot of people—a fact that caused me trouble on one occasion. I was driving with Shalom Bahat, who later became Labor Council secretary, to a gathering of the Mapai party congress in Tel Aviv. It was drizzling, and Bahat and I were engrossed in conversation, when suddenly at Atlit, near Haifa, the car in front of me pulled to a stop; I had no time to brake, and in trying to avoid a crash, I swerved and my car turned over and ended up on the side of the road with its wheels up in the air. Bahat and I got out unscathed through the windows. Because I was supposed to chair the meeting I decided to hitchhike and caught a ride to Tel Aviv. I left the Chrysler where it was, upside down at the edge of the road.

I reached the auditorium where the meeting was held and did my day's work—and only then did the thought enter my mind that someone might have spotted the car and its number and told my wife about it. That had in fact happened, as I discovered when I got home. I rushed back to Haifa and found my wife beside herself with anxiety; I had a hard time trying to calm her.

When I returned home Wednesday afternoons, I changed from my Knesset "Saturday best" into my Haifa Labor Council work clothes. It was quite a change—passing from the "upper house," as it were, where speeches were made and votes taken on issues of national and worldwide significance, to the "lower house," where the prosaic and day-to-day affairs of working people were dealt with. I devoted almost the whole period from Wednesday to Monday, including Saturday, to my work in the Labor Council. Friday night was all I allowed for myself and my family.

During my early period in the Knesset I became acquainted with the people, the events, and the problems that were constantly looming into public view.

Haifa, of course, was frequently front page news. My first problem was to get my order of priorities straight: should I content myself with merely sitting out my term so I could then advance my own goals, or should I really dedicate myself to parliamentary work and make the best contribution to it that I could? The decision came almost of itself: I decided to get down to work and learn, and make myself part of the Knesset. Despite my crowded schedule I took the time to study parliamentary procedure and the laws and rulings which governed the operations of the Knesset; and I read as much material as I could lay my hands on about the subjects being debated on the Knesset floor.

I soon discovered that I had one undeniable advantage over many of my colleagues: I was already familiar with most of the problems the Knesset dealt with; and I had come to know them not merely in theory, but had learnt them directly from life. I therefore decided to use my advantage of having unmediated experience with the issues. After doing my homework in the Knesset library I would appear in the assembly hall of the legislature whenever speeches were being made or questions put before the government, and also when legislation and agenda were being presented to the Knesset on economic and social issues.

I became one of the most active MKs in the Third Knesset—a fact attested to both by the number of my appearances at plenary sessions and by my participation in two Knesset committees, the committees of Finance and Labor. Dr. Binyamin Avniel of the Finance Committee and Akiva Gubrin of the Labor Committee—both of whom I worked closely with—put me at the head of several subcommittees. I was therefore able to bring before the Knesset a respectable number of bills for second and third readings, among them the Army Retirement Law.

Colleagues versus Friends

When I began feeling at home in the Knesset and became a familiar figure there, I was also made a member of its most important "club"—the Knesset dining room, where one was introduced to other MKs and could hear the news and also the political rumors. Most important, this was the place where pressing Knesset affairs were settled. I also discovered that at Knesset plenums one spoke, in committee one discussed, and in the dining room one chatted—and that all three types of discourse were closely tied up with one another. I realized, too, that although an MK may have colleagues among parliamentarians in his party, his real friends are at times in the opposition; he may be at ideological odds with a member of another political party but not involved in internal party rivalry with him, so that ties of personal friendship can often be formed more easily for that fact alone.

Akiva Gubrin—who was chairman of the government coalition, factional chairman, and chairman of the Work Committee—was very friendly with me. He had a way with a joke and used to entertain me with witty lessons on Knesset facts of life. He advised me, for example, that if I wanted to know if the speech I was making in the Knesset was any good, all I need do is to look at the faces of the members of my own party faction: if they were looking happy and content it was a sign I was making a bad job of it, but if they looked downcast I could take it as a certainty that my speech was a triumph.

At the end of one of my speeches (in which I had argued against the contention of the right-wing parties that Histadrut law was at odds with the law of the state), I received an invitation from the Knesset usher to see Knesset Chairman Yosef Shprintzak in his office. On my way up, I kept thinking that Shprintzak had caught me out in a parliamentary indiscretion he was especially sensitive about—namely, putting long questions to the government, which encouraged speech marathons. But Shprintzak was smiling and gave me a warm reception, and said to me, "I listen to the speeches of all members of the Knesset either directly or by means of the intercom in my office, and I must say that I've been pleasantly surprised by your speeches. You're one of the few in the Knesset who has brought to it the refreshing spirit of real life."

Shprintzak, who had been Histadrut secretary-general, had decided to pay me the compliment after hearing me speak on Histadrut law and other social and economic issues that touched on the Labor Federation. But much as I appreciated Shprintzak's kind words to me, they made me feel more than ever the great responsibility I had undertaken by joining the Knesset: noblesse oblige, I thought—and I resolved that from then on I would conduct myself on the Knesset floor with greater care than ever in order not to disappoint my constituency.

The Mapai party found itself in a great quandary over economic policy during the mid-1950s. Levi Eshkol, then finance minister, and Pinhas Sapir, minister of commerce, proved themselves to be acrobatic whizzes at explaining the state of the nation's economy. When they talked about wage policy to Mapai members, they painted a black picture of the country's financial situation, but when it came to debating economic issues with the opposition (which they often did on the same day), they appeared as perfect optimists and laid it on with the rosiest colors in their rhetorical palette.

In my own speeches on the economy I tried to strike a balanced view, and avoided being either overly sanguine or excessively pessimistic, but I always spoke from the perspective of the wage earner. This seems also to have been the attitude of the majority in the party.

The Sinai Campaign

When in October 1956, the Sinai Campaign had ended in one hundred hours with the whole of the peninsula in IDF hands, the battle shifted from the desert to the UN. There, member nations refused to come to terms with Israel's astounding victory by which its armed forces had managed not only to reopen the nation's sea route through the Straits of Tiran but to push forward all the way to the banks of the Suez Canal, whose nationalization by Nasser had been the cause for the failed Anglo-French operation undertaken in coordination with the Israeli campaign. There was a pressing need now to intensify our information operations abroad if we wished to guarantee free access for Israeli shipping not only through the Straits of Tiran, but through the Suez Canal as well, which had been closed to us for a long time. We had to see to it, too, that there would be no one-sided Israeli withdrawal from the Sinai Peninsula without a political return.

Golda Meir, who was minister of foreign affairs at the time, asked me to go to Europe on an information tour, during which I would meet with trade-union leaders, especially of the seamen's and longshoremen's unions, whose support, along with that of their governments, I was to try to enlist in behalf of Israel's right to enjoy the same freedom of the seas as did all other countries. Since I knew the unions of France and Italy to be under Communist influence, I decided to pass those countries by and concentrate on Belgium, Holland, Denmark, Sweden, Norway, and Finland. Golda told me before I left that if my campaign went well, she would ask me to take in England and West Germany as well.

I received great assistance from all our ambassadors in the countries I visited. In Copenhagen I had the pleasure of once again seeing Harry Beilin, who had represented the Jewish Agency in Haifa as our liaison agent with the British army in the prestate days. He was now Israel's ambassador to Denmark. Our ambassador to Sweden and Norway was another friend, Dr. Haim Yahil, who had been coordinator of the Cultural Committee in the Haifa Labor Council. My talks with Scandinavian leaders bore fruit, and they promised to support our interests.

In Finland I met Shlomo Zablodowicz, a Jewish businessman who had survived the Holocaust and settled in Helsinki, where he had cultivated strong ties with the Finish armaments industry. He was later able to secure significant cooperation between Finish industry and Israeli factories; his crowning achievement was the establishment of the Sultam plant in Yokneam. Zablodowicz helped greatly to make my mission to Scandinavia a success.

While I was still in Scandinavia, I received a wire from the Foreign Ministry, asking me to go on with my campaign and visit London and Bonn. In the capital city of the Federal Republic of Germany, I met both trade-union leaders and the heads of the Social-Democratic party. I was the first official visitor from Israel to have come to Bonn, and was asked by the chairman of the West German parliament if I would like to be welcomed by the Bundestag. The memory of the Holocaust and my own years in German captivity were still fresh in my mind, and I refused his offer. In The Hague I was received by the prime minister of Holland, Dr. Willem Dreis, who was also a popular labor leader. During our conversation, the prime minister announced that he had instructed Holland's ambassador to the UN to support our cause. I thanked him for his sympathetic attitude and invited him to pay Israel a visit. Dr. Dreis took up my invitation and in 1960 made an official visit to Israel. He even participated in the opening of the Ninth Mapai Party Congress when I was party secretary-general.

In England we were in a delicate situation because the British Labor party had come down hard against the conservative government of Anthony Eden for the failure at Suez; in the end Eden was forced to resign. In any case, the man who assisted me on my visit to England was G. S. Watson, a leader of the coal miners whom I had met during his visit to Haifa sometime earlier; Watson helped open all doors for me. At the end of my visit I was invited to dine with the leadership of the Labor party. During the dinner, which was held in the houses of Parliament, the conversation went along quite freely, and I had no need to ask for help from Gershon Avner, then counsellor in the Israel Embassy in London. When the leftists began badgering me about our part in the "imperialistic" Sinai Campaign, Watson jumped up from his place at the table and manfully came to my aid.

All in all the trip came off well. When I returned to Israel, I reported on the results of the tour to Golda, who expressed her satisfaction at the way I had stood up to the test of my first attempt at international diplomacy.

A few days later I was sitting with Yitzhak Navon in his office (he was Ben-Gurion's personal assistant then) when the Old Man walked in and, seeing me, said, "I hear you get on well with Gentiles. . . ."

"Only with Gentiles," I replied. I was to have quite a few meetings with Gentiles.

A Grenade in the Knesset

On October 29, 1957, a hand grenade was tossed from the visitors' gallery onto the floor of the Knesset. It exploded between the government's table and the speaker's dais. As was later found out, the grenade thrower was Moshe Douek, a mentally disturbed young man. The episode was not the work of any political group. In the explosion, minister of religion Moshe Shapira (who also had the name Haim, meaning "life," in accordance with an old Jewish custom intended to assure a long life for the name's bearer) was seriously hurt. Golda Meir, Moshe Carmel, and David Ben-Gurion were slightly injured.

At the time I was sitting with Arieh Bahir very close to the government's table. The moment we heard the explosion, Arieh Bahier rushed to Ben-Gurion's side to get him out of the assembly hall, but the Old Man wouldn't budge from his seat. A few minutes later, he was obviously beginning to feel the pain from the wound in his leg, and his face went white. Bahir and I helped Ben-Gurion rise and then accompanied him to Ziv Hospital, where he received medical attention. His wife Paula arrived presently and, as was her custom where Ben-Gurion was concerned, took over. When Ben-Gurion came to himself a little, he asked if the name of the assailant were known. He was evidently relieved when he heard that the man involved was mentally ill and that the attack had not been politically motivated.

Election Reform

After Ben-Gurion had recovered from his injuries and resumed his responsibilities as prime minister, reform of the electoral system became a public issue.

Election to the national legislature in Israel is not personal. It is based on party lists of candidates, who enter the Knesset in the order of their appearance on the lists and in accordance with the number of seats made available to the party by the percentage of votes it has received nationally. Israel does not have regional elections to the Knesset and government, with a candidate standing for election in a particular electoral district. The movement for electoral reform involved an effort to introduce the system of local constituencies for Knesset candidates.

In the summer of 1958, during a conversation with Ben-Gurion, I put forward the idea of proposing a bill for a national referendum on the issue. After I had had a talk with the centrist General Zionist Party, I told Ben-Gurion about their readiness to support a national referendum if we could come to an agreement with them about the number and extent of the electoral districts. The General Zionists were proposing that ninety MKs should be elected by regional constituencies and thirty on the basis of national lists drawn up by the parties. The thirty elected from the national lists would allow for the possibility of surplus votes going to the smaller political parties, which would probably lose in constituency elections but could hope to preserve their representation if the old system were retained at least in part.

I expressed the opinion that we ought to come to an understanding with the General Zionists to bring the proposals of both parties up for a vote. Should one of the party's proposals seem to have the better chance for passage, the second party would throw its support behind that proposal.

I had no illusions that my bill would receive a majority in the Knesset. I knew that all the small parties would band together in order to block any change in the electoral system that would reduce the number of parties to only two or three, and wipe out the half dozen minute and ephemeral political entities that had been complicating parliamentary existence in Israel for years. What I wanted was to challenge the sanctity of small political factions and to strengthen the ties between the electorate and its representatives. An electoral system based on local constituencies seemed to me to give a chance to candidates other than those groomed by party secretariats—to people who were worthy of representing the public because of their personal abilities and achievements. I asked Ben-Gurion to help me convince the party to support my proposal, and he gave me his word that he would try.

The subject was close to Ben-Gurion's heart. As early as 1954, he had proposed at a meeting of party headquarters held in Rehovot that Mapai should include electoral reform in its campaign platform, and he called the system as it existed "corrupt and corrupting." His proposal received the support of an overwhelming majority of the party.

On December 9, 1958, I put my proposal before the Knesset. The various parties managed to get all of their members to attend the debate and be present for the vote, and the Knesset was completely filled with MKs as I began to speak. I was heckled from all sides, both by colleagues in the coalition and by members of the opposition parties. At the close of a stormy session, the vote was taken: my bill had failed to pass by a slim margin of three votes—sixty-one against, fifty-eight for. The anti-Mapai alliance had a field day, and was even able to pass its own legislation, according to which a proposal to change the electoral system would require a two-thirds majority in order to pass—a majority which electoral reform has yet to receive in the Knesset.

It is likely that the victory of the opposition parties was what led to the election of Dr. Nahum Nir of the Mapam Party as Knesset chairman after the death of Yosef Shprintzak. It was the first and only time that the Knesset chairmanship was held by someone who was not a member of one of the big parties. Dr. Nir had been brought in by a "coalition of opposites" formed against the common enemy—Mapai.

In the Third Knesset, Mapai held only forty seats, which represented a significant drop in strength from the forty-six sets it had held in the Second Knesset. The opposition parties were certain that this boded the end of Mapai. However, the returns for the Fourth Knesset, which were held that year, completely overturned the expectations of the prophets of Mapai's impending doom.

Yoram Injured

On the afternoon of April 1, 1957, I was making my routine trip to Jerusalem and trying as usual to reach the Knesset in time for the session. Not far from Jerusalem, at the Abbu Gosh Junction, I saw the wreckage of a military command car overturned at the side of the road. I remember that as I continued driving I felt both regret at the fact that the soldiers involved in the road accident must have been injured and anger at the army for not making more sure that its men obeyed the rules of road safety.

When I got to the Knesset, I was told to call Shaarei Zedek Hospital immediately. I had a terrible premonition that the phone call had to do with what I had just seen on the road, and I was right. When I arrived in a rush to the hospital, I was told that my eldest son Yoram had been injured in an automobile accident near the village of Abbu Gosh and was now in the operating room. His knee had been crushed, and he was still unconscious. I put in a call to my wife in Haifa.

With the help of friends, I threw myself into the task first of trying to save his life and, then, if possible, his leg. The best physicians in Israel spared no effort in treating him, and the hospital staff worked tirelessly to ease his suffering. Throughout the crisis I was painfully aware of the reversal in his fortunes: only a few days before he had been an energetic and happy young man holding the rank of second lieutenant in the Tank Corps, and now he was lying helpless in a hospital bed, groaning with pain, and facing the possibility of having his leg amputated above the knee. Why? was all I could ask myself.

There was no choice—his leg had to go. When Yoram was conscious once more, his first question was whether he would be able to return to duty. I promised to look into the matter. After making inquiries among people in authority, including Ben-Gurion, I was able to tell Yoram that he could back to the army if he wished. He was overjoyed.

After a period of recovery, during which he met other disabled people both in and out of the army who had lost limbs, he was able with their help to get back to active life. I was not surprised. I knew he was made of strong stuff, and I believed he would find a way to compensate for his physical disability by making full use of his mind. That was how things turned out. Despite his artificial limb, Yoram was able to give an excellent account of himself in his chosen field, the military.

18
The Ata Strike

After a month of having almost altogether absented myself from the Haifa Labor Council, I returned to find the Ata file on my desk. It was a thick file, describing the events leading up to the Labor Council's approval of a strike at the Ata Textile Company's plant. I was sure that we had a tough fight ahead of us, with an employer of the old school—a man who was demanding exclusive right to firing people without giving the least consideration to their seniority or the rights that had accrued to them during their time on the job. Everything else—wages, work conditions, social benefits—had long seemed to me trifling matters when compared with this one, central issue.

Hans Moller wanted to run the plant along paternalistic lines, handing out benefits to workers as if they were personal favors rather than on the basis of impersonally established rights. He regarded as a personal offense any attempt by his workers to stand up for their rights and put matters of wages and work conditions on an orderly and permanent footing.

In 1956 the Histadrut executive decided on a general wage increase, of which two-thirds was to be paid out to the workers during that year and one-third in 1957. Hans Moller refused to honor the agreement, which had been signed by the Histadrut and the Association of Industrialists.

When the time came for paying the cost-of-living increment, Moller announced that he would only pay it in exchange for efficiency layoffs. So his employees wouldn't think he was bluffing, he put out a list of 116 candidates for firing. This was clearly a declaration of war, and in my conversation with Pinhas Lavon, secretary-general of the Histadrut, which took place after all sorts of attempts at mediation had already been made, I said that it seemed unlikely to me that we would have any choice but to call a strike.

"If I were in your place," Lavon answered, "I'd have a secret vote taken among the employees." I agreed without hesitation, and the balloting was carried out under the supervision of the Haifa Labor Council. The results did not surprise me: 96 percent of the workers voted to strike. The results apparently took the Histadrut's secretary-general by surprise, however. No sooner had they become known, than the wheels of the government and the Labor Federation began to turn rather quickly. Meetings were called and talks held to keep the Ata affair from getting out of hand.

I had already made up my mind. On May 10, work stopped at the Ata plant. At a strike meeting, I summed up the issues in one sentence: "The question is whether we are going to be Ata's workers or Hans Moller's slaves."

My own situation in this dispute was a difficult one from any angle, personal or public. I decided on taking the extreme step, striking not only out of a sense of loyalty to the men working at Ata, but out of a conviction about the utter right-ness of this strike. I took that position knowing full well that the strike could send tremors through the whole Labor Federation and might undermine even further my relations with the Mapai party leadership. Nevertheless, I could not make peace with the idea of not doing everything we could—even to the point of declaring a long strike—to avoid a situation in which management would have the sole right to fire employees. That would turn the clock of labor relations back a whole century. It wasn't efficiency that was at stake here, but arbitrary layoffs, putting working people's security and well-being into the hands of any tyrant who happened to bear the title of manager and creating an atmosphere of fear, toadyism, and corruption on the job. I doubt, too, that the kind of fear created by efficiency layoffs can help to increase productivity in our technological era. We need only consider the wretched productivity levels in totalitarian states, where workers live and work in a state of unrelieved fear, to see that terror accomplishes the opposite results.

Support and Opposition

The Ata strike had repercussions throughout the country and gained support-ers from some quarters and opponents from others. In the forefront of the opponents stood the old guard of the Mapai party leadership, which began to inspire fear among the membership concerning the hidden motives of Yosef Almogi—fears whose real nature I only discovered years later.

After the strike had entered its second month, I was called to Ben-Gurion's home for a meeting with the institution that went by the name of "Our Crowd." The participants included all of the government ministers who were then in the country, Party Secretary Giora Josephtal and Histadrut General-Secretary Pinhas Lavon. Lavon led off by addressing himself to Ben-Gurion: "So as to free you from any fears I declare to you that I greatly respect Almogi. But the matter under discussion here is the very soul of the Histadrut. Almogi shows a degree of independence and aggressiveness displayed by no other union secretary or Labor Council secretary. Things have reached such a point that workers are making a distinction between the 'reactionary' Executive Committee and the Haifa Labor Council. The moderates among them are complaining that we are letting Almogi take a radical line, and so they, too, are forced to make their demands more extreme."

Then Finance Minister Levi Eshkol spoke up: "We are now responsible for a *state* and not just the Jewish Agency. Our workers aren't working and no one can fire them because they are being too zealously defended. Then one 'screwball' called Hans Moller shows up, who is ready to fight for his right to fire employees and change once and for all the bankrupt practice of featherbedding. And maybe this deserves a try. I just don't understand why Almogi has to go after him and fight him with all he's got. And the same goes for wages: it wouldn't hurt Almogi a bit to bend a little."

At this point, Sapir drew out his famous little black book and started quoting statistics from it to show that the country was on the verge of bankruptcy. Eshkol wound up by saying, "Moreover, Moller is a Zionist and a liberal Jew. Why should we suspect that he, of all people, would be firing workers for no cause?"

The other ministers kept quiet, preferring to hear what I had to say first.

I thanked Eshkol for having spoken so frankly but took exception to his whole approach to the matter at hand. I then said that I thought that Moller's proposal represented a catastrophe to working people and that Moller's way of doing things was not only rejected by me but by all the employees in his plant. It was clear that Lavon had made a mistake in asking me to have a vote taken by the Ata workers, for almost 100 percent of them had voted for a walkout. I said I was not about to hide behind them, however—that I personally was utterly opposed to arbitrary layoffs. I would never suggest calling a strike just because we had gotten a smaller wage increase than we would have wished. When it came to laying off workers, however, we could not agree to a system which differed from the one in force in the whole country. I wound up by saying that before the strike took place, we had brought the matter up with the Histadrut Executive and heard no opposition from that quarter. I also pointed out that Lavon might have tried to mediate the crisis.

The discussion went on for about three hours. Ben-Gurion spoke only once and then only to make a few general observations about the needs of the economy and the party and to urge us to be mindful of the need for comradely relationships in our camp. Finally, I told those gathered: "Friends, your opinions differ from mine. The choice is yours as to whether the Histadrut executive should be called into session to decide the conditions for terminating the strike. But we retain the right to decide whether to accept and carry out the conclusions reached by the executive or to reject them. Should we reject them, I would resign so you can come to terms with Moller on your own. That you should decide in some inner sanctum about policies which we oppose and which the Histadrut constitution does not oblige us to carry out is totaly unacceptable!"

19

Confrontation and Reconciliation with Ben-Gurion

The Ata strike continued. Morale among the striking workers remained high. Hans Moller, too, was in good spirits, especially when news headlines spoke of a rift in the Mapai and of the party secretariat's refusing to support the strikers. With this kind of news making the rounds, it was little wonder that Moller was in no hurry to settle the dispute.

Then I received word from the prime minister's office that Ben-Gurion was coming to Haifa. I immediately got in touch with Levi Eshkol and asked him what role Ben-Gurion had defined for himself for this trip. Eshkol replied that Ben-Gurion was coming down as a "one-man arbitrator."

There was no doubt that Eshkol had reported my stand to Ben-Gurion. Nevertheless the Old Man arrived in Haifa as scheduled and in the company of his personal secretary, Yitzhak Navon. In the entry of July 19, 1957, in his personal journal, Ben-Gurion writes:

> In the morning I left for Haifa. Earlier, I had spoken with our friends in Mapai and on the Ata shop committee. Almogi regarded the new step . . . as a move against the party, because this had not been decided on. I returned to Jerusalem empty handed.

I had not intended things to take such a depressing turn. I had spent a sleepless night considering the problem from all angles. I knew that my rejection of Ben-Gurion's arbitration attempt would draw highly unfavorable reactions and would certainly push the prime minister into our opponents' camp. On the other hand, a rejection by the general meeting of the prime minister's proposal would be taken (and quite rightly) as a serious blow to Ben-Gurion's prestige.

I plucked up my courage, therefore, and at the meeting of Mapai party activists in Haifa gave Ben-Gurion a detailed account of my position, which had the support of all Mapai members on the Labor Council. I then explained to him that if I backed the proposal for arbitration, my action would be taken as a breach of the workers' trust.

Ben-Gurion did not try to argue and went back to Jerusalem. The press did what one would have expected with the story of my refusal to arrange for Ben-Gurion to meet with the workers. This sensational bit of news even made the headlines of the *New York Times*.

Tempers flared. When Ben-Gurion returned to Jerusalem, Mapai Central Headquarters called a meeting to settle accounts with Almogi and perfidious Haifa. Abba Khoushi and I decided we would not attend. I knew that if I went to the meeting I would find myself having to say things that would make my relations with the party even worse than they were already.

Unexpectedly, Ben-Gurion took an objective tack in the deliberations. "The trouble with Almogi," Ben-Gurion observed, "is that he has another view of economics and labor. He is no demagogue. He is serious in his opinions. But these opinions do not square with the line of Mapai." Ben-Gurion went on to say that just as Menahem Begin took very seriously his concept of the historical rights of the Jewish state to "both sides of the Jordan," I took seriously my social and economic convictions.

My confrontation with Ben-Gurion troubled me deeply, even though it had been unavoidable. So when Yaakov Dori, who was president of the Technion in Haifa, rang me up on the morning of August 12 and proposed personally to arrange a meeting on that very day between me and Ben-Gurion, I consented without a moment's hesitation. Later the same morning the first meeting in Haifa took place between the city's Mapai activists and the Commission of Inquiry sent down by Party Central Headquarters. Before deliberations on the question of "the Haifa rebellion against the party" could begin, a telephone message came through from the prime minister's office inviting me for a meeting at Ben-Gurion's home in Jerusalem. When I told those present the news, Namir and Josephtal were greatly disturbed and decided to break off discussions immediately and return to Jerusalem.

I arrived at Ben-Gurion's residence in the evening. Two representatives from party headquarters and Ehud Avriel were already there. Ben-Gurion asked me to sit next to him and with no futher ado asked me where I stood. When I asked him what he meant, he became specific: What would happen, he asked, if the party decided to go against my views on the Ata question? I replied with no hesitation that in such a case I would hand in my resignation.

At this Ben-Gurion asked, "And will you stay in the party?"

I replied that the question was insulting. Was it conceivable that because of a dispute in one factory I should leave the party? What was I expected to do—found an "Ata party"?

Ben-Gurion smiled in the direction of Namir and Josephtal and then, looking very much relieved, turned to me and said that if I were putting out my hand in friendship so would he. "Come," he said, "let's just forget all about your mistakes in the Ata affair and wind things up." I was quite surprised and thanked him. Then I asked him if he would care to listen to the other side. We agreed that the Ata shop committee would come up to Jerusalem the next day to have a talk with Ben-Gurion.

As I was leaving Ben-Gurion's room, Paula Ben-Gurion caught sight of me and, in her usual tone of bantering affection, said, "Ah, there's our little Stalin!" When Ben-Gurion saw that his wife had got after me, he said to her, "Now, why are you holding Almogi up?" To which Paula replied, "What's wrong? I happen to like Almogi!" And Ben-Gurion returned, "So do I. . . ."

A week later the Histadrut executive, with our agreement, approved the proposal to take over the responsibity of dealing with the Ata case. Mapam and Ahdut Avoda attacked the decision and found fresh opportunity to excoriate Mapai.

All I had to do now was to get approval for the proposed agreement from the general meeting of Ata employees. Tensions ran high among Ata workers, who were feeling bitter about matters having been taken out of the hands of the Labor Council. Rebellion was very much in the air at the Ata workers' meeting, which lasted for four uninterrupted hours. My voice grew hoarse from my efforts to parry the loud attacks by Mapam and Ahdut Avoda members and defend the gains we had made. When the vote did come finally, the proposal to end the strike was carried by a small majority. A procession then formed up spontaneously, in which hundreds of Ata workers, led by the representatives of the Haifa Labor Council, marched through the streets of Kiryat Ata toward the plant and there removed the "On Strike" sign from the entrance.

I returned home exhausted; there was a telegram waiting for me from Ben-Gurion: "I congratulate you on your comradely and wise conduct." I was touched, and in my reply to Ben-Gurion I said that his words to me were like "drops of dew in a political wilderness."

A few months after the affairs of the Ata employees were put back in the hands of the Haifa Labor Council, amicable relations between Lavon and myself were restored. At a congress of labor councils, Lavon compared us both to a pair of old war horses and said, "Almogi erred, but his motives were honest. What he did was done out of loyalty to the workers."

The atmosphere of reconciliation had little effect on the press. Even after the Ata strike had ended, the newspapers continued giving it space and predicted that I would soon resign from my post on the Haifa Labor Council. The afternoon paper, *Maariv,* even published the following dialogue, which was given special prominence by being put into a box:

> "Say, did you hear Almogi's finished?"
> "How's that? He's still secretary of the Haifa Labor Council and an MK."
> "Tell you a story about what took place in Russia. One day Ivan says to his friend, 'Say, did you hear they hanged Vanka?' So his friend says, 'What are you talking about, I just saw him at work this morning!' And Ivan answers, 'Yea, he doesn't know it yet'"

It wasn't hard to figure out the moral of that tale.

20

The Youth Wing versus the Bloc

Nineteen fifty-eight was a year fraught with crisis for Israel, both internally and abroad. It was the year in which Egypt and Syria formed the United Arab Republic, Jordan and Iraq announced their intention of forming a federation, and the monarchy in Iraq was overthrown, with the new regime proclaiming union with Syria. On the heels of the coup d'etat in Bagdad, the United States sent the Marines to Lebanon, where a leftist revolution threatened. Israel's border with Syria began to heat up, and settlements in northwestern Galilee came under frequent Arab fire.

With the Arab military ring tightening around the country, Ben-Gurion sought to meet the threat by developing closer relations with France where de Gaulle had assumed power, and by putting out diplomatic feelers to secure cooperation with West Germany. The development of political relations with Germany was a potentially explosive issue at the time. The Israeli public, memories of the Holocaust still very fresh in its mind, was simply not ready to accept such a move. When it became known that Ben-Gurion had sent then Chief of Staff Moshe Dayan on a secret mission to Bonn, there was a monumental public scandal. The public was also greatly disturbed by Israel's having to relinquish the advantages it had gained by the Sinai Campaign.

The internal situation was stormy as well. The "Who is a Jew?" issue, which concerned the extent to which secular religious law should determine Jewish identity in Israel, was straining relations with the religious political factions in the government coalition. Then the public revelation of the chief of staff's visit to the Federal Republic of Germany became the source of another crisis—this one with the Ahdut Avoda. Finally, within the Mapai party itself, the conflict between the "Youth Wing" and the alliance of the "Bloc" and veteran party members was coming to a head.

152

The most prominent personalities in the Youth Wing, who were by then quite grown up, were Shimon Peres, Aharon Remez, Ehud Avriel, Avraham Offer, Shlomo Hillel, Asher Yadlin, Ahuvia Malkin, David Golomb, and Shulamit Aloni. Moshe Dayan—the hero of the Sinai Campaign who had just retired from a highly successful term as chief of staff of the IDF—joined the group.

In joining the Youth Wing, Dayan brought to it not only his qualities of leadership and political daring but a sense that the Old Man himself was behind them. He opened his campaign to establish control of positions in the party by focusing on the Histadrut. He took a position in favor of compulsory arbitration in labor disputes and supported the National Health Insurance plan, issues that appealed to members of the Moshav settlements (agricultural cooperatives), recently demobilized soldiers, members of the free professions, and young people who regarded themselves as belonging to the vanguard of change.

Opposing the Youth Wing were the Bloc and Mapai's veteran leadership. At their head stood Shraga Nezer, who worked for the Tel Aviv Department of Sanitation and, as a consequence, did not rely on political activity for his livelihood. The Bloc included most of the secretaries of the party's local branches, Mapai mayors, and heads of townships. It tended to be relatively balanced and fair in distributing offices and positions of influence, especially among second-line party activists.

Shraga Nezer and his wife Dvora, who had, in her own right, achieved prominence and influence in the party, were the pith and marrow of the veterans of Mapai's upper echelon. Because of the complete identity of the Nezer's cultural, social, and ideological attitudes, they were able to take the same positions on the major political issues of the day. Moreover, younger party members whom the Nezers had taken under their wing—those belonging to the middle generation of party activists headed by Pinhas Lavon and Pinhas Sapir and including Zalman Aran, Mordecai Namir, and Golda Meir—felt thoroughly at home with the pair. Relations between the veteran Mapai leadership and the Bloc were based to a great extent on reciprocity; leadership positions in all sectors were made accessible to members of the Bloc, who were able to keep tabs on developments and make certain they would follow a desirable course.

Attempts at Reconciliation

When relations between the Youth Wing, which was supported by Ben-Gurion, and the Bloc, sponsored by the veteran higher-ups of the party, were growing increasingly strained, Shraga Nezer offered to ease Ben-Gurion's burden of responsibility: "You take care of matters of state," Shraga proposed, "and leave party matters to me." Ben-Gurion would not accept Shraga Nezer's proposal. Instead, he took up Levi Eshkol's suggestion to invite all factions of the Mapai for a weekend get-together for the specific purpose of bringing about a reconciliation. The conference took place at the Green Village Agricultural School on a Saturday, and when one Saturday proved to be insufficient for the task, another Saturday meeting was arranged. However, even the tranquil rural setting of Green Village could not ease the strain in relations between the opposing party groups.

Neither I nor other members of Mapai in Haifa participated in any organized factional activity, and neither of the sides maneuvering for control could lay claim to our support. Consequently, we returned from the meetings in Green Village in a bleak mood. Pinhas Lavon had absented himself altogether from the discussions, because he could not bring himself to be in the same forum with Shimon Peres, and this raised fears among us for the party's future. The rift between the two men, although news to me at the time, was actually of long standing. It dated from the days when Lavon was minister of defense and Peres director-general of the Defense Ministry. Lavon charged that Shimon Peres had tried to undermine his authority at that time and that when Peres had testified before the Olshan-Dori Committee in the early stages of its investigation of the secret-service scandal now known as the "Lavon Affair," he had represented Lavon in a bad light. Lavon then demanded that Prime Minister Moshe Sharett relieve Peres of his duties, but Sharret refused, relations between himself and the defense minister having reached the breaking point.

The reconciliation attempts were unsuccessful, and relations within the party remained as strained as ever. The Youth Wing was quite open about wanting to replace the old-timers, whom they accused of "refusing to take any notice of the biological clock," and take over the key posts in the government, the Histadrut, and the party. Ben-Gurion, conscious of the need to prepare a reserve of potential national leaders, gathered about him some of the more promising younger members of the Mapai, who later became important political figures. None of this was the least likely to improve Ben-Gurion's relations with Mapai veterans and the Bloc; if anything, his differences with them grew until they became irreparable.

Neither camp in the struggle was overly fastidious in its choice of weapons. The most destructive of them were the news leaks, which became a regular pestilence that not only exacerbated personal relations but did great damage to the party as a whole. They deeply upset party veterans. Thus, for example, Ziama Aran would not allow journalists to be present at meetings he attended, and on the few occasions when he agreed to the presence of newsmen, he did so on condition that he would edit their stories, himself. In Ziama Aran's view, the leaks represented a serious threat to stable democratic government.

Golda Meir, too, had been deeply offended and hurt by the manipulation of the news media, and with good reason. For a long time, she castigated herself for having allowed herself, out of unquestioning loyalty to Ben-Gurion, to be used as a cat's-paw in turning Moshe Sharett out of the Ministry of Defense, only to be humiliated, in turn, when Ben-Gurion was in control of the ministry with Shimon Peres as his director-general. Her life was made perfectly wretched by the news leaks about her illness (herpes zoster) and by uncomplimentary articles published in the British *Jewish Observer*, a weekly partially funded by the Defense Ministry. When *Newsweek* came out with a report about her illness and predicted her coming replacement by Abba Eban—an item which she believed to have

been planted as part of the effort of the Dayan-Peres group to undermine her—
Golda felt she had enough: she decided to quit. But when she presented her
resignation to Ben-Gurion he refused to let her go. I do not think Golda believed
Ben-Gurion personally had had a hand in the business, but she could not forgive
him for failing to get rid of those who were responsible for her having been so ill
used.

Veteran party leaders were incensed by intentional leaks from "sources close
to Ben-Gurion" that predicted a coming change of personnel in the country's
leadership, by which was meant the impending removal of the old-timers from
their positions of power.

In all this, Levi Eshkol occupied an exceptional position. Originally a member
of Hapoel Hatzair, he had always remained a member at heart. As early as 1930,
he was working with Ben-Gurion, who belonged to the Ahdut Avoda, to amalga-
mate their factions of the Labor Zionist movement and form the Mapai. After so
many years of working together so closely, it was only natural that the two men
should understand one another well and be bound by ties of mutual sympathy.
Like Ben-Gurion, Levi Eshkol had volunteered for the Jewish Legion in World
War I—this at a time when his own party was officially opposed to participation.
By nature he was a man of compromise for whom taking a one-sided view of
things went against the grain; now, with the party riddled by disputes, he was
scrupulous to avoid being drawn into giving his support to any faction. By
remaining aloof from the factional infighting he actually increased his own influence in the party.

I liked Levi Eshkol even when we happened to find ourselves on opposite
sides, which happened when I had to represent trade-union demands to him in
his role as finance minister. I enjoyed following his train of thought as he developed his position before coming to a final decision on an issue. He had a fine
grasp of up-to-date organizational and administrative theory, in keeping with
which he would make it a point to test any proposal put before him by highly
perceptive counterarguments. After carefully weighing both sides, he would
reach a decision that was at once considerd and logical.

As tensions in the party kept mounting, Eshkol made up his mind to try to
calm things down. He met with Ziama Aran to try to convince him that it was in
Mapai's interests to involve younger members in the political life of the party. In
an effort to charm Ziama into a more amenable mood, Eshkol brought his
characteristic sense of humor into play, telling how he had established his own
"young guard": "I take a young man and toss him into the water. If he swims—
well, what could be better? And if he sinks, that's pretty good too—because we've
just saved ourselves from an incompetent official."

Ziama, however, was not impressed. Party veterans remained convinced that
Ben-Gurion was intent on getting all of them out of power and putting his young
protégés in their places—an intention Ben-Gurion constantly denied. But under
the impact of the news leaks engineered by Ben-Gurion's associates, the old-
timers persisted in feeling jittery even though they had no real grounds for their
fears. Ziama used to tell anyone willing to listen that the situation in the party
reminded him of how Eskimos abandoned their old people to freeze to death in

the snow, to be eaten by the bears. He seemed to have forgotten though, that this was exactly what he himself wanted to do to Ben-Gurion.

Still, Levi Eshkol kept trying to champion the veterans to Ben-Gurion. He spoke up especially on behalf of the top echelon of the Histadrut, which was under constant verbal fire from the party's young bucks. In this Eshkol was no more successful than when he put the case of the Youth Wing to party veterans.

The Elections Approach

In the second half of 1958, elections took place for the Mapai's Ninth Party Congress and its local branch councils. Foreseeably, in addition to being marked by the usual personal rivalries for posts, the party elections were characterized this time by wrangling between the Youth Wing and veteran Mapai members. The internal conflicts virtually paralyzed Mapai; in twenty-three of the party's ninety-five branches activity virtually ground to a halt. Mapai's rivals could not have asked for anything better, and they were not slow in reaping the rewards.

Early in 1959, the so-called Nir Coalition named for Dr. Nahum Nir of Mapam—was formed to promote his election as Knesset chairman to replace Yosef Shprintzak, who had recently died. The move was a classic instance of the maxim coined, I believe, by Beni Marshak that "parties go their separate ways but beat Mapai together." Dr. Nir's election to the chairmanship of the legislature was as much a morale booster to Mapai's opponents as it was a blow to the morale of Mapai party men. Everyone knew that in normal times members of other labor-movement parties would never even contemplate joining forces with the right-wing Herut party against Mapai. The internal situation in Mapai, then the leading party in the government, and the losses the party had sustained in the previous elections to the Knesset, convinced Mapai's rivals on both left and right that it was due for a real drubbing in the coming Knesset race.

Events had taken so bad a turn that many of us began thinking the time had come to push more energetically for electoral reform. The idea had Ben-Gurion's wholehearted support, and I decided to throw myself into the effort. Even after the proposal I had put to the Knesset for a plebiscite to change the electoral system fell through, I did not stop trying. I followed up with a suggestion that a public commission be established to keep the issue alive and even submitted the name of the man I thought best suited to lead it—Yigael Yadin. Ben-Gurion accepted the idea, and as for Yadin, Ben-Gurion smiled and said, "Well, why not? We'll give it a try." When I asked him why he had smiled, Ben-Gurion explained that although Yadin was a gifted man and a celebrated scholar, he was by nature inclined to be hesitant and overly cautious. Ben-Gurion had several times offered Yigael Yadin important posts, among them the Education Ministry, but Yadin would always waver and end up by not accepting. "My one consolation," Ben-Gurion concluded, "is that Zioma Aran is a good minister of education."

I had had two opportunities to meet Yigael Yadin when he was chief of staff; on both occasions, I was favorably impressed. I particularly remember the sigh of relief he breathed when I succeeded in convincing Ben-Gurion to give up his notion of having locomotive engineers called up to the army when they had gone out on a wildcat srike. Yadin was unstinting in his support of my position that the armed forces should not be involved in labor disputes. When I went to see Yigael Yadin this time, he was retired from the army and pursuing an academic career in biblical archaeology. He had no trouble recalling the efforts we had made together to dissuade Ben-Gurion from using the army to put an end to the railway strike. On the matter of my current proposal for him to head the electoral reform commission, we were able to settle things very quickly: Yadin accepted.

Ben-Gurion was immensely pleased. The associates of the Youth Wing, however, were less than enthusiastic about Ben-Gurion's show of favor to Yadin and took issue with the Old Man on his high opinion of Yadin's personal qualifications. They considered it ill advised to have a man who had spent so many years in scholarly seclusion suddenly elevated to the top of the political hierarchy. They felt that Yadin, having detached himself from public life, deserved no such reward. Besides, he had had no experience in the rough-and-tumble of political life. Better, they thought, for a public appointment to go to someone who had actually made his way through some of the more disreputable back alleys of politics, been bloodied, so to speak, and made some enemies as well as friends. I had to admit there was some truth to what they were saying.

Meanwhile, the elections were drawing near. One day during the winter of 1958, I was called in for a meeting with the then party secretary-general, Giora Josephtal. Giora was a tall, broad-shouldered man. He had originally come from Germany and was a member of Kibbutz Gilad. He and his wife, Senta, had held important posts in the Zionist movement both back in Germany and after they had settled in Israel. During the the time I was a prisoner of war, Giora was doing a first-rate job of helping to get recruits for the British army; he had also been in the administration of the Jewish Agency and, in that capacity, involved in the work of immigrant-absorption. Before his appointment as party secretary he had been treasurer of the Jewish Agency.

Giora was without doubt a good party secretary. He was, however, mistaken on one important point. He was associated with the group of Ben-Gurionists who argue to this day that Ben-Gurion wished not only to move members of the Youth Wing into positions of national leadership, but intended to push out the old-timers to make room for those he wished to advance. The suspicion was groundless. For all the ten years I was in close touch with Ben-Gurion—during which time we had had many occasions to talk about individual party workers—there was no instance I can recall of Ben-Gurion speaking with anything but respect of veteran members of Mapai or discussing the advancement of the younger generation to leadership positions in the party and country in terms other than their *gradual* introduction to office. True to that position, Ben-Gurion had, in the 1950s, advanced a "young man of promise" called Pinhas Lavon, until the latter was ousted by the veterans in the Mapai leadership. Another "young man" whom Ben-Gurion had helped to the top without making gray heads roll was Pinhas Sapir. In not a few cases, Ben-Gurion could have forced a "changing of the guard"; yet not only did he refrain from doing so, he later made it a condition of his continuing in office as prime minister that Pinhas Sapir and Golda Meir be retained in their posts.

Among the rumors released during the highly sophisticated campaign of news leaks that hit the country then was one claiming that a list of names had actually been discovered in Giora Josephtal's office and that it laid out in detail a coming government reshuffling in which the veterans were to be replaced by members of the Youth Wing. This and similar rumors had vexed the members of the Bloc and party veterans to such an extent that they began seriously to discuss ways of getting rid of Josephtal.

In a meeting I had at the time with him on Knesset matters, Josephtal suddenly took off his glasses and gave me a sad look. He made no effort to hide what he was feeling. Speaking straightforwardly, Giora explained that he had been planning to lead the party's 1959 election campaign and then retire as secretary-general, but that the party leadership felt that he did not have enough organizational experience to run the campaign—this despite his reputation, up until that time, for having excellent organizational abilities. "So there's no choice," Giora sighed. "In the name of the party I have to ask you to take on the responsibility of organizing the next election campaign."

I was surprised by the offer. We talked a little about the twist of fate by which I was being offered the job of running the election campaign by the very party leadership with which I had been at such odds only a year before. I promised Giora he would have my answer within ten days. The challenge of organizing the party's election campaign greatly attracted me, but I thought I should have a talk with Ben-Gurion and Lavon before making my decision.

Ben-Gurion was very cordial and told me how happy he was that my candidacy had the approval of all the party groups. "But why," he added archly, "did Lavon, the Bloc, and the Youth Wing all give you their support?" I explained that it was not because I was too old to be a threat to the Youth Wing and too young to be one to the old-timers, but because I was one of the last of the "neutralists" left in the Mapai party. Ben-Gurion recommended that I continue hewing to my neutral line; it was one way to reduce party tensions. At the end of the meeting, Ben-Gurion said, "My door will always be open to you. I won't act the way you did when you closed the door of the Ata employees to me." When I tried to answer his barb, Ben-Gurion gave a wave with his hand, as if to dismiss the matter. "Never mind," he said, "I have already forgotten the whole thing."

My talk with Histadrut Secretary-General Pinhas Lavon lasted longer, since we had to deal with the coming elections for the Histadrut executive. My relations with Lavon were quite good—sufficiently so for even the long-drawn-out Ata strike not to have put a great strain on them. I had been a dinner guest at the Lavons' a number of times, on which occasions I had enjoyed Lucia Lavon's wonderful cooking. Pinhas was always an interesting man to talk to; he had a brilliant way of formulating a position and was a fascinating raconteur. He was also a sage man, and aboveboard—especially considering the usual standard of behavior in conflicts among political figures. I had followed his career with interest from the time he had become minister of agriculture and had been responsible for food rationing. Not infrequently, we found ourselves at odds, but in our clashes we always treated one another with respect. During his term as defense minister, I had helped him in establishing Upper Nazareth. Once I accompanied him to a reception on one of our naval vessels: I remember his pleasure at the ceremony when he was whistled aboard and saluted by the ship's crew.

But now, as I came to see him about the election campaign, he was a changed man. Lavon was tense, and when he spoke of the Youth Wing—and of Dayan and Peres—his rage was unmistakable. He even asked me to set up party campaign headquarters in the Histadrut Executive Building rather than in the offices of the party, where I would be surrounded by Youth Wing intrigue. I told him that it was impossible to do as he advised and that he could rely on me to make sure that the elections would be properly run from the building already rented by the party on Ben Yehuda Street in Tel Aviv.

By chance I ran into Shimon Peres and Moshe Dayan at Ben-Gurion's office in Jerusalem. In the course of our conversation about the coming elections, they asked me if it would not be worthwhile having, in addition to a general campaign headquarters, a "select headquarters" which would act as a kind of active secretariat. I was quite explicit in rejecting the idea: I told them that I intended to hold frequent meetings at election headquarters, of which there would be no more than one. Dayan and Peres took the rebuff without a murmur.

In January 1959, I handed over the affairs of the Haifa Labor Council to Avigdor Eshet—an exceptionally modest and loyal man who had stood by me whenever the going was rough. I then moved to Tel Aviv to get the party's election campaign underway.

21
The 1959 Elections

I began my work at Mapai campaign headquarters by introducing a number of changes in the procedures that had been the rule up until then. For some of these changes, we even proposed bills in the Knesset and they became part of the law. Changes proposed by the other parties were also dealt with on their merits.

A change in campaign tactics we introduced was to end the use of popular entertainment. At the time, these performances were regarded as a necessary adjunct to the party's election rallies; they were thought to sweeten the pill of having to listen to the speakers. Although the rallies drew large large crowds, we had no way of knowing whether they came for the sake of the party, the speakers, or the show. Usually, the entertainers were the star attraction, and their antics on stage were bought at an exorbitant price.

My view was that the shows were not doing us much good, and at times did actual harm. Ben-Gurion and a score of other party figures had enough drawing power in themselves to need no help from show business. On the other hand, less popular speakers tended to irritate the audience, which was impatiently waiting for "that nudnik" to finish his sermon so their favorite songstress or pop group could come on. A good part of the crowd had come not to hear campaign speeches, but to have fun.

I decided to shift our stress from spectacular rallies to meetings of smaller groups of sympathizers gathering in private homes. I also opposed serving refreshments at campaign meetings. Our information campaign would begin with meetings of party leaders and activists, after which the message would be passed on at gatherings by talking *with* the voters and not at them.

To qualify a solid core of people who could put our point across to the voters, I organized countrywide meetings of Mapai party workers at which the audience could put the most difficult questions they could think of to the party leaders, from Ben-Gurion, Meir, Eshkol, and Sharett down to the members of the Central Committee. The first of these gatherings, held at Kibbutz Einat, was a great success. The party workers who participated returned to their local branches both recharged with enthusiasm and armed with information that would serve them in good stead in the election campaign.

At the first meeting of the campaign headquarters staff, I was somewhat taken aback to discover that some of my colleagues were given to superstition. I wanted to use the Solel Boneh building on Ben Yehuda Street for election headquarters, since the building was unused at the time. But Namir and some of the others resisted the idea with surprising vigor, only because the same building had been the site of campaign headquarters in 1955 when the party had done badly. I could hardly believe my ears; it was hard for me to understand how normally level-headed people could allow themselves to take such nonsense seriously. Despite my colleagues reservations I decided to tempt fate and set up our office where I had planned.

On May 17 the elections for the Histadrut went off as scheduled, with very satisfactory results: Mapai received more than 55 percent of the vote—a drop of only 1.5 percent in comparison with the previous election. At a special session of the Central Committee, Pinhas Lavon spoke admiringly of the way the Histadrut campaign had been conducted; privately, however, he complained that not all the leadership of Mapai had really thrown themselves into working for the Histadrut campaign. For his part, Ben-Gurion told me that a Mapai victory in the Histadrut was no great trick: the real battle would begin only now. In the coming national elections, we faced a serious contest against the Herut and General Zionists on the right, and Ahdut Avoda and Mapam on the left.

Mapai versus Herut

The week after the Histadrut elections, the papers reported that "reliable sources" claimed Mapai was about to change its staff at election headquarters, and the man heading it, for people who were better suited for running a Knesset campaign. Nothing of the kind had been said to me. It was simply another news leak originating with the Youth Wing, whose members wanted to take over for the elections to the Knesset.

Some days later Lavon asked me to accompany him to a meeting with Ben-Gurion about the makeup of Histadrut institutions. Ben-Gurion was in good spirits and asked me if I felt rested up enough to get back on the job. "Up to now you've been looking after Pinhas," he said, "Now you'll be looking after me!" Before I could say anything, Lavon asked Ben-Gurion if there was any truth to the rumors about a change of personnel at campaign headquarters. "God, no!" Ben-Gurion replied with conviction, "Just don't pay those machinations of the press any mind." We put off our discussion of Histadrut institutions until after the Knesset elections.

In June we rolled up our sleeves and got down to work. Abba Eban, Moshe Dayan, Moshe Sharett, Shimon Peres, and Shulamit Aloni joined the muster of party campaigners. All the ministers, Central Committee members, mayors, and the rest of the party officials joined as well.

Among the general public the feeling was growing that this time Herut would take a big chunk out of Mapai's representation in the Knesset. Talk was not just about Mapai losing, but by how much. On one occasion during that period I was chatting in the Knesset with Dr. Shimshon Yunichman, Eliezer Shustak, and Menahem Begin, who expressed sympathy with me for my being ill used by my party. My party colleagues (they said) had only chosen me to head the campaign to make me the scapegoat for a certain Mapai defeat, so that they could finally get rid of me. I thanked them all for their friendly concern and asked what would happen if Mapai won. Dr. Yunichman promised me a bottle of cognac. It was the only wager on the elections I allowed myself.

Early in the contest Herut threw in its "big gun"—Menahem Begin. Begin opened with a series of fiery orations throughout the country. His first appearance was in the north at Migdal Haemek, at that time a problematic and somewhat violent town. We made a recording of that address, and when we listened to it, we realized that we could put it to good use in our own behalf. During his talk, Begin had turned to one of his listeners and pointedly asked him: "Did you get ten thousand liroth from the government?" That was an enormous sum of money in those days, and the poor man whom the question had startled could have hardly answered otherwise than, "No, I did not." It was exactly the answer Begin was waiting for, so he could release his rhetorical clincher. "Of course not!" he said. "But the Jewish Agency received tens of thousands of liroth for you, and it is wasting them without giving you the portion that's coming to you!"

We immediately sensed that this kind of unrestrained talk was bound to anger a large part of the public and would help close ranks in our own camp. I gave instructions to have scores of copies of Begin's speech made up and distributed, among other places, to kibbutz settlements and farm cooperatives. In a short time Begin's speech was in popular demand in Labor circles, and the Herut leader's words did yeoman service in helping us to enlist support among members of the kibbutz movement. As election day drew near, I even received a request from the Herut people to sell them a pressing of the authentic recording. Within an hour they received a copy of the record with the following letter attached:

The Worker's Party of Eretz Israel
Headquarters
July 30, 1959

Mr. Avraham Drori
Secretary, Herut Movement

Dear Mr. Drori:

In response to your letter I am happy to forward to you a copy of the recording of the speech by Mr. Menahem Begin, as per your request.

We ask no payment from you in return, as you had offered, since we are convinced that the record has already done us an inestimable service and constitutes one of the most important contributions to have been made to the Mapai Party's election campaign.

We believe that everyone hearing the speech of the leader of Herut—whatever party he may belong to—and even many who supported Herut in the past—will be made to realize why they should not support or vote for that party.

We therefore present you with a copy of the record free of charge.

Yours truly,

(signed)

Y. Almogi

Chairman, Election Headquarters

The contest grew more heated as election day approached. Our right-wing opponents were not above trying to break up election rallies, and it was only Mapai gatherings that they went after, allowing the other parties to hold their meetings in peace. The attempts were mostly made in socially problematic communities, such as Kiryat Gat, Givat Olga, Migdal Haemek, Safed and Wadi Salib, in Haifa. In the face of the assaults coming at us from both right and left (Ahdut Avoda was stirring up the public about the government's secret contacts with West Germany), I worked hard to reduce the wrangling within our camp. The conflicts occurred partly because municipal races, which were slated to take place on the same day as the national elections, had increased tensions among local party workers. In my effort to reduce the rivalry on a local level, I proposed to Eshkol that he should lead an arbitration body of Mapai especially created to iron out the party's problems. I was delighted when Eshkol agreed, and he really did a first-rate job of local trouble shooting. We had some assistance in this from the external pressures being exerted on us from all sides.

The arrogant style in which Herut conducted its campaign brought over to our side younger members of the artistic and cultural community, whose support we never dreamed we could get—personalities such as Haim Topol, Uri Zohar, and Dan Ben-Amotz. At one of our campaign rallies, organized for information purposes, Pinhas Lavon spoke brilliantly about our struggle with Herut. It was the opening shot in the contest with our right-wing opponents. Ben-Gurion, who was sitting near me then, could hardly contain his admiration the whole time Lavon was speaking. The thousands of campaign workers who were there left the meeting with excellent campaign material.

Party leadership did its job in the campaign without a hitch, except in one instance when Moshe Dayan took issue with my instructions that no separate party organization be formed to work in the development towns. This had been proposed by the Youth Wing, and I suggested to Dayan that he either bring the proposal up at a meeting of campaign headquarters or present the matter to Ben-Gurion for his consideration. Dayan chose the second alternative. When Ben-Gurion heard Dayan state his case, he cut Dayan short and told him directly: "If Almogi differs with you he must have a good reason. You'd better rely on him." That ended the matter, and a conflict was avoided between the Bloc and the Youth Wing, which gave us one less squabble to contend with.

When the party list of candidates for the Knesset was being made up, I saw no reason to interfere. The only time I did so was when Lavon's position on the list was being considered. While Lavon was on holiday, it was decided to place him below all the ministers and the Knesset chairman, moving him from fourth in line—the place he had had in the previous Knesset race—to twelfth. I appeared before the party's High Committee of Appointments, chaired by Ben-Gurion, and asked for Pinhas Lavon to be allowed to remain in his original place on the list. The veteran leadership was strongly opposed, arguing that the Histadrut secretary-general could not take precedence over state ministers. I persisted, however, and pointed out that Lavon had been a government minister long before Namir and should not be punished for having responded to the party's call for him to take over the top post in the Histadrut. Moreover, in Israel, the Labor Federation's administrative head is no less important than a minister of state. Ben-Gurion decided in Lavon's favor.

Advice Givers

The head of a party campaign headquarters does not enjoy anything like the authority of a prime minister or, for that matter, a city mayor. He has no right to decide on his own between opposing positions. At all hours of the day, he is at the mercy of all sorts of bearers of good counsel. Listening to them, he must preserve both his calm and good manners no matter what the circumstances.

Ziama Aran was one of the most insistent of these advisors. In his day, he had headed two election campaigns, and so he regarded himself an expert. He missed no opportunity to shower me with the wisdom of his experience, even though when he headed elections for the party he wouldn't take lip from anybody. Shprintzak used to say about Ziama that he was nervous only one day of the week; the trouble was you never knew which day.

I would begin my week at campaign headquarters at five o'clock Sunday morning. I started the workday by going over the press, after which I would often rouse one of our campaign spokesmen and between apologies for having gotten him out of bed at that ungodly hour, I would give him a rundown of what and how I thought we should respond to an item that had appeared in the news. In trying to reach the voting public, I not only kept to well-beaten paths, but was always trying to reach the independent voters. For example, I approached religious groups that were not identified with the National Religious Party. In our appeal to the religious sector, we did quite well. I believe that, at the time, there were more religious people to be found among Mapai supporters than among voters for the religious parties. Ben-Gurion thought our activities in this sphere to be important enough to make himself available for meetings with religious audiences.

In the closing days of the campaign, I proposed having a giant rally of independent voters at the Tel Aviv theater. I thought we could draw a crowd by inviting our three top guns to appear together—David Ben-Gurion, Pinhas Lavon, and Moshe Sharett. Ben-Gurion accepted without hesitation, but doubted whether Sharett would oblige. On the same occasion, he repeated his view that Sharett should be appointed minister of education. "Well, why don't you do it?" I asked him. "You're right," Ben-Gurion said, "I have to find a way to placate Sharett—it's important to me he feel right." As we know, the reconciliation between the two men never did take place.

On November 3, election eve, the Voice of Israel interviewed the heads of the election campaigns of the parties in the race. Every one of them predicted an increase in his party's strength in the Knesset. Had all their predictions been realized, the Knesset would have been bursting at the seams with no less that 250 MKs, whereas the number of places is fixed at 120. I was the only one of those interviewed who made no prediction about the number of seats his party would win. I did, however, appeal to Israeli voters to renew their mandate to Mapai.

Herut put on a spectacular show in Tel Aviv, mounting a motorized parade in which the "next prime minister," Menahem Begin, rode in his car with a convoy of outriders on motorcycles. It was a spectacle long to be remembered in Israel, though not necessarily to Begin's advantage. As Tel Aviv echoed with the sound of cheers from the crowds that had turned out to greet Begin, spirits at Mapai campaign headquarters began to sink. I was still confident though. I kept assuring party leaders who dropped by—among them David and Paula Ben-Gurion and Abba Eban and his wife Suzy—that those who had organized the parade and really done us a favor. I was certain that the people running Herut's campaign had egregiously misread the public mood. I returned to Haifa that night so that I could vote early the next day and get back to Tel Aviv for the Day of Reckoning.

After I had done my duty as a voter I was able for the first time in months to sit back in my car seat and, at my leisure, consider the exhausting election campaign now behind me. My friend Shlomo Wirt—who acted as my chauffer on long journeys—seemed to feel the same relief I did; he drove to Tel Aviv slowly. I was grateful that I had kept my patience during those long months, had not allowed myself to be worn down by all the bickering—about the size of our campaign posters and the printing on them; about radio and newspaper items which had slighted one person and played up someone else; about injustices, real or imagined, committed against all sorts of people in Beersheba, Afula, Givatayim, and God knows where else. I had tried to keep my temper in check through it all and, as far possible, to keep smiling. Looking angry, I've found, is of no help in public work, especially at election time. I remember talking to Abba Eban, who was then new to electioneering in Israel. I advised him to speak Hebrew in a more popular style when he appeared at large gatherings and to avoid elegant turns of phrase. After giving some more helpful hints, I sent him off to the hustings, where he did well.

When I arrived at campaign headquarters in Tel Aviv, I experienced the kind of empty feeling anyone has who just finished a task in which he had totally involved himself and has nothing left to do but wait and see the results of his work. On election day at a campaign headquarters, even the best organized staff is utterly at loose ends.

By evening the returns began coming in from the smaller districts. Even then I sensed (and I told this to my nail-chewing colleagues) that we were already past the point of danger—of falling below the forty-seat lower limit, which would have put our control of the government and Knesset into question. As the hours wore on, my mood became increasingly sanguine. Foreign correspondents and local newsmen trickled into campaign headquarters, and we got some of the "bohemian set" coming in, too, with their infectious gaiety helping to dissipate some of the strain. By 5:00 A.M. I knew we had clinched forty-three seats. I asked the crowd to go home, and an hour later, at six, I shaved and ordered a helicopter, and then left for Sde Boker to see Ben-Gurion.

When I arrived the Old Man was waiting for me at the door of his cottage, and he gave me a warm hug. As I congratulated him, I felt a deep sense of satisfaction. We went in to be photographed together, and then I made my report and told him that I thought there was a chance we might get as many as forty-six places in the Knesset. While I was talking the Voice of Israel radio reported that Mapai had received forty-seven seats. Still later we discovered that the Arab List, which we supported, won five seats, so that altogether we now had fifty-two seats in the next Knesset!

When I asked Paula for a cup of coffee, she started her usual banter and demanded to know why I had not managed to bring in sixty-one seats. "What's all the noise about fifty-two seats?" she asked, only half in jest, I thought. "What's the matter—isn't Ben-Gurion worth sixty-one?" Only after Ben-Gurion did a little coaxing did she finally come across with my cup of coffee—despite my "poor showing."

Ben-Gurion excitedly ran over the list of Mapai candidates with me to see who had got into the Knesset and who had not made it. He was disappointed when he saw that his friend Yosef Izraeli, who was sixtieth on the list, had missed getting in.

Jubilation

Returning to Tel Aviv, I found the whole country celebrating. Congratulatory letters and telegrams poured in from all over Israel and abroad. My political opponents were among those sending me greetings. Dr. Shimshon Yunichman from Herut wrote me:

I must admit that I am far from feeling the same joy as you, but you people have received heaven-sent tidings and I am happy that *you* were the bearer of them to your party. Believe me, the architect of victory was you.

Abba Eban sent a letter from Rehovot:

I feel a personal need to express to you my great admiration for the enormous undertaking you organized and brought to a successful conclusion in the last weeks. . . . Over and beyond the organizational efficiency, I shall always re-member what a fine spirit—a spirit of partnership, service and joy of battle—you inspired among us all every step of the way in the campaign. . . . It was a wonderful experience for me to work together with you in my first encounter with this sphere of activity.

On Friday night I took part in two party rallies, one in Haifa and one in Tel Aviv, and at each I felt myself among happy people. In Tel Aviv I walked in on the middle of a speech by Namir, who had won the city's mayorality contest, and the crowd broke into applause that made my cheeks go red. Two days later the entire party leadership was sitting on stage at the Habima Theater, which was jammed with people. I regretted letting Ben-Gurion talk me into having the rally held here rather than in the larger House of Culture. Ben-Gurion had failed to appreciate the extent to which our victory had excited the public. When he came up to speak, he was cheered long and enthusiastically. He made a moving speech. At the end of his address and before the rally closed, I turned to Giora Josephtal, who was sitting at the table together with all the party leaders and told him I was handing the party back to him and returning to Haifa. When some of the ministers overhead, they said, "Why the rush?"

Well, I *was* in a hurry. I felt I had to get back home to recuperate from the strain I had been under for so long.

22
Secretary-General of the Party

I thought that before returning to my duties on the Haifa Labor Council I should take a holiday and go with my wife to the United States. It would be an opportunity for us to see our son Yoram, who was studying naval architecture at MIT. The manager of Israel Bonds was able to set up a lecture series for me in about a dozen American cities. I bought the ticket for Shifra, and we got ready for the trip.

Many of my friends thought I was being unwise. With the congratulations rolling in and the headlines I was making, it seemed to them I should be making career capital out of it all. I disagreed.

The day before our flight, I went to Ben-Gurion to pay my respects. I told him, "Even though I'm only Haifa Labor Council secretary now, and all I'm really required to do is notify Lavon of my departure, I thought that since we have worked together so closely these last few months, I could allow myself to take up a little of your time to say good-bye." Ben-Gurion was very friendly, asked about Yoram and told me that as soon as the returns were officially proclaimed, he would begin negotiations for putting together the government. As I turned to leave, Ben-Gurion accompanied me to the door of his office and embraced me in front of the people who were waiting to see him in the next room. Then he said, "Yosef, you're a wise man. Have a good trip. When you get back, come in to see me."

I did not quite know why Ben-Gurion praised me for being "wise" at this particular moment. I thought it unlikely that it was because he thought I was sure I would get an important post without actually having to put my own name forward.

When I returned to Israel, Ben-Gurion set up an appointment for me to see him. When I got to his home in Jerusalem, he was ill in bed and running a high fever. I was about to take my leave of Paula after telling her I hoped Ben-Gurion had a quick recovery, when the Old Man overheard us talking and called me into his room. He began by telling me about the posts that had to be filled in the party and then observed that the secretary-general of the party would have to be someone acceptable to all groups. Finally, he asked me to accept the position of party secretary. I asked him if we could put off the discussion until he was well, but he wouldn't hear of it. I told him that I doubted I was the right man for the job. After all, we were not just talking about running an election campaign, which was basically a matter of organizational work and no more, but about being party secretary, which was a full-time, long-term proposition. Besides, the post needed someone who had more knowledge and virtues than I could lay claim too—someone more affable and polite than I was.

Ben-Gurion would not accept my reservations and asked to have my answer— favorable, of course—in a few days. He explained his rush by the fact that Giora Josephtal was joining the goverment as minister of labor, so the need to find a replacement was pressing. He added that the party leadership had decided that a delegation made up of Pinhas Sapir and Shraga Nezer would ask the Haifa branch of Mapai to free me from my duties on the Labor Council so I could take over as party secretary.

I spent the week debating with myself whether I should accept the post. I did not feel happy with the thought of taking on the job. I feared that after our signal victory at the polls had released party leadership from anxiety about the elections, internal strife would erupt all over again and that the man who would have to settle the disputes would be me. It also occurred to me that a man who combined both the psychological makeup and the organizational skills required for the job would be hard to find; so it might be advisable to divide the office in two and appoint a political secretary and an organizational one. But I realized that if that were to happen I could not agree to accept the second office. Time was beginning to run out, and I had to return an answer.

In the end, I accepted, but I did so with no great show of enthusiasm. At a special meeting of party headquarters, Giora, Sharett, and Ben-Gurion introduced me as the coming secretary-general of Mapai. My candidature was received with a round of applause. After the vote was taken and my appointment secured, Ben-Gurion rose to speak; I quote a part of what he had to say:

> I have asked permission to speak in order to say a few words about the new secretary. There are many in the party who regarded Almogi (and there are still those who do today), and not without reason—as a "boss." That is not something we find likable or desirable. It was especially revealed in the Ata strike, and I myself was perhaps a victim of that very "bossism." . . . And I may not have been too happy about the way he acted. However, I knew it did not arise from his "bossism . . . but out of his exceptional devotion (sometimes to the point of blinding him) to working people. And those of our colleagues who have heard something about Almogi's internment, when he was a prisoner of the Germans, know of the national pride, the courage, and the extraordinary devotion he revealed in his relation to fellow prisoners. . . .
>
> Nevertheless, I am not surprised that there are colleagues who feel great anxiety about Almogi's "bossist" qualities. But I have seen Almogi in the last few months, when he revealed a marvelous trait. We all remember what was going on among us and around us in the months before the elections, in almost every party branch and among the members of any one branch . . . we all saw how Almogi in a short time not only succeeded in making himself liked by party members, but in the course of his work introduced such a degree of

unity as we have not seen for a long time. True, we should not give credit for this only to Almogi; many colleagues worked for it. . . . All the same, Almogi is the man who kept the structure together and inspired full confidence even among those who could not forgive him his "bossism." . . .

Almogi did not find it easy to accept this post . . . , and I am sure he is aware of all the difficulties awaiting him on this job. But I believe that Almogi is the one colleague who has the inner spiritual resources to see this thing through . . . because he is qualified by one personal trait, and an important one for all public work, namely—love. He loves people, he loves the movement, he loves work. And love can overcome many difficulties.

Whoever knows Almogi as he is in his heart of hearts and to the full extent of his ability, not only in the specific ambience of Haifa—for it was no new Almogi who appeared to us during elections, and had he not possessed those traits for a lifetime, he would not have achieved what he did at election time— [knows] he is the man who can bring together people who stand far apart . . . and I hope that after a few months of work, even Shaul Avigur will come and say, "I was wrong."

I made a short speech thanking Ben-Gurion for his warm words The next day I started work; Some aspects of the job were not altogether new to me. I was under heavy pressure from the outset because I had to set up the party conventions and prepare the way for the elections to the party institutions. At the same time, I had to get the routine business of the Secretariat out of the way. Right at the start, I announced that the activity of the organizations at party headquarters would be intensified: they would meet at least once a month, and the secretariat once a week—and these meetings would convene punctually, at prescribed times.

It was hard to enforce punctuality at the Secretariat, which included all the country's leaders and heads of the Zionist movement. In time, however, my colleagues got used to my little quirks and, I suspect, even grew to like them. From this time forward, they knew not only the exact time meetings were to start but when the sessions would end, so they could plan their other meetings around those they had with me.

At the first meeting, only two participants and the stenographer managed to make it on time. I didn't bother to wait for the rest and began the meeting by considering an important item on the agenda. By the time most of the members of the Secretariat arrived, we had already finished considering a number of respectable issues, and the latecomers were taken aback. Namir took umbrage about my not waiting for him before discussing a question he had a special interest in. I replied that we had all agreed to be on time to meetings and that he had been late. "And while you were out we managed to finish our deliberations on that point," I told him, and added, "but you have the privilege of lodging a protest, of course."

Namir never did, and within only a month, members of the Secretariat had learned to appear on time for our meetings. For me it was a matter of principle. Punctuality is part of the whole pattern of civilized behavior. In public life, it is a factor which in no small degree determines the efficiency of elected institutions, whose members are some of the busiest people in the country. In formal deliberations punctuality prevents the taking of hasty and ill-advised decisions. I discovered that it was important to schedule the time a meeting would end; otherwise participants will inevitably have other meetings overlapping your own, and keep walking in and out of the session until you feel as though you are holding court in a railway station. Not infrequently you end up speaking to an empty room, or decisions are taken that are arbitrary and merely the reflection of the few peole who happened to have more patience and a greater respect for the body they are privileged to belong to than the rest of their colleagues.

I was pleased to see the effect of my innovations: the party leadership quickly adjusted to the new way of doing things, and the rule of punctuality was adopted at meetings other than my own.

Another thing I did was to call in an interior decorator to make the Party Headquarters Building more suitable for its functions and its facilities more efficient. We changed the arrangement of the auditoriums and offices; I believe my alterations still serve today. This had been my practice in all of the posts I have held, although I made certain to keep the costs of alteration down to a minimum. I had learned that interior arrangements had an important effect on work efficiency: offices and meeting rooms had to be comfortable and pleasant; dank and ill-lit interiors with rickety furniture and tables piled high with papers are the signs of neither modesty nor thrift, but of incompetence and neglect. An insouciant bohemian style is no virtue in a public body and utterly unsuitable to work in the public service.

Reorganization

As the time drew near for Mapai's Fifth Party Congress, scheduled for March 23, 1960, I prepared a memorandum on the proposed structure of the party and submitted it for consideration by our local branches and by the Standing Committee, which was chaired by Meir Argov. My basic assumption was that if we took the same means and energy we had concentrated in the six months before the last elections and spread them over the four-year period between elections, we would be sure to get a clear majority in the Knesset at the next contest. I suggested the establishment of a permanent corps of party workers at each local branch. Such a procedure, I argued, would strengthen routine ties between party workers and rank-and-file members, and could eventually lead to the introduction of a regional electoral system both within the party and in the nation as a whole. To my regret, I was unable to get this reform adopted.

Shortly after taking office, I was one of those invited to the convention at the Bureau of the Socialist International in London. Our delegation, which also included Shraga Levenberg and Esther Herlitz, was warmly received. Mapai's victory had been a surprise in London, too. Hugh Gaitskell said to me with a smile that he was looking for someone to run the British Labor party's election campaign, and he asked if I had anyone I could suggest for the job. It was also my first opportunity to meet the leaders of the Socialist movement in Europe, among them Bruno Kreisky. Our delegation proposed making Haifa the site of the next conference of the International, and our proposal was enthusiastically endorsed. In general, sentiment in the International was running high in Israel's favor, as a mark of which the Socialist-International Bureau arranged a luncheon in honor of Mapai.

When I returned to Israel I had an emergency to deal with: there was a problem with the starting date of the party congress. Ben-Gurion would be out of the country on opening day and could only make it the day after, on February 24; it was suggested that we postpone the session. Mapai old-timers loved delays, whereas I was allergic to them. I met with Ben-Gurion and proposed to him that the congress meet as scheduled and that he join it the next day. Ben-Gurion was agreeable, but my colleagues thought I had gone mad: "What," they said, "open the congress without Ben-Gurion?" I suggested that Moshe Sharett deliver the opening address, on the tasks facing the party at that time. Sharett was greatly pleased by the idea.

The congress opened on schedule with a large crowd in attendance and in a festive mood. Among the guests were the foreign diplomatic corps, leaders of the government coalition parties, the president of Israel, and many guests, both from home abroad. Dr. Dreiz, prime minister of Holland, appeared, having taken me up on the invitation to visit Israel I had extended in 1956.

The party congress provided us with many exciting moments. Enthusiasm reached a height when Ben-Gurion arrived on the second day. He was put at the head of the meeting, which marked the thirtieth anniversary of Mapai and aroused strong feelings of nostalgia in us all.

It was also the occasion on which elections took place for the party institutions. After some hard deliberations in the Standing Appointments Committee, membership in the party secretariat was fixed at thirty-one. Another decision taken was to establish a forum, which took the name Haverenu ("Our Comrades"), which would include, in addition to the ministers, the secretary-general of the Histadrut, the Knesset faction leader, and the party secretary. The prime minister was supposed to chair its meetings, but for some reason Ben-Gurion decided that I should be the one responsible for running the meetings and even determining the agenda—which was what I did until the end of my term as secretary of the party.

I should add here that among the positions I have held in my public career, that of chairing the meetings of Haverenu was among those that gave me the greatest satisfaction. We usually met in Ben-Gurion's Tel Aviv office. When all the ministers arrived, I would announce the agenda, and deliberations would begin. In the course of these meetings, I often had to maneuver very gingerly in calling on members to speak. This was particularly true when we neared the end of a session because this body took no formal decisions and only summed up its conclusions on policy. I tried as much as possible to find a common ground for agreement among the opinions, which were often opposed in the extreme. It is to the credit of the ministers that they usually avoided sharpening their differences and even helped me to close the gaps in their positions.

Careful Sailing

At meetings of the secretariat, too, I was often faced with problems that required delicate handling. I always maintained that only members should participate in meetings of the party secretariat. However, a custom had been established by then for the secretary to invite nonmembers who held various posts in the movement. It was a practice which had turned the secretariat into a kind of general assembly, with all the problems that implies. One result was that elected members stopped coming. Their places were taken by nonmembers who persisted in showing up and were eventually coopted into the secretariat by a retroactive decision of party headquarters. I regret to say that the practice has been reestablished and still exists.

On the October 31, 1960, at the first meeting of the new party headquarters, I was reelected secretary of Mapai. My desk was piled high with reports on the problems of the economy, the trade unions, the income tax, the high school teachers, and more. I tried to negotiate between strongly opposed views, but Giora Josephtal would become irritated with what he believed to be my exaggerated inclination for compromise. That was what the Youth Wing was saying about me, too. I admitted my failings, but continued my efforts to try to bring peace to the party. I sometimes had the suspicion that the Youth Wing wanted to force me into taking extreme positions, and that they had a low opinion of compromise. In any case, I thought it an obligation that I should help preserve party harmony, and in this I was in agreement with Ben-Gurion.

Pressures on me in this respect were mounting at the time. The party was deliberating over serious political and economic problems, and every group, great and small, represented in the party, was trying to gain support for its position. I concluded that without making a continuous effort to stress the points of contact among the positions put forward, party unity could easily break down. Mapai is a broad-based movement unified on basic issues but often at odds with itself on questions of detail. I therefore did not let myself take the criticism of my penchant for compromise to heart.

At the end of April, Haifa played host to the convention of the Socialist International. Most of the leaders of the labor movement in the Free World came, and Mapai organized a mass rally to receive them at the Histadrut stadium in Kiryat Haim, one of Haifa's northern suburbs. As party secretary, my duty was to introduce our guests both in Hebrew and in English; needless to say, I felt more comfortable in the language of the Bible. Another difficulty was having to introduce a German, Erich Olenhauer, for the first time to a large public in Israel. I was a little afraid that someone from the crowd might interrupt me in protest. I introduced him in Hebrew and told of his anti-Nazi past; then I welcomed him. When Olenhauer approached the microphone to speak, he was visibly moved, and as he talked you could hear the catch in his throat. The crowd applauded him loudly. That evening on the Carmel, Olenhauer came up to me and shook my hand; he asked me if it was true that I had been a prisoner of war in Germany. He then strongly urged me to accept his invitation to visit his country as a guest of his party. To my sorrow, Olenhauer died only a short time after leaving Israel.

That summer the party organized a series of seminars on fundamental problems in various fields. Yizhar Smilansky opened with a lecture on the younger generation for which he coined the term "Espresso Generation," referring to their apparent preference for idling away their time in cafés and their seeming lack of social commitment. Another subject of discussion was agriculture in Israel. The level of discussions was high, and sessions lasted for many hours.

Early in June I was appointed to lead a parliamentary delegation to England, the story of which is told in the first chapter of this book. When I came back to Israel the controversy over "Ben-Gurion and Zionism" was in full swing. The problem had been brought up by Zalman Shazar at a meeting of the secretariat. He complained that Ben-Gurion was attacking the Zionist movement and refused to be a delegate to the Zionist Congress. I suggested we hold a thoroughgoing discussion on the subject of Zionism and its role in our day and reach some decisions which would be binding on us all. Shazar and Sharett smiled at what they took to be my naiveté. They told me that they accepted the suggestion and that I should see Ben-Gurion about it. We scheduled a meeting of the secretariat for the purpose, but when I asked Shazar to start the discussion, he refused; so did Moshe Sharett. "If that's the case," I said, "I declare the meeting open and give the floor to the first debater." Shazar and Sharett were taken by the new formula and took the floor.

After the discussion in the secretariat, I met with Ben-Gurion, and we fixed a date for a discussion on the same subject at party headquarters. On this occasion Ben-Gurion repeated his well-known opinions about the Zionist movement. Then he added: "Do not imagine that the idea came to me just now, and only because I am prime minister. Let me show you something."

He groped around in his cabinet and drew out a piece of yellowed paper. "Take a look—it's a letter I wrote to my parents back in 1908!" I took it from him and began to read what Ben-Gurion had written when he was still David Green, and only twenty-six: "With the establishment of a Jewish state, the only ones who will be called Zionists will be those who settle in Eretz Israel. The others who do not come will be organized into a Congress of World Jewry and will be called on to give help to Israel."

I knew I was not going to get anywhere with Ben-Gurion by debating this line, so I appealed to him on the grounds of party discipline and the need to accept the views of the majority. I knew that a man of Ben-Gurion's makeup was sensitive to those issues and could not ignore the validity of my point on that score. With his agreement, I established a time for a Central Committee meeting on the subject. He also agreed to my suggestion that we invite Dr. Nahum Goldmann and Rose Halprin. Just to make sure that the discussions would not become too diffuse, we decided to have three meetings, which would take place on the same day—morning, afternoon, and evening. These meetings were exceptional both for the level of debate and the atmosphere in which they were conducted. The debate was serious and conducted in a friendly spirit, although Ben-Gurion did call Dr. Goldmann "The Wandering Jew". The highly serious tone of the discussions was relieved somewhat by Rose Halprin's colorful hats, which she changed from one meeting to the next.

A number of resolutions were passed at the end of the discussions. Ben-Gurion submitted no proposal of his own, arguing that nothing he suggested would get a majority anyway. When the resolution to keep the Zionist movement alive was passed, Ben-Gurion and a number of colleagues voted against it. When the Twenty-fifth Zionist Congress was about to open at the Binyanei Hauma in Jerusalem in December 1960, we sent Ben-Gurion a delegate's card, and he came. When he mounted the rostrum, the whole congress, including the representatives of Herut both from Israel and abroad, rose to its feet and greeted him with tumultuous applause. Only one man demonstratively kept his seat—Pinhas Lavon.

The "Lavon Affair" was beginning to cast its pall over the country, and a new, self-destructive episode in our history was about to open: the fight between the Youth Wing and the Bloc was on again, as was their wrangling with the Histadrut. Ben-Gurion's proposal for agreed arbitration in labor disputes became a point of contention between the "supporters" of the Histadrut (read: Lavon and his followers) and "opponents" (Ben-Gurion and his followers).

Meanwhile, Lavon went on a short holiday abroad. A large farewell committee saw him off at the airport, where Lavon let it be known that when he got back he would have something to announce.

23
The Lavon Affair, 1960

On September 25, 1960, I met Shalom Rosenfeld over a cup of coffee. Rosenfeld's paper, *Maariv,* had just published a scoop that morning: the scandal of our secret-service failure in Egypt in 1954 was being dredged up again. This time, however, the talk wasn't about *haesek bish* ("that shameful business"), as it was then called, when eleven Egyptian Jews were arrested for espionage in Egypt and two of them were executed and the rest sentenced to long prison terms. Now it was the "Lavon Affair." "Ben-Gurion Orders New Investigation of Evidence behind Lavon Quitting Gov't" was the headline blazoned over *Maariv*'s story.

After Rosenfeld filled me in, he asked me what I, as party secretary, had in mind to do in light of the developments. I was not yet aware of their explosive nature and had no way of guessing that in a very short time we would all be swept up in the maelstrom of one of the bitterest controversies in our history. I assured Rosenfeld we would be able to iron it all out; that was what I honestly believed then. I had never dealt with the matter before, neither with its original manifestation when the scandal first broke nor with any of its ramifications as it developed. I was still naive enough to believe that it was just another one of those internal party problems we would manage to overcome.

Shalom Rosenfeld was an experienced journalist, and I suspect he believed that I was trying to cover up. In any case, he ventured that the affair was going to snowball and that there was no telling when it would stop and with what result. Knowing Rosenfeld to be a mine of information, most of it reliable, I began to feel uneasy—exactly about what, though, I didn't really know.

The next day the story was spread across the front pages of all the papers. By then there could be no doubt that something serious was in the wind. I decided to speak to Ben-Gurion about my fears. To my surprise, Ben-Gurion did not share my concern. He told me that a week and a half before, on September 15, a military commission of enquiry, presided over by Chief Justice Haim Cohen had, in fact, been established to study the district court's findings on the 1954 espionage scandal and to investigate some other security matters from the period Pinhas Lavon had been defense minister. However, the investigation did not touch on Lavon himself, and he would not even be required to testify before the commission. "There's no reason to worry," Ben-Gurion assured me.

The facts in the original case were these. In July 1954 a series of acts of sabotage were carried out in Egypt by an intelligence ring that included both Israelis and locally recruited agents and that took its orders from Israel. The uncovering of the intelligence ring not only led to the death and imprisonment of its leaders, but did untold damage to the nation's security. It also did great political harm to Israel both abroad and at home, where it raised a public storm and became known as "that shameful business." At the request of Defense Minister Pinhas Lavon, Prime Minister Moshe Sharett appointed the president of the Supreme Court, Isaac Olshan, and Major General (Reserves) Yaacov Dori to investigate the security blunder and discover who was responsible. When the commission failed to assign responsibility unequivocally, Lavon, on February 17, 1955, resigned from his post as defense minister. Lavon never stopped insisting that it was not he, but the chief of intelligence at general staff who had given the order for the operation in Egypt.

In the spring of 1960, Pinhas Sapir received information from a senior IDF officer, Yosi Harel, which Sapir believed proved Lavon's innocence and confirmed the former defense minister's claim that not only had he not given the order for the operation, but that the operation had been carried out without his knowledge. Sapir advised Harel to pass the information on to Lavon. In April, Lavon handed it over to Ben-Gurion, who was once again prime minister and asked him to investigate. In May, Ben-Gurion ordered his military secretary, Haim Ben-Dor, to check out the material received from Lavon to see if there was any truth to the information it contained of two IDF officers having suborned witnesses into giving false testimony to the Olshan-Dori Commission in order to shift the blame for the operation onto Lavon. According to the information, one of the officers in question had even gone so far as to forge documents so as to make it seem as if Lavon had actually given the order for the operation to be carried out.

In June, when Haim Ben-Dor's investigation was well underway, Lavon left the country and returned only in mid-September. The report which Ben-Dor had meanwhile handed in stated that "changes in the documents were indeed made in the Intelligence Department of the IDF after the failure in Egypt." Some days before Lavon's return from abroad, Chief of Staff Haim Laskov, acting on instruction from Ben-Guiron, appointed a commission of inquiry headed by Chief Justice Haim Cohen to review the evidence against the two officers. Ben-Guiron's instruction to Laskov came after the Jerusalem District Court had ruled, in sentencing Avraham (Avri) Elad, the intelligence operative known as the "Third Man," that there had been false testimony given and witnesses suborned to give false testimony before the Olshan-Dori Commission. The appointment of the military commission went unreported at the time.

On September 26, 1960, Lavon was invited by the prime minister for a meeting. After the meeting, when Lavon was asked what had taken place, he replied, "Each of the participants made his position known." There was no longer any doubt that Lavon and Ben-Gurion were at odds. Lavon had insisted that there was enough evidence in Yosi Harel's testimony to clear him of the charges leveled against him in 1954 and that there was no need to make him wait for the findings of a commission of inquiry. However, Ben-Gurion took the position that he was not empowered to clear Lavon since he had not been the one to charge the former defense minister in the first place; only an investigatory legal body could adjudicate in the matter. In reply, Lavon said that he wanted to put his case before the Knesset Committee of Foreign Affairs and Security. "That is your privilege," Ben Gurion told him, "go right ahead."

Ranging In

Lavon had good reason for asking to testify before the Foreign Affairs and Security Committee. He had absolutely no confidence in the party leadership, which had forced him to resign as defense minister. He regarded himself as the victim of a conspiracy that had led to his frame-up. So thoroughly was he convinced of his innocence that he privately told close friends that if his name were not cleared, he would take his own life.

Nor was any love lost among party leaders for Lavon. They had been incensed when he was promoted over their heads to the second most important office in the country. Party veterans regarded Lavon as an arrogant newcomer, riding roughshod over their privileges; his conduct and policies in office shocked them deeply. Lavon would have to seek elsewhere for a fair hearing, and he decided to put his fate in the hands of the Knesset committee, where members of the opposition parties were represented. Among them Lavon would find allies against what he believed to be the machinations of Mapai—and against the party's most sacred values and symbols as well, including the Old Man himself.

Meanwhile, on September 29, Lavon appeared at a meeting of the party secretariat. We received him warmly, and after several members had spoken on different subjects, Lavon was given the floor. He said, among other things, "I certainly support the position taken by the party secretariat. The party has no forum for dealing with this matter. It should not involve itself. . . . I returned to Israel on the twenty-sixth of the month to find the whole country in a turmoil over the issue, while this stupid censorship, I regret to say, is causing things to be published in the form they are. . . ."

The party secretariat reconfirmed its position that the matter would not be taken up in a party forum, and after the meeting, I invited myself to Lavon's home. After lunch, Lavon and I withdrew to his room without his wife Lucia, and we talked over the painful business. I told Lavon that if high state secrets were involved I could see no possibility of having a party committee deal with the matter. Should we do so, we would all have to have access to secret documents, and our opponents would be sure to make something of that, and quite justifiably too. They could accuse us not only of taking illegal action, but of working against the state. If anyone believed that such deliberations by a party committee would not become known outside, he was only dreaming.

I thought it right to tell this to Lavon, even after the party secretariat had made that very decision with his agreement. I felt I had to explain to him why the party was unable to help him in a matter so very important to him. Up to this point, Lavon was in complete agreement with me. But when I went on to observe that in appealing to the Knesset Committee he should exercise restraint, he responded with a fury I thought had subsided in him long ago. Lavon's face turned white with rage such as I had never before witnessed. "I am ready," he shouted, "to make common cause with any element, even an antiparty one, in order to expose the conspiracy against me!"

Our conversation lasted an hour and a half, in an atmosphere which became almost unbearable. When I left I was worn out and very anxious. I decided to go to Sde-Boker to talk to Ben-Gurion. Once again I discovered that Ben-Gurion did not share my premonitions.

When I described Lavon's reaction, which was like a banked flame ready to leap to life at the mere mention of the 1954 episode, Ben-Gurion repeated his opinion that Lavon had nothing to fear. He himself would help Lavon in every way he could. The prime minister even suggested that Yaacov Shimshon Shapira, an undoubted friend of Lavon, should head a commission appointed to determine who had given the order for the operation in Egypt. Lavon rejected the idea out of hand and chose to appear before the Committee of Foreign Affairs and Security.

In those days Ben-Gurion still had a "weakness" for Lavon. Ben-Gurion remembered the brilliant speech Lavon had made during the Fourth Knesset election campaign on the nature of the Herut party. The speech had been an inspiration to the whole labor movement, and Ben-Gurion was lavish and persistent in his praise of it. Yet it seemed to me that Ben-Gurion relied too heavily on the prospect of being backed on the issue of government regulations by the party's veteran leaders, who were on the whole unsympathetic to Lavon.

On that particular day, Ben-Gurion was unperturbed by the storm gathering on the horizon. On April 10, 1960, he wrote in his journal:

Almogi came here at 9:30. He is seriously worried over the Lavon affair. He had a long conversation with him yesterday and it seems to him that a demon has gotten into him [Lavon] and all he has on his mind is that business. I told him I do not share his alarm. It is clear that *Herut* and *Merhav* and the sensationalist newspapers will seize on the issue to attack the Party, and me perhaps most of all, and that is just why I am not anxious. No intrigue, stirring-up or attempt to create a distorted view among the public can hold up for long in the face of the truth. . . . Incidentally, Almogi told me that in his talk with him, [Lavon] again argued that it was up to me to clear him.

An Unprecedented Scene

At about the time of my meeting with Ben-Gurion, Lavon made his first appearance before the Knesset Foreign Policy and Security Committee. From that day forward to the end of his testimony, the country witnessed Lavon's animus as he heaped charges against the Foreign Ministry, the armed forces, the system of arms acquisition, and the intelligence service. It seemed almost as if no one could escape unscathed from Lavon's wrath. Both the press and Mapai's opponents on the committee encouraged Lavon in his fury and poured fuel on the fire.

I had stood at Lavon's side when he clashed with the Youth Wing on Histadrut matters. Now, however, when in his access of anger he had gone so far as to enlist the enemies of Mapai in his own cause, I found myself gradually moving toward Ben-Gurion's side in the confrontation between the two men. Lavon's appearance before the Foreign Policy and Security Committee shocked the whole party, and even those in Mapai who had supported him at first now turned away from him. And Mapai's opponents looked on with evident glee at the spectacle of Lavon's uninhibited assault on the party that had raised him to a position of power and prestige.

I feel sure that a commission of inquiry of the kind Ben-Gurion was suggesting would have taken circumstantial evidence into account in its deliberations. Moreover, it seems to me that the chances were very good that such a commission would have cleared Lavon of the charge of having issued the order for the failed operation. Lavon, unfortunately, did not think so and opposed the creation even of a commission of an evidently nonpartisan character. As a consequence he let out all the stops, and deliberations of the Foreign Affairs and Security Committee were even leaked to the communications media.

Although he was attacking the party with unrestrained fury, Lavon entertained the hope that he would get the support of those members of the Bloc who had backed him during the clashes between the Histadrut and the Youth Wing. But even they told him that there were limits to their support; if he should attack Ben-Gurion, not only would they withdraw their support, but they would even turn against him. Their warning had no effect on Lavon, who continued his attack to the point of threatening that if the Defense Ministry did not desist from slandering him, he would expose it by making public the contents of a "secret file" which he claimed to have in his possession.

The party was in deep trouble. We were hard put to it to find a way to avoid a split in the movement. Fortunately, Golda Meir and Pinhas Sapir finally returned from abroad; the next day Levi Eshkol came back, too. I went to meet Eshkol at the airport, and joined him in his car so as to take advantage of the time afforded by the trip back to give him a firsthand report on the situation. Sapir, who was reluctant to leave Eshkol alone with me, came along, too; naturally Sapir's views were not entirely in agreement with mine. All the same, when Eshkol got back to Jerusalem that night he immediately opened talks to reduce tensions.

Eshkol first met with the party group known as the "Cooperative" (also known as the "Troika"), whose members were Golda Meir, Ziama Aran, and Pinhas Sapir. The Cooperative generally supported the Bloc, although it was not a part of it. Ziama Aran was the most problematic figure among the members of this extraordinary circle: he was angry with Ben-Gurion for having demanded Moshe Sharett's resignation in 1955, was very friendly with Golda Meir, had little esteem for Levi Eshkol, and was the sworn enemy of the Youth Wing. When he had been party secretary, he had closed down the weekly newspaper of the Mapai's young guard, Ashmoret, because it had published an article he did not like. Later he devoted himself to problems of education and reduced his activities in party affairs. He was a man of extremes and, like Golda Meir, was inclined to categorize people into one of two groups—good and bad. Ideologically, he was utterly opposed to the positions of the Youth Wing, and in matters of security and foreign affairs, there was no one more given to worry than he.

Golda Meir was the group's Ben-Gurionist in her social and political convictions. She disliked Lavon and threw herself into the efforts to force him out of office. And although she had no great enthusiasm for Dayan and Peres either, she initially rejected the claim that there had been a conspiracy in the Ministry of Defense against Lavon.

The third personality to make up the Cooperative, Pinhas Sapir, presented himself as a neutral in party conflicts—one who, to use his own words, "was not an adherent of the rabbis." His friendship with Eshkol ran deep and ended only when the latter died. Sapir and Golda were drawn together by their common suspicion of the Defense Ministry. Sapir used to say that every time he found himself in the same room with Dayan and Peres, he had the feeling that there were knives hurtling through the air.

It was Sapir who had the most important function in the Cooperative: it was he who acted as the contact between the Bloc and the party as a whole, including all its leaders and branches. Ziama was the ideologist of the group, and Golda its moral authority. The Cooperative neither opposed Ben-Gurion nor sided with Lavon; although Sapir, its man of action, maintained a close friendship with the Histadrut secretary-general. The group was dedicated first and foremost to fighting Ben-Gurion's young adherents who, the three believed, were building a wall around the Old Man in order to cut him off from the party veterans.

On this issue, Ziama was the most realistic of the three. He once told me privately that he was aware that his generation could remain in control for only a few years longer; it was for this reason they were preparing younger members like Sapir and others, who had roots in the labor movement, to take over from them. However, Ben-Gurion was doing this with Dayan and Peres and their set.

When I asked Ziama what was wrong with that, he began to rage against some of the younger members of the party who, he thought, could bring down Mapai and the whole labor movement. He even believed them capable of preparing a putsch and, with Dayan at their head, taking over the government by military force. Like Golda and Sapir, Ziama feared the influence, almost magical in their view, of the Youth Wing on Ben-Gurion.

After seeing Ben-Gurion, I met with Eshkol, Sapir, and Ziama. My friends in the Cooperative and their supporters said that Ben-Gurion would probably agree not to establish a state judicial commission of inquiry. I argued that the Old Man would never come to terms with such a decision. "Although I don't know Ben-Gurion as well as you do," I told them, "I'm afraid that you have no grounds for your optimism. I think that this time Lavon has gone for the jugular: this is the first time in the history of the country's public life that the defense establishment and the IDF have been besmirched by a key personality in the party, and with the encouragement, and to the malicious pleasure, of the party's sworn enemies."

My colleagues in the Cooperative were not convinced, and the next day we went to see Ben-Gurion again. In a last-ditch effort to get Ben-Gurion to change his mind, his old party comrades reminded him of Lavon's threat to reveal the contents of his "secret file." "You just don't know the man," they all urged; "he's capable of anything." "It will be a Pandora's box!" Eshkol added. It was the first time he used the expression, which soon became common coin among the Israeli public. Another expression used on this occasion was "mass grave"—Moshe Sharett's contribution. "The episode and the secret file could develop into a mass grave," he said.

Ben-Gurion could not be moved. "If I have to choose between doing harm to the party or to the state, I must choose to do harm to the party," he declared, and explained that he regarded the issue to be of the highest importance both to the state and to the education of its citizens.

We left having achieved nothing. In the party secretariat a debate began to unfold on which should come first—truth or domestic tranquillity. Everybody had something to say, quoting sources ranging from Scripture to socialist tracts. And all this time the Foreign Affairs and Security Committee remained in session to hear Lavon's less-than-aboveboard testimony.

A little later news was out that Ziama Aran had proposed to Eshkol to put the matter in the hands of a ministerial commission in which all the coalition parties would participate, rather than leave it to the Knesset committee. The ministerial commission would determine the procedures and ways of dealing with the material gathered by the Committee of Foreign Affairs and Security. Toward the end of October 1960, a commission of ministers was established, against Ben-Gurion's wishes. It was headed by the progressive minister of justice, Pinhas Rosen, and was called the Commission of Seven. Not only did it fail to bring an end to the dispute, but it created a public furor over the validity of its authority, procedures, and findings.

At the time I saw Ben-Gurion frequently, either in Jerusalem, Tel Aviv, or Sde-Boker. With each passing day his anger grew against Lavon. Paula tried to convince Ben-Gurion not to hurt Lavon because the man had a weak heart. She had a high opinion of Lucia Lavon and wondered why she had not restrained her husband.

Ben-Gurion would eat his breakfast while looking through the morning papers. (When he finished eating he would always take the dishes to the sink, much to Paula's delight.) Ben-Gurion's anger would grow worse each time he read about Lavon's testimony to the Foreign Affairs and Security Committee. He was upset later when intellectuals organized themselves in support of Lavon.

Lavon's "secret file" was always on his mind, and during our many talks he repeatedly asked me what I thought they might contain. I told him that I did not know, but that I guessed they bore on money matters having to do with the elections. "Really?" he said, surprised; "If that is so, what assurance have we that his threats would end if a nonjudicial commission of enquiry is appointed to clear him? Tomorrow he will want something else, and if he does not get it, he will again threaten to use his secret file, and the matter will never end."

The Lavon Affair became a public issue, and groups of intellectuals and students organized in support of Lavon and demanded his "total exoneration." This development was part of the ongoing debate in Israel at the time over the question of whether defense was a national value in its own right, as was being maintained by the security-minded, or a mere accessory required for survival, as the country's intellectuals argued.

"Lavon Acquiesced in the Order"

On one of the days when the public storm over the Lavon Affair was at a height, I was invited to a talk at Golda's home. There I met Isser Harel, Moshe Dayan, and Pinhas Sapir. Golda repeated her question to Isser: "What do you think?" Isser replied, "I do not believe Lavon gave the order. But he gave it his retroactive approval." Golda then put the same question to Moshe Dayan, who answered in almost the exact same words: "I don't think that Lavon gave the order, but he acquiesced in it and issued it retroactively." It was the first part of Isser Harel and Moshe Dayan's judgment, the one freeing Lavon from the responsibility of having given the order, which was important to Golda and Sapir. They tried to make use of these opinions to influence Ben-Gurion. Ben-Gurion, however, was no longer interested in the problem of who issued the order; for him the crux of the issue lay in determining the character of the commission that would have to reach a decision on the question.

There was a flurry of talks and meetings. Eshkol, who was actively involved in the business, would pop back home between meetings for a short rest and some tea. I would often accompany him during his recesses. Once home he would stretch himself out on the bed, his legs propped up on a chair, so as not to soil the bedspread, and give free rein to his troubled thoughts. I remember him saying:

"See, Yosef, what we've come to? Every day we eat ourselves up. Is it worth being in public life at all? Just look—the kids have become goats, they've grown up. . . . I just don't recognize them anymore. Golda, Ziama . . . why, Ben-Gurion was their oracle, unique in his time. They used to drink up everything he'd say, flatter him endlessly. . . . Me?—less so. I was with Ben-Gurion even before the union between Hapoel Hatzair and Ahdut Avoda, and at the time of the union I worked with him as an equal. I never toadied to him. I often went along with his policies, but not every time. Now look what's happening—an insurrection of the small fry, the revolt of the sons. . . ."

24

Ben-Gurion Resigns;
Lavon is Ousted

On the December 21, 1960, the Commission of Seven cleared Pinhas Lavon of responsibility for ordering the intelligence operation in Egypt. Four days later the government confirmed the committee's findings. Four government ministers, among them Ben-Gurion, had abstained in the voting.

On the last day of that year the party secretariat and Mapai representatives in the Knesset held a meeting that lasted twenty-four hours, almost without a break. We all had the feeling we were present at a momentous event, which might well determine the fate of the party and its leading personalities.

Most of the key figures in Mapai took part in this marathon session. Golda began by saying that although it was true that Lavon had been greatly hurt, his harsh language was inexcusable. Then, in the same breath, she said that even the most admired person in the party could err. Her words revealed the depth of her anger at Ben-Gurion when she said, "It's a certainty he saw Almogi more often than me." But she was insistent in denying that Ben-Gurion had said he would resign from the government if a judicial commission were not appointed to deal with the Lavon Affair.

On that last point, Golda and I were in disagreement. I had heard Ben-Gurion repeatedly say that if a commission of inquiry were not established, he would not remain in the government. Golda, however, persisted in claiming that if the Commission of Seven had found against Lavon there would have been no fuss, and that only because he had been cleared that we now assembled. That comment brought shouts of disagreement from many, including Dayan, Josephtal, and Gubrin. But Golda went even further: she opposed the motion being put before the secretariat that Mapai should not continue in the government without Ben-Gurion. Such a decision was unnecessary and superfluous, she said. Then to make her point, she dramatically announced her own resignation from the government. Earlier, at the government meeting which confirmed the findings of the Commission of Seven, she had handed her letter of resignation to Levi Eshkol when she found out that Ben-Gurion would not accept the Commission's conclusions.

The debate became heated. Israel Kargman attacked Golda in the strongest terms while praising Sharett "for having freed the public from Lavon's services." He then urged that we now free ourselves from Lavon's services in the administration of the Histadrut. It was the first time the idea of ousting Lavon was aired in the party.

Ziama Aran took Golda's side, and said that under no circumstance should a judicial commission of inquiry be created, as demanded by Ben-Gurion. He called on party members to remember Sharett's forebodings about a judicial commission's becoming a "mass grave." At this David Hacohen interrupted, saying, "The Commission of Seven is a mass grave—not a secret commission of inquiry!"

At this point in the proceedings, I thought it time that I interfere, and I asked the participants in the debate to keep us out of graves of any kind.

Moshe Dayan took the floor. He stated that in his opinion Lavon did not give the order, but that the 1954 episode did not interest him in the least; it was the year 1960 that interested him. He thought the Commission of Seven had taken over a function not properly belonging to it. Then he accused Eshkol of running party affairs in a spirit contradicting the spirit of Ben-Gurion and observed that now when everyone was attacking Ben-Gurion, the party had abandoned him, too. He then warned that the line being taken by Eshkol would lead to the end of both the party and Ben-Gurion.

For all that, Dayan also opposed a party decision not to return to the government without Ben-Gurion. "I support 99 percent of Ben-Gurion's policy," he said, "but if by some miracle I should be called on to participate in a government without Ben-Gurion—a government in harmony with the interests of the nation—I shall participate in it, because the nation stands above Ben-Gurion!" The last, superfluous sentence was meant to be a hint to Golda, who was also opposed to disbanding the government if Ben-Gurion were not a part of it, that one could "do business" even with Dayan and that he was not Ben-Gurion's "Siamese twin." Summing up, Dayan reminded us that Ben-Gurion would not join the next government without Golda Meir and Pinhas Sapir and that they had to be persuaded not to resign.

Pleading with Golda

We had two resignations hanging over our heads—Golda's and Ben-Gurion's. Ben-Gurion had announced his decision the moment the findings of the Commission of Seven were confirmed, but because of outstanding matters having still to be attended to—such as the World Zionist Congress and some defense problems—he put off taking the final step. For the time being, he was on vacation.

Early in January I chanced to meet Sharett at a meeting of the party's Central Committee, and we spoke about Golda's resignation. A few days later I received a letter from him:

> Dear Yosef,
>   What you told me during Levi Eshkol's speech in the Central Committee has caused me concern.
>   I certainly am in favor of Ben-Gurion's return to the prime ministry. And I also favor Golda's remaining in office as foreign minister. I am aware that the effort of convincing her to withdraw her resignation will be very hard and require summoning up every available means of persuasion. And on this point I am concerned lest the supposition that there is, or can be, a replacement for Golda in that office will weaken the effort and cause it to fail.
>   I therefore regard it as my duty to declare emphatically, and in the most positive terms, that any attribution to me of such a supposition is utterly erroneous. On no account will I accept any portfolio, not even that of foreign minister, in the government which is to be formed under the leadership of Ben-Gurion. I need hardly explain—stating the fact suffices. I think I have had enough opportunities to demonstrate—since my resignation from the Government in 1956—that if I say no I say it absolutely, and all of the attempts aimed at throwing me into confusion are only a cause of distress and a loss of time both to me and to those colleagues who keep themselves busy at it. Moreover, they can sometimes lead to missing other opportunities.
>
>   Yours,
>
>   Moshe Sharett

It seemed that between the lines of the letter there was a little slap meant for Golda: Sharett was implying that he would not do to her what she had done to him.

On January 23, 1961, about five weeks after the ministerial commission had submitted its findings, Ben-Gurion handed in his resignation to the president. In his letter of resignation, Ben-Gurion set out his position on the Lavon Affair and stated that he would not be a party to a distortion of justice. There was little public understanding for Ben-Gurion's motives; general feeling in the country at the time was anti-Ben-Gurionist. If anyone gained the reputation for integrity and being a defender of democracy it was Pinhas Lavon.

The local branches of Mapai had not received information about the developments and complications in the Lavon Affair, and their morale was generally low. As differences between the groups in the party grew more marked and when it became a certainty that Ben-Gurion would not acquiesce in the exoneration of Lavon, I thought it wise to determine party attitudes on a local level and discover if all the members of Mapai had in fact turned their backs on Ben-Gurion. It certainly seemed as if the whole country had. All the other parties, the entire press, as well as the veteran leadership of Mapai and joined against Ben-Gurion's demand for the appointment of a judicial commission of inquiry in the Lavon Affair. Not a word, though, from Mapai's branches. Could it possibly be they had nothing to say? If such indeed were the situation, it was unfair and could not be allowed to continue. I decided I should try to put it right and thought the most natural way to go about it would be to get the local branches actively involved. I therefore called down the branch secretaries and informed them that the most important task we had before us now was to reverse Ben-Gurion's resignation. Once we got past the crisis and returned things to normal, we would hold a series of consultations and full information would be made available on what had taken place up to that point.

The papers had dubbed my efforts a "revival campaign" *(masa hitorerut)*; Lavon called it a "campaign of undermining" *(masa hitarerut)*. But whatever fanciful name had been attached to the undertaking in public, the fact is that every local branch of the party, without exception, sent letters and telegrams to Ben-Gurion urging him to withdraw his resignation. Our initiative was, in part, a response to the one undertaken by the secretaries of the trade unions and Histadrut organizations, who had sent telegrams to the party secretariat demanding an end to all investigations of the Lavon Affair and calling for Lavon's name to be cleared without involving a commission of inquiry of any sort.

Ben-Gurion himself was not particularly pleased with what we were doing, and on January 6, 1961, I received a letter of protest from him:

> Dear Yosef,
> For God's sake stop those rallies and meetings that are asking me to go back on my resignation. This is taking names in vain; the nation's, the movement's, and maybe even mine. After all, there is some respect due even to a mortal man.
>
> Sincerely,
>
> David Ben-Gurion

I did not agree with him, but there was no longer any need to proceed with the campaign since all of the party branches had already done what had been asked of them. They had held discussions of a subject that had thrown the whole party into a turmoil, and for the first time in months, members of Mapai had made a public show of sympathy for Ben-Gurion.

Concomitantly, I tried to find a way to iron out the differences between Ben-Gurion and the veteran leadership of the party. To that end a meeting was arranged between the members of Haverenu and Ben-Gurion at the Sharon Hotel in Herzliya. The tensions were palpable even before the meeting actually began. I asked Ben-Gurion to open the session, and when he began to speak, the first thing he said was: "Two colleagues are destroying Mapai—Ziama Aran and Golda Meir."

Ziama made an effort to smile, but he turned pale. Golda just burst into tears. I accompanied her to the next room, and after I gave her a small glass of whisky to calm her down, we returned to the meeting. There was no breakthrough, only a rehash of old positions, and the meeting ended without achieving anything.

That night I arranged for a meeting between Eshkol and Ben-Gurion, which took place the next morning in Ben-Gurion's room at the hotel. After a night's sleep, Ben-Gurion seemed calmer than the day before, and Eshkol was his usual aimiable self. Ben-Gurion repeated his position, but to greater effect this time because he was able to do so calmly.

Getting Free of Lavon

An hour and a half later, I took Eshkol in my car to Tel Aviv. On the way he hummed Hasidic tunes. As we came in to the city, I asked him what proposal he would make at the meeting of the party secretariat that day. He answered that up to now he had fulfilled all Lavon's requests; now the time had come to get free of him.

I did not inquire into the details, but I understood that in his talk with Ben-Gurion, Eshkol had gathered that Ben-Gurion was for "freeing" Lavon from his duties as secretary-general of the Histadrut. Ben-Gurion had not said so explicitly, but Eshkol was fast on the uptake.

At 4:15 in the afternoon, Eshkol arrived at the meeting of the secretariat, and I let him take the floor. He opened his remarks by saying, "I have reached the conclusion that in the light of existing circumstances Lavon cannot represent the party as secretary of the Histadrut."

There was sudden silence. The members of the Cooperative looked furious; they were clearly very angry at Eshkol, and surprised.

After some moments had passed with no one having said a word, I proposed that the meeting be adjourned until the following morning. I also proposed that the Central Committee be convened immediately. That, I explained, was the proper forum for such a proposal to be put forward and for its author, Levi Eshkol, to give his reasons for having made it; there those who opposed it would have a chance to speak as well (Moshe Sharett volunteered for that role). Finally, I proposed there be a prior announcement that the voting at the Central Committee would be by secret ballot.

The motions I put forward were passed. Right after the meeting, I met with Ben-Gurion's supporters to make an assessment of the situation. We had to take into account that for months Ben-Gurion's opponents had had a field day in the press and on radio. Every day the newspapers and hosts of organizations, intellectuals, and spokesmen of opposition parties had been proclaiming their support for Lavon, while our party was split. On one side, the old leadership accepted the findings of the Commission of Seven and opposed Lavon's ouster from his office as head of the Histadrut—except for Eshkol, who, though he had joined in supporting the commission's findings, had in the last couple of days come to the conclusion that Lavon had to be removed from his post. On the other side stood the local party branches, many of whom—thanks to the revival campaign—would certainly support Eshkol's motion. The task we had at hand, therefore, was to line up the party branches, whose representatives would be taking part in the vote.

The following day, a Friday, February 3, the secretariat session lasted a full day, at the end of which a vote was taken. The results: 28 in favor of Eshkol's proposal, 11 against, and 6 abstentions.

The outcome was a shock to the public.

Lavon's supporters were quick to organize themselves in response. The next morning a rally was held by students, intellectuals, members of the Haolam Haze movement, and young members of the parties opposing Mapai. They gathered in front of the Ohel Auditorium, where the Central Committee was meeting. The demonstrators heard speeches and shouted slogans in support of Lavon and against Ben-Gurion. One could hear them call over and over again for Ben-Gurion to go back to Sde-Boker.

I called the meeting to order on schedule. The speeches of Eshkol and Josephtal for Lavon's ouster and of Sharett and Rotenstreich against it were listened to attentively and without interruption. At the end of the debate a secret vote was taken, after which the results were read out in an atmosphere fraught with suspense and tension: 150 for Eshkol's proposal, 96 against, 5 abstentions.

The prevading mood in the hall was one of gloom, and there was total silence as I rose to bring the meeting to a close. In the remarks I made to sum up the day's proceedings, I said that the party was still in a state of shock and had just gone through one of the most painful meetings in its history; nevertheless, it had succeeded in making a responsible and democratic decision. I went on to say that Mapai would do everything in its power to heal the wounds and close ranks to meet the tasks that lay before it. The crisis we had gone through had at least left us with one consolation—we had preserved our unity.

After the close of the Central Committee session three of us—Yitzhak Navon, Shraga Nezer, and I—rode out to the Sharon Hotel to report the results of the vote to Ben-Gurion. The Old Man showed no pleasure at the news, but it was evident that he considered the results to be just.

25
The Bloc of Four

On February 6, 1961, the president of Israel, Yitzhak Ben-Zvi, began consultations with the representatives of the parties on the makeup of the new government. Mapai's representatives proposed to the president that he reappoint David Ben-Gurion, whose resignation from the office of prime minister had caused the whole government to resign. However, with feeling against Ben-Gurion at a peak among the public and in the news media, Mapam, Ahdut Avodah, the National Religious Party, and the Progressives declared that they would not take part in a coalition under Ben-Gurion and formed the so-called Bloc of Four.

The situation was now precarious, and so as not to have to call new elections, Ben-Gurion proposed that Levi Eshkol undertake the formation of a government. The party secretariat and Haverenu met at Golda Meir's home in Jerusalem, where Mapai rejected Ben-Gurion's proposal and decided to risk an election. Eshkol and Aran predicted defeat at the polls; I maintained that, at worst, we would lose seven seats.

This is not to say that I was unaware of the potential hazards in the situation. I had expressed my opinion in the strongest terms that Ben-Gurion's ouster from office with the agreement of his own party would lead to the disintegration of the country's public life.

If, on the other hand, elections were held in an orderly and legal fashion and the Bloc of Four defeated, not only would public confidence be returned to Ben-Gurion, but the lid would finally be put on the whole sorry affair.

At the meeting of the Central Committee on March 19, Haim Gvati and M. Margalit of the kibbutz movement Ihud ha-kvutsot ve-ha-kibutsim proposed that negotiations be continued with the left-wing parties so as to avoid having to go to the polls. The motion received only six votes, with all the rest of the committee members voting to hold national elections. When the meeting came to a close I rose to make the official announcement that the Israel Workers' Party was "resigning from the affair" *(poreshet me-ha-parasha)* and would now get ready for elections. It was the first time in a year that I felt satisfaction at a meeting of the Central Committee. There was a new spirit in the air.

When I felt that we had finally gotten all the major party controversies out of the way, I decided to take a few days out to recover for the election campaign. I went to the Megiddo Rest Home on Mount Carmel in the expectation of doing nothing but lie back in an easy chair. But before I had even had a chance to unpack Abba Khoushi and Avigdor Eshet visited me with the news that the party leadership had come to an agreement whereby Eshkol would be prime minister and Ben-Gurion minister of defense, on the understanding that in a few months Eshkol would give the senior post back to Ben-Gurion. I was surprised and puzzled by this latest move.

At breakfast the next morning the phone rang in the dining room. Paula Ben-Gurion was on the line; Ben-Gurion wanted to speak to me. But before she turned the phone over to him she took the liberty, as always, to speak her mind about all the items on the agenda. Although I was a "little Stalin" she fully supported my position that Ben-Gurion ought not to accept the proposed personnel change. Finally, she gave the phone to Ben-Gurion, who asked me to come to see him. We set a meeting for the next day in Jerusalem.

When I saw him I realized quickly that although he had formally agreed with Eshkol to the ministerial change, the move did not meet with his wholehearted approval. Indeed, he did not like it at all. As we spoke I realized that Ben-Gurion did not believe this to be a solution, since all the rival parties would like nothing better than the opportunity a collapse of Mapai would afford them to build themselves up and get the Workers' Party out of power; it was the reason they all wanted elections. The only reason he had originally agreed to the idea was that he did not wish to be a stumbling block to the attempt to put things in order without having to go to the polls. To me the whole idea of Ben-Gurion returning as defense minister to a government headed by Eshkol seemed futile—not because it would represent a loss of face for Ben-Gurion, but because his agreement to such a scheme would be interpreted as surrender to the dictates of Mapai's rivals and tantamount to admitting he had been wrong in demanding the appointment of a judicial commission of inquiry to resolve the Lavon Affair.

In the end the scheme proved abortive: the Knesset voted to have national elections in August.

The Fight Is On Again

I did everything I could to have the elections take place in October or November rather than August, which is when a great number of Israeli's are away at resorts. I was afraid that voter turnout would fall in the summer month, and a reduced electorate was usually to the disadvantage of the larger parties. I thought that at least Mapam and Ahdut Avoda, most of whose voters were wage-earning working people likely to be on holiday in August, would go along with us in opposing elections being held then; but the anti-Mapai coalition in the Knesset put up a solid front. We had no choice but to accept the inconvenient scheduling and put ourselves in immediate readiness for the contest. Our local branches, in any case, were ready for action—a fact that helped considerably in getting the campaign organized and bringing election information to the voters.

The election results, I thought, were quite good. We had received forty-two seats—significantly more than I had expected in the circumstances. As after the last elections, I went to see Ben-Gurion in his home to inform him of the results. Only now I found him in low spirits: he was brooding over his worsening relations with the party's "old guard" and full of foreboding. I later appeared at a farewell gathering of the workers at election headquarters. I told them that the people had once more put their trust in Mapai with Ben-Gurion at its head; the people had decided differently from what our rivals had hoped when they forced us into early elections.

When the results of the election were officially proclaimed, Mapai once again asked the president to invite Ben-Gurion to form a government. But the Bloc of Four had no intention of gracefully bowing out: oblivious to the will of the voters, they persisted in putting obstacles in Ben-Gurion's way. To get round the obstructions Ben-Gurion proposed tht Levi Eshkol be appointed to form a government in which Ben-Gurion himself would still be prime minister; as to its makeup, he indicated he was ready to form a coalition with the General Zionists, who were then united with the Progressives.

Only toward the end of October did the Party Secretariat meet to make a final decision. The Central Committee was scheduled to convene on November 1 and the Knesset on the second of the month. At the secretriat meeting, we were informed of developments in the negotiations with Ahdut Avoda: their last condition for joining the government was that they be given two portfolios—the ministries of Transport and Labor; on fundamentals of policy, they were approaching our positions. As the meeting proceeded I visited Ben-Gurion at his home several times to report on our progress and get his approval for various steps we were taking.

At our last consultation, just before the formation of the government, Ben-Gurion accompanied me to the door, and then he suddenly asked me: "Do you know Yosef Krelenboim?" I gave him a puzzled look, wondering what the punch line was going to be. "Yes," I said, "I think I know him. . . ."

"Well, if you see him," Ben-Gurion went on, warming to his joke, "tell him he's going to be minister without portfolio in the next government."

"I certainly will!" I assured him, falling in with his playful mood, "And I'm sure he'll be very thankful to you."

On my way back to party headquarters, I felt heady with excitement. It was like a dream. I had made no request on my own behalf; proposed myself for no post, and out of nowhere I was being offered the office of minister in the government of Israel. Would it really happen?

Meanwhile I had my present duties to attend to. At the November 1 meeting of the Central committee, I reported on developments in the negotiations and then gave Ben-Gurion the floor. Ben-Gurion spoke briefly, saying that if anyone deserved a prize for bringing peace to the party, it was Levi Eshkol. At this the whole Central Committee broke into applause.

Then Levi Eshkol got up to read the names of Mapai members of the government: David Ban-Gurion—prime minister and minister of defense; Golda Meir—minister of foreign affairs; Levi Eshkol—minister of finance; Pinhas

Sapir—minister of commerce and industry; Giora Josephtal—minister of housing and development; Moshe Dayan—minister of agriculture; Behor Shitreet—minister of police; Abba Eban—minister of education and culture; Dov Joseph—minister of justice; Eliahu Sasson—minister of the posts; Yosef Almogi—minister without portfolio.

It was the first time my name was officially mentioned as a member of the proposed government. I do not deny that my heart skipped a beat when I heard it read.

Eshkol spoke, and Mordecai Surkis then moved that the list of proposed ministers be accepted without debate. The Central Committee then passed the list by acclamation.

This marked the end of a period of internal party conflicts that could not be matched for vehemence. I hoped we had finally put an end to the Lavon Affair.

My next immediate task was to hand over the party secretaryship to Reuben Barakat, Golda's candidate. I convened the Central Committee in November, and Barakat was unanimously elected. I had finished my term as party secretary, and Ben-Gurion rose to make a speech in honor of the occasion of the secretaryship changing hands. He was unstinting in his praise, and said I left my office bearing the fond esteem of the entire Central Committee, that all those in the party who had regarded me as the "Boss of Haifa" had been pleasantly disappointed. I had not only proved my organizational abilities but had shown I was able to listen to an opponent's views. He concluded by saying that he was certain I would continue to serve the public faithfully in my new post.

26
Minister with and without Portfolio

The change from party secretary to government minister eased my work schedule. As secretary of Mapai during the very tumultuous years between 1958 and 1961, I bore an enormous burden of responsibility. There had been two election campaigns, and in between the Lavon Affair had resurfaced. These alone were enough to exhaust a man. In addition, I was driven by my sense of duty to involve myself in every aspect of my office, and was unwilling to let slip any opportunity to act.

Quite suddenly, I could relax. I was no longer confronted every day with problems clamoring for attention. I now rose in the morning looking forward to the day's work with positive pleasure. The meetings of the government were never a cause of emotional strain. Most of the members of the government I had already had experience with as partners in working sessions within the party, and both the style of deliberations and the manner in which decisions were reached by the government were familiar to me. Nor were the official residence and car put at my disposal anything new; I had enjoyed these privileges when I was party secretary.

What was new to me was the ministerial dignity which was from now on to accompany me in all my assignments. I began to appear for the government at celebrations throughout the country and often to represent it abroad—especially at ceremonies marking the independence of new states. On behalf of the Independence Loan and the Foundation Fund, I frequently met with Jewish communities of the Diaspora. In Israel I was actively engaged in the work of the Emergency Economic Committee, whose job was to ensure vital manpower for agriculture, industry, and the public services during national emergencies and, in case of an enemy attack, to oversee the supply of water, fuel, and electricity; the maintenance of transportation; the mounting of rescue operations; and the provision of adequate hospital facilities.

In May Giora Josephtal, minister of housing and development, fell ill, and I was asked to fill in for him. I was aware of the delicacy of the situation and was careful to behave accordingly. I avoided using Josephtal's office and did all the work connected with the absent minister's duties in the small office set aside for me as minister without portfolio. I assisted the general directors of the Housing and Development Ministry's offices and replied on the minister's behalf to questions and agenda proposals in the Knesset, where my earlier experience in parliamentary procedure stood me in good stead.

Putting a Man on the "Fifth Floor"

Aharon Becker's appointment to the secretary-generalship of the Histadrut after Lavon's departure from the office was causing deep concern among the veteran leaders of Mapai. The choice seemed to them insufficiently "strong," and they advised Ben-Gurion to free Golda from her duties in the government and give her the job of "saving the Histadrut." Ziama Aran, who was strongest in advocating this course, declared himself ready to work in the Histadrut at Golda's side. He proposed that Israel Kargman, regarded as an expert in trade-union affairs, should also go over to the Histadrut executive.

Ben-Gurion at first refused to go along with the advice of the party's leadership, but eventually, as I learned later, gave in to pressure. I wasn't present at the meetings in which these steps were discussed, and my only source of information about the matter were the rumors making their way through the corridors of the prime minister's office.

The suggestions of the Mapai leadership got a poor reception in the press; the newspaper *Ha'artz* proposed that I be given the administration of the Histadrut. At the time, Becker was on holiday in Cyprus; as soon as he returned he went to see Golda Meir to hear what she had to say about what was happening. Golda told him explicitly that she did not want the office of Histadrut secretary-general because she had no wish to appear again in the guise of someone instigating an ouster. I don't know if Golda had initially intended to move onto the "Fifth Floor," but I am certain Ben-Gurion faced a touchy situation because of the deterioration in his relations with veteran leadership after the Lavon Affair.

I was in Buenos Aires when I received the sad news of Giora Josephtal's death. I was not asked to return from my tour, and I kept to my original schedule. In Israel deliberations were already underway over the two portfolios left unattended on Giora's death; and by the time I got back around mid-September the matter had become a public issue of central concern. Ben-Gurion was on a visit to Scandinavia then, and while the chief was away, the rumor mills began to turn. In any event, no one mentioned the matter to me.

When Ben-Gurion returned to Israel in the second half of September, he called a government meeting to report on his Scandinavian tour. An hour before the meeting took place, he called me into his office and said he had decided to turn over both of the unattended portfolios—Housing and Development—to me. At the end of the government meeting the prime minister announced my dual appointment; none of the ministers present offered a comment or asked any questions. So, in an atmosphere of subdued reservation, I went from being minister without portfolio to minister with—in possession, indeed, of two portfolios.

The Ministry of Development

The Ministry of Development had under its jurisdiction the area of the Dead Sea Plain and the Negev; this was an exception among government ministries, which were organized on a functional rather than regional basis. The situation had a history all its own. When Mordecai Bentov of Mapam became development minister, he had insisted on holding onto the Dead Sea Plain and Negev Department. I discovered that the department employed about twenty people who spent their time riding around the wilderness in a couple of jeeps. They seemed to be contributing little to the development of the region, so I closed down the departmennt and transferred its personnel and equipment to the appropriate ministries. My colleagues were somewhat surprised by my munificence, but they accepted their portion of the largesse without a murmur.

I found other irregularities within the jurisdiction of the ministry. The beaches of the country were being disfigured by gravel mining. After complaints began pouring in, I did some hard and long negotiating with the parties involved, and finally got out an order putting a stop to the gravel mining. I then appointed Colonel (Reserves) Michel Shaham to the job of seeing to it that the order was enforced, and the depredation of the seashore was brought to a halt.

Another ministry project was the search for oil. An international expert in the field recommended changes in the law to make it easier to obtain oil-drilling concessions. Before I took office, the country had been divided into four districts in which three companies, partly owned by the government, held onto tracts of land without actually taking advantage of the concessions they had been granted. The expert had suggested that the companies be merged so that they could pool their resources. Naturally, the companies did not take to the idea and argued that competition was the best guarantee for finding oil. Nevertheless, I appointed a commission headed by Professor Yigael Yadin to study the problem, and on its recommendations, we introduced changes in the law. But it required more than that to get oil.

I met many experts on the subject, Jews among them, who shared the belief that there was oil to be found in Israel; unfortunately, there is no instrument that can pinpoint the exact location of oil underground. A number of regions are regarded as promising, but just to verify the existence of oil requires a lot of drilling, and at enormous cost. Only the very large oil companies in the West can afford the investment, and they are unprepared to risk their international undertakings just for drilling in Israel.

The same problems exist with regard to underground mineral resources, in which our country seems to be, unfortunately, quite poor. I remember that, during a tour of the Negev I took with Sir Ben Lockspeiser, the Anglo-Jewish scientist who was a member of the Technological Advisory Council to the Development Ministry, I observed to him that Moses must have been so highly impressed by the Land of Israel because he had not seen a country with real natural wealth, like Canada or even Saudi Arabia. Sir Ben advised me to stop murmuring against our greatest prophet because one day we will find that he was right. He then ran through a list of countries whose natural resources were discovered only after generations of searching.

Problems at the Timna Mines

The Timna copper mines were never off the Development Ministry agenda. The problems were endless: heavy financial losses, chronic labor shortages, frequent strikes—and, at the same time, demands by the enterprise for an enormous additional investment in order to excavate and develop a new mine. Experts had drawn up a plan that would cost forty million liroth. There were geologists who doubted that so large an investment was worthwhile and suggested that only 600,000 liroth be initially allocated for research at the site. But the dynamic manager of the Timna Mines, Eliezer Bodankin, opposed investing even a penny more in research and demanded approval for the whole vast sum—with an adjustment upward, of course, to compensate for the inflation that had taken place since the request had been submitted. The subject was debated for weeks, and I was torn by doubts the whole time. The engineer Yitzhak Vilentchuk, for example, insisted that as things were, it was useless to expect profits from Timna and that for the enterprise to go on and Jews to be able to live in nearby Eilat, the Jewish people would have to foot the bill. However, to my question as to why it was necessary both to lose money and force Jews into hard labor, Vilentchuk had no answer. I came out of every meeting feeling greatly depressed by the proceedings. All the same I kept applying to the government for approval of the Timna budget. Sapir decided to pass the buck to me: he gave his approval to having forty million liroth set aside for the Timna project, but left to me the final decision on whether the money would be used or not. That left me even more worried than before, and I decided to proceed with caution.

I went back to study the Timna problem again and discovered some strange facts. The Israel Mining Industries Company in Haifa, under the management of Dr. Abraham Bniel, was funded by the monies set aside for the Timna Mines. The director of Timna visited the mines once a week at most. Finally, around one hundred engineers of Timna worked in Tel Aviv and, at intervals, would make the "hop" to the site of the mines in the far-off south of the country at Eilat.

I consulted with Givoni, Preminger, and Yosef Tulipman—the last a fine engineer and a first-rate man who became, at my suggestion, deputy director-general of the ministry. Both Givoni and Tulipman agreed with the decision I finally came to—that a large investment in Timna should not be made at that time. I was aware that I was letting myself in for a fight whose outcome I could not be sure of. In any event, I informed the Timna management that I had decided to withhold approval of a large investment at this stage, but would approve the smaller sum for further research by Israel Mining Industries. I also announced that all Timna employees living in Tel Aviv would either have to move to Eilat or resign and take their severance pay; the same applied to members of the Timna management.

Bodankin and the mines' management let me know that if I insisted on my demands they would all resign. I did not let the threat shake my resolve. I called in the mines' shop committees—both that in Tel Aviv and the one at Timna—and explained my decisions to them on both the question of investment in the mines and the matter of requiring employees and management to live in Eilat. To my surprise and relief, the shop-committee members rose one after another to commend my decision. I learned that they had already gotten word of the details of my decision, but had not quite believed that I would have the courage to go through with it.

The accommodating attitude of the shop committees made it easier for me. Sapir was taken by surprise when he learned about my having canceled the plan for making a large investment in Timna and was subsequently to boast that it had really been his doing, because it was, after all, he who had had the idea of putting the final choice of what to do with the money up to me. As expected, the Timna management quit. I asked Yaacov (Yanek) Ben-Yehuda to take over the administration of the Mines. Yanek Ben-Yehuda was an economist with excellent patriotic credentials—a former member of Kibbutz Usha, he had been active during the Second Aliya and had served in the security services. He accepted my offer and moved down to Eilat. I gave Givoni the job of negotiating with the Timna employees in Tel Aviv who had refused to relocate in Eilat, and I sent Tulipman down to Timna to run things until Yanek could take up his post. I also appointed a new management.

The choice I made to approve only the research budget for Timan proved to have been wise. The testing showed that an investment of tens of millions would have been a complete waste, and I felt immense satisfaction at having been able to save the country such a vast sum, which could now be put to better use.

The Zarchin Project

Desalinization of sea water was another subject that occupied me during my term as Minister of Development. Alexander Zarchin, an engineer and inventor who immigrated to Israel from the Soviet Union, had devised a system of sweetening sea water by freezing, which he claimed to be less costly than the methods currently in use throughout the world. My predecessors in the ministry had established a company, in partnership with the Fairbanks-Whitney Company in the United States, for the construction of desalinization plants. According to the agreement with the American company, plants of the type designed by Zarchin were to be built in Israel and the United States, the assumption being that there would be a large world market for such installations because of the simplicity of the technology and the relatively low cost involved in their production and operation. However, the many engineering problems that were encountered in the course of constructing the plants held up production. Zarchin publicly criticized the engineers at work on the project for failing to understand his design and asked for a half million liroth to build a plant by himself and prove the project workable. My predecessors were unconvinced of the wisdom of risking so much money, and suggested to Zarchin that he submit his project to study by another engineer of his own choosing: if it should pass the latter's review, the required funds would be set aside. Zarchin responded by sending off letters of protest to the prime minister and other members of the government; he also found supporters among professional colleagues whose qualifications were beyond dispute. Finally, at a meeting with the inventor in the office of Ben-Gurion, who found himself forced to intervene in what was purely a technological matter, it was agreed that Zarchin would go to the United States to seek the opinion of American experts. Should his project meet with their approval, he would receive the money he had asked for.

For my part, I decided to have built in Eilat four desalinization plants operating according to Zarchin's scheme and one conventional water-sweetening facility based on the heating principle and served by an electrical power plant. We then waited to see which system was better technically and economically.

Some time later in 1963, when Levi Eshkol visited the experimental station, I was able personally to treat him to a drink of water that had been sweetened by the Zarchin process. Eshkol was delighted. Zarchin was present, too, and the money for his project was approved, but the choice between his system and other desalinization processes has yet to be made.

I took advantage of Eshkol's good mood and got his support for my own project of extending the railway south to Oron and Dimona from Beersheba. I had wanted to have track laid down all the way to Eilat, so that our southern port city would have an overland link with the rest of the country. The economic advantage to the nation of such a link was, and is, beyond doubt. So I was rather surprised when the plan met with resistance from army command. The military problems protecting a line of track as long as the one I had in mind would have put an unacceptable strain on the resources of the IDF. I had no choice but to compromise and accept only a modest extension of the line.

The Electric Corporation

The problems of the Israel Electric Corporation occupied much of the Knesset's time in the summer of 1962. The opposition took advantage of Mapai's internal strife, and hammered away at the government over the issues of labor relations and employee involvement in management at the Electric Corporation. The grand debate on the Electric Corporation was mounted in the Knesset while the Development Ministry budget was under deliberation. The MKs participating in the debate were Shneur Zalman Abramov for the Liberal party, Benjamin Avniel for Herut, Michael Chazani for the National Religious Party, Abraham

Hartzfeld and Israel Kargman for Mapai, and Moshe Carmel for Ahdut Avoda. Most of the speakers were critical of policies in the corporation.

Responding to the critics, I vigorously defended both the program of having employees participate in the administration of the Electric Corporation and the job the company's heads and workers were doing in managing the enterprise. I had had no small part in the coalition's decision to require worker participation in the management of the company and had helped push through the policy despite opposition from some members of Mapai, who objected that workers' representatives would serve simultaneously in management and in the shop committee. At the end of a long debate, Akiva Gubrin, Knesset head of the coalition, submitted a motion affirming that the Knesset took "a favorable view of workers' participating in the management of the Electric Corporation at a time when the government is working for a continuation and improvement of that partnership." The motion was supported not only by the coalition factions, but even by some of the MKs in the Knesset opposition who were members of the religious Poalei Agudat Yisrael party. The motion passed, and the policy of employee involvement in the corporation's administration now had the imprimatur of the nation's legislature. The addition of the final phrase "improvement of that partnership" to the motion contented the doubters in Mapai and left the way open for them to find ways of making the policy of employee-management collaboration work better.

In supporting the policy, I felt sure of my ground. I knew that enlisting workers in management would raise the level of their involvement in the enterprise as a whole and increase their sense of responsibility for its work. As for the better-than-average wages and benefits of Electric Corporation employees, it was the founder of the company himself, Pinhas Rutenberg, who started the policy. It should be remembered, however, that these advantages have, in the course of time, been much reduced. Nevertheless, the bargaining power of Electric Corporation workers—employed in what is after all one of the most vital enterprises in the country—remains strong to this day.

After the battle over the Electric Corporation administration, I set to work on improving the venture of employee-management collaboration. I appointed a committee to study the corporation's problems in this area. The committee was led by Israel Kargman—this despite the fact that some party colleagues thought Kargman's position during the Ata strike had cooled our relations to the point that we would find it difficult to work together. I disagreed, and I never had cause to regret Kargman's appointment. As usual, he did a thorough job. There were, however, some disagreements, one between Kargman and the head of the shop committee, Yaacov Khoushi. Kargman had recommended that workers' representatives who were active in the company's administration give up their membership in the shop committee; Yaacov Khoushi took the view that being on the shop committee should, in fact, qualify an employee to represent labor in company management. Still another point of disagreement was over the rotation of employees in management and the method by which workers' representatives in the administration should be chosen. In none of these disagreements did I think it necessary to intervene. What I regarded to be most important was ending the internal conflicts that were wearing down the company's employees. To that end I concentrated on bringing about the merging of the corporation's two shop committees and the cooperation of the two Mapai cells of the company in the north and south of the country. I also had to work hard to convince the director-general of the company to extend its high-tension lines to Mitzpe Ramon and Midbar Paran in the Negev. We also continued to expand the electrical network supplying the settlements of the country's ethnic minorities. In Ashdod we had got the new power plant into operation, and in Haifa gas-operated facilities were put up to serve in emergencies. Our production of electricity was now nearing the one-million-kilowatt mark.

This was also the period in which the government began to consider the possibility of constructing an atomic power station. There had been some talk of taking the project out of the hands of the Electric Corporation, and the board of directors threatened to resign if such a plan was carried out. I, too, thought we would be ill advised to establish a second electric company for this project. Nevertheless, I put off taking the matter further, since it was clear that the realization of the atomic power project was still long way off; it seemed to me a waste to squander energy on the controversy prematurely.

With the recommendations of Kargman's committee in hand, I established, in May 1963, a board of directors on which three representatives of the Electric Corporation were represented: Feivel Kantor and Zvi Yifan from Tel Aviv and Moshe Flieman from Haifa. As a temporary measure, I took on the duties of board chairman. In January 1964, a national council of Electric Corporation employees was finally established after I had spent some months preparing the ground. I was able to achieve the much-needed balance between the northern and southern shop committees of the corporation with the help of the company's Jerusalem employees, who were represented in all the workers' organizations.

The Chemical Industry

In 1957 the chemical engineer Aleksander (Sasha) Goldberg founded Fertilizers & Chemicals, Ltd., equipping the plant with machinery he had acquired from Europe and the United States. The company experienced financial difficulties, and I found it necessary to secure a loan for it from the Savings and Loan fund so that its workers, most of them new immigrants, could be paid.

Phosphates were the most important raw material used by the enterprise, and there were fifty million tons of phosphates underground at Oron. There was a hitch, however: the phosphates were low in oxidized phosphorus (only 23 to 25 percent) and the cost of mining would have to be compensated for by a sizable increase in marketing. This in turn would have meant higher freight costs. Another way of dealing with the problem was to use chemical enrichment to raise the content of oxidized phosphorus to 29 percent, for which one of the largest available kilns, capable of processing half a million tons a year, was needed.

The plant in Oron was established by Brigadier General (Reserves) Shlomo

Shamir, a highly idealistic person with a strong pioneering background who had worked unbelievably hard to build the operation in the face of stiff competition from phosphate enterprises in Morocco, where deposits were vast and rich. A somewhat richer deposit of phosphates was found in the region of Arad, where Fertilizers & Chemicals, Ltd., had the mining concession.

When natural gas was also discovered near Arad, the basis was laid for the development of a really large chemical enterprise built around phosphates, potash, and natural gas. We set about planning the undertaking, while at the same time looking for investors. We opened negotiations with a Dutch company that had applied for a concession to extract the raw material, but in the end the Dutch company had to pull out because of Arab pressure.

While I was looking for ways to get these projects underway without having to turn to companies abroad, a dispute suddenly broke out between the phosphate enterprise in Oron and Fertilizers & Chemicals in Haifa over mining concessions in Arad. It seemed to me that the best way to resolve the problem would be for the two companies to merge, so that they could pool their resources in exploiting the mineral deposits in the north and south; I also suggested that Sasha Goldberg be general director and Shlomo Shamir deputy director of the company that would be formed as a result of the merger.

Goldberg agreed with the idea of a merger and was amenable to the proposed appointments. Shamir, however, rejected my proposals and turned for support to Ben-Gurion, whom he had been close to for years. I tried my best to get Ben-Gurion and Shamir to see things my way, but Shamir wa adamant and handed in his resignation. Then the newspapers got to work and began to publish dire warnings of the "epidemic of resignations" that was sure to follow if I went ahead with my plan. I had no intention of giving up on the project, and I turned over the task of putting it into operation to a committee under the leadership of Menahem Bader. Bader, it turned out, opposed the scheme and announced that he was in agreement with Shamir and that he supported the idea of a limited partnership of the two firms, which would work together under an umbrella organization.

My attempts to put Fertilizers & Chemicals, Ltd., back on its feet brought me into conflict with the finance minister on the question of the handling of company finances. I rejected the view of the Finance Ministry that because the company did not exist primarily to accumulate capital, it could afford to lower the prices at which it sold fertilizers to farmers in Israel. My experience, however, had taught me that once an enterprise begins to take its losses in stride, both management and labor turn lax; in such a situation they will even expand manpower against all reason, having gotten used to the public's footing the bill. A public enterprise can never be put on its feet again if it makes peace with chronic deficit and turns it into a matter of principle or ideology.

After studying the company's problems, we decided to inject new life into it by changing its capital structure, canceling its deficit, and raising production to increase profits. To begin with, we would have to close experimental plants, which were bringing in no profit, and cut down on manpower by letting go 205 employees. Administrative costs also had to be lowered, and production increased.

Pinhas Sapir became reconciled to my scheme, even though making Fertilizers & Chemicals profitable had destroyed his theory that a development industry had to run at a loss. He did not believe that we would manage to close down experimental facilities and lay off employees. It was for this reason he had made his participation dependent on the rehabilitation of the company's finances and the complete implementation of the scheme.

The company's employees met the challenge of getting the firm on its feet. The chairman of the shop committee, M. Maza, put himself fully behind the effort. Fertilizers & Chemicals, Ltd., was well on the way to recovery.

A Family Note

My son Yoram married his sweetheart, Yuta, in a ceremony performed in November 1962, witnessed only by the family. The reception, however, was a grand affair. It was held in the Solel Boneh factory in Haifa harbor. The announcement in the papers brought thousands of well-wishers, among them government ministers and David and Paula Ben-Gurion.

Seeing the great crowd of friends who had come to celebrate filled me with a pleasure I have rarely experienced. The sheer number of friends who attended led Ben-Gurion to ask whether there was anyone left in Israel who had not come. Shifra and I felt at the time that we were not being sufficiently attentive to our guests, which, under the circumstances, could only have been expected. We hoped that the celebrants would understand and forgive. That night we also resolved that when our younger Zvika married the celebration would be confined entirely to family—if, that is, all concerned agreed when the time came.

27
The Ministry of Housing

My first contacts with the Ministry of Housing occurred when I filled in for the housing minister, Giora Josephtal, after he had taken ill. When I was named minister of housing, I took over an office that had been functioning without an official custodian for some time. The ministry was then under heavy pressure to alleviate a serious housing shortage, although it had at its disposal neither an adequate budget for construction nor manpower skilled in the building trades. In addition, it was hampered in its work by bureaucratic inefficiencies.

After first delegating more authority to the ministry's district offices and adding people with first-rate organizational skills to the staff, I turned my attention to the most urgent problems confronting us. I soon discovered that in financing housing we were taking the pauper's view—buying cheap and paying dear. The Finance Ministry, by adopting a policy of thrift in the short run, found itself having to pay high in the long and even the middle run. The quality of housing put up was bad: planning was poor, the size of apartments small, and construction shabby. The result of all the cheap building was that in a relatively short time a fortune had to be disbursed to correct not only the built-in physical shortcomings, but the social ills attendant on them. On our own, we had actually created new poverty neighborhoods to join the old ones we had inherited.

I managed to persuade Levi Eshkol to change the Finance Ministry's policy. Then, with his backing, I issued an order to increase the size of existing apartments and improve neighborhood services. I put a stop to the practice of moving people into uncompleted apartments and unfinished neighborhoods, without pavements, landscaping, or street lighting. I also made a special effort to improve the appearance of housing complexes. I regarded ugly buildings as not only an aesthetic blot on the landscape, but a threat to our education, health, economy, and society. I therefore invited the best architects in the country to submit proposals for housing projects which would be less bland and more attractive than the standardized apartment blocks being put up. I also established a Tenant Home-Culture Association, which was funded by the Housing

Ministry; the National Corporation for Immigrant Housing, Amidar; and the Department of Immigrant Absorption of the Jewish Agency. The association worked with women's organizations and tenant house committees and was active in neighborhoods and, in particular, at schools. I made it my business to participate personally in a number of the association's meetings to encourage its activities.

After I had succeeded in having immigrant housing units increased in size from 102 to 124 square feet and brought about a vast improvement in the infrastructure of neighborhoods, I came under fire from less recent immigrants, who complained that they were being made to put up with undersized and poor quality housing only because they had arrived in the country earlier. There was certainly some justice in what they were saying, but I was unable to meet their demands at a time when great masses of immigrants were still living in transit camps, tent villages, canvas huts, tin shacks, and abandoned Arab dwellings.

During the Knesset debate on the 1963–64 national budget, I promised to put an end to the transit camps. It was a promise I kept, even though the operation laid a heavy financial burden on us. The operation had shortcomings because of the great speed with which it had to be carried out, but despite this we managed to move many thousands of families from temporary shelters into permanent homes.

Housing for Young Couples

While we were still principally at work on the problem of getting immigrants permanently housed, the complaints kept growing among old-time settlers about their own deprivation in housing. Particularly hard hit were newly married couples, who could not afford housing, and many of whose parents did not have the means to help them. An average of twenty thousand couples married every year; I estimated that at least fifteen thousand of them would have to receive public financial aid, either from the state or from the municipalities, in order to acquire an apartment. I decided that top priority had to be given to finding solutions to the housing problems of young couples.

After talking the problem over with Eshkol and Sapir, I drew up and put into the works a savings plan called Bar Mitzvah, whose aim was to anticipate the housing needs of future young couples. Parents possessing limited means were given an opportunity to put away money for their children, beginning at each child's Bar Mitzvah. On reaching marriageable age, the children would thus have a tidy sum toward the purchase of an apartment. The plan was taken advantage of by thousands of parents. At the same time I encouraged young couples to move to newly established development towns, where the quality of their lives would certainly be greatly improved and where they would be contributing to the achievement of an important national goal—a balanced distribution of population, which was too heavily concentrated in the narrow coastal strip between Tel Aviv and Haifa. By providing housing for young married couples in the development towns, we would also be working toward a better mix of ethnic communities in Israel. Then, too, land prices in development towns were lower than in established cities, and this reduced building costs.

To attract settlers to the development towns, I worked to improve services and lower the cost of living in those communities. The new policy was applied to all development towns. However, I gave special attention to two new cities whose establishment I had sponsored—Arad in the southern desert and Carmiel in the Galilee region. Carmiel was an unprecedented achievement in at least one respect: I was able to demonstrate that with good planning a large-scale undertaking of this sort could be carried out quickly and efficiently. Just one year after the cornerstone of Carmiel's municipal building was laid, the first residents moved into their homes. The "miracle" was accomplished by completing the building campaign as planned. Contrary to the usual practice in Israel, we did not introduce changes during construction, and each step of construction was scheduled carefully, including the time-consuming finishing touches. I urged the builders to apply advanced building techniques and to use ready-made units for doors, windows, cupboards, and the like—yet to preserve architectural variety and good taste.

During the Knesset debate on the Housing Ministry's 1963 budget I had to respond to a question about nationally owned land. On that occasion I was able to disprove the widely made claim that because 90 percent of land in Israel was nationally owned, it should be sold at low prices to builders to appreciably reduce construction costs. I was able to demonstrate that most public land was not located in the crowded coastal plain, but in regions where land price was an insignificant factor in the cost of construction.

I asked the Ministry of Interior to prepare a master plan for construction to meet the needs of a national population of five million; the plan would lay out in detail the requirements in housing, public buildings, industry, education, and health. I also appointed Major-General (Reserves) Yaacov Dori to study possibilities for technological research in construction and for the application of the results of such research to the building industry. We set aside a budget for building research to be carried out, in particular, at the Technion. I took these steps because I had become convinced that we were less advanced in the field of housing than, say, in agriculture, industry, and shipping. Under conditions of a chronic housing shortage, incentives had to be created for builders to adopt advanced construction techniques. For this, the initiative had to come from the government.

Rehabilitation of Impoverished Neighborhoods

When I took over the Ministry of Housing, conditions in our poor neighborhoods became a matter of immediate concern to me. For a long time prior to taking office, I had regarded them as being not only a serious flaw in our society, but a potential menace to the country as a whole. Although I pushed to increase the budget for home construction for the disadvantaged, I soon realized that rehousing the poor was a painfully slow process involving unlooked-for difficulties. Often the hovels left behind by those we had rehoused were occupied by people from development towns before we got demolition work underway. Some slum dwellers refused to leave their old neighborhoods despite having been offered new homes. We were in danger of having another generation grow up in poverty. It was a problem no system of education could cope with.

After studying the matter carefully, I concluded that the population of poor neighborhoods could be rehabilitated without straining the economy beyond its capacity. Most of the poverty districts occupied expensive land in the heart of the large cities—locations ideal for modern housing developments and trade and entertainment centers. The redevelopment of these areas could be financed on a purely commercial basis, and sufficient funds could then be made available for relocating residents in new homes and in healthier and less crowded environments.

I put out a pamphlet called *A Plan for Slum Clearance and Redevelopment* with the help of senior workers in the ministry and of my old friend from British army days, Baruch Gross, who threw himself wholeheartedly into the task. The pamphlet was distributed among members of the Knesset, city mayors, builders, and building engineers. Its publication prepared the ground for a proposed law for slum clearance and redevelopment, which I submitted to the government in November 1963. Getting the government to agree to put the law before the Knesset was not achieved without difficulty.

After a long talk with Eshkol, I was able to get his backing for the plan. However, when I revealed to him that Sapir was opposed to the project, Eshkol said to me, "Well, you're both from Kfar Saba, so why don't you fight for your opinion?" I then brought the plan up for consideration at a meeting of the party's Central Committee where, because Sapir did not participate, it was accepted unanimously. But I still had a struggle ahead of me.

When the Mapai faction in the Knesset met to discuss the project, Sapir opposed it on the grounds that we would never find investors and the government would, in the end, have to shoulder all the costs. I replied that the mere submission of the proposal would not oblige the government to finance the scheme by any specific date. There was also flack from other members of the government. Ministers have the right to submit their objections to a proposed law before it is introduced for debate in the Knesset, and some of my colleagues did exactly that. Nevertheless, I succeeded in bringing over the members of the government to my view, and on the April 5, 1965, I finally was able to submit my proposal to the Knesset, where it was passed. Unfortunately, because of the split in Mapai which occurred shortly afterwards, I was unable to put the project into operation.

Visit to Turkey

In May 1964 I was host to the Turkish minister of housing, an intelligent man with an excellent command of English; he was also a noted novelist. Because of the sensitivity of our relations with Turkey, the Foreign Ministry had requested that our reception of the visitor be restrained. I played host to our Turkish guest as best I could and took him to see our achievements. When we parted, he thanked me for my efforts and promised to send me an official invitation for a return visit to his country. To the surprise of our foreign minister, Golda Meir, the invitation actually arrived, making me the first Israeli minister to be invited to visit a neighboring Moslem country.

When I set off for Ankara in November 1964, I was accompanied by Yosef Sleifer, one of our best experts in the Department of Housing. On arrival we were warmly greeted by our chargé d'affaires in Turkey, Moshe Sasson, the son of the former minister of posts, and were taken by him to our rooms in one of Ankara's luxury hotels. I noticed that, contrary to the rules of protocol, our flag was absent from the hotel entrance; on my request our national colors were put up. It was the first time the flag of Israel was publicly shown in Turkey. Sasson informed me that the display of our flag was made possible by the absence of the Turkish foreign minister, who was then on a visit to the Soviet Union.

During my meeting with my opposite number in Turkey and with senior officials in the Turkish Housing Ministry, we discussed the country's housing problems. In the course of our discussion we agreed that a Turkish mission would be sent to Israel to learn from our experience in the field.

I had a particularly interesting meeting with the Turkish prime minister, the aging Ismet Inönü— a statesman with strong pro-Western leanings and suspicions of the Arab countries. Inönü inquired after Ben-Gurion's health and asked me to tell Ben-Gurion not to give in to Arab demands. He told me that Turkey was using its influence on Pakistan to convince that country to establish ties with Israel and that he believed that the day would come when Israel would be an active partner in an alliance of pro-Western countries in our region against the Soviet Union. As he conceived it, the alliance would include, in addition to Turkey and Israel, Pakistan and Iran. When I reported on Inönü's views to Ben-Gurion, he was skeptical and observed that although this might be the position of the Turkish prime minister, it was not that of the Turkish government, which was trying to preserve a balanced policy toward Israel and the Arab states. It should also be noted that on the day before we left Turkey, the Turkish foreign minister, having just returned from Moscow, announced that his country and the Soviet Union had a common interest in strengthening ties, in particular because of the Cyprus issue. Nevertheless, two weeks later an official delegation did arrive in Israel from Turkey, and an agreement for the exchange of technical and scientific information was signed between the two countries.

Transit Camps

In the summer of 1964, during the visit of a United Jewish Appeal (UJA) fact-finding mission, Arye Pincus, who was treasurer of the Jewish Agency, contended that there were twenty thousand people in Israel still living in transit camps. He said that unless the UJA could come up with enough money, Israel would have no choice but to continue to house new immigrants in the camps. Only a short time before, I had reported to the Knesset that the transit camps would soon cease to exist and that no more than about three thousand people remained in them. The disparity in our figures and predictions was hardly insignificant, and a sharp dispute developed between Pincus and myself.

After the newspapers got hold of the story, I was asked to explain the contradictions. I insisted that the facts I had given in the Knesset, which had been reported as well by the finance minister, were correct. I added that whatever amount of money the UJA managed to collect, the government had no intention of establishing transit camps again unless there was an unexpected wave of immigration. To my regret, Moshe Sharett, who was then chairman of the board of directors of the Jewish Agency, found it necessary to intervene in the controversy. Sharett said he hoped that my announcement about closing down the transit camps was not made on behalf of the government, since he could not believe that the government of Israel was ready to relinquish the aid being given by Jews abroad to house new settlers. I had to repeat my statement, this time making it clear that I was speaking for the government. Although the newspapers still devoted space to the story, most of them accepted the statistics put out by the government, and the matter was essentially at an end.

At the heart of the controversy is the publicity approach followed by the leadership of UJA. Most of them seemed to believe that the more wretched the situation in Israel appeared, the easier would be the task of collecting contributions. My own experience in canvasing for contributions, which goes back to 1946, has taught me that this attitude is fundamentally in error. Any appeal calculated to inspire tears may get its pennyworth of alms, but tears have a way of drying up quickly, as do contributions, once the pity that called them forth is forgotten. More abiding results are obtained by a balanced account of our problems and achievements; in this way contributions are made out of a desire to take active part in the Zionist enterprise—in both its struggles and its triumphs. I fear that the beggar's view still dominates among those who collect money for Israel.

A case in point occurred during a tour I made on behalf of the Histadrut in North America in 1952. At a dinner given by the UJA in Boston, an Israeli representative who had spent some years in the United States and fallen victim to the prevailing attitude equating donations to Israel with charity rose to speak. He spoke to his audience accusingly, reminding them that while they were enjoying their feast, there were still hungry children in Israel who had never tasted milk in their lives. When my turn came to speak, I dismissed the time-worn story of hungry children as fiction and urged my hearers not to take the representative's tale of woe to heart. "Take a look at me," I said, "someone just arrived from Israel. Do I look like skin and bones to you?"

In February 1965 I presented the proposed Housing Ministry budget for 1965–66. I reported (with some pride, I admit) that in the preceding year more than thirty thousand dwellings had been built for immigrants and old settlers and that 60 percent of these had been put up in development towns. The average size of apartments had increased to 177 square feet, and there had been an attendant improvement in apartment construction and neighborhood development. In addition, Amidar had added about sixteen hundred rooms to existing apartments and moved close to one thousand families into larger quarters. The Bank Hatfahot, which had just gotten started and had become the major mortgage bank in Israel, was financing most of the projects for slum rehabilitation and housing for the underprivileged. I was also able to report the start of construction of a Bedouin housing project near Beersheba and the setting aside of 25 million liroth for construction in agricultural settlements. It was a record of achievements we could all be proud of.

I enjoyed my work in the Housing Ministry. During the three years I served there, I introduced reforms in its organization and created close working relations between myself as minister and the senior staff. The initiative and momentum that resulted were felt particularly during the weekly meetings I held with the ministry's top officials. It was with real regret that I left the ministry only a few months after having presented its annual budget and seen passage in the Knesset of the Slum Clearance and Rehabilitation Bill. I found myself forced to resign from the government in the wake of the split in the Mapai party.

28

The Lavon Affair Again, 1964

The years between 1962 and 1965 were among the best and most creative in my career. I had immersed myself completely in my work as minister of housing and development, concentrating my efforts in particular on the social advancement of the common man in Israel and the broadening of the country's economic base.

Although hardly a ripple could be discerned on the surface of the country's political life, there were stirrings underneath. After the formation of the new government in 1961, the ghosts of the secret service failure in Egypt in 1954—"that horror of Goshen," as Sharett called it—returned to haunt us. The assistant legal adviser of the Ministry of Defense, Mrs. Herzliya Ron, began to collect material on the incident, and before she left for Washington with her husband, she handed over the information she had found to Hagai Eshed, a journalist who enjoyed Ben-Gurion's confidence. In 1962 Eshed took a leave of absence without pay from his paper, *Davar*, and signed a special contract with the Defense Ministry whereby he took on the job of collecting information on the 1954 scandal and its revival in 1960.

It was a sign of Ben-Gurion's growing disquietude over the Lavon Affair in both of its successive manifestations. In addition, Ben-Gurion's relations with party veterans took a turn for the worse, and he was finding himself increasingly isolated on matters of policy. His differences with the older leadership in Mapai reached their peak over the incident involving German rocket scientists working in Egypt, when Golda Meir openly sided with Security Chief Isser Harel, who had made a public issue of the matter against the judgment of the prime minister and minister of defense. Ziama Aran and Pinhas Sapir, too, had disappointed Ben-Gurion by refusing to support him on this and a number of other issues. He was also still upset over the decision of the 1960 Commission of Seven to clear Lavon of responsibility in the security failure.

Then the break came. On June 16, 1963, Ben-Gurion resigned from the government, and Eshkol took over as prime minister and minister of defense. News of Ben-Gurion's resignation reached me in New York. I received two telephone calls from Israel bringing me up to date: Teddy Kollek gave me a rundown on events, and Abba Khoushi told me about how he and a group of party members had failed in an eleventh-hour effort to prevent Ben-Gurion's resignation. He was barely able to get Ben-Gurion to agree to remain a member of the Knesset. Both of them felt that even though there was no chance of changing Ben-Gurion's mind, it would be best if I came home. I cancelled all my remaining appearances for the Independence Loan in the United States and boarded the first plane for Lydda Airport.

Broken in Spirit

I was not surprised by Ben-Gurion's move. For a long time I had watched his relations with the party's veteran leadership deteriorate. The old-timers worked to bring the "Age of Ben-Gurion" to an end, and the members of the Cooperative and their adherents tried to impose their brand of politics on the Old Man—a politics based primarily on negation and aimed to prevent the rise to power of Dayan, Peres, and their supporters.

I remembered my last meetings with Ben-Gurion, during which he had seemed depressed and irritable. He had poured out his anger especially on the office of the prime ministry: "It's just a dirty marketplace," he would way, "don't ever become prime minister!" Paula was keenly aware of the change in her husband. She asked me to do my best to persuade him to be head of state and leave philosophy alone and complained that all he was interested in was reading, study, and contemplation, which left him with hardly any mental energy for running affairs of state. Even Dr. Moshe Feldenkreiz, Ben-Gurion's personal physician, whom Paula described as a "miracle worker," was unable to raise Ben-Gurion's spirits. Paula would change Ben-Gurion's sleeping tablets from time to time, hoping that in this way they would take effect.

When I visited Ben-Gurion at his home in Tel Aviv the day after my return, I found him in an unexpectedly good mood. He began telling me about his plans and revealed that he had definitely decided to retire to Sde-Boker and write. He seemed relieved that the whole business was over with and that he had gotten free at last from a painful situation. Henceforth he would devote himself entirely to what gave him the most pleasure—reading and writing.

I tried to get him to explain why it was that when he had resigned the first time, at the end of 1953, he had made it his business to see to a change of personnel in the government by appointing Lavon minister of defense and Dayan chief of staff, whereas now he was leaving the field open for anyone to take over. Ben-Gurion had no satisfactory answer, allthough the situation was likely to have a significant effect on political developments. My impression was that Ben-Gurion only wished to live at peace with the political coalition, so to speak, between the veterans and the Youth Wing—an alliance then still in force in both the party and the government. He may also have deluded himself into believing that Eshkol's government would meet him halfway on the Lavon Affair, which had once again begun to bother him.

I began to wonder at the time if Ben-Gurion had ever had the intention to replace anyone at all in the leadership. In this regard, my own case seemed to be instructive. The party veterans had not been keen on my joining the government, but Ben-Gurion was determined to have me in, and my appointment was accepted without anyone daring to oppose it. I had been appointed minister without portfolio, so no one was put out of office to make way for me.

Eshkol, however, took a different approach. He had made a number of changes in his government which favored the veteran leadership. Ziama Aran was minister of education and culture once more, and Abba Eban, who was free of suspicion of being rebellious, was appointed deputy prime minister. Dayan was minister of agriculture, but he was unhappy about the distribution of offices in the government and talked about resigning. What he found particularly irksome was that Sapir, a member of the Cooperative and now serving as minister of commerce and industry, was holding onto authority in matters that would have seemed more properly to belong to the minister of agriculture's domain, such as the import of food and export of agricultural products and the determination of levels of subsidy for agricultural produce. The Youth Wing, whose chief representative, Dayan, was in the government, wished Dayan to have a say in determining policies in foreign affairs and defense—something Eshkol was none too anxious to agree to. Still, Dayan's threats to resign were not unequivocal. From my talks with him, I gathered if he could be satisfied on at least some points in his disagreements with other members of the government, he would remain in office. I decided to try to help, even though my relations with Eshkol, though good, tended at times to be a little one sided, as I had occasion to point out to Ben-Gurion.

One summer evening I took the liberty of dropping in at Eshkol's home. He was reading a book when I came in, and when he looked up he had a mischievous twinkle in his eye. "Well, what have you to say about your Abu Jilda?" he asked. (Abu Jilda was a daring ringleader of one of the Arab bands in the 1936–39 riots, whose name Eshkol had whimsically attached to Dayan.) I responded by telling him that Dayan's demands were exactly what I had come to talk about. After a brief chat, I found that the veteran leadership was not really interested in seeing Dayan leave the government. That, at least, was a good starting point. In September 1963, Dayan, Sapir, and I met in Sapir's office in Tel Aviv, and in only half an hour, we were able to come to an agreement on the problems outstanding between the two men. Dayan then officially notified Eshkol of his intention to remain in the government.

A short time after Ben-Gurion resigned, he received the material gathered by Hagai Eshed, which contained a good deal of information on the Lavon Affair both in its original guise and in its 1960 revival. Ben Gurion had also accumulated a file of his own on the subject, gathered from party sources. As he studied the material, he became increasingly engrossed in the case. His friend Aharon Hoter-Yishai, a jurist and former judge advocate-general, and the then

Chief Military Prosecutor, Yitzhak Tunik, volunteered to go through the evidence and make an assessment—which turned out to be highly critical. In particular they took exception to the work of the Commission of Seven, which they felt had done a woefully incomplete job. When the results of Hoter-Yishai and Tunik's review, which had taken them several months to complete, were received by Ben-Gurion, he became incensed at what he felt was a "perversion of the law." He made up his mind to demand from Eshkol that the case be put under legal investigation once more.

When I came to see Ben-Gurion in Sde-Boker, I tried to convince him to leave the case alone, or at least to give Eshkol time to get used to his new office before dropping this hornet's nest into his lap. Ben-Gurion allowed himself to be persuaded by the last argument and promised to let the matter rest for a few months. He had his doubts, though that the government would agree to his demand to appoint a new commission of inquiry.

During the conversation, I had the impression that Ben-Gurion was becoming increasingly convinced that a conspiracy was being formed against him and that his enemies were using Lavon for the purpose. Ben-Gurion did not say this explicitly, but he did repeatedly ask me about the real opinion of the party leadership about Lavon, and he seemed unable to understand how they could have behaved as they had toward him in 1960. He once again analyzed the characters and behavior of the party comrades who had turned their backs on him. Was it possible that Eshkol, who had been in agreement with him for all those years, now rejected a governmental approach? And what of Golda and Ziama—especially Ziama, that man of principle and moral probity? Didn't he see the terrible injustice in what was being done? But maybe the whole thing was a conspiracy born of fear, fear that Ben-Gurion was going to replace the party old-timers with his young followers—to get rid of the veteran founders of the movement? On the last point, I suspect that Ben-Gurion may have heard Ziama Aran's fanciful comparison of his own situation to that of old Eskimos being abandoned in the snow to die. It did not seem to occur to Ben-Gurion that this was exactly what was being done to him, except that the setting was the desert rather than the arctic tundra.

Ben-Gurion was unable to come to terms with what was going on, and when I spoke with him in late February 1964, he reminded me of a similar situation that had occurred in the past, but he was unable to find the relevant documents at that particular moment. However, Ben-Gurion was not in the habit of forgetting, and a little later I received from him a letter dated June 20, 1964:

> My dear Almogi,
>   After you rode off, I found in the notebook I was holding before you left my room the things I was looking for and wanted to read to you. Here they are:
>
>> Tuesday, July 13, 1954
>> In the afternoon Dayan, Luz and Namir arrived. It wasn't the Ein-Harod dispute that brought them. They came to ask me to return. The initiative is Dayan's, but there were consulta-

tions with many party colleagues. Namir claimed: no sense of security among the public. No one knows what the security situation is, what our situation in the world is. No authority. Although his fears at the time I resigned proved false—they are now about to become worse. How will they go to the polls? No peace internally. Members of all sorts of *landsmanshafts* are already fighting for position. According to [Israel] Yeshayahu there is a wave of xenophobia among Yemenites in Rosh-Ha'ayin. It may spread.
Dayan and Luz added more of the same.

And from what I wrote in my journal later, some passages:

The external situation doesn't worry me so much—everything depends on the situation internally. . . . [elipses in the original]. The renewal must come from the young. . . . The earlier way of working is not suitable to new conditions. All of the contexts are becoming fossilized. . . . We won't be saved by the State. Volunteering from within is needed—it is about to succeed. I won't return. I went back to Sde-Boker—and here I'll stay.

Yours,

D. Ben-Gurion

P.S. You can show what I wrote to Luz, Namir, and Dayan.

Ben-Gurion rushed to finish the material which had been collected by Hagai Eshed and studied for its legal aspects by Hoter-Yishai and Tunik. When he was unsuccessful in getting Eshkol to accept the material and put his support behind the appointment of a legal commission of inquiry, Ben-Gurion went to Jerusalem and on October 22, 1964, handed over to Minister of Justice Dov Joseph a very thick file, containing both the original documents and his own analysis of the Lavon Affair.

About five weeks later Dov Joseph submitted to the government a "Proposal of the Minister of Justice for a Government Decision," based on a review of the material by Attorney General Moshe Ben-Zeev. Although the justice minister did not support Ben-Gurion's demand for the appointment of a commission of judges to review the findings of the Commission of Seven, he nevertheless recommended: "There is reason to appoint a commission of inquiry for the purpose of making a full, inclusive and exhaustive investigation of the . . . affair, and of determining who was responsible for it; if it was the Defense Minister at the time, or someone else who did or did not give the order to have it carried out, and if the senior officer had acted in it or not on his own initiative and without the knowledge of the Minister."

The attorney general's opinion and the recommendation of the minister of justice represented an important moral victory for Ben-Gurion, and we all tried to convince him to consider the matter closed with that; after all, Dr. Dov Joseph's proposal made it clear that if the commission of inquiry were to reject the findings of the Commission of Seven, Ben-Gurion's demands would have been fully met. Although Ben-Gurion was encouraged by the position taken by

Dov Joseph and Moshe Ben-Zeev, he was not satisfied with their having re-
stricted themselves to proposing an investigation merely of the security scandal
of 1954; Ben-Gurion was asking for an investigation of the 1960 events connected with it—specifically the work and findings of the Commission of Seven,
which had come under heavy fire in the attorney general's report. Ben-Gurion
rejected, as well, a proposal published by MK Haim Zadok in *Davar* that the
government merely put on record the findings of the attorney general respecting the Commission of Seven and consider the affair closed. I think that had
Zadok's suggestion been adopted, it would have provided Ben-Gurion with an
honorable way out and might even have allowed him to conclude the controversy
with a moral victory.

But things took a different turn. The opinions of leading jurists concerning
both the 1954 and 1960 events helped ease Ben-Gurion's isolation among party
workers, and on the basis of some of those legal opinions I was inclined to believe
that at some stage in the developments there might even be a chance for the
investigation of at least the 1954 scandal to be reopened. I had a lot of talks with
both Ben-Gurion and Eshkol on the matter, and there was also a group of Mapai
MKs who went to see Eshkol in order to pressure him to give in to Ben-Gurion's
demand. Concurrently I tried, with the help of Hoter-Yishai and Tunik, to
persuade Ben-Gurion to be content, under the circumstances, with the appointment of a commission of inquiry that would investigate only the 1954 episode. A
group of party workers from the Bloc, the Haifa branch, and the Youth Wing
leadership drew up a proposal for a party decision supporting Ben-Gurion on
this point and calling for the appointment of a judicial commission of inquiry
into the 1954 security scandal. Since Eshkol had declared that under no circumstance would he agree to the appointment of a commission to investigate the
findings of the Commission of Seven, there could be no question of a review of
the Lavon Affair in its 1960 manifestation.

At last, on Friday, December 16, 1964, I got Ben-Gurion's agreement to an
investigation that would be limited to the events of 1954. I later succeeded in
getting Eshkol to agree "to appoint a commission of enquiry for the purpose of
making a full, inclusive and exhaustive investigation of the . . . affair, and of
determining who was responsible for it," as proposed by Dov Joseph. When the
party secretariat met on the same day, Ben-Gurion announced, "The decision of
a commission of judges will bring the matter to a close."

Hearing Ben-Gurion's explicit statement I was exhilarated and left the meeting to have a talk with Eshkol. To my surprise he, too, spoke unequivocally:
"Yosef, do everything you can when you talk to the Troika; if the Cooperative
does not get in the way, maybe we've gotten somewhere."

I recall that conversation with Eshkol very well. He spoke quietly and with
restraint, and it seemed to me that his thoughts were elsewhere, fixed on a power
absent at the time but still capable of determining the outcome of things. It was
the first time he had fully admitted his dependence on the Cooperative, and it
was obvious he now wanted to be free of them and of the whole nightmare of
their struggle with Ben-Gurion.

Immediately after the meeting of the party secretariat, I told Shraga Nezer about my talk with Eshkol and asked him to get the Bloc to put pressure on Sapir and Golda, who had not been present at the meeting. I felt particularly encouraged by the apparent willingness to go along with a commission of inquiry revealed by Ziama Aran, the third partner in the Cooperative; this, at least, was the impression I had from one of the questions he had asked Ben-Gurion during the meeting.

That evening I was informed of the decision to establish a three-man committee consisting of Dov Joseph, Party Secretary Reuben Barakat, and Yitzhak Navon, which would prepare a letter of authorization for a commission of inquiry to investigate the 1954 episode, but not events in 1960 or the findings of the Commission of Seven. I was greatly relieved at the news, as were many others. It appeared that the rift between Eshkol and Ben-Gurion had finally been healed. By the time I appeared at a meeting of Mapai in Kiryat Haim, the agreement was reached, and morale in the party was evidently on the rise.

My exhilaration was suddenly cut short by bad news from Shraga Nezer: The agreement was off. There was a meeting of the secretariat scheduled for the next evening, Saturday night, in Jerusalem.

What had happened in the five short hours that had passed between the time Eshkol had given his blessing to the agreement and his cancellation of it? None of us could figure it out. My phone did not stop ringing until well into the night—everyone kept asking why, how this sudden change for the worse. Speculation was rampant. There were even those who said that Eshkol's wife Miriam, whom he had recently married, had been the one responsible for Eshkol's sudden about-face. I did not know her well, although I had frequently availed myself of her services while she was librarian in the Knesset library, but it seemed unlikely that she should have been the only one influencing Eshkol to change his mind.

Arieh Tsimouki, the Jerusalem reporter for *Yedioth Ahronot,* seemed nearer the mark; his sources were usually dependable. He wrote:

> After the compromise had been reached, there appeared on the ministers' platform Golda Meir, Sapir and Aran, who announced unequivocally that since it had been decided to appoint a commission of inquiry, they would resign. Moshe Sharett applied his whole moral and personal weight in the effort to avoid the appointment of a commission, and the leaders of Ahdut Avoda put pressure on the Prime Minister to oppose a commission of inquiry.

Tsimouki then added:

> There is no denying the role played in this campaign by the Prime Minister's wife, who was revealed as a woman of keen political sense.

The Price of Justice

The fact was that when Eshkol returned to Jerusalem after the meeting of the party secretariat on Friday, he had come under enormous pressure. Moshe Sharett would perhaps have agreed to an appointment of a commission of inquiry to review the findings of the commission of Seven, with which he was unconnected; but he was unalterably opposed to an investigation of the security scandal of 1954. Such an investigation would have laid bare the unfortunate state of affairs then in the government, where Sharett had failed to impose his control and all the members did as they pleased without bothering to coordinate their efforts. The revelation that a partisan ministerial committee for defense existed during his administration would have also hurt Sharett's reputation; it was what lay behind Sharett's warning about creating a "mass grave."

For her part, Golda felt that the appointment of a commission of inquiry, even if limited in its work to the 1954 episode, would mean one thing only—a triumph for Ben-Gurion. That, she thought, would inevitably lead to more party workers joining former Minister of Justice Pinhas Rosen in saying, as he had said early in the game, "What is shocking and dangerous is that in the final reckoning Ben-Gurion is always right." To Golda, the appointment of a judicial commission of inquiry would have been tantamount to conceding once and for all that Ben-Gurion had been fighting all along for the principle of justice and that he was now being backed by leading jurists whose objectivity was beyond doubt. Moreover, Ben-Gurion's comeback would seriously undermine the possibility of building an alliance with Ahdut Avoda, which had never forgiven Ben-Gurion for the split in Kfar Vitkin, and forgave him even less for having disbanded the Palmah. Finally, the appointment of a commission of inquiry would strengthen Ben-Gurion and his young protégés, and Eshkol—who was just beginning to show signs of independence—would find himself once more standing in the giant shadow of Ben-Gurion. This was clearly also the opinion of the other two members of the Troika, Sapir and Aran, who feared that Eshkol's "capitulation" to Ben-Gurion would lead to Ahdut Avoda pulling out of the government. Without Ahdut Avoda, there was no possibility of forming the government, so Mapai would return to the untenable situation it had been in before its coalition with Ahdut Avoda.

The meeting of the party secretariat on Saturday night, December 12, at Elisheva House in Jerusalem, was one of the saddest I have ever attended. It was the first time, as I said during the meeting, that party members showed no desire to resolve an internal conflict. The result of the meeting was inconclusive: by a vote of 124 to 60 Eshkol received the right to make a final decision.

Eshkol tried to prevent discussion by the government (whose composition remained unaltered) of the justice minister's recommendation. The reasons he gave were purely formal—that because only two government ministers, Dov Joseph and myself, supported the justice minister's proposal, there was no need to put the question to a vote, since the rules require the support of at least four ministers.

At this I asked for the floor and said:

Since the party has left it up to government ministers who are party members to decide on their own conscience what their position would be in regard to the recommendations of the justice minister, I wish to make my opinion known and to give my reasons for supporting Dr. Dov Joseph's proposals. I support the opinion of the attorney general and the proposals of the minister of justice, who was not involved in the affair, neither in 1954 nor in 1960, and whose motives are beyond suspicion.

I then made some references to rumors of goings-on other than the Lavon Affair, and Eshkol became enraged: "That kind of argument hasn't been heard here before," he said, "What is it we are supposed to know—what went on in the streets?"

I responded:

I will not speak of what went on in the streets. And by the way, I heard that myself from the minister of transport, Israel Bar-Yehuda, who claimed there is not only this affair, but others as well. I can certainly rely on a specific opinion heard within the government. Those who say this affair is not easy to investigate because there were also other incidents do not themselves perhaps realize that by saying this they are adding fuel to the fire. Because if there were other incidents, this only adds force to the demand, and to our obligation, to investigate the affair we have before us.

Amid all the noise being made in the street, one fact has been lost sight of— that the affair was not of David Ben-Gurion's making but Pinhas Lavon's, who maligned the defense system. The statements are recorded and signed in the minutes of the Knesset Committee of Foreign Affairs and Defense. The Commission of Seven in no way considered, stated reservations about, or responded to those smears of Pinhas Lavon—the man who created the affair.

No doubt political interests are legitimate, but David Ben-Gurion, the citizen, is no mere object of political enmity—he was prime minister and defense minister for close to fifteen years. And if David Ben-Gurion, the citizen, is worthy of any respect at all, it should at least be given him for his achievements up to 1960; and if he is making a demand for a just verdict, and that demand is being supported by noted jurists, how can we explain our refusal to appoint a commission, such as he is demanding, to review the matter.

I know that there are two slogans making the rounds in the street: "We've had enough," and "The people are tired." Both these statements have led to wild statements that give off the stench of a political lynching. Words of that sort will one day set the monster against his makers, and none of us will emerge unscathed.

If it be decided not to appoint a commission of inquiry, there will certainly be none. But the real significance of such a decision is that the affair will continue running out of control in public and will do us all further damage. The choice is this: either we get the affair out of the limelight and give it over to three or five legal experts, and so finish with it once and for all—or it will continue to harry us for years to come. In order to put an end to the affair, we must adopt the proposal of the minister of justice. Ben-Gurion, I, all of us deserve for this to be done.

My speech, needless to say, did not change Levi Eshkol's mind.

With Julius Ginsburg and B. Jacobson on a visit to the office of M. Feinclas, a trade-union leader in Chicago, 1953.

A gathering of members of the Hoffman family living in Dallas and Houston, Texas. From left to right, Leo Hoffman, Shalom Omri, Sarah Hoffman, unidentified, Gloria Hoffman, Harold Hoffman, Maurice Hoffman, Virginia Hoffman.

Four generations of the Hoffman family. *Left to right:* mother, Sarah; son, Morris; grandson, Charles, with great-grandaughter, Ronit-Leah. Charles Hoffman, a Zionist, is one of the young Hoffmans who came to Israel. He and his wife, Annie, established a family in Jerusalem. Charles is now an editor on the *Jerusalem Post.*

At the ORT convention in Israel. On the dais, to Almogi's left, Teddy Kollek, mayor of Jerusalem; to Almogi's right, General Chaim Herzog and Yigal Allon, respectively Israel's ambassador to the UN and deputy prime minister at the time.

At the opening of the academic year of the University of Tel Aviv in 1969. On Almogi's left, A. Doron, then director-general of the university; the late Arye Pincus, then chairman of the Jewish Agency; David Horowitz, president of the Israel National Bank. On Almogi's right, Dr. George Weiss, then president of the university, and David Ben-Gurion.

At the International Conference on Technology and Human Development, Jerusalem, 1969. On the dais, the chief representatives of various countries.

Almogi handing over the Ministry of Labor to Yitzhak Rabin.

Almogi receiving guests at a cocktail party for delegates of the ILO convention in 1969. Among the guests, American labor leaders George Meany and Jacob Potofsky.

In a gesture of friendship, President of Israel Yitzhak Ben-Zvi invited Almogi's younger son, Zvika, to repeat the ceremony of his bar mitzvah, 1961.

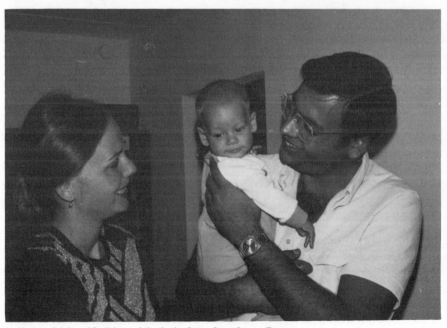

Avika and his wife Liat with their first daughter, Renat.

The Hoffman family observing Hanukkah. *Left to right:* Saul Hoffman; Frieda Hoffman; David Hoffman; Francis Hoffman; Sol Edell; Dr. Mark Levy and Lisa Levy, daughter of Saul and Frieda Hoffman, with the Hoffman grandchildren Jo and Robie.

Almogi's older son, Yoram, receiving his Ph.D. at the Technion, Haifa. With him are, *left to right:* Mindi, who was among the first Hoffman children to come to Israel, where she married Jacob Swissa and gave birth to two children; Almogi and his wife, Shifra; Uta, Yoram's wife; Yoram's younger brother, Zvika; Uta's parents Mr. and Mrs. Blauerstein; and Yoram's children.

Greeting Marc Chagall in Haifa, 1958. *Left to right:* Z. Aran, minister of education; Dr. J. Pomoroff, chairman of the Marc Chagall Painting Center; and a representative of the Haifa Art Association.

Gordon Zwicker, a childhood family friend, from whom Almogi parted in Poland in 1929, when he set out for Israel and Zwicker went to Canada.

29
My Resignation; Mapai Splits

The Eshkol government remained in power, and its makeup did not change. I continued in office as Minister of Housing and Development, but my relation to it was not as before. I was in a moral quandary. I had no doubt that justice was on the side of Ben-Gurion in the all-out war being waged against him by the political parties, the newspapers, and all those in whose political interests it was to get rid of him. The sole sin that could be charged to Ben-Gurion, who was then seventy-nine, was that he had not been sufficiently flexible to make his peace with a reality he was unable to change. His opponents had made a cold calculation. They had concluded that the old, isolated man had few favors to bestow on them, and so they made light of what he was fighting for and left his side, although they were perfectly aware that he was right. As for myself, I had no illusions about there being any chance that Ben-Gurion's battle could be won. It was almost a certainty that his was a lost cause. After giving the matter a great deal of thought, I realized that I had no choice but to obey the call of my conscience, and I joined the small minority that remained loyal to Ben-Gurion. Once I had done so, I did it wholly, and as my first task, I joined in helping to prepare for the Twentieth Party Congress, which promised to be decisive: not only would the issue of Mapai's unity be decided there, but also what the political structure of the country would look like at a particularly critical time in our history.

I did not direct my activities especially against Eshkol, who was a man of many accomplishments and merited respect independent of his office. I did not share Ben-Gurion's opinion that Eshkol was almost solely responsible for the decline in the nation and the party. It was clear to me that it was not Eshkol who was to blame, but the highly personal nature of the political ambience in which he moved. I continued meeting with him, and in the course of our talks, I became more and more convinced that if things were up to him, he would find a way of resolving differences with Ben-Gurion. Eshkol, however, was surrounded by old associates intent on preventing the advancement of one set of young party members who saw themselves as Ben-Gurion's protégés; they were also intent on advancing other young party workers whom they found more amenable. In our talks, Eshkol would chide me that I, of all all people—the man who had coined the phrase "resign from the affair"—was abetting the one person who was bent on reviving the business. When I insisted that we had to find a compromise, Eshkol answered that it was, in fact, Ben-Gurion who had advised him when he handed over the government to him not to make a habit of compromise.

The veteran leadership in the party began gathering its forces for the confrontation, which would take place in mid-February 1965. Most of the Bloc lined up squarely behind Eshkol; other young party workers, too, such as Abba Eban, Avraham Offer, Asher Yadlin, and Lyova Eliav joined the old guard, as did the party branches of Jerusalem, Tel Aviv, the Moshav settlements, and the development towns.

By contrast, minority headquarters was undermanned. Dayan was busy writing his book on the Sinai Campaign and was still undecided about joining our camp. Peres was Eshkol's deputy in the Defense Ministry and was therefore unable to work with us full time. We made Joseph Yizraeli minority chairman. We tried to put out printed material. However, Nahman Tamir, who had been in charge of printed campaign publicity in the 1959 elections, said he could not run off printed matter for us without money, and money was what we were short of. We set to work as best we could.

Weak Minority, Secure Leadership

I continued working for the minority, which was revealing appalling weakness. Our numbers kept shrinking. At a meeting in Beersheba, for example, I was shocked to discover that in a city which had a reputation of being strongly Ben-Gurionist there were practically no supporters of Ben-Gurion left. Even in Haifa, the minority stronghold, we were beginning to lose support; there, Abba Khoushi, who was still backing Ben-Gurion, would soon leave us. As the date of the congress drew near, my meetings with Youth Wing headquarters under the leadership of Elhanan Yishai grew more frequent; every bit of strength we could pick up counted now.

When, finally, we did appear at Culture House in Tel Aviv for the party congress, we did so without illusions; we knew that we had no chance of obtaining a majority in favor of our demand for a judicial commission of inquiry to review the Lavon Affair. If any of us harbored a faint hope of at least a sympathetic response to our cause, it was crushed in the congress's standing committee, where representation was based on relative strength in the congress.

At the start, the congress received Ben-Gurion, Dayan, and Peres with applause, just as it had Eshkol, Golda, and Aran. Then it turned on Ben-Gurion with a vengeance. Moshe Sharett, who had come to the congress in a wheelchair, made a vigorous speech against Ben-Gurion:

A leader cannot subjugate the movement, stop it from thinking, merely by some aristocratic right. I hope and believe that the party will close ranks on this point, and once and for all shake off this nightmare, exorcise this evil spirit."

Golda, too, spoke accusingly:

Why didn't you resign as soon as the Commission of Seven came into being? Why did you appoint Pinhas Lavon? Why didn't you reveal the secret to us that you would demand an investigation when you resigned and appointed Eshkol to take your place?

Golda and Sharett's speeches, which gave the meeting that evening the name "night of the knives," so deeply wounded Ben-Gurion that he walked out of the congress not to return, even when the vote was taken.

We knew we would not get a majority in the congress. The pessimists among us reckoned on 30 percent of the vote, the optimists 40. When we received 40 percent of the ballot on the issue of the Lavon Affair, we considered it a triumph. We also thought it a coup for the congress to have been forced to discuss the Lavon Affair and pass a resolution that "the question of the appointment of a commission of inquiry is handed over to our party members in the government solely for them to decide."

We were in high spirits, and four of us—Peres, Surkis, Navon, and myself—went to Ben-Gurion's home on Keren Kayemet Avenue to tell him the good news. Ben-Gurion did not share our enthusiasm: "Victory means a majority," he said. He was still brooding over the attacks made on him by the party leadership on the "night of the knives." We, however, felt encouraged by the results of the voting; in our innocence we were convinced that the party leaders would want to avoid deepening the rift in the party by risking the alienation of close to half the membership. We quickly learnt how wrong we were. The results of the voting had put party leaders on the alert, and they immediately mustered all their forces against us.

After the congress, the division in the party became even more sharply drawn, with two distinct camps having formed: on one side there was Eshkol's camp, which enjoyed the favor of the press; on the other was ours, consisting of Ben-Gurion and his followers—of whom there were fewer and fewer as time went on. Many among us were beginning to reconsider their loyalties in the light of personal advantage, and the movement from our camp to that of our opponents began to look like a headlong flight. Those who were leaving us knew that we were in the right but chose to preserve their political futures. Moreover, for all our criticism of Eshkol, we had not yet put forward a candidate of our own for the prime ministry. In this regard, I have the feeling that had Ben-Gurion announced his intention to return as prime minister, we could have obtained a majority, if only a slim one. As it was, in the absence of any real contender other than Eshkol, about a hundred delegates to the congress who were sympathetic to us decided to cross over to the other side. It was they who tipped the scales in favor of Eshkol.

No Quarter

Minority headquarters was made up of representatives of the Youth Wing, mayors of some of the development towns, part of the agricultural-settlement movement, and some of the party's old hands. We were not happy about the prospect of a split, and we met a number of times with Eshkol and Barakat to try to find some way of avoiding a break. To no avail. The party had decided on an all-out struggle against the minority and made no effort to reach a compromise with us. The majority began to reduce our representation in the party organizations to a point well below our actual strength at the congress.

As the party leadership hardened its position, Ben-Gurion, too, took the offensive, making Eshkol his particular target. In characterizing Eshkol, Ben-Gurion said of him: "On the one hand he does not have the qualities that are appropriate to be a prime minister, and on the other he has qualities that are inappropriate in a prime minister." The rift widened, and in a last-ditch effort to patch up differences Shraga Nezer and Abba Khoushi came up with the offer of giving the top spot on the party's Knesset list to Ben-Gurion "without hurting party members who are leading the movement and the nation." Nezer invited Ben-Gurion to the party's branch office in Tel Aviv for a meeting to make the offer official, but Ben-Gurion took a poor view of the good intentions behind the offer and declared that he would not work with Eshkol who, "in any event, would not last long in office, even if the Central Committee does elect him." Ben-Gurion's declaration put an end to the Tel Aviv branch's offer, in which the Haifa branch had also joined. It was a blow to the supporters of Ben-Gurion who were seeking to heal the rift in the party.

Eshkol was greatly angered by Ben-Gurion's harsh judgment, and at a meeting of the national secretariat the next day, he demanded that members of the government either go on record as rejecting Ben-Gurion's statement or draw the proper conclusions concerning their future in office. Hearing Eshkol's announcement, Golda responded with evident approval, and said, "At long last!" It was a spontaneous outburst which summed up, better than any amount of objective testimony, Golda's position with regard to the developments around the events of 1954 and 1960.

My own reaction to Eshkol's announcement was to decide finally to resign from the government. It was not an easy decision for me—I had a heavy price to pay: I would have to give up working in fields in which I had a special interest, and I would have to make a break with Eshkol even though my opinion of him was very different from the one held by Ben-Gurion—a fact I could not make public because my saying so would have been interpreted as an attempt to stay in office by betraying Ben-Gurion.

I talked to Peres, who was sympathetic but felt I should give the matter a little more thought before sending in a letter of resignation to Eshkol. He also asked me as a friend not to hand in my resignation before he did.

Shimon was in a difficult position. He did not believe we should resign. If it turned out that we had to, then my resigning first would put him in a bad light, especially because he was one of Ben-Gurion's closest associates. If I should be the first to go, my action would be judged against his, and it would appear that he had reservations about Ben-Gurion's attack on Eshkol. He was concerned that at the very least he should not seem to have been dragged by me into resigning, and so he urged me to delay my resignation until he had a chance to make up his mind. Since the matter of prestige was of little consequence to me, I agreed to wait for his decision. I handed in my resignation immediately after the Voice of Israel announced that Peres had resigned from his post as deputy minister of defense.

In my letter of resignation to Eshkol, I stated that my opinions about him and Ben-Gurion were surely known to him from our many conversations, and that he must also know that I had done everything in my power to avoid the break which had taken place between him as prime minister and David Ben-Gurion. Then I went on to say:

> Your clamorous appeal to ministers in the government and your public demand for recitation of a personal "confession" is, in my view, a provocation unprecedented in the life of the movement, and could be interpreted as an attempt to personally degrade ministers who are in sympathy with . . . David Ben-Gurion and his outlook, even if they may not necessarily agree with every one of his opinions and observations about key figures in the movement.
>
> Since you have placed me in the position of having to make a choice of conscience and either disavow this new political way of thinking or relinquish my membership in the government, I hereby submit my resignation as a member of the government of the State of Israel.
>
> My letter to you bears the date Friday, May 14, 1965, but in response to a request made by close party friends, I have delayed sending it until now.
>
> Yours respectfully,
>
> Yosef Almogi

That evening I told my family about what I had done. Their response moved me deeply: unstinting sympathy and support despite the implications of my action, some of them affecting the family in very real terms.

Publicly, my resignation from the government had accelerated the process that was leading to a party split, which only a few in our camp actually wanted but which so many in the leadership were helping to bring on. At meetings of the party minority with Ben-Gurion, there were those who took the view that Peres and I had been wrong to resign. The reason they gave was that as "part of the intraparty coalition" (the status in the Mapai that many members regarded us as having), we had a right to more portfolios than we actually held in the government. I, however, did not take that view and insisted that given the situation there was no alternative but to resign. I also argued that the whole development had not been of Eshkol's making, but that he was unwittingly manipulated into the conflict by the real instigators.

Back to Haifa

I renewed my ties with Haifa, where my public career had taken shape. I took up visiting places of work once more, met with groups of friends, and tried to get the feel of the mood in the city. I concluded that Mapai members in Haifa were, on the whole, sympathetic to Ben-Gurion, but were anxious to avoid a split. That assessment guided me in my actions outside of Haifa as well. Actually, I could only devote a small part of my time to the city, since I was required to participate in the meetings of minority headquarters, which took place in Tel Aviv and Jerusalem. Shimon devoted most of his time to getting party minority operations into shape. Our headquarters was now permanently installed in the El Al Building in Tel Aviv.

On the days I spent in Haifa, I had long conferences with Abba Khoushi, who told me frankly that he had made up his mind not to break with the party. The reasons he gave were, first, he did not believe we could succeed, second, our constituency was made up largely of working people whose mood was strongly against a break with the party, and, finally, were he younger, he might have been ready to make the gamble, but at his age he just could not take the risk of losing. Listening to him, I could not decide whether he was justifying my activities in behalf of the party minority as proper to someone younger than he, or if he was hinting that he had an interest, for reasons known to himself alone, in my opting for a break with the party. At all events, Eshkol and Sapir were now taking steps to strengthen their hold on Haifa, and Khoushi, who was mayor, had just received the go-ahead to establish a new university in the city. At the ceremony in which the agreement for an alliance of Mapai and Ahdut Avoda was signed—an event that took place at the Technion, where the Histadrut had been founded—Khoushi made a speech in which he spoke against factionalism and moves to split the party. Some minority members were angered by what he had said, and felt that his words bordered on betrayal. I felt that Khoushi was perfectly within his rights to choose sides, and I had no quarrel with him on that account. Still, I thought he might at least have tried to speak in public with a little more restraint. However, looking back, I think that Abba Khoushi's position was of far less importance than it seemed at the time. Even had he joined us and left the party with us, it would have made little difference to the relative strengths of the factions. We might perhaps have received more votes in Haifa, but not enough to tip the scales in our favor.

On May 26, 1965, three thousand members of the minority met at Beit Hagdudim in Avihail. The major topic of the meeting was the anticipated split with the party. Abba Khoushi was one of the speakers, and he came out against a break. In private he warned me against the careerists who were climbing on Ben-Gurion's bandwagon only to advance their own interests. Nevertheless, Khoushi went on attending minority meetings until the split actually took place.

At the end of May the Mapai Central Committee met to decide on the party's candidate for prime minister in the coming elections, which would take place in early November of that year. At the meeting Khoushi proposed a compromise: Ben-Gurion would head the list, Eshkol would head the country. It was a lame compromise and Ben-Gurion turned it down flat. July 3 was when the decisive vote was taken in the Central Committee, and Eshkol was chosen as the party's candidate for the office of prime minister by a majority of 60 percent. Despite all the pressures, the minority still could boast of having the support of nearly 40 percent of the Central Committee's membership. Our impressive showing had as little effect now as at the party congress: when a proposal was put forward for calling a special party conference at which a final choice would be made between Ben-Gurion and Eshkol, it was rejected by the majority—even though Dayan had explicitly stated that the choice would be binding on both sides.

I had no doubt now that the majority in the party was making an all-out effort to force a split. When I was interviewed by the *Jerusalem Post*, I was asked for my opinion of Eshkol. I answered, "We may have a prime minister, but we have lost Eshkol." Implicit in that statement was my assessment of the true will of the party as represented by the younger members about to inherit it and the veterans about to bequeath it: they were all intent on getting rid of the party minority, which was disrupting their well-laid plans.

At minority headquarters there was uncertainty. The members of the Youth Wing in our camp were pushing for us to run in the elections on a separate list. I had my doubts about the wisdom of taking such a step. The situation is nicely summed up by Ben-Gurion in the June 16 entry in his journal:

Shimon, Almogi, Moshe and Surkis arrived. In Shimon's opinion reconciliation talks are without results. We must decide on a separate list, if not—our colleagues will disperse. Moshe Dayan, if he would have to choose now, would decide against a [separate] list. He would also choose not to join. Almogi says the list would need nonparty people, money needed, newspaper needed. Asks for decision to be made on matter of list no later than July 1. Shimon also asks same.

Ben-Gurion's opinion is recorded in an entry made ten days later:

Yesterday morning Shimon, Dov Joseph, Yizhar, Almogi, Yitzhak Navon, Uzi [Feinerman] met at my place. I stated my opinion that we should not form a party, but should make a trial by appearing in elections. If we succeed in reforming the party, we will eliminate the moral decline that will open the way for Begin to take power. If not—I will not join any faction and will do my literary work without interfering in political affairs. Moshe and Uzi announced that they will not join a separate list.

We really did have a hard time deciding what to do. In the talks we had away from Ben-Gurion, we were inclined to be against breaking with the party. Dayan and I thought we were better off "staying home" for a while and remaining publicly inactive. We knew that in the end the choice lay with Ben-Gurion, but he was still torn. I had had enough experience in election campaigns not to hesitate in letting Ben-Gurion know the enormous difficulties we would have in putting up a separate election list so late in the game—there were only four months to go. I pointed out that we had no experienced campaign workers, no money, and no well-organized group of leaders. Nevertheless, I let Ben-Gurion know that if he decided in favor of putting up a separate list I would join him. Despite the tactical errors he had made, I felt that Ben-Gurion had been right in essence in all he had said about episodes that underlay the split in Mapai. Although many of my colleagues may have thought it naive, there was the matter of personal loyalty—something I could not simply brush aside. It seemed to me there was nothing to be ashamed of in remaining loyal to a man of Ben-Gurion's stature— especially when he was in such great difficulty, when so many colleagues had left him, not for any ideological differences, but because he had lost the power to bestow political favors on them and because he had grown old, too old ever to return to power. Indeed, loyalty to Ben-Gurion seemed to me to rank as a positive value for both the nation and the labor movement. This was a man to whom not only Mapai but the whole people owed a debt of gratitude. To pay pious lip service to his cause and then to desert him for the reward of a ministerial post, a seat in the Knesset or some advantageous appointment seemed to me the epitome of antieducational behavior—an encouragement to public hypocrisy and fawning on authority.

Leaving Mapai

On the question of loyalty, my choice was clear, but I still had to make up my mind whether to support a break with the party or to help avoid one. In the end I took a middle course: I took no initiative that would lead to a break, but I made it clear that if Ben-Gurion decided to leave Mapai I would support him without reservation. Knowing that the decision on this issue was entirely in Ben-Gurion's hands, I took no active part in the conference at Avihail, nor did I speak there. Nor did I think it right that I should set straight those of our potential supporters who were making their membership in the party minority conditional on there being no break with Mapai. In effect, they were asking for the wolf to have eaten and the sheep to live. Some of the participants at Avihail were honestly of the opinion that we would have a better chance by struggling within the party than outside it. I now think that they were right, but that is the wisdom of hindsight.

In line with my decision, I also took no part in the seminar being conducted by members of the party minority in Haifa. The idea of a discussion series was apparently intended as a way of influencing Abba Khoushi. Although Khoushi had helped organize the seminar, he did not participate in it.

Haifa was not in favor of a split. Nevertheless we stuck together, and I felt completely at home at the party branch and with the Mapai leadership of the city. When the final break was close at hand, representatives of the party in Haifa came to me and asked me not to join in establishing a separate list. They argued—and I was inclined to agree with them—that a split among Mapai members in Haifa was unnatural. For my part, I even talked some party members—people working in Histadrut organizations in the city—into remaining in Mapai, since I could be of no use of them or their families in helping them find jobs to replace those they might lose were they to join me.

The moment of decision for the minority came on July 26, 1965, at a meeting in the El Al Building. Peres was just about to make the decision to remain in the party when Ben-Gurion suddenly appeared to lead us across the Rubicon. That morning I told Shimon that although I was not for leaving the party, I would nevertheless join Ben-Gurion if he decided to run in the elections on a separate list. As it turned out, Shimon had no more choice than I in supporting an independent election list.

30
Rafi

The decision to found Rafi (the Israel Workers' List) was taken during a tension-charged meeting at Ben-Gurion's Tel Aviv home on July 27, 1965. I went to work on Rafi's behalf in Haifa. Shimon Peres got down to the job with great energy at our Tel Aviv headquarters.

One of the things Shimon did was to bring in people belonging to circles outside the labor movement. The first question we had to resolve was whether we should participate in the Histadrut elections on September 19, just seven weeks before the Knesset race. Opinions were divided, and we had to come to an immediate decision on an issue of principle which had become a point of disagreement among us, namely, whether Rafi was a Ben-Gurionist–Mapai election list, or a centrist party in its own right, holding an ideological position between Mapai and the parties of the General Zionists and Herut.

The debate between the Histadrut-oriented wing and the Centrists, whose chief spokesman was Peres, went on throughout the brief history of Rafi until it was finally won by the former when Mapai, Ahdut Avoda, and Rafi merged to form the Israel Labor Party in 1968. Nor was this the only point of disagreement in our ranks, although despite our differences, there was never even a hint of personal animus between Shimon and me, and we never competed over positions within Rafi. Shimon Peres and his friends did all they could to disassociate themselves both from the issue of the Lavon Affair and from Ben-Gurion himself.

As the Histadrut and Knesset elections drew near I became more convinced than ever that the political line being taken by Peres and his associates were alien to me. There was no question of conflict over control of positions and offices; our differences were over ideology. Shimon kept pressing to the right and talked about our need for "liberation from Marxist nostalgia," and my position was that Rafi's existence was justified in the first place because of its support of Ben-Gurion and his struggle, rather than its fostering of nonsocialist ideologies. To me it seemed more than a little strange that Rafi, which had been conceived and created by and around Ben-Gurion, should now not only seek to ignore Ben-

Gurion and replace his venerable image in the public mind by that of some anonymous youngster bearing new tidings to the nation, but attempt as well to introduce political creeds alien to us. Was our break with Mapai over economic and political issues? Surely not, I thought.

With these differences dogging us, it was not easy to organize ourselves quickly for the Histadrut contest. Even on the subject of the Histadrut—a field in which I innocently believed I had some degree of expertise—I found myself in sharp disagreement with my fellow Rafists over the status of labor councils, the structure of trade unions, and the whole complex of Histadrut and labor affairs, which in an access of ambition my colleagues wanted to reform radically. Fortunately we were joined by a number of Histadrut old-timers who were well versed in these matters, and they took over our election campaign in the Labor Federation. With their indispensable help, we garnered about eighty thousand ballots, 12 percent of the vote. Our showing was encouraging, and all the more impressive for the fact that this was the first Histadrut contest in which the Herut party had put up an election list of its own. It gave us a solid basis for running in the elections for local government and in the Knesset race.

I was in no doubt that Rafi's real constituency was among Mapai members in the Histadrut and that it was to them that we should primarily appeal. My views were, in fact, vindicated in the Knesset race: we received only sixteen thousand votes more than we had in the Histadrut election.

When Dayan, after having spent some time on the fence, finally joined Rafi, these differences became even more acute. I was present at the meeting in Ben-Gurion's home when Dayan's entry into Rafi was solemnized. In the course of the meeting, Ben-Gurion told Dayan that although the Lavon Affair was not the whole Rafi program, it was the principal element. Dayan responded by saying, "I do not agree to having the affair represented as a principle." I was very sorry to see Ben-Gurion give in on that point. Dayan's joining did much to raise morale in Rafi, but it also hastened the process of Rafi's detachment from Ben-Gurion, and its departure from the causes that had originally brought it into being.

The top spot on the Rafi election list was set aside for Ben-Gurion, and second place was reserved for Peres. Moshe Dayan, however, was dissatisfied with this arrangement and proposed that the order of appearance of candidates on the list be random rather than hierarchically determined. His proposal was accepted, with the result that Dayan appeared in seventh place.

Peres and Dayan and their group were not satisfied by merely turning to the young voter. In attempting to give the new party as young an image as possible, they worked at developing a constituency among the very young and organized entertaining picnic parties for their benefit. In a move calculated to flatter potential non-Histadrut voters, they made a target of the corruption of the establishment and its apparatus.

As Election Day drew near, some Rafi speakers who had no experience in organizing an election campaign began to let their enthusiasm run away with them. Going on nothing better than the applause we received at campaign rallies, they began making fantastic predictions that we would take between twenty and thirty seats in the Knesset. Even Shimon Peres estimated that we would win twenty places. The argument ran something like this: in the Histadrut election Rafi received eight and a half mandates, and the voters who had given them to us were as good as in the bag; now, taking into account that our list contained outstanding personalities in the defense establishment and that everything connected with Ben-Gurion and the Lavon Affair had been swept under the carpet, and adding our potential supporters outside the Histadrut, why, there wasn't a scintilla of doubt we would double our vote.

I was highly skeptical about the forecast. I suspected that, if we went on as we had, we would both alienate our constituency in Mapai and fail to add to our strength elsewhere. This was exactly what happened. Our list for the national election received merely two mandates more than we had won in the Histadrut, and we ended up with only ten seats in the Knesset. This was all that was achieved by placing our bets on the non-Histadrut voter and talking about the "scientization of the country." It all went to prove that compromising on the issue of Ben-Gurion's struggle, and seeking an artificial alliance with groups that had nothing in common with Ben-Gurion or his moral zeal, had not only failed to help us, but had done us positive harm. Looking back, I feel certain that had we stuck to backing Ben-Gurion's cause and had we concentrated our efforts on the 40 percent of Mapai members sympathetic to Ben-Gurion, we should have done immeasurably better in the Knesset race.

In the Original Spirit of Rafi

The day after elections, the pressure was off. At last I was free of the burden of having to be at the center of things and could return to Haifa. The first few days after elections I fretted over our failure to gain the number of seats we ought to have gotten. We had turned our backs on our potential backers within the ranks of Mapai and from among Ben-Gurion sympathizers and sought our support, instead, among the purely marginal constituency which remained after the voters of Herut, the Liberals, and the "Citizens for Eshkol" had been accounted for. I soon stopped brooding over facts that could not be changed, and made up my mind to establish a local branch which would hold to Rafi's original spirit.

At the end of January 1966, I was chosen by secret ballot in the Rafi Council to sit on the Executive Committee of the Histadrut. There I was given responsibility over the Department of Vocational Training, and once again I had an office at my disposal with all the attendant perquisites. I did not continue in that post for long. I had already decided to concentrate my activity on Haifa and in the Knesset and give up all my responsibilities in Tel Aviv. I therefore left the Department of Vocational Training in the Histadrut executive and turned my attentions once more to the Knesset. I submitted motions for the agenda and participated in debates on economic and social issues. Most of my free time I spent in the library doing research. Every week I wrote three short articles for the newspapers: one for the main weekly of Rafi, *Mabat hadash* [*New View*], one for the Haifa weekly, and one under a pen name for *Yediyon*, the Rafi bulletin for

Haifa. The bulletin was published by Binyamin Ivri and Motke Levanon and became popular because of the high level of its content. I found these activities immensely satisfying.

In May 1966 Rafi held a party congress; its first and—unknown to anyone at the time—its last. Delegates were elected by thirty-three thousand registered party members, of whom nearly three thousand were Haifaites. Rafi gathered strength among agricultural settlements as well, where the great majority had formerly been Mapai supporters. Here was proof positive that all the flirtation with sections of the population that had no roots in the labor movement had been in vain. The congress was successful, and it was conducted in an atmosphere which was stimulating without being divisive. A good many of the decisions taken at the congress had to do with the merger of the factions and parties of the labor movement, as laid down in the Rafi platform, which was drafted by Avraham Wolfensohn and had the support of Ben-Gurion. That such a merger was not far off occurred to none of us. It was closer, in fact, than some may have wished.

An Early Sign of Merger

In the summer of 1966, Israel experienced a serious economic slump, and national morale was sagging. Bitter jokes began making the rounds about Eshkol, the government, and growing unemployment. The most popular of all told of the last person leaving the country being asked to make certain he switched off the light at Lydda Airport. In the prevading mood of national gloom, the momentum of Rafi's growth stood out all the more, especially so in Haifa, where relations were improving between the Israel Workers' Party and the Israel Workers' List.

The relations between the Haifa branches of Rafi and Mapai had improved to the point that the secretaries of the trade unions came for coffee at the Rafi club. Nevertheless, I continued to insist, both locally and nationally, on the justice of Rafi principles, and repeatedly called for having the problems brought on by the Lavon Affair resolved. With regard to the economic slowdown, which I regarded as an antilabor phenomenon, I demanded legislation that would secure people against unemployment and called for the implementation of policies that would stimulate the national economy. I also worked for the creation of a government health insurance plan that would be based on existing sick funds.

31

The Six-Day War and After

The threat to our security caught us unaware. For months defense experts had been predicting there would be no war within the next few years. Quite suddenly, on Independence Day afternoon, 1967, the Egyptian army entered Sinai. The Arab radio stations poured out streams of martial slogans and blood-curdling threats of our imminent annihilation. The round-the-clock propaganda campaign terrified our Arab-speaking citizens; even the taste we got of it in Hebrew translation had a chilling effect on us all. Concern mounted as Jordan joined the military alliance with Syria, and command of the Jordanian army was handed over to an Egyptian general. Our sense of danger grew all the more once it became clear that the West and the United States were unable to act in the crisis. The withdrawal of the UN Emergency Force from Sharm el-Sheikh and the West's failure to take practical steps to reopen the Straits of Tiran which had been closed by Egypt to cut off shipping to and from Eilat, augured the worst. As the threat to Israel became more palpable, national morale took an upward swing. The nation instinctively closed ranks, and all at once the political differences that had divided us were set aside.

Saturday, May 20, 1967, Rafi's secretariat met on my request in order to consider the security situation. The entire membership showed up, including Ben-Gurion, Moshe Dayan, Yaacov Dori, the poet Nathan Alterman, and Zwi Zurr. Dayan and Dori had just returned, exhilarated, from a tour of inspection arranged for former chiefs of staff. They spoke enthusiastically of the state of readiness and high morale of our reservists, who were just waiting for the order to break through the tightening ring of siege. Dayan believed that if war broke out, we would succeed in breaking the blockade of the port of Eilat. Ben-Gurion observed sadly that he could allow himself no opinion because he had no information on what was going on. During the meeting, Dayan announced that he intended to volunteer for military duty.

From that day forward we would meet almost every day either in Tel Aviv or in Jerusalem. Ben-Gurion felt like a caged lion; it was the first time since the establishment of the state that he had to stand on the sidelines as an event of supreme historical importance to the nation unfolded. The newspapers put forward the idea of forming a government of national unity, and at Ben-Gurion's request, we met to discuss the subject. Ben-Gurion asked for a resolution that Rafi would not participate in a coalition headed by Eshkol, and I agreed with him.

Pressures on Eshkol began to mount from within Mapai. Yehoshua Rabinowitch together with many members of the Mapai secretariat and the party faction in the Knesset turned against Eshkol. They demanded that Dayan be appointed to the government as minister of defense and that the leaders of Gahal—the Herut-Liberal bloc—be co-opted into a national unity government.

Dayan was away in the north at the time, and Shimon Peres and I were appointed to the Knesset Committee of Foreign Affairs and Security, which was then meeting in Tel Aviv. Shimon initiated a series of meetings with representatives of the Herut-Liberal Gahal bloc, the National Religious Party, Mapam, and the Independent Liberals to get their agreement to Dayan and Ben-Gurion's joining the unity government. Menahem Begin proposed to Eshkol that Ben-Gurion be taken into the government in view of the national emergency, but Eshkol refused, saying that two horses such as he and Ben-Gurion could never be hitched to the same wagon.

The government's continued postponement of military action was nerve-racking both to the army and the civilian population. Nevertheless, when the government came to vote on the issue, the ministers were divided equally—half of them supporting a preventive strike and half opposed. Eshkol had the deciding vote but refrained from casting it. In the meantime Nassar was being photographed in Sinai, where he issued his well-publicized challenge, "If Rabin wants to come and get us out—*ahalan wasahalan* [he's welcome to try]." Pressures kept increasing within Mapai for changes in the government. A party delegation from Haifa led by Abba Khoushi confronted Eshkol with the demand to appoint Dayan as defense minister.

The public kept tuned to Arab stations and listened with growing unease to the festival of jingo and the prophecies of an Arab victory that would soon sweep us all into the sea. The combination of our isolation in the world community and Arab saber-rattling was especially frightening to survivors of the Holocaust, in whom the memory of their ordeal and fear of its repetition were cruelly awakened.

On Saturday night, May 27, Shimon and I took part in an unprecedented meeting between Ben-Gurion and the Gahal leadership, represented by Menahem Begin, Yosef Sapir, Arieh Ben-Eliezer, and Elimelech Rimalt. Ben-Gurion observed then that if matters rested with him, he would have a ship run the blockade at the Straits of Tiran. "I am certain," he added, "that Nassar would fire, and then no one would charge us with having initiated hostilities." For the internal situation, Ben-Gurion blamed Eshkol and thought the government should be changed; he insisted, however, that Dayan not be appointed to it.

Begin promised to use his influence to have Rafi invited to take part in the national unity government. I thought that Ben-Gurion should be taken into the unity government with or without Dayan, and that if Dayan were not in the government, he should be given a military post.

Despite the fact that nearly everybody—the National Religious Party, Gahal, Rafi, and part of Mapai—was working hard to have Dayan taken into the government, Ben-Gurion persisted in wanting Dayan to be kept out. Many in Rafi disagreed with Ben-Gurion, and toward the end of May I saw, in the corridors of the Rafi executive, party members preparing posters and petitions urging Dayan's appointment as defense minister. There was even a demonstration of women in support of Dayan.

Finally, late in the afternoon of June 1, Eshkol gave in and put Dayan in charge of the ministry of defense. The Rafi secretariat met immediately, and a decisive majority voted in Ben-Gurion's absence, to support Dayan's joining the government. We then went to inform Ben-Gurion of the decision. Dayan behaved with restraint this time and observed, "If the decision receives final approval, well and good. If not, I'll just have to think things over again." To our surprise Ben-Gurion wasn't put out. He said that since he had become aware of the prevailing mood in the army, he had changed his mind and now agreed to having Dayan take over the ministry of defense in Eshkol's government. My own opinion remained unchanged—I still opposed the appointment. In this I remained alone. The entire Rafi leadership surrounded Dayan to congratulate him, and I joined them. Then Dayan turned to me and said, "You'll see yet that the decision was a good one."

Rejoining at Any Price

I thought otherwise. I was certain that the army was ready for battle and that we would win no matter who was defense minister. However, Dayan's entry into Eshkol's government knocked the spirit out of Ben-Gurion's followers and Rafi's exponents. That evening Ben-Gurion himself gave up the fight for lost. Henceforth we would all have to work in behalf of Eshkol and his government, since we were all part of it. Moreover, it was inconceivable that Dayan, now that he was minister of defense, would work against Eshkol. And what of Ben-Gurion's fight against the miscarriage of justice? After all, it had been our support of Ben-Gurion on this issue—and not differences on policy or ideology, as some argued—that had led us to break with Mapai. With that gone, there seemed to be no justification for our continuing an independent existence as a party. I had the distinct feeling Rafi's fate was sealed.

Several days later, at a meeting in which Golda, Barakat, Shimon, and I participated, the cat was out of the bag. To Golda's surprise and mine, Shimon said, "If our participation in the government in order to strengthen our position in the face of the enemy requires that Rafi enter Mapai, then we are ready to enter unconditionally and to dismantel Rafi's organization framework." In effect Shimon was doing away with Rafi without so much as a by-your-leave to its membership. Golda and I replied on the spot that Rafi's entry into Mapai was something to be decided by Rafi's party organizations.

On June 5 the Knesset Committee of Foreign Affairs and Security had scheduled a tour of inspection in the South. We arrived at Dov Airfield and were about to board our plane when the sirens sounded. We were ordered into trenches, from where we could see Hawk missiles being transported to the edge of the field. Before the all clear sounded Dayan arrived to tell us that hostilities had begun and that the IDF had swung into action.

I went with Shimon to his home, and from there we were able to keep in touch by telephone with all the government and military authorities. I was able to get through to my wife in Haifa to let her know I was well. In the evening I was called to the Knesset in Jerusalem to hear the proclamation of a national unity government and to witness the swearing-in of its members.

In the late afternoon Shimon and I went to Ben-Gurion to give him the information we had received from the IDF general staff about the annihilation of the Egyptian airforce. We joined Ben-Gurion in his car for a lift to Jerusalem, and on the way we saw army units moving toward the capital. Soldiers who recognized the Old Man clapped their hands and called out, "Hurrah for Ben-Gurion!"

The Knesset was within shelling range of Jordanian guns, and we were ordered down to the shelter. As we were waiting for the all-clear siren, Randolph Churchill, Winston Churchill's nephew, who had come to Israel as a reporter for the British press, approached me and asked me to introduce him to Ben-Gurion. I was glad to be of help, and Ben-Gurion made an appointment to meet him in Tel Aviv. Ben-Gurion was greatly excited, but for all his enthusiasm over our successes in the war he felt cut off from events for the first time in his life.

Moshe Dayan could not get to the swearing-in ceremony at the Knesset and was also unable to take the time to report to Ben-Gurion on the situation at the front. The job of keeping Ben-Gurion up to date was taken on by Haim Israeli, one of the Defense Ministry's most talented and dedicated men, and Major-General Zvi (Chera) Zur, who was appointed aide to the new minister of defense. As a member of the Foreign Affairs and Security Committee, I had frequent occasion to meet with Dayan, and at the end of our sessions I proposed that he appoint Shimon Peres deputy minister of defense. I told Dayan that although I had not spoken of the matter to Shimon, I assumed that he was unhappy to be sitting out one of greatest events in our history. Moshe did not accept my proposal.

At the end of six days, the war was over. All of Sinai, the Gaza Strip, the Golan Heights, the West Bank, and East Jerusalem were in our hands. The nation was ecstatic. And the younger generation had undergone something of a metamorphosis. They, who up to the eve of the war had been called the Espresso Generation, had proven themselves worthy successors to the Maccabees. Politically, the achievements of the Six-Day War were immeasurably greater than those of the Sinai Campaign. No one was threatening us with dire consequences if we did not withdraw. This time we were awash in a tide of sympathy such as we had never before experienced.

When the noise of battle subsided, the internal debate on the future of the territories began. A public group was formed to preserve the integrity of the historical Land of Israel, and Herut took a solemn oath that Eretz Israel would never again be divided. Jerusalem was unified as one city, and by decision of the Knesset, the residents of East Jerusalem were put under Israeli law.

Sentiments of Union

The sentiment for political union was growing among the labor parties in Israel. Rafi opened talks with Mapai on the possibility of reunifying the party. Within Mapai itself a movement among former minority supporters was calling for a three-way union of Mapai, Ahdut Avoda, and Rafi. Just then we got the news of the quickening pace at which the merger with Ahdut Avoda was being achieved and of the difficulties being put in the way of union with Rafi. Abba Khoushi, Amnon Lin, and the Bloc were trying to influence the Mapai leadership to complete the union with Rafi either at the same time or even before union was achieved with Ahdut Avoda.

Shimon and I met with Mapai Party Secretary Golda Meir, Pinhas Sapir, and others. Sapir advised me that to talk privately with Golda. I took his advice and had a series of meetings with Golda at her home. Golda had misgivings, and I did my best to convince her that the reunification of the historical Mapai was a real possibility.

Not everyone in Rafi was enthusiastic about union. Among its opponents were some of the most prominent men in the Rafi's leadership, including Baruch Ber, Mordecai Ben-Porat, Meir Avizohar, and Yitzhak Navon. Ben-Gurion remained neutral. Although he was convinced that we would never succeed in replacing the leadership of Mapai, he announced that he would not oppose union and, that if, moreover, the merger succeeded, he would readily join in. Until then he would wait and see—even if it meant doing so alone.

Dayan and Peres sat on the sidelines and watched the battle in the Rafi Secretariat between the supporters of union, at whose head I stood, and its opponents. It was astonishing that they could be so apathetic about an issue which was likely to determine their political future. They, apparently had their reasons. For my part, I continued to fight for union with Mapai and had the backing of Avraham Wolfensohn and Professor Ernst Bergmann as well as others.

On June 19 the Central Committee of Rafi was called into session in Jerusalem, and the subject of union with Mapai was aired publicly for the first time. I spoke unhesitatingly in favor of union. I based my arguments on the decisions taken at the first Rafi congress calling for our full merger with the country's labor movements. In the end my position won out, and the secretariat resolution to open negotiations with Mapai was carried by a majority of fifty-five to thirty-two. After the vote, Shimon announced that he was going abroad and named me to take his place. After he left I held a series of conferences with representatives of Mapai, with the Bloc, and with the Haifa branch of Mapai, I also kept Ben-Gurion abreast of developments. Ben-Gurion did not oppose the negotiations by "those of our colleagues who are convinced that this is the only way to reform the situation in Mapai and in the country," as he wrote in his diary, adding: "and therefore they are entitled and, by their own lights, obliged to merge. I am not."

Rendezvous at the King David Hotel

In an effort to get Ben-Gurion to soften his stand a little, I asked Golda Meir at one of our meetings if she were prepared to have a talk with him. I thought that, despite everything that had taken place between them, Golda still admired the Old Man, and Ben-Gurion retained a soft spot for her. Golda replied she had nothing against such a meeting but doubted that she could persuade Ben-Gurion to alter her position. When I asked Ben-Gurion if he were ready to meet Golda, he said, "Certainly, but she has to ask me." I went to the Knesset dining room to tell Golda, and she immediately wrote out a note to him and handed it to me. I did not bother to read what she had written, and to this day I have no idea what it was. When Ben-Gurion read her note, he blushed and put it away in his pocket. "All right," he said, "she can come to the King David Hotel, which was where Ben-Gurion was staying. I made arrangements for chauffeurs and bodyguards, feeling like a marriage broker setting up a meeting between two youngsters.

The next day Golda told me that for two hours Ben-Gurion had tried to persuade her that Eshkol was unsuitable for his office. "Well," she said, "what was I supposed to do?" Ben-Gurion's version was that Golda stubbornly refused to concede that Eshkol was inadequate for the job.

The papers were full of stories about the difficulties being experienced within Rafi over union with Mapai; most of the reports concerned the positions of Ben-Gurion, Dayan, and Peres. I continued to appear at local Rafi branches to explain my position favoring a merger. One of the arguments I put forward was that if we continued as an independent party, we could not remain in the government, and Dayan would either have to leave his office or break with Ben-Gurion. Although it was true that the Lavon Affair and relations with veteran leaders in Mapai could not be ignored, they would have to be attended to within the context of a unified party.

The prediction I made publically when I opposed Dayan's entry into the government without Ben-Gurion came true earlier than I had expected. At a meeting called by the Rafi Central Committee on September 24, Ben-Gurion spoke at length about the significance of our having broken with Mapai, and stressed that the issue of the distortion of justice was the fundamental source of our difference with Mapai. Not unexpectedly, he spoke in unflattering terms of Eshkol.

When Ben-Gurion finished speaking, Dayan took the floor. Part of what he had to say was the following:

> I know that collective responsibility exists in the government. The prime minister is perhaps more responsible than others for its actions or blunders . . .

but the responsibility for what the government does or does not do falls on all members of the government. . . .I did not sneak or smuggle myself into this government on my own. I entered for and on behalf of Rafi. And all Rafi need do is even hint that it does not want to bear responsibility for this government—all of Rafi, including you, Ben-Gurion—and I will leave the government. . . .If this government is not doing its job, and Rafi is of that opinion, Rafi needn't participate in it since there is such a thing as collective responsibility, and I, Rafi's representative, will have to leave the government. Nothing would be easier—the government will continue to exist even without me.

This was Dayan's rejection of Ben-Gurion's effort to cast him in the role of the people's rather than Rafi's representative in the government.

Surely Dayan was right at least on this point: the moment Ben-Gurion had agreed to Moshe Dayan's joining the Eshkol government he was no longer in a position to attack either Levi Eshkol or the government in which there was a representative of Rafi—or, in effect, of Ben-Gurion himself—and especially so if that representative held the key post of defense minister. On this issue I took Dayan's part and said, "What has changed since the beginning of June? Are we better off? Have the dangers passed?" Then I appealed directly to Ben-Gurion and asked him to give us leave to fulfill his own wish—the union of the labor movement. "It was because of a distortion of the law and the justice of Ben-Gurion's position that I quit Mapai and joined Rafi," I went on, "But this is a momentous time in our history, with its prospects and perils, and we cannot stand in its way."

At the end of a trying discussion, it was decided to convene a second session of the First Party Congress of Rafi to resolve the question of merger. Rafi's local branches were torn by disagreement, and both sides mustered their forces in anticipation of the meeting. When the session opened on December 12, 1967, Avraham Wolfensohn spoke on behalf of those supporting union, and Meir Avizohar for those opposed. They were followed by speakers from both camps.

Ben-Gurion was present throughout the discussions. The fact that Yitzhak Navon, one of Ben-Gurion's close associates, spoke against union was interpreted as being a sign of Ben-Gurion's opposition to merger. The debate was closed by Dayan and Peres. Dayan said "it appeared" that he would vote for union; Shimon was no less equivocal. The opponents of union let it be bruited about the numbers opposing should be increased as much as possible—if only for the purpose of having a better bargaining position with Mapai.

"With That Kind of Majority You Don't Merge"

The vote was a 58 percent majority in favor of union. I felt gratified, but was a little suspicious of the conference Dayan, Peres and Meir Avizohar were having off in one corner. As I approached the huddle I heard Avizohar say heatedly, "With that kind of majority you don't merge." Moshe and Shimon looked hesitant, and I decided to intervene. I said that even 51 percent of a vote was a majority, and 58 percent was a respectable majority! I then made it clear I would not tolerate a misrepresentation of the results of the voting. Nevertheless, such attempts were made. Meir Avizohar demanded that the Standing Committee meet to consider the situation, since there were many who would not accept the decision, and it might be advisable to have a referendum or elect a new party congress. Avizohar's words were drowned in cries of protest from, the supporters of union, whose patience he had taxed to the limit. Dayan proposed that since the voting was over, the congress should adjourn and anyone having further proposals should submit them to the Rafi secretariat. Shaul Ben-Simhon spoke in favor of Dayan's motion, but added that the congress had *voted but had not decided*. Shimon, who tried to convince his listeners that this had been a "fair congress," was jeered by supporters of union. He found it difficult to assert control over this particular variety of "friendly debate" and together with Dayan tried to calm the crowd. From what they had said I learnt something I had not known: there would be a meeting of the secretariat to discuss and decide on the results of the congress. That sounded suspicious to me, and I rose and said simply: "The congress has convened, voted, and decided." With that I voted for Dayan's motion to close debate and wind up the congress. The delegates then rose and sang "Hatikva."

After the congress I sat down with some of my freinds to consider the result. What impressed us was the sudden change in mood revealed by the opponents of union once the results of the voting became known. They seemed to have lost their confidence and were ready to do almost anything to change an accomplished fact. We suspected that anyone who could reject the results of a vote taken by secret ballot would be ready to torpedo the efforts for union.

Our fears turned out to be justified. After the congress there was a deliberate dragging of feet in carrying out the decisions that had been made. On December 17, the Rafi secretariat met to approve the text of a letter to Mapai Secretary Golda Meir on the results of the Rafi congress. The text proposed by Peres was as follows:

> To the Secretary of Mapai, Golda Meir:
> I hereby inform you that the second session of the Rafi Congress, which took place on 12–13 December, has decided in favor of a unified labor party, with Rafi participating.
>
> (Signed) Shimon Peres,
>
> Secretary-General

The coldly worded text, Peres's attempt to place the secretariat over the congress, and the invitation of nonmembers to the secretariat to take part in debate and, possibly, even to vote were not exactly signs of an intention to undertake real and intensive negotiations for union. They had to do with hope still being entertained by some of the opponents of merger that the union would be sabotaged by the veteran leadership of Mapai—and especially by Eshkol, after Dayan announced at the Rafi congress that he was going into Mapai in order to get Eshkol and Sapir out of the leadership. Mapai members were asking how a government minister could proclaim his intention of getting rid of the prime minister. This accounted for the belief that negotiations could be dragged out until they broke down. To meet the threat, I warned that I would do everything in my power to see to it that the decisions of the congress were carried out; if necessary I would not hesitate to muster all those who had voted with the majority and have a negotiating committee appointed with their help.

Finally, after exhausting negotiations during which I frantically worked (with help from Khoushi, Sapir, and Nezer) to close the gap between Shimon and Golda, an agreement between Rafi and Mapai was reached. The formal signing took place in January 1968 at an official ceremony in Elisheva House in Jerusalem. Shimon Peres was elected deputy-secretary of the new Labor party— now embracing Ahdut Avoda as well as Rafi and Mapai—and the tripartite union became an established fact in the political life of Israel.

During this whole period I remained in close touch with Ben-Gurion. The veteran leadership of Mapai finally made its peace with Ben-Gurion. Golda played host to Ben-Gurion at a banquet in Beit Berl and asked him to return to the labor movement. Ben-Gurion refused—but he did stop fighting, and he came to terms with all his former opponents.

I feel very proud of having been privileged to work, for a time, with one of the towering figures in Jewish history. His letters to me and the dedications in his hand in books and on pictures remain in my possession—treasures to be passed on to my children and my children's children.

32

Rejoining the Government

The signing of the agreement establishing the Labor alignment on January 21, 1968, signaled the end of a phase in my public career. I announced publicly that I was no longer in Rafi and was now a member of the Haifa branch of the Labor party. I had dedicated myself to bringing about the merger of Mapai, Ahdut Avoda, and Rafi because I had regarded the union as something made necessary by realities both within and outside the labor movement.

An Offer and Its Complications

In June 1968 items appeared in the press saying that I might be chosen as Histadrut secretary-general in place of Aharon Becker, who was about to leave after having held the post for seven years. Reporters were letting it be known, too, that my name had been put forward as a candidate for minister of labor to replace Yigal Allon, who would appointed deputy prime minister and minister of immigrant absorption. These rumors apparently started after a chance meeting I had with Golda a few weeks earlier, when she had surprised me by asking what I would do were I to have a choice between being secretary of the Histadrut and serving as a minister in the government. I answered that I had problems enough as things were, but if she really wanted to know, I was not particularly drawn to the secretaryship of the Histadrut and would prefer to be back in the government. After that the matter seemed to have been dropped, and I received no offers.

The press items kept cropping up. My friend Arieh Tsimouki, *Yedioth Ahronot* Jerusalem correspondent, swore to me at lunch that what he had written about the posts that might be offered to me was absolutely true. While we were still chatting, Golda and Israel Galili arrived at the restaurant, and I was invited by Golda to join their table. Then, without a hint of what was coming, she said: "I've got a hypothetical question: If you were offered the Labor portfolio, would your response be favorable?" I said that my answer (hypothetical, of course) was yes.

That evening Sapir phoned to ask if Eshkol had already spoken to me. When I said no, Sapir promised that Eshkol would invite me for a chat and make me an interesting offer. Eshkol, believing that the offer had already been made, did not speak to me and brought up the matter directly at the meeting of the party faction on June 12, 1968. Eshkol's announcement was followed by a long and stormy exchange, mostly between former members of Mapai and Rafi. The Rafi people were enraged by both of the proposed appointments. In Yigal Allon's proposed appointment as deputy prime minister, they saw as an attempt to put the brakes on Moshe Dayan's advancement; as for mine, they thought they should have been consulted first. Shimon argued hotly that Rafi had committed itself to a struggle against the veteran leadership of Mapai and that if a government reshuffle was being contemplated, the leaders of Rafi should be asked who were their candidates for the ministerial posts. Shimon's hint was obvious enough. Mordecai Surkis agreed that I was the man for the job of minister of labor, but took exception to my being approached directly on the matter. Mordecai Ben-Porat asked Eshkol if I would be representing the Rafi faction in the Labor party—to which Eshkol replied, "Almogi will be taken into the government as someone suitable to be labor minister."

The storm over the appointments lasted two more weeks. The National Religious Party (NRP) and Gahal were incensed that a deputy prime minister should have been appointed and a new minister brought into the government while two ministers from Gahal remained without portfolio. Among the Rafi leadership, a proposal was put forward to make common cause with the NRP and Gahal against the new appointments.

My former colleagues in Rafi seemed to have forgotten two matters of principle: first, that it had been Rafi itself which had urged the dismantling of former factions in order to form a united party: second, that the right to bring ministers into the government is reserved for the prime minister and must be approved by the Knesset. Moreover, had the Mapai faction been officially required to make a concession to the Rafi faction in the matter of ministerial appointments, it would have had to do so on the basis of Rafi's proportional representation in the Labor party. In this case, Rafi—a minority faction representing only 21.5 percent of the party—was not eligible to have one of its people receive the portfolio of defense. Concerning the value of that office, Gabi Cohen of Ahdut Avoda had once said, at a meeting of the Labor party faction, that in exchange for the defense portfolio he was ready to give us three ministers with portfolios. There was no reason, therefore, for me to refuse the appointment. I assured Sapir, who was afraid I would withdraw my candidacy because of the opposition of so many of my colleagues, that I would remain firm in my decision to accept the post.

The opponents to my appointment remained firm as well and convened a special meeting of Rafi to consider the subject. I decided to take part in it and speak my mind. I never did. When I got to the place of the meeting, the President Hotel, I had a sudden dizzy spell and began feeling weak. Dr. Haim Doron, later chairman of the Board of Directors of the Sick Fund, had me rushed down to Hadassah Hospital. I was afraid that I had suffered a heart attack, one of the occupational hazards of public life. To my great relief the doctors diagnosed my symptoms as a "mere" collapse. When the fact became known, I was inundated by get-well telegrams, flowers, and wishes for an early recovery from Ben-Gurion, Eshkol, Golda, and many others. Shimon Peres visited me at the hospital. I few days later I was released and went home to rest.

Early in July Menahem Begin phoned. He wanted to be the first to bring me the news that the government had confirmed my appointment by the prime minister to the post of minister of labor. Begin revealed that his party had voted against the proposal, but assured me that the vote had not been taken against me on any personal grounds. My colleagues in the opposition who participated in the Knesset debate on the new appointments did not speak against me personally as a candidate for the post. Shimon Peres was among those who welcomed my appointment. When Eshkol took the floor to answer for the government, the lights in the Knesset auditorium went out because of a power failure. He said that after hearing all the praises being heaped on me, he was surer than ever that his choice had been the right one.

When I mounted the dais for the swearing-in ceremony, the lights suddenly went on again, which was interpreted as a sign of good luck. Afterward I went with my wife and some of our Haifa and Jerusalem friends to the Holyland Hotel, where we raised a toast in honor of my appointment.

The following day I met with my predecessor in office, Yigal Allon, and senior officials of the Labor Ministry and the social security services. Yigal graciously introduced the office staff, at their head the ministry's director-general, Hanoch Lev-Kochav, a young and gifted man from Kibbutz Palmahim, who died in the terrible Swissair catastrophe in 1970. I got down to work immediately, first answering hundreds of letters of congratulation. Many friends dropped in to see me, and in Haifa a party was thrown in my honor, complete with speeches of praise.

I was put off by all the praise I was receiving. Some of it struck me as insincere and even cynical. I could not avoid giving some thought to the successive changes in my fortunes. I had fallen from a great height to the nadir in my political career and stayed there for three years. Now I was at the top again.

Notes on Mapai Leaders

My return to the government was a propitious moment for me to take stock. I considered the years I had been active in political life, and the opportunities I had had to work with some of the great personalities in the state, the party, and the Histadrut, people who were giants in our time. I had seen them in times of joy and sorrow, observed them in their glory and pettiness, witnessed their capacities for great personal warmth and chilling hate. Taken all in all, their merits outweighed their faults. The riddle of whether the age makes the man or the man the age remains unsolved, but from my own experience of great events in the making, I would venture to say that this revolutionary epoch of Jewish history was graced by leaders who did it justice.

In the decade between 1958 and 1968, I had the opportunity of working closely with Ben-Gurion, who towered over all of that great company. As one who had observed Ben-Gurion from close up when he confronted a variety of challenges, I think I can say, without ascribing superhuman powers to him, that David Ben-Gurion was a great man who possessed all the gifts and virtues of leadership that were called for at a fateful turning point in the history of our people.

I had seen the Israel Workers' Party at the zenith of its power and Ben-Gurion when his reputation was at its height. I am not certain that in 1960 Ben-Gurion's abilities were still at a peak, but I do think that were it not for the Lavon Affair he would have succeeded in laying the foundation for an essential change in the electoral system—which is the same as saying that he would have changed the country's social system. We lacked only nine votes in the Knesset for our proposed law of electoral reform to have passed. I had been carrying out intensive negotiations, trying to gather support for the law during the Fourth Knesset, when all our efforts were nullified by the Lavon Affair and its aftermath.

I had seen Ben-Gurion bursting with ideas, alert to every event both in Israel and in the world at large. I had watched as he excitedly held forth during the discussions of the Bible study group at his home. His wife Paula, who planned the seating arrangements and saw to the refreshments at these gatherings, would looked on with evident pleasure. I remember coming to him with a question just before a government meeting was about to take place; he responded by lecturing to me for a full quarter of an hour on how many Jews had followed Moses out of Egypt.

The only error Ben-Gurion made in the period during which I was close to him (and it may have been his last) was in the attitude he took toward the Lavon Affair. None of my attempts to persuade him of the gravity of the situation, nor any display I made of my unhappiness over developments, had any effect on him. I remember once talking the situation over with Ben-Gurion's political aide, Yitzhak Navon. Ben-Gurion entered the office, and one look at my face was enough to tell him how depressed I was feeling. Without even asking why I was looking so glum, he pointed at the map in the room and said: "Don't let it get you down. Just look at the Negev—one day millions will be living there." And when I interrupted him and said, "But what about the present?" he cut me off and answered, "There is no present. There is a past, there is a future. The moment you said the word "present" it was already in the past." Ben-Gurion would not let me continue with my tale of woe.

Ben-Gurion never imagined that Moshe Sharett, the man who, when he was prime minister, had to cope with the mess brought on by Lavon, would join Golda Meir and Ziama Aran in defending Lavon. He also failed to grasp the significance of the anger of the veterans in Mapai. When the press published leaks about Ben-Gurion's plans for reshuffling personnel, he did not imagine that party veterans would believe that he was trying to replace them with younger members of the party, when all he really wanted to do was to bring younger talent into positions of authority but without undermining the older party workers. Some of the younger party members on the make may have been in a hurry, but not Ben-Gurion.

Ben-Gurion had been convinced that, if he abstained from voting on the issue of establishing the ministerial Commission of Seven to inquire into the Lavon Affair, it would not come into being. It took a long time before Ben-Gurion was finally able to realize what Eshkol had tried to tell him, namely, that his disciples and followers had grown up, and when he did, it was already too late. His correspondence with Sharett clearly showed Ben-Gurion's inability to come to terms with changes in circumstances and in people. Ben-Gurion believed that Moshe Sharett knew more than any other man about the Lavon Affair and could not imagine how a man of Sharett's decency could possibly withhold what he knew.

Although Ben-Gurion may have made a number of tactical blunders over the Lavon Affair, his fundamental position on it was sound. On the matter of principle he was backed by a number of prominent jurists, including Minister of Justice Dov Joseph, former Attorney General Moshe Ben-Zeev, the lawyers Aharon Hoter-Yishai and Yitzhak Tunik, and Haim Zadok. I thought that Zadok had suggested the best course to follow to resolve the issue, namely, that the government put on record the findings of the justice minister and the attorney general.

As I look back, it seems to me that if the split had any positive achievements, they were to be found in the lesson it taught to the nation that the holding of public office was not the ultimate value in public life. It is true that had Ben-Gurion held his ground in insisting that our fight with Mapai was not about party programs, but on the issue of a distortion of the law, Dayan and Peres and groups from outside the labor movement would never have joined Rafi; for them Rafi represented a new political direction. We might have lost a few Knesset seats—although not inevitably because on the issue of the Lavon Affair alone, we might have made inroads among Mapai supporters—but we would have righted a grave miscarriage of justice and done so without making pretentious bids for political power.

Ben-Gurions's greatness remained with him to the last. When he finally let go of the Lavon Affair, he renewed his friendships with the comrades he had broken with and welcomed them warmly to Sde-Boker when they came to congratulate him on his birthday. In his will he gave expression to his desire to leave this world on good terms with his former friends.

Paula Ben-Gurion was an exceptional person. She knew all the people around Ben-Gurion well and had strong opinions of her own on the events and issues of the day. Although there were those among Ben-Gurion's associates whom she disliked, she never said a word against them to Ben-Gurion. She enjoyed grumbling about aches and pains and Ben-Gurion would take her complaints very seriously, indulge and soothe her. She, for her part, had consciously chosen to live in Ben-Gurion's shadow. Yet in her own way she played an active role in public life: she was an advocate of good will and peace in domestic political disputes. During the period of the Lavon Affair, she did everything in her power to restrain Ben-Gurion's anger. She used to praise Menahem Begin to Ben-Gurion, speak of Begin's honesty and integrity, and try to influence BG to avoid coming into personal conflict with him.

Moshe Sharett was a favorite figure in the movement. His learning, knowledge, precision of thought, manner of speaking, and gentlemanly behavior made him greatly admired and loved. He had a notable capacity of sympathy for others.

From 1955 on, after Sharett had been compelled to give the prime ministry back to Ben-Gurion, and especially after Ben-Gurion's Givat-Haim speech, in which he implied that the change in the defense ministry had made it possible for Israel to receive arms, Moshe Sharett was a deeply frustrated man and remained so, I think, until the day of his death. He succeeded in hiding his frustration and behaved with admirable loyalty toward the government and Ben-Gurion. From Sharett's personal journal, published after his death by his son Yaacov, we learn of his unrelieved anger at Ben-Gurion, but of his admiration as well. His journal teaches us why Ben-Gurion could never stop writing to him. The pity is that even Sharett's attitude in the Lavon Affair was based on considerations of party politics. He had argued that Lavon was responsible for the secret—service failure in 1954 even if he hadn't issued the actual order for the operation, but he believed that the opposition to Lavon at the time the details of the scandal were revealed was working to the advantage of *ha-kat* ("the clique")—by which he meant the Youth Wing.

Golda was a clever and gifted women, with a capacity to take a subject and concentrate on it wholly. She brooked no opposition. She saw things only in black and white, and recognized no intermediate shades; people were either good or bad. Ideologically, she was a dedicated Ben-Gurionist. During the debate that took place before the establishment of the state on the issue of political action or restraint, Golda took on the job of representing Ben-Gurion's point of view while he was away in Paris. She was the one who carried on the struggle against Kaplan, Shprintzak, Lavon, and others, while Eshkol chaired the Standing Committee, which took the decision favoring activism.

When Golda was asked whether she had had hesitations about accepting a government ministry, she replied that if Ben-Gurion had asked her to jump from the fifth floor she would have done so. Nevertheless, her clash with the ministry of defense and her belief that there was a conspiracy against her despite her sacrifices on behalf of Ben-Gurion drove her closer to Sapir, who was an avowed dove, and to Ziama Aran, who was also dovishly inclined. She eventually became the mainstay of the Cooperative and its dominent personality.

As an opponent she could be hard and merciless, but she was also a good friend and comrade. She was generous in her conduct toward those who worked for her, and when I entered the Ministry of Labor, the love of those on the staff who had worked with Golda was still very much in evidence. Ben-Gurion admired her greatly, but he observed that she had a weakness for intellectual men and Hebraists and would sometimes fall under their influence. So it had been with David Remez, Ben-Gurion claimed, and now it was with Israel Galili.

Ziama Aran resembled Golda in his attitude toward people, with one difference. For him, most people were bad. He, too, thought in terms of black and white, with very few of the latter color. He was not as steady a type as Golda.

Ziama took a fatalistic view of life; he regarded himself as someone for whom trouble lay in wait. Once, when he took a train trip, the train was derailed; on a flight from England to Israel, his plane made a forced landing in Libya. When both of us made the voyage on the *Negba* to Marseilles and arrived sound and hale, Ziama claimed that the only reason the ship had not sunk was because there were so many passengers on board whose good luck outweighed his bad.

Pinhas Sapir was the youngest member of the Cooperative. In effect his role in the country was very much like that of a general director in an enterprise. His virtues were his capacity for hard work and his ability to make quick decisions, but overwork and hasty decisions also accounted for his failures. Sapir, unlike Golda and Ziama, never either smoked or took a drink. Other than his family, which he loved to distraction, Sapir's only real joy was his little black notebook in which he noted down all the facts and figures on the development of the country's economy and which he kept always with him. He did have another small pleasure; he enjoyed listening to a racy bit of gossip now and then.

Pinhas Lavon was Ben-Gurion's favorite during the early days of the state. He possessed all of the qualities of a man after Ben-Gurion's heart: he was young, intellectual, bright, a leader in the pioneer movement, a member of Kibbutz Hulda, and he also regarded the state as the chief institution of the country. It was he who, just after the foundation of the state, determined the direction the Histadrut would take in a Jewish country. And it was he who put the Labor Exchange in the hands of the state. Lavon was also an excellent speaker, and one of the most brilliant polemicists in the country.

Lavon's dovish views did not bother Ben-Gurion, who regarded Lavon as his successor. In anticipation of Lavon's succeeding him, Ben-Gurion gave Lavon the defense portfolio. When misfortune overtook Lavon, Ben-Gurion considered it a great loss to the country.

Eshkol was second only to Ben-Gurion in stature among the party leaders. He possessed earthy common sense and was a good-hearted, loyal friend. He immersed himself wholly in the country's life, experiencing it with every fiber of his being. It was a pleasure to share his company. I had occasion to go with him on a number of inspection tours of development projects, and I still recall with what love he gazed at every bush and tree we passed. I think Eshkol may have been the man most loyal to Ben-Gurion. Only those who knew both of them can understand the depth of the tragedy in their estrangement.

During the conflict between the Youth Wing and the party veterans, Eshkol prevented the ouster of Giora Josephtal. Eshkol never joined the controversy between the two camps and had no serious complaints against the Youth Wing. During the bitter debate in the Fourth Party Congress of Mapai in 1965, Eshkol spoke without anger; he only appealed to Ben-Gurion to give him a chance in office for four years. Had Ben-Gurion allowed him that, the history of Mapai would have been very different.

I remember the day after the voting when I mounted the podium; Eshkol rose from his seat and shook my hand. His gesture of peace was greeted by applause from the public: both he and they wanted a reconciliation. But it was no secret that part of the leadership—especially those in its second and third ranks—

wanted a split in the party. Eshkol did not and for a time withstood the pressures from the Cooperative to bring it about.

Eshkol and I worked together for the election of Moshe Sharett to the chairmanship of the World Zionist Organization. During the 1959 election campaign, I asked Eshkol to do the troubleshooting at local party branches. He threw himself into the job heart and soul and gave it all of his talent and time. He worked night and day without making the headlines: there are few who knew how great was his part in our victory in that election. A great wrong was done to Eshkol when he was prevented from straightening out his differences with Ben-Gurion and when, on the eve of the Six-Day War, he was deprived of the office of minister of defense.

End of an Era

My duties in the Labor Ministry left me with little time for party activities, but I made it a rule to devote one day in the week to the Haifa branch of the party. I wasn't happy about the way things were going there, but I continued to hope that there would be changes after the 1969 elections.

Early in April of that year, Abba Khoushi took part in a conference of young party members belonging to the Haifa branch. Like myself, Khoushi was not pleased with how things were shaping up at the meeting and walked out greatly upset. The next day he suffered a heart attack, brought on, in part, by the strain of walking up three flights of stairs to his apartment. He was rushed to Rothschild Hospital in Haifa, and there he died. His death marked the end of an era in the history of the city he loved so much and to which he had dedicated most of his energy. Before he was laid to rest, I met with a group of Abba Khoushi's friends, among them Sapir, and we decided to assist Moshe Flieman, Haifa's deputy major, to fill Khoushi's shoes.

After Abba Khoushi's death, an attempt was made to make me responsible for dealing with the affairs of our Arab minority. It was a field in which Abba Khoushi had been very active, and one for which he was eminently suited: he spoke Arabic, knew Arab customs, and was at home in their neighborhoods. I refused to accept the responsibility, just as I would not allow the responsibility for development towns to be palmed off on me when I was labor minister. That job had been in my province when I was minister of housing and development. I believed then, as I still do, that a government minister should concentrate on the work of his office; if he must have extracurricular activities, party work is quite enough. Any additional task he takes on will only interfere with his work and that of his staff.

Late at night on February 26, 1969, I was startled out of my sleep by the telephone in my hotel room in Toronto, Canada, where I was on tour on behalf of Israel Bonds. Our ambassador to Washington was on the line to inform me that Prime Minister Levi Eshkol had just died; I was asked to return immediately to Israel. My Canadian bodyguards, whose efficiency was a marvel, went into immediate action. With their help I was able to arrange a flight to New York and from there to Israel with no delay. As I boarded the plane in New York I met Zeev Sharef, then minister of housing, and we began speculating about who would replace Levi Eshkol as prime minister. We both thought that Golda was the ideal choice: not only because of her abilities, but because any other candidate was likely to split the party.

When we reached Israel, Sapir informed us that all of the members of the government, including Galili and Allon, were agreed that Golda should be prime minister. Peres, however, told me that the Rafi faction would oppose her candidacy. Dayan spoke with great anger about the fact that the veteran leaders were holding unofficial meetings on government matters, and even discussing questions of national security, without including him in their deliberations. Despite the general way in which he couched his complaints, it was clear that he was thinking about the deliberations being held about Golda's appointment. I therefore asked for a meeting with Sapir, Yaacov Shimshon Shapira, Allon, Galili, and Dayan. I put my cards on the table: I recommended that the prime ministry be given to Golda, but I also spoke out against the factionalism that was being revived and protested against Dayan's being treated as an outsider by his colleagues in the party. The deliberations were friendly. Still, as Dayan and I left party headquarters, he told me that he had not made up his mind yet about Golda's appointment.

Nevertheless, despite the reservations of two of Rafi's leaders, I followed my own convictions on the matter and worked for her appointment. I held talks with a group of former Rafists. We decided to vote for Golda and asked Avraham Wolfensohn to announce our support for Golda at the meeting of the Central Committee.

The Central Committee met at the Ohel Auditorium. Sitting beside Golda in the front row, I watched her face as Wolfensohn spoke with great warmth in her support. I was sure she now knew that she had strong backing even from Rafi. When she mounted the stage to thank her supporters, she was in tears. It was still too soon to realize that we were looking at a woman who would soon hold a place of special honor among the prime ministers of Israel.

As the date of Histadrut, Knesset, and local elections approached, members of Rafi who were unhappy over the merger with Mapai grew increasingly restive. There were complaints about the lack of dialogue and the co-opting of former Rafi members; Shimon Peres was regarded as a case in point, after the failure to find a way to move him into the government. The communications media became the battlefield in the war of nerves between party factions. Once again the press leaks were coming fast and furious. Former members of Rafi who were in the Labor party's Central Committee were meeting constantly and were demanding the right to be represented as a faction in the Knesset and government. I avoided these meetings; I had already made it clear more than once that I did not regard myself as a member of any party faction, but so long as factions still existed within the Labor party I would consider myself a former member of Mapai. When I was asked what I would do if no faction put my name forward as a candidate for the election list, answered that it was a risk I was willing to take. I also said that although it was Rafi that had made the dismantling of factions a condition of its merger with Mapai, so long as an elected assembly had not met to vote on candidates (an event that was scheduled to take place only after the 1969 election), each faction should be allowed to chose its own candidates.

Call for a Real Merger

During that period I met frequently with Moshe Dayan, who, unlike some members of Rafi, was not particularly happy about the prospect of a split in the Labor party. I also raised the matter at meetings with Prime Minister Golda Meir and Party Secretary Pinhas Sapir. I wrote an article outlining my demand for a real merger of all groups in the Labor party and published it in *Davar* on April 4, 1969. The article drew sharp criticism from Rafi against both me and Sapir. In my article I pointed out that the controversy on all of the issues having to do with the government, society, and the party was, in fact, a debate among colleagues within the Labor party—one taking place within a single, all-embracing political context. Moreover, harm done to the Labor party was done to the nation as a whole and could lead to national catastrophe. Our political situation and the state of our national security called for unity, not division. "The requirements of a party in the process of consolidation," I wrote, "and the growing trend toward unity, in accordance with the organizational agreements and the founding compact of the party are the determining factors, not former "historical" factions. . . . We must continue our meetings for internal rapproachment. This is the positive and constructive meaning of 'the turning of a new page' (as it was called by Moshe Dayan) so greatly needed by our party today."

At the Rafi convention at the end of April, it was decided that so long as the elected assembly of the unified party had not met, representatives of Rafi would be elected by the faction. I saw nothing terrible in the decision, since I could well understand Shimon Peres' concern over his position in the next government.

Chaim Herzog observed about my stand on the merger: "I have no quarrel with Almogi, since from the very first he has made clear what it is that he wants and has achieved what he wanted to achieve. Would that we had many like him, although not working toward the same goal as he." Murik Bareli remarked: "I don't agree with Peres's opinion, nor with Almogi's. We have to reach a synthesis."

An agreement on Peres's joining the government was concluded before the elections, and relations between Golda and Dayan had improved to the point that they could almost be called cordial. Dayan's popularity was then at its height, a fact made very evident by the expression of public concern for his health when he was injured while at an archaeological excavation. I was then in the United States and witnessed the great concern of the Jewish community there. When I returned to Israel I visited Dayan in the hospital. Even though he had evident difficulty in talking, he kept speaking of the security situation, which was what preoccupied him most. He assured me that he would do all he could to eliminate the problem of terrorist incursions into Israel. I tried to tell Dayan that Rafi was getting into trouble again, this time over its strong opposition to a party align-ment with Mapai; Dayan indicated, however, that the subject was of no interest to him.

During the 1969 election campaign I was active only in the Haifa branch of the party, although even there the role I played was limited. I kept somewhat aloof because I was less than enthusiastic about the way in which the campaign was being run, and I felt particularly dissatisfied over the way our publicity depart-ment was working. I believe that were it not for the fact that Sapir lead the campaign and that Avraham Ofer was campaign-headquarters coordinator and Yosi Sarid responsible for publicity, there would certainly have been a thor-oughgoing investigation of the causes of our serious losses at the polls. The Labor party fell from sixty-three seats in the Knesset to fifty-six, and so had taken one more step in the direction of handing over the government to the right. This happened when the party's election campaign was in the hands of a team that failed to get results in every contest it had directed before then—and since.

It should be remembered that the election took place after the Six-Day War, at a time when the country was riding the crest of an unprecedented economic boom and international political gains. In the 1961 election—which took place after the ruinous Lavon Affair—we lost only five Knesset seats, and that was enough to raise an uproar among our local party branches. The drop of seven seats this time—even if we discount the two mandates gained by Rafi in 1968 from non-Labor sectors—represented a considerable loss to the Labor party.

33

The Ministry of Labor

When I took over from Yigal Allon in the Labor Ministry about a year after the Six-Day War, I found it necessary to introduce changes in the Ministry in order to accommodate its operations to the needs of the state and the economy. The Six-Day War had far-reaching consequences for the whole country, and my office was no exception.

The Employment Service

When I first started in the Labor Ministry the staff tended to regard me as a dreamer out of touch with the real world. Honoch Lev-Kochav, the director-general made no bones about his misgivings. Ministers, he said, needed publicity: they announced ambitious projects that made headlines, but when it came to carrying them out, well, that was another story. Then he asked, "Do you really intend to put those plans of yours into effect?" When I said that I did, he replied, "Well, every minister has his madness, I suppose."

I announced the cancellation of locally initiated work projects, which were really a form of fictitious employment, and I ordered a check to be made on the number of people registered as working in Hameshakem ("Rehabilitation"), the large institution for the employment of senior citizens. The steps I took created an uproar and drew heavy criticism from city mayors and people in the Histadrut. But these work programs, which employed between thirty and forty thousand people and cost between forty thousand and sixty thousand liroth to maintain, seemed to me to be a prodigal waste of money and manpower which the nation could put to better use.

Despite all of the opposition and criticism, I went ahead with my plan. With the help of the Employment Service staff, some of those employed in the work projects were put to work in industry, and others were sent to job-retraining courses and received wages during their training nearly equal to the minimum wage in industry.

The lack of manpower in industry was becoming increasingly severe. In my meetings with employers, I called for them to introduce more automation rather than depend on manual labor, which only seemed cheaper. I also asked my staff to begin preparations for the latent work force, especially women who would soon be entering the industrial labor market.

Another social group I set my sights for was the teenagers who were neither going to school nor working. The Employment Service sent teams of workers to Bat-Yam and Rosh-Haayin, where they sought out young men and women and tried to get them to join vocational training programs that had been organized at local places of employment. The experiment proved to be successful, and we introduced it in other localities. The grants received by the young people who joined these vocational training programs were only a little below the starting wage in industry and were a good incentive for enrollment. The process by which young people were absorbed at work was improved, and the apprenticeship law of 1953 was applied to all trades. There were also special units established for the purpose of placing pensioners in jobs, and wage ceilings were raised for people receiving state pensions so they could work without losing their retirement benefits.

I took a special interest in technical workers and senior technicians. It seemed to me that encouraging advanced training for youths who, for economic reasons, were unable to study at the Technion or to complete their training at a regular technical college was not only good for the economy, but was also a social duty. The fact that a far greater number of oriental Jewish youth were registered in technical schools than studying engineering convinced me that a special effort had to be made in behalf of technical education. I therefore set aside a budget of fifteen million liroth for the establishment of a technical college on the Neve Shaanan campus of the Haifa Technion. The school was first housed in a temporary structure and later replaced by a permanent building. In its first year, 1969, the school enrolled about two thousand students; by the time I left the Labor Ministry eleven thousand students were studying there. This sizable increase in the number of technical workers and senior technicians was indirectly responsible for organizational problems arising from professional rivalry between senior technicians and engineers. To deal with the situation I appointed Professor Efraim Katzir (later president of Israel) to head a committee to define the professional areas of technicians and engineers respectively. The findings of the committee were applied to reduce tensions between the two groups.

Employment of Arabs from the Territories

In the first few months of my work in the ministry, I had to face the difficult problems that had arisen as a result of the employment in Israel of Arabs from the West Bank and Gaza. Thousands were working in the country without supervision, and the absence of control not only involved a security risk, but had led to serious exploitation of the Arab laborers, whose work conditions were substandard. The military government had initiated a program of public development projects for the employment of the jobless in the territories, and I agreed to have the Department of Public Works oversee the planning and building of a road network in the West Bank to create jobs for several thousand unemployed Arabs.

The ministry's policy on the employment in Israel of Arabs from the territories took shape after long negotiations between myself and various state agencies—among them the IDF, the Ministry of Defense, the Histadrut, and various economic bodies. We established a number of principles, the chief of which was that we assumed an obligation to assure employment for the population in the areas under military rule, both by initiating work projects in the territories themselves and by the employment within Israel of Arabs from the territories. We decided to open employment bureaus in the territories, to place them under the direction and supervision of the Employment Service, and to keep unorganized labor in this area to a minimum. We also resolved that the Arab laborers from the territories whom we employed would receive the same salaries and enjoy the same social benefits as Jewish workers. The salaries of workers from the territories were to be disbursed through the employment bureaus, which would also be responsible for the bookkeeping; the procedure was the same as the one which had been in use in the past for work projects in Israel. We would also take off the standard deductions, including income tax, social security, and health insurance, and transfer the amounts to the proper agencies. Finally, all amounts deducted for social benefits would be deposited in the workers' names.

On the last point, I had quite a tussle with Moshe Dayan. The deductions for social benefits taken off the wages of Arab workers from the territories had accumulated, and their accrued value was beginning to run into the billions. The question now arose of what to do with this money. I was of the opinion that personal files should be opened for all the workers to keep a record of the amount of money in social benefits accruing to each of them, so that when the time came they could take advantage of the services coming to them, including social security retirement pensions. Dayan proposed to put the whole sum at the disposal of the military government and to have the money used for development projects in the West Bank and Gaza.

I argued that we had no moral right to dispose of workers' money without their knowledge and express permission. What, I asked, would happen if there were ever peace and the same Arab workers came to us and demanded, quite rightly, the benefits for which we had deducted money from their hard-earned salaries? Surely we could not renege on our obligations. My arguments had no effect even on Golda, who backed Dayan on this issue. All the same I stuck to my guns and brought the matter up for a vote in the government. The result was a surprise: I think it was the first time that Golda and Dayan were in the minority. The government decided in my favor, and personal files were started on all the Arab workers from the territories. In 1980 I had the immense satisfaction of learning of the first two workers from the territories applying for and receiving retirement pensions.

The policy we had set concerning the numbers of Arab workers from the West

Bank and Gaza to be employed and the way in which they would be processed received official approval from all the relevant authorities, and responsibility for its implementation was taken on by the Ministry of Labor. During my period in office thirty-five employment bureaus were opened in the territories, and serviced more than fifty thousand Arab workers. We also established about thirty vocational training centers in Judea, Sumaria, and Gaza, and helped start a number of cooperative companies, among them enterprises for water supply and freight transport.

We experienced quite a few difficulties in putting our policy on employment in the territories into effect. We had particular problems over the employment of agricultural workers from the territories during the heavy seasons. At such times whole families, together with their children, were hired by agricultural settlements and farms and were put to work under substandard labor conditions. Many, including authorities in the military government, took a tolerant view of this shameful practice. I imposed strict measures of control to eliminate the abuse. As a result I came under fire from farmers, who began to protest loudly against what they called "Almogi's patrol." I persisted. I agreed to lift severe controls when I finally gained the farmers' agreement to hire workers only through the employment bureaus and to refrain from using children as laborers and quartering families of hired hands on the farms.

I also disagreed with Dayan on his support for cancelling the limit set on the number of Arabs from the terrritories that were allowed to be employed in Israel. I was particularly worried that, in the building industry, Arabs from the West Bank and Gaza accounted for 65 percent of the labor force. I felt that if the trend continued, the manual labor force in our economy would be largely composed of Arabs from the territories, and Jews would confine themselves to the skilled trades and posts in management. It seemed to me that if we did not put a stop to this pattern, we could find ourselves one day faced by the threat of Arab workmen shutting down vital sectors of our economy. The massive employment in Israel of Arabs from the territories could be stemmed by the introduction of more automation and advanced technology in Israeli enterprises. Until that could be done, I preferred that during the fruit-picking season, for example, Jewish volunteers, including high school students, be employed, in exchange for incentives, to free us from our dependence on labor from the territories.

Absorption of Soviet Immigrants

In the early 1970s a crack appeared for the first time in the iron curtain, permitting Soviet Jews to emigrate to Israel. We quickly organized to help them find jobs. To cut red tape and save the new immigrants from having to run around in their search for employment, the Employment Service stationed a man at each of the Jewish Agency's Immigrant Absorption centers. In this way we were able to secure employment for most of the immigrants from the Soviet Union, including nearly 80 percent of the women. We faced a difficult problem in finding jobs for immigrants in the academic and free professions, who accounted for nearly 40 percent of the new settlers—or about triple the rate in the general population. The upshot was that every year we had to find employment for about ten thousand professionals. Golda and Pinhas Sapir asked me to submit a memorandum on the subject for consideration by the government. After consultation, the government appointed a ministerial committee chaired by me to formulate proposals to alleviate the problem. Our first step was to propose the establishment of a vocational information center for professionals and a policy of giving assistance to enterprises with a sizable staff of academic employees. I also suggested to Victor Shem-Tov, the minister of health, to study the possibility of setting up modern hospitals to serve patients from abroad, which could employ scores of immigrant doctors; for a variety of reasons, the project, unfortunately, never got underway.

Department of Social Security

The director of social security, Dr. Israel Katz, worked closely with me on the vast number of activies under his department's jurisdiction. We established a planning and research unit headed by Rafi Roter, who later became director of social security. Together we succeeded in vastly improving the public reputation of this all-important social agency. In the twenty-five years of the existence of the department, one of whose founders was Golda Meir, about twenty-five laws and emendations of laws had been passed in the field of social security. I had introduced thirteen of these in the Knesset. My work in this field at the legislature was greatly eased by the chairman of the Knesset Labor Committee, Shoshana Arabelli-Almozalino, who was keenly conscious and very knowledgeable about social problems. It was a pleasure to see her fight in the Knesset to push through improvements in the law in addition to those which I had initiated.

The field of social security occupied me more than any of the others in my jurisdiction, even though my activities in other areas made more impressive newspaper headlines. In my first years in office, I worked hard to get the finance ministry to increase the sums paid out in all kinds of social benefits being dispensed by the department. I spent long sessions with Avraham Agmon, finance ministry director and his loyal aides, trying to squeeze out just a bit more of the money I thought was important for the needy. To ease the problem of the ongoing devaluation of benefits as a result of inflation, we raised benefit payments to unprecedented levels, which brought in train a corresponding expansion in our budget and activities. In a number of instances I thought the increases in payments exaggerated. For example, in 1970 social security benefits suddenly rose from seven hundred liroth to fifteen hundred liroth per month. However, I had no part in the decision leading to the increases, which were the result of an agreement made by the government, Histadrut, and employers. I was afraid that steep increases of this kind might be interpreted by the public as a step to siphon off more public funds. To preserve the good name of the department, I called frequent meetings of the agencies concerned in the work of the department and carefully explained to their workers the difference between taxes and social security deductions.

In July 1972, the Knesset passed an amendment to the Social Security Law. The amendment had taken over a year to prepare and contained fully seventy-eight sections which, taken together, vastly improved the social benefits available. One of the achievements of the amendment was to guarantee more effectively the value of old-age pensions by linking them to the average national income rather than, as formerly, to the cost-of-living index, which does not adequately reflect the rise of wage levels in the country. Another item in the amendment established a special fund for grants to deal with social problems not specifically covered in the law.

Particularly important was the improvement in benefits in child allowances received by large families. We simplified procedures and made all families in the country—both of wage earners and the self-employed—eligible for child-allowance benefits. The decision to impose income tax on all earnings, including child-allowance benefits, was a step in the direction of greater social equality. About 75 percent of the real beneficiaries of child-allowance benefits were wage earners with large families who payed almost no income tax; by taxing the benefits of higher income brackets, we were able to recoup a significant part of the money paid out to those in need.

During the five years in which, as minister of labor, I had responsibility for social security, a number of respectable advances were made in the field. Social benefit payments in that period rose at the rate of 25 percent annually. At a meeting of the Public Council of the Social Security Department I spelled out the significance of these increases. On the same occasion, I gave a detailed account of the effects of the reform we introduced in the matter of child-allowance benefits. The statistics I quoted to demonstrate the improvements that had been achieved were a credit to the government and could only enhance its reputation among the public.

I knew that Sapir would read what I had said, but I was not sure what his response would be. He had invited me to his office for a chat. I arrived in the afternoon. Sapir was taking his usual short rest on the couch in his office. He was clearly upset and began by complaining to me that although he had gone out of his way to help me, Dr. Israel Katz was attacking him at every opportunity. "Look, you have just told the public about our achievements," he added, "and it is good that you did. But why, for heaven's sake, is Dr. Katz slandering me?" I calmed him down and promised I would have a talk with Dr. Katz.

Dr. Katz was certainly a good director-general, he was both knowledgeable about his job and devoted to it. But he had a penchant for interviews with the press, to which he would come without being properly prepared, and would make highly critical statements about the government and the minister of finance. The more he was praised by the press the more pleasure he seemed to find in his role of public gadfly. I asked him to exercise greater restraint, but I could not really get angry at him; I knew he behaved as he did in all innocence. But even innocence can be a cause of great annoyance. The late Michael Chazani, who was minister of welfare at the time, would go into a rage even at the mention of Dr. Katz's name. Sapir knew me well enough to realize that I was not in sympathy with Dr. Katz's public expressions of criticism, but Chazani suspected that the director of social security was making his statements with my approval and so directed his anger at me as well. And indeed it seems to me that little if anything is ever achieved by behaving with hostility toward one's colleagues in the way Dr. Katz did.

Accident and National Health Insurance

The introduction of a law for national health insurance was a subject of public discussion since the foundation of the state. It was a plank in the Mapai platform in every election campaign and the subject of deliberations by countless committees, some of which even made practical recommendations acclaimed by everyone. Moshe Soroka, chairman of the Histadrut Sick Fund and an expert in the field, was an enthusiastic supporter of it. I regarded such a law as a cornerstone of social legislation, and although I was aware of the opposition to it by some members of the Histadrut, I felt they were in error. It was not our intention to nationalize existing health insurance programs, but to base our legislation on them. I regarded the existing situation as an intolerable drain on our resources and decided to work to change it. The government appointed a committee under my direction to investigate the subject, as did the Labor Alignment. I found myself immediately at odds with just about everyone; I was even accused of betraying the Histadrut. In the end, with an able assist from Dr. Haim Doron and Gideon Ben-Israel, we came up with a detailed and practical proposal. We submitted a memorandum to the government, and I appeared before the party faction, which—after stormy debate and an excellent speech by Professor Andre de Vries—gave its approval. Then, after I ran the gauntlet of debate in meetings with doctors, people from the Histadrut, public groups, and members of the government, a bill proposing a national health insurance law was finally presented at the Knesst by Minister of Health Victor Shem-Tov.

Unfortunately the proposal was late in being presented in committee, and we were therefore unable to bring it up for second and third readings. We did, however, chalk up one victory: in 1972 we were able get Knesset approval for the Parallel Tax Law, which increased health insurance payments to health insurance programs and eased the strain on their finances. It was an important step in the direction of a national health insurance law. My reward for helping obtain passage of the Parallel Tax Law was the establishment of a center for industrial medicine in collaboration with Tel Aviv University and funded by the Histadrut Sick Fund. By another package deal, the Department of Social Security took two new units under its wing: disability insurance and unemployment insurance.

The unemployment insurance law was welcomed by both the Knesset and the Knesset Labor Committee. Among the law's provisions was one which made it possible to set aside 5 percent of the annual income of the unemployment insurance fund for the use of the Bureau of Economic Efficiency, set up in collaboration with the Labor Productivity Institute. Enthusiasm for the work of the bureau was so great in the Labor Committee that a proposal was introduced for the amount to be raised to 10 percent. In the end we compromised by stipulating that in case of need the bureau could apply to the Labor Committee for up to 10 percent and receive the amount upon approval by the committee. For only a nominal fee or, in some cases, free, any enterprise or organization could apply to the bureau for advice for improving its economic and production efficiency. The bureau offered advice as well on subjects such as internal personnel shifts, vocational training, and job retraining. In the first months of its existence, the bureau proved its worth by helping to increase the efficiency of many enterprises, saving the economy millions of liroth.

34

The Change That Never Was

In mid-August 1970, Prime Minister Golda Meir called to ask if I would come to her office in the Knesset. I had no idea what she wanted to see me about.

Golda began by speaking warmly about how well I was carrying out my duties in the Ministry of Labor. Then she spoke about the difficult situation in the Ministry of Posts and of its becoming worse all the time. She asked if I would be willing to exchange ministries and take over the Ministry of Posts from Israel Yeshayahu. She was recommending Israel Galili to take over the Ministry of Labor and suggested that I take on, in addition to the Ministry of Posts, the Ministry of Development, which I been responsible for from 1962 to 1965. Golda was trying to sweeten the pill: she knew I had a sentimental attachment to the Development Ministry because the Electric Corporation and the chemical industry, which were under its jurisdiction, were centered in Haifa.

Although I had not had any advanced warning, I told her on the spur of the moment that although I would be sorry to leave the Labor Ministry I felt that as prime minister she had the right to distribute ministerial offices as she saw fit. Golda was surprised at my reply and the rapidity with which I made it. I was being frank, and I did not regard my acceptance of the change as any sort of sacrifice. I certainly did not consider Golda's suggestion a personal slight. I was well aware of the problems in the postal ministry, and knew that it would require a lot of work to get the office on its feet. By comparison with what would be required there, my work at the Ministry of Labor might almost be described as a bed of roses. I had never in my life asked for the easy jobs.

To my amazement, almost all the newspapers came out with editorials attacking the planned reshuffle of ministers and full of praise for my work in the Ministry of Labor. In *Davar* Eliyahu Agress and Zalman Yodi came out with articles opposed to Golda's proposals. Similar articles were written by the editor of *Haaretz*, Gershon Schocken, and the editor of *Maariv*, Arieh Dissentshik.

Golda suspected me of organizing the opposition to the cabinet change, which was not the case. I was heartily sorry about what was happening, and to put an end to it I went to a meeting of Golda's group of Mapai party members, Haverenu, intending to ask for the change to be put into effect immediately. Before I had a chance to speak my piece, Golda angrily announced that the reshuffle was called off. It took a long time before she became convinced that my initial acceptance of her proposal was made in good faith and that I had had no part in the public protest over the change. In any case, I remained minister of labor.

The Chinese Connection

As minister of labor I had frequent occasion to travel abroad, either on ministry business or on behalf of national organizations and fund drives. In 1969 I went on a Far Eastern tour during which I visited Singapore, Hong Kong, Japan, Australia, and New Zealand. When I returned to Israel, the day after the opening of the Labor Party Congress, I told Moshe Dayan about an interesting conversation I had had in Singapore. The foreign minister of Singapore, who was a member of the Singapore Labor party and a Chinese, arranged an official dinner in my honor. It was held in the government building, and leaders of the country's labor party and trade unions were invited. Between courses we spoke of the international situation, and at one point the foreign minister told me, offhandedly, that the world was in for a surprise soon when the United States and China began putting out diplomatic feelers in one another's direction. I expressed my own surprise at the news and then mentioned that long ago Ben-Gurion had prophesied this development. The foreign minister answered that he was not a prophet, but was stating a fact soon to be made manifest. Then he advised that Israel would do well to send a representative to Hong Kong to watch events from up close, so as to determine the possibilities of developing ties with China. It was his assessment that China would be ready to deal with any country that was at odds with Russia because Chinese foreign policy was about to take a strong anti-Soviet turn.

All this had taken place before the "ping-pong diplomacy" between China and the United States, and Moshe Dayan thought the whole thing a little farfetched. But he thought that Ben-Gurion would get a kick out of the story and advised me to tell him about it to cheer the Old Man up. When I did, Ben-Gurion took the story as something perfectly natural and reacted as if all that had happened was that the Chinese had taken his advice.

Labor Shortage

One of the chief problems faced by the country after I "returned" to the labor ministry was the critical labor shortage, which was beginning to make itself felt even in the occupied territories. Pressures were being applied on us to approve the introduction into Israel of unskilled laborers from Turkey, Spain, and Cyprus. Although we withheld permission, cases were cropping up of foreign laborers in Israel, many of them claiming to be tourists who remained in the country for lack of funds and were only working temporarily to earn enough money for their fare home. It was hard to decide just what to do about them.

Women represented one labor resource that had still to be fully tapped. However, it was clear that to draw women into the labor market, something would have to be done about lightening the heavy tax burden born by working couples. A second difficulty had to do with the small number of available and reasonably priced nurseries where working mothers could leave preschool children. I raised the problem with a number of agencies and asked for it to be taken up at a combined meeting of the party secretariat and the Knesset party faction. We succeeded in improving things somewhat, especially in the matter of child care centers. Pinhas Sapir managed to collect contributions for the purpose, and the project began to gather momentum. Our efforts resulted in an impressive increase in the number of working women—to the benefit of a number of new industrial fields, among them electronics.

During my term as labor minister, I gave my full backing and support to the Labor Productivity Institute, whose work I regarded as vital in raising production, establishing work norms and increasing industrial efficiency. I recall the vain efforts government agencies made at one time to improvise norms at the port of Ashdod, and the stubbornness with which the institute fended off attempts to interfere with scientifically determined labor norms, whose establishment has a direct bearing on salaries and taxes. For its work the institute earned a deservedly high reputation among both workers and employers.

Problems in Labor Relations

The conditions created in Israel after the Six-Day War had all of the ingredients for labor unrest in most of the sectors of the economy. Overemployment, high taxes, and inflation, in combination with strongly organized trade unions, created pressures and counterpressures.

During the pre-State period, the Histadrut carried out what were essentially governmental functions, and by its epic struggles in behalf of labor, it was able to secure inestimable gains for working people. Once the State of Israel was established, the achievements of the Histadrut were made to apply to all citizens by being turned into law. For example, laws were ratified regulating working hours, rest periods on the job, paid vacations, pregnancy leaves, work contracts, unemployment insurance, overtime pay, women's labor, apprenticeship, industrial accident prevention, and the settlement of labor disputes. Israeli labor law requires that labor contracts to which both parties are signatories be registered with the Department of Labor Relations of the Ministry of Labor, whereby they take on legal force. The department, however, was not intended to replace collective bargaining. It was designed to act as an arbitrating agency, to help the parties in labor disputes come to an agreement.

The Labor Dispute Settlement Law was passed by the Knesset as early as 1957, and before I took office as labor minister, an amendment to the law was submitted, requiring both parties to declare a labor dispute two weeks in advance of taking measures such as strikes and shutdowns. The Knesset was also asked to consider a bill establishing labor courts which would be authorized to rule in disputes over interpretions of particular provisions in labor contracts already in force. Both these laws contributed greatly to resolving labor difficulties, but not all such difficulties. Laws designed to cool off labor disputes are powerless to deal with the really tough labor problems.

In many political parties, including the Labor party, there was a clamor for a law requiring compulsory arbitration in essential services and industries. I had many grounds for opposing such a law, not the least of which was that it had already failed in every advanced country in which it had been tried. It also seemed to me that such a law would put in jeopardy the whole principle of free collective bargaining. Finally, it seemed to me less than fair for a liberal attitude to be taken toward the accumulation of profits and for the law of supply and demand to be held up as an economic model, while the wages of working people should be made a target for legal restraint. I took the position that legal sanction should rather be given to the rules applied by the Histadrut to labor relations. Accordingly, I proposed legislation that would make it illegal for a strike to be called so long as a labor contract was still in force. My proposal was approved, but with strong objections from the Histadrut secretary-general, Yitzhak Ben-Aharon. I therefore agreed that the law should only be applied to vital enterprises which were publicly owned. I explained that the proposed legislation would define once and for all what a strike was, who was entitled to call a strike, and when it could be called. The law would also make it illegal for a group of employees to strike an enterprise if the majority of its workers were opposed. It would, in addition, encourage the establishment of norms of conduct in honoring contractual obligations and promote more precise consideration of the provisions of a labor contract before it was signed. Once an agreement was signed, it would remain in force for the period specified in it, so that labor peace would be assured. I proposed, in addition, that the law include among its provisions the Histadrut procedure of secret ballots in voting on a strike call.

Getting acceptance for the amendment to the Labor Dispute Law involved a long and difficult struggle. Golda supported the bill but wished to avoid a confrontation with Ben-Aharon, and she tried to work out a compromise between me and the Histadrut secretary. After submitting the bill to endless reviews, starting with the committee led by I. S. Shapira and ending with Haverenu, I brought it up for approval before the Labor Alignment faction in the Knesset and Alignment members of the Central Committee of the Labor party. Both Yigal Allon and Israel Galili backed the proposed amendment. Golda did not take the floor and only let her position be known by an interjection during debate. She also did not participate in the voting. The bill received a majority and was then submitted to the Knesset, where it passed.

Aware of the lack of a tradition of labor relations in Israel, I tried to encourage research and the training of academic personnel in the field, so that it could be taken out of the hands of amateurs. My efforts were rewarded by the establishment of centers for labor research in Tel Aviv University and the Hebrew University in Jerusalem, as well as centers for industrial safety and hygiene, and for industrial medicine.

Secretary of the Histadrut

From the start of 1973 up to the Yom Kippur War in October of that year, my name was continually brought up in the news media as the man who was to be tapped for the post of secretary-general of the Histadrut. On January 12, Amnon Barzili wrote in *Haaretz* that, according to a secret poll, were I named a candidate for the post of secretary-general of the Labor Federation, the Labor party would make a stronger showing in the Histadrut elections: the poll indicated that with Yitzhak Ben-Aharon standing for the Histadrut the Labor party would receive 5 percent of the vote, and with me heading the list the party could expect between 55 and 56 percent of the ballots cast. The prediction for Yeruham Meshel was 47 percent.

I was abroad when the article appeared, and when I returned I made no attempt to verify the poll figures. Nevertheless the story would not die, and a few months later the papers came out with a story that the Bloc had had its heart set on me at first, but pressures had been exerted to force it to decide to name Meshel as the party's candidate. One of the papers contained a statement by Sapir that the reason I was not the candidate was because I had refused.

Sapir's version was the true one. While in Geneva attending an ORT (Organization for Rehabilitation through Training) congress, I was invited one morning by Sapir to see him at his hotel. Over a glass of fruit juice and a cup of coffee, Sapir asked me if I wanted the post of Histadrut secretary. My reply was a flat no. When Golda asked the question, I returned the same answer. The simple truth is that I never wanted the job. I also have the feeling that Golda and Sapir were not sure that I was the suitable candidate for them. At least that was the impression one got from an event about which I heard somewhat later.

After Ben-Aharon's speech at the Metalworkers' congress, which took place at about the same time and in which he took the government sharply to task, a delegation of party veterans approached Golda and asked her to remove Ben-Aharon from his post. When Golda asked them whom they would have in Ben-Aharon's place, one of the members of the delegation replied, "Yosef Almogi." At this, according to the version I heard, Golda began laughing and said: "You don't know Almogi. Maybe Almogi won't make speeches against the government and the wage policy, but if he ever decides anything, no one will be able to move him. At least with Ben-Aharon you can talk. I have the feeling that, in addition, Golda never quite forgave me for our differences over the Ata strike.

I have good reason to believe that this story is perfectly true.

35

The Yom Kippur War

In the early spring and summer of 1973 life in Israel was running its normal course, with social and economic pressures and internal political wranglings no different from what they had always been. Despite rather worrisome news filtering through to us about goings-on just across the border, no one guessed the extent of the violence which would shortly be unleashed against us.

On May 25, the mayor of Haifa, Moshe Flieman, died of a terrible illness, and a frantic search began for a replacement to fill the office he had left vacant. The city, which had got used to Abba Khoushi's style of administration, was looking for a suitable candidate who could carry it on. Flieman's death was a hard blow to Haifa: it was the second time in only four years that the mayor of Haifa had died in office. A Citizens for Haifa organization was formed to look for a nonpartisan candidate for mayor, and the opposition parties began to view control of the city government as being within reach.

The Labor Alignment seemed to have no doubt at all about its choice of a candidate, and I found myself being urgently prodded to make myself available for the job. For some months I refrained from responding to the urgings, oral and written, to which I was subjected. Finally, as summer drew to a close, I decided the time had come for me to decide.

National and local elections were coming up in November, and I would need time to organize an election campaign. There were other pressures as well that were forcing a quick decision. Sapir told me that if I were not the party candidate for mayor we might lose Haifa, and this at a time when we were facing a similar prospect in Tel Aviv. Golda invited me for a chat and told me she had received many letters supporting my candidacy for the mayoralty. Among other letters she mentioned one that was especially enthusiastic in my support written by the Haifa correspondent for *Davar,* Mendel Singer, who had praised me to the skies. She stressed that I was one of the best ministers in the government and that she enjoyed working with me, but Haifa was causing the party considerable anxiety and a solution had to be found. After all, she too had once been asked by the party to run in a mayoralty contest in Tel Aviv, and she had not refused the party's call, she said. I tried to fend her off by saying I had never had much of an interest in municipal issues, but she replied by saying that once elected I was likely to do a good job. We agreed that the matter would be settled at a meeting of Haverenu and the party's head office.

The decision reached at the meeting, which was held in the prime minister's office in Jerusalem, was that it was in the party's interest that I accept the candidacy for mayor of Haifa, but that the final decision would be left to me. After much hesitation I reluctantly agreed to head the party list in the municipality race. After the meeting, Sapir joined me for the ride to the Knesset to perk up my spirits and assure me that I would have to serve in Haifa for only four years, enough time to groom a replacement, and then I could return to the government.

I was not particularly concerned about what I should be doing in another four years, and despite my initial feelings, I had begun to take an interest in municipal affairs. As the High Holy Days approached I began to collect material about municipal administration in general, and the Haifa municipality in particular, and made an intensive study of the subject. I expected no trouble being elected, since the Likud candidate was not a serious rival.

On the morning of the Day of Atonement, Yom Kippur, everything suddenly changed.

At 9:30 A.M. Government Secretary Mike Arnon was on the phone inviting me to a cabinet meeting in Tel Aviv, scheduled for noon. I called my driver out of the synagogue and set out immediately. Along the road we passed young men in and out of uniform waiting for lifts to get back to their units, and we picked up three of them. By the time I reached the meeting room, there were already several ministers waiting, Haim Bar-Lev among them. I tried to pump him for information. All I got out of him was one short sentence, which he pronounced in his usual slow and deliberate manner. It spoke volumes: "Looks like there's going to be a war."

Defense Minister Moshe Dayan opened the meeting by telling us that information had been received that the Egyptians and Syrians would be launching an attack at 6:00 P.M. We were in touch with the United States, and our reserves had been called up, he said. The question was brought up whether we should launch a preventive strike while there was still time, but Golda said that our information about enemy intentions, which had reached the Americans as well, still had to be verified; so it would be best if we did not take hostile action now, otherwise we would be accused of starting a war. At the time I had no way of knowing that even had we wanted to take the offensive, we would have found ourselves in no condition to do so.

While the cabinet meeting was still in session, and Sapir was warning us against being the first to attack, the air-raid sirens began to wail. The prime minister's military secretary came in to announce that at that moment—at 1400 hours—Egypt and Syria had gone to war against us.

I immediately got in touch with Lt. Colonel Meir Chechik, the labor ministry's man in charge in national emergencies, and within a few hours our Department of Emergency Manpower was in full operation.

The Surprise Attack

Like the rest of the cabinet, I was in a black mood. I made no contributions to cabinet discussions at the time on our problems of defense and foreign policy. I was not sufficiently knowledgeable about either. Nor did I have at my disposal highly classified secret intelligence, to which only a few of our ministers had access. So I thought it better to listen than talk, especially when operational military decisions came up for discussion. Still, I was unable to free myself of the shocks and anxieties I experienced in the course of the cabinet sessions held during the Yom Kippur War. The intelligence blunder was in itself upsetting enough, but the botch in logistics was even worse—and even less excusable. In the first hours of the war, our munitions depots were in terrible disarray, with hardly an item that was not in low supply. Among its other baneful consequences, the mismanagement of supplies had a very bad effect on fighting morale.

I was shocked at the difference between what was being reported at cabinet meetings and what I heard from doctors at Haifa's Rambam Hospital during my frequent visits there. The battlefield descriptions heard by doctors from wounded servicemen differed completely from the reports in the cabinet, where in the first days of the war our mood kept shifting from depression to relief and back again. Dayan was pessimistic and very much down, as was Israel Tal ("Talik"), who kept lighting one cigarette from another, Chief-of-Staff David Elazar ("Dado"), on the other hand, and later Bar-Lev, were optimistic and exuded confidence. Bar-Lev's announcement after the first week of fighting that the Arabs had gone back to being Arabs and that we were back to our old selves again lit up the faces of everyone in the cabinet. Golda showed nerves of steel throughout.

The people experienced a brutal shock in the war, and the crisis was primarily one of credibility. The nation's pride in the defense system—the apple of its eye—had been dealt a hard blow. The arrogant boastfulness with which some of our senior officers rode the crest of victory after the Six-Day War now appeared, in the light of the conduct of this war, to have been empty posturing.

When the cabinet took up the question of whether to attempt a crossing of the Suez Canal and carry the war into enemy territory, I decided to voice my opinion on a military matter. I said that I thought the attempt should be made to guarantee that we would suffer no further setbacks, whose ultimate effects could do us irreparable harm. I asked Dayan, who was seated beside me, whether there was no possibility of pushing the Egyptians back to the other side of the canal. Dayan's reply was, "The Americans wouldn't like that." He went on to say that we were in need of munitions: he did not elaborate. Finally, we decided to approve having the Army Engineers Corps attempt to span the canal with a bridge so our forces could attempt a crossing. We were told that construction would take about three hours.

The experience of that night I will never forget. Every hour I would pester Colonel Israel Leor and other officers with questions about the state of the operation. At midnight I was told we had established a bridgehead on the other side of the canal. We had not managed to span the canal, though; it took until the following day for the bridge to be put up.

From the day the Yom Kippur War started until the day it ended I could not get the notion out of my mind that elements in the American intelligence community and others in the United States were privy to Egyptian intentions while preparations for the Egyptian attack were underway. Although I have no actual proof of this in hand, I have no other explanation for the fact that it was the Americans who turned out to be the real winners of the Yom Kippur War.

What happened in the Yom Kippur War was that the Egyptians gained a military success which, although only partial and short-lived, had the effect of redeeming their national honor. Israel suffered a hard blow, though not too hard, which both took down its pride a peg and raised its dependence on the United States. The result was that Egypt returned to the Western fold and the United States reestablished its influence in the Middle East. The moves involved occurred too rapidly and were carried out with too great a precision and a bit too adroitly for them to have depended on chance. It is difficult to believe that the Americans could exploit so efficiently, to their advantage, unexpected situations and sudden turns of events, without having known the scenario in advance.

In any event, this suspicion greatly disturbed me, and I tried to check out some relevant hints and some details that came my way, but without result. All the experts and those in the know kept to the version of events contained in the official announcements. I remained unconvinced.

During the war I was surprised at the optimistic forecasts that kept streaming out of the Pentagon. I could never quite accept the explanations about the absence of transport facilities for the American munitions which had been approved for us, nor the story of the supposed argument over that issue between Secretary of State Henry Kissinger and Secretary of Defense James Schlesinger. Again, I have no proof that the scenario of the Yom Kippur War was prepared in advance by some group in the United States, but I continue to suspect that this was the case.

The Yom Kippur War came as a profound shock to Israelis and Jews throughout the world. The Six-Day War had raised the prestige of Israel's armed forces in the eyes of the people to such a height that it became the object of national adulation. The IDF popularly came to be regarded as the army with the best intelligence in the world. Everyone in the country was aware of how highly Israeli intelligence was esteemed abroad. And then quite suddenly it had failed, failed abysmally, and that failure became the talk of the day everywhere in the country. The whole people shared in the humiliation.

Everyone in the country was aware that more was involved than a failure to know the time of the Arab invasion. Our tanks were confronted on the Egyptian front by antitank weapons which were being used for the first time, and in the first couple of days of the war these weapons had inflicted terrible losses on our armor. There was a story about our men suffering heavy casualties on the Egyptian side of the Canal because of ignorance of the terrain. The confusion between the Sharon and Bern divisions in Sinai became common knowledge among ordinary Israelis even before the ministers knew about it; soldiers passed the story on to friends and relatives. In that way the public learned very quickly about a whole series of foul-ups that doubtless cost many lives.

In his summation of the Yom Kippur War, Dayan wrote in his book *Avnei derekh:*

> In any event among us too, in the army and the Mossad, the assessment was . . . that the Arabs were not set on a war immediately. Hence our forces at the front were too few in the defensive phase. Even the reinforcements rushed out there came in small units, without proper organization. There had not been sufficient time to make the preparations necessary for a counterattack.

Dayan was right, without a doubt, but among the people complaints were rife about the mess in the munitions stocks and about tanks and equipment being in no condition for use. A story was passed around by word of mouth about the Americans having been surprised to learn that not enough blankets and clothing had been stocked for emergency use. None of this was malicious gossip; it was told by soldiers who were deeply troubled by the injury being done to the reputation of the army.

The bungling and attendant damages were partly the result of the shattering of a cherished conception in Israel that in any war with the Arabs we would have to win in a matter of days, at most in a week. The administrative and economic measures and manpower resources prepared for emergencies had been planned on this assumption, which had been vindicated during the Sinai Campaign and the Six-Day War. In such short wars, it was possible for the economy to hold its breath, so to speak, as part of the country's industry was shut down, all means of available transportation requisitioned, and all able-bodied men put into uniform. As the Yom Kippur War began to drag out, it became apparent that factories and agricultural settlements would be hard put to it to continue functioning without men and that the country could not go on with its public and freight transportation at a standstill. Large numbers of trucks now had to be acquired at great cost. Even the money that had to be disbursed to pay our soldiers began to weigh heavily on the economy.

People in Israel, and in the world at large, had developed a fixed notion of what military conflicts between ourselves and the Arabs were like. Accordingly, the scenario was of a war in which we had the Arabs beat and were back at the canal within forty-eight hours, after which it was only a matter of time before the enemy would be asking for a truce. Even the Americans, with all those computers at their disposal, predicted a quick Israeli victory. That this was not to be was evident already within the first week of fighting, and when the fact came home morale in Israel and among Jews abroad plummeted. Among the latter disappointment was especially keen when they realized that the one place they had assumed Jews could be sure of a refuge had turned out to be very much less than the secure haven they had imagined it to be. And how could it have been otherwise? For our whole physical survival depends entirely on our quality. Clearly we cannot allow ourselves the luxury of weakness that other nations perhaps can in matters of security, intelligence, and military preparedness.

Somewhat later, after Israeli forces had closed a ring around the Egyptian

Third Army, I happened to be in Washington, where I met Golda. She was in a rage after talks with Henry Kissinger, during which the secretary of state had flatly demanded from her that Israel permit the opening of an access route to the besieged Egyptian forces. I was subsequently told that after President Nixon had intervened and settled the differences between the two on that particular issue, Henry Kissinger said to our ambassador in Washington, Simcha Dinitz, that he pitied Golda because she would have many more bitter pills to swallow.

Relief to Enlisted Men's Families

On my return from a tour on behalf of the UJA to the United States early in November 1973, I found that Knesset and municipal elections had been put off until the end of December. During the two months I had left in office, I devoted myself to trying to alleviate the social and economic problems created by the war.

Morale in the country was at a low ebb, and I thought that the nation's citizens were troubled enough psychologically to be spared the indignity of having to endure the social and economic hardships arising from the procedures by which benefits were paid out to families of reservists who had been called up in the war. It was an area beset by difficulties. The Equalization Fund, participated in by both workers and employers and under the jurisdiction of the Ministry of Labor, which was supposed to provide for this purpose, had all but ceased to function. Instead of receiving their regular wages through the fund, the men were being paid by the army according to a flat scale without regard to professional ranking or job seniority. When I found out what sort of pay the men were receiving from the army, I proposed that in this war they should get their pay from the Equalization Fund, which would at least free them from worry about the welfare of their families. The board of directors of the fund responded to my proposal without delay, but I knew that because of the vast number of men that had been called up the fund's coffers would soon be empty. I therefore applied to Finance Minister Pinhas Sapir with a request for the government to cover the deficit likely to accrue to the fund (it would come to several tens of millions of liroth) and debit the fund for repayment at a future date. Sapir agreed. He also gave his approval to another of my proposals—for the benefits to be paid retroactively to the month of October, when the war started.

We also found a way to pay benefits to the families of soldiers who, for one reason or another, were ineligible for Equalization Fund benefits, and we arranged for advances on benefit payments for large families. Finally, we met more than halfway the needs of reservists who were self-employed, whose financial losses while on duty were often greater than those of salaried workers: we allowed them to correct the income they had declared before their call-up, so that the new figures rather than the old would form the basis of benefits received from the Equalization Fund. We set up a fund in the amount of ten million liroth from which loans on easy terms were made to the self-employed. To expedite matters, I arranged for information sessions at which social security personnel were briefed on the new procedures. About sixty workers in the department then made a tour of military units to inform soldiers of their rights under the program.

The government gave me the especially difficult job of dealing with the problem of getting vital manpower back to work—a task that required obtaining the release from military service of workers in vital trades and professions. The men involved were those whose absence from work could lead to the closure of factories and the creation of pockets of unemployment. There were nearly ten thousand such workers, and the coordinating committees, which normally dealt with the matter, were unable to cope with an operation on the monumental scale now required. Just how thorny a problem we were up against became clear when I met with General Herzl Shapir, chief of the IDF Manpower Branch. We were faced by a conflict of priorities: many of the reservists who held key positions in industry and in the economy were also doing vital service in the air force, tank corps, and paratroops.

Once it became known that I was the government's man responsible for obtaining release of vital workers from military service, I was inundated with requests from enterprises all over Israel. Hard hit were kibbutz and moshav settlements-and particularly recent moshav settlements, all of whose men had been called up, leaving only women to work the fields. Unfortunately, the reservists from agricultural settlements turned out to be the most difficult to release.

To come to grips with the problem I established a ramified system of committees representing all branches of industry. The committees included representatives of both the army and the employers and were headed by members of the Labor Ministry staff. We were gradually able to get the situation under control.

The elections took place in December, and I was elected mayor of Haifa. I continued to hold office as minister of labor until the new government was installed. In the interim, I had my hands full at the ministry. At the end of January, reservists were being released in the thousands. At a cabinet meeting held at the time, I pointed out the dangers in our not having established a single key agency authorized to deal with problems in the field of housing, employment, and economic recovery. I proposed that we establish nine interministerial centers, to any one of which released soldiers could go with problems and get immediate advice. Golda was delighted with the idea and told me to put it into operation. I tried to get out of it by reminding her that I had just been elected mayor, that I was a member of the Knesset, and that to top it all I was still busy with the work of the Labor Ministry—so where was I supposed to find the time for this project? "So you'll work overtime," she replied. I couldn't very well refuse after that, but I did stipulate one condition—that the ministers send representatives with authority to the centers I proposed, so that problems brought there could be solved quickly and efficiently. My condition was agreed to, and the very next day ministerial representatives were chosen and the heads of the centers were appointed.

To get the centers into operation, I had to get the Knesset to pass a number of bills quickly. I approached the opposition leader, Menahem Begin, with a request not to make passage of the bills too difficult. He agreed and the bills were passed. The centers were established, and they did their work efficiently and well—so well that I got the idea to establish similar centers for the absorption of new immigrants.

A National Emergency Government

At the end of January 1974, the president of Israel asked Golda Meir to form a new government; the Labor Alignment had lost five seats in the elections, which were postponed because of the war, and was facing a rebellion among the public and within its own ranks. The Likud party had won thirty-eight seats in the Knesset, and its candidate, Shlomo Lahat, had been elected mayor of Tel Aviv. Dejection was felt everywhere in the Labor party and the Labor Alignment. At a convention of young party members held in Beit Berl, a demand was made for the replacement of government ministers; Avraham Offer called specifically for the removal of the ministers of defense, foreign affairs, and finance. Only after pressure had been brought to bear on her did Golda agree to take on the responsibility of forming a government.

There were three alternatives: for the new government to be constituted in the same way as the one before the elections, which would require having to cope with the difficulties being made by the National Religious Party; for new elections to be held and party election lists opened to new prospective candidates; or for a national emergency government to be formed in which all Zionist political parties would take part.

The last alternative was the one I advocated, in writing and orally at meetings and rallies. The formation of an emergency government seemed to me to be the only way in which we could free ourselves of the atmosphere of gloom that engulfed the nation. I do not know why Golda was so dead set against the proposal. I assumed Mapai would be against the formation of a broad coalition government; I understood that in a coalition with Likud it would have difficulty continuing the negotiations on the separation agreements with Egypt and Syria. I expected even greater difficulties if a narrow coalition government were formed. Demands were coming from all groups in the party for changes in the makeup of the cabinet, with Moshe Dayan the target of a large-scale assault. In the end, Dayan announced his resignation, followed by Peres, and Rafi went into emergency session. Dayan proposed new elections. For her part, Golda went to the president with a proposal for the formation of a minority government without the NRP and with two cabinet posts left open in reserve for Peres and Dayan. Her choice for minister of defense was Yitzhak Rabin.

Once again I took on the job of mediating between Golda and both Dayan and Peres. Peres announced that the Rafi faction would vote for the government, but no more. I expressed the opinion that Peres and Dayan's refusal to join the government was tantamount to another party split. Negotiations went on for weeks. Early in May the party's Knesset faction and the secretariat convened in the Knesset building, and Golda presented her proposal for the makeup of the cabinet to the party for confirmation. Ben-Aharon and Avraham Offer angered Golda by attacking her proposal. Then I took the floor and appealed to Golda to withdraw her opposition to the formation of an emergency government based on a broad coalition. I again spoke about the depressed mood in the country and of the people's awaiting word of national unity.

Golda decided to remain silent no longer. She took the floor to reply to the speakers, particularly to me. She, too, knew the mood of the people, she said, but she did not believe that news of a broadly based government would be what they wanted to hear from her. Then, to the surprise of everyone, she announced that she was returning her mandate to the president. Aharon Yadlin, party secretary, hurriedly declared the meeting adjourned, and a delegation rushed to Golda to try to persuade her to withdraw her resignation.

The press had a field day once the story of the meeting broke. Several correspondents were inspired to write that Golda was unimpressed by the criticism of Ben-Aharon and Offer, who were notorious oppositionists, as everyone knew, but that when Almogi, a man rooted in the soil of the labor movement, demanded that the Likud party be taken into the government, *that* could only mean the end was at hand. So, according to the press my words made Golda decide to return her mandate to the president.

Today I am more convinced than ever that I was right. I am entirely persuaded that our social situation would have taken a more favorable turn than it did had we then formed a government of national unity.

As it was, events took a different direction. On March 6, the central committee of the party met to ask Golda, Dayan, and Peres to return to the government. Yitzhak Rabin's speech made a highly favorable impression: it was clear, considered, and persuasive. It was suddenly clear that there were, after all, candidates in the party for key posts who had not been involved in the "wars of the generals" or in internal party struggles. By evening, Dayan and Peres had decided to accede to Golda's renewed request for them to join a government under her leadership. Even the National Religious Party had had second thoughts and returned to the coalition. Rabin, the party's rising star, replaced me in the government to take over the Labor Ministry.

But the crisis had only apparently been resolved. In the beginning of April, the first part of the Agranat Report on responsibility for the lack of preparedness for the Yom Kippur War was published, raising a storm of outrage among the public, in the party and the government. There were again demands for Dayan's resignation, and at party headquarters Sapir rose and said that if he were in Dayan's place he would resign. Haim Gvati, Golda's close friend, defined the situation as having reached a rock-bottom low. Golda gave up and resigned. This time no one dared ask her to change her mind.

I proposed that no radical steps should be taken until the second part of the Agranat Report—which was to deal with ministerial rather than military conduct in the war—had come out, but there was no response. The party was in the grip of a crisis that holds it to this day. But unless new elections were to be called there was no choice but to seek a new candidate from the ranks of the Alignment, and the frenzied activity began anew. All eyes were on Sapir, who announced flatly that he was not a candidate. This time he was believed, but everyone realized that any other candidate who was put forward would be "Sapir's candidate." In the meantime Haim Zadok, too, had said he would not be a candidate; and Abba Eban did not have Sapir's backing. Only two candidates remained, therefore— Yitzhak Rabin and Shimon Peres.

A Troubling Proposal

My name, too, was brought up, and among the groups supporting my candidature were some I never dreamed would consider me for high office. A few articles published in *Davar* spoke of me as "a good candidate for the prime ministry in present conditions," and as someone capable of bringing together all sections of the party. In its editorial on April 4, 1974, *Haaretz* recommended me as a choice for prime minister and, in the editorial on April 15 entitled "The Real Choice," wrote the following:

> If the Alignment is ready to form a broad coalition, it has a natural candidate—Mr. Yosef Almogi, known for his support of the idea of a broadly based government, and, in respect of his personality and his place on the political map, preferable to every other candidate.

During that period Rachel Yanait Ben-Zvi called me and tried to persuade me lead a government that would rescue the nation from its despair and revitalize the party. Of all the requests I received on that score, Rachel Yanait's appeal was the most moving. I had became acquainted with the Ben-Zvis during the period of the Lavon Affair, when I was party secretary. I had visited them often at their home. I was witness to the warmth of the relations between them and Ben-Gurion and to the sympathy and friendship Yitzhak Ben-Zvi and Rachel felt toward Ben-Gurion all their lives and preserved even when they opposed his stand on the Lavon Affair. Each time I visited them I was impressed anew by their nobility of character and decency. I remember how, after I had invited the Ben-Zvis to the Bar Mitzvah of my youngest, Zvika, and they had had to turn me down because coming would have meant violating the Sabbath, they offered to have a second ceremony in the president's residence. They were as good as their word. Our whole family was deeply moved by the gesture—my son more than the rest, when he delivered his Bar Mitzvah oration with the president of Israel looking on.

Shortly after Rachel Yanait had spoken to me, Shimon Peres contacted me and announced that if I were "running" for high office, he would not put his own name up as a candidate, but that if I intended to stay out of the race he would enter. I assured him I was not a candidate for the prime ministry.

For the whole week I was off my stride. I found myself unable to work properly, and I slept irregularly. During my life I have learned to live with pressures and still function more or less efficiently. Pressures and emotional strain can result from success as well as failure. This time I was suffering from the crisis of an excess of a good thing—and it troubled me greatly. I was certainly flattered by the proposals for my candidature being made in the press, and the approaches being made to me on the subject by individuals and groups. But I was aware of my limitations: I had neither the educational background nor the experience that would qualify me to move with ease and assurance through the complexities of international politics and take on the responsibility for foreign affairs at the level a prime minister of Israel inevitably must. Had I been offered the post of deputy prime minister for internal affairs, I would have thought myself qualified. I think I might even have been able to make some important contributions in that capacity. But that was not what I was being offered, and I was not prepared to be prime minister.

At the end of April, Rabin was chosen by a slender majority over Shimon Peres to head the government. His government, as everyone knows, was short-lived. I returned to Haifa, which I regarded henceforth as my main arena of activity. I had even wanted to give up my seat in the Knesset, but the party would not agree. More's the pity: those were my leanest years in the legislature.

36
Mayor of Haifa

The Alignment's election list for the Haifa municipality received 58 percent of the vote; in the Knesset election it received only 45 percent.

I began my term as mayor of Haifa in February 1974. My reception by the public was warm, as was the reception I had from municipal employees, who showed themselves ready to give me their full cooperation. With great hopes being pinned on me by so many of my townsmen, I felt my responsibilities very keenly. I immediately went into high gear, dividing my working day into three shifts—6:30 A.M. to noon, 4:00 to 6:00 P.M. and 8:00 P.M. to late at night. The last shift I set aside for meetings and reading reports.

From my first day in office, I discovered that since the death of Abba Khoushi, no one had dared to alter working procedures or introduce any change whatever; everything was exactly as it had been in the days of Hassan Shukri. Even the mayor's office still had the look of a village official's reception room. I had no objection personally, but times had changed and Haifa was no longer a small provincial town but a major urban center. I gave the order for alterations to be made.

On the principle that the opportunity for democratic expression should be a routine part of public life and not confined to election time, I made it my business to give the city's residents more efficient access to municipal offices and authorities. I insisted that every application, by letter or orally, to municipal agencies should receive attention in the shortest possible time. I called the city council into session regularly and at close intervals and made it a rule that its meetings be open to the general public and to the press, who were encouraged to bring up questions on city affairs. Administrative meetings were held once a week. I maintained an open-door policy in the mayor's office and in those of his deputies and the chairmen of the city council, even though it added greatly to the workload of city officials: it was an efficient way of keeping tab on what disturbed the public, as well as a way of keeping informed on the performance of the administrative machinery. I spent hours of my working time listening to the

complaints of ordinary Haifa residents, many of whom came to me simply because they had found no other authority they could turn to.

Haifa is a patchwork of many neighborhoods. Only a few of them had active
community committees that were in touch with city hall. I therefore encouraged
the establishment of voluntary regional and neighborhood committees that
acted as both the municipality's representative to the people and the public's
representative to the municipal administration. The committee coordinators
kept in regular touch with the municipality and the Association for the Encouragement of Home Upkeep *(Aguda Letarbut Hadiur),* an organization I had established while I was minister of housing. I also set up a network of municipal
information bureaus staffed by specially trained receptionists. I proposed to two
of the city's large publicity firms that they publish a city weekly to be distributed
free of charge and financed by advertisements. Even though I demonstrated
that the undertaking would be profitable, the advertising men remained unconvinced. The idea was later picked up by a Haifa resident, and today there are
three such weeklies being distributed in the city. Another of my innovations was
to institute the office of municipal ombudsman, a post which Yaacov Levav,
formerly of the administration of Haifa University and a secretary of Solel
Boneh, filled with great devotion.

In my tours of inspection through the city I observed that guardrails and
protective fences were badly in need of repair; that facades of buildings needed
renovation, and that road markings and directional signs required repainting. I
enlarged the city budget for the maintenance and repair of public facilities, and
we set to work to freshen up Haifa's appearance.

Efficiency and Budget Problems

After making a study of the city's administrative organization, I called in an
internationally recognized efficiency expert to examine the subject in detail. I
also called in the Labor Productivity Institute to test our organizational machinery. To ease the strain on the budget that financing these activities incurred,
I took advantage of a provision I had introduced while labor minister for the
purpose of financing the activities of the Committee for Prevention of Unemployment. In this way we were able to make some progress toward efficiency in
our municipal services—one of the more neglected aspects of municipal government in Israel.

I worked to change the structure of the municipal budget, to free it from the
burden of establishing and maintaining organizations and institutions which
were more properly the concern of national rather than city government, such as
the University of Haifa and Rothschild Hospital. I also saw to it that in housing
and slum rehabilitation Haifa's share in the national budget should remain level
with that of other cities.

As I became increasingly acquainted with the municipality's budgetary problems, I realized how many activities which were really outside the domain of local
government were being financed at very great cost by the city budget. In this

Haifa was not alone. Mayors in Israel seemed simply to have come to terms with budgetary deficits and had come to regard them as a permanent and inevitable feature of municipal finances. Budgets had a way of falling into deficits which grew steadily, and there seemed to me to be no reason to encourage the process by burdening local finances with extraneous costs. Further investigation showed that deficit spending was not accompanied by a parallel expansion of services. City deficits kept growing because of borrowing: loans were linked to the cost-of-living index, and with the constant and steep rises in the index, the interest payments accumulated and grew at an appalling rate. The going assumption among mayors seemed to be that bankruptcy was around the corner anyway, so why bother saving?

At the same time, municipal income was constantly decreasing, particularly the municipal business tax, and all my efforts to improve things in that area ended in failure. Haifa did not have officials responsible for the various departments of municipal services—men holding "portfolios" like ministers in the government cabinet. In this respect Haifa was behind Tel Aviv and Jerusalem, where such posts existed. I therefore had no one to go to about budgeting problems. The members of municipal administration chaired public committees that lacked authority to put decisions into operation, and in the absence of a municipal director-general, senior municipal employees oversaw the operations of the city's services without being answerable to a single elected official who bore ultimate responsibility.

We established a development company, and transferred responsibility for the buildings and grounds of the science industry in Haifa from the office of the City treasury to the development company.

When I discovered that Haifa's parks, for which the city is famous, were beginning to show dangerous signs of neglect, I began to look around for a suitable landscape architect. I found one, finally, in Jerusalem, and brought him to Haifa. I also saw to it that the ugly billboards that were defacing the city were replaced by attractive signboards.

At the same time, I addressed myself to a number of practical problems which for one reason or another my predecessors had failed to attend to, such as the completion of a parking lot near the new Haifa Auditorium. I also succeeded in altering the purpose of what had originally been intended as a new maritime school being built near the Kishon Beach. With the donor's agreement I arranged for it to house a school of industrial trades.

I was able to do something for the arts in Haifa as well. I found a solution for the storage and exhibition of the municipal art collection, part of which was inadequately housed in the municipal building and the rest scattered in a variety of inappropriate sites throughout the city. Since we lacked funds to build a municipal museum as planned, I had a building—formerly a school—in the Hadar neighborhood modified to serve the purpose. It is now used for the storage and display of the more important works of art in the city's possession.

Years before, the artist Mane Katz had acquired a house at a beautiful location on Panorama Road on Mount Carmel. After his death his paintings were crated and stored there. The house was neglected, the roof leaked, and the paintings were now in real danger of suffering irreparable damage. I founded the Society for the Mane Katz Museum and had the building restored. It is now a public museum for his works.

The sculptress Ursula Malvin who had come to Israel from Switzerland and was living in the cooperative artists' colony at Ein-Hod, proposed to bequeath her works to the city, on condition that they be placed in one of Haifa's public parks and cared for by the city. After consulting experts in the field, who praised her works, I accepted the artist's offer. Today her sculptures stand in Haifa's Sculpture Garden, one of the city's most beautiful parks.

Of the religious sites in Haifa the Cave of Elijah is unique because it is sacred to Jews, Christians, and Moslems. The problem was that the area around it was badly neglected and unbelievably filthy. The situation had grieved me for a long time, and during the election campaigns, I was so annoyed over it that I said that it was not Elijah's Cave but "Elijah's Shame." After taking office I reached an agreement with the Ministry of Religion, which is responsible for religious sites, that a tender would be published for the submission of plans to rehabilitate and beautify the area.

The zoo in the Gan Haem Park was for some reason badly neglected. After appointing a new manager for the zoo, it became a star attraction in the city, enjoyed by young and old alike.

Mayor or Minister?

Toward the end of 1974, there was talk of the Labor party's intention to invite me to rejoin the government. It was claimed that because I did not want to resign from the Haifa municipality I would be made minister without portfolio and retain my office as mayor; to ease my workload I would give up my seat in the Knesset. I paid little attention to the rumors, imagining them to be another fantasy cooked up by the press. But then Yitzhak Rabin invited me to see him and asked me officially to join his cabinet.

Rabin had begun his term as prime minister backed by the party's good will and high expectations. But it took only a short time for him to feel the effects of the wrangling and intrigues around him. A political novice still, and inexperienced in party infighting, Rabin wanted to form a centrist group to resist the efforts to undermine his administration. I had a good opinion of him and was ready to support him not only because he was the party's choice for his office, but because I believed him to be a sincere man with the right qualities for leading the country. Rabin, may have made the offer because he sensed my attitude toward him.

The news of Rabin's offer was not well received in Haifa. Although I had no doubt that my holding two posts, mayor of the city and minister in the government, would even prove to Haifa's advantage, I felt constrained to reject the prime minister's proposal. I had no wish to have my having run for the mayoralty interpreted as a political trick engineered by the Labor Alignment to retain control of Haifa through my election victory—then only to return me to the national government.

Rabin had applied to the minister of justice, Haim Zadok, for his opinion on the legal issue involved in holding the two offices. Only after I had rejected the prime minister's offer was Zadok's reply that the two posts could not be simultaneously held, finally published. Nonetheless, even thouth I turned down Rabin's offer of a cabinet post, relations between us were strengthened, and I backed him in his struggles.

I remained mayor of Haifa and set myself the goal of establishing the broadest municipal coalition in city history. At the time I believed that such a coalition was desirable, not only nationally, but in local government as well. After the issue had been debated in the party, my plan was approved, and a wall-to-wall coalition was formed in the municipal government. That marked the beginning in Haifa of a successful cooperative venture in municipal government, in which all the city's elected officials, regardless of party, collaborated to the benefit of Haifa's residents and the city as a whole.

A special committee under the direction of Professor Elhanan Elon drew up a new master plan for Haifa. The plan was exhibited in the Municipal Hall for all to see—for both experts and the general public to have a chance to examine it and express their opinions of it. It is still bottled up in the District Committee of Planning and Construction.

Haifa is a city of excellent beaches and offers a variety of cultural activities, features that should make it a good draw for tourists. To encourage the development of tourism in the city, I initiated a number of large-scale, organized tourist events and sought ways to make them permanent features of Haifa. Thus, I was able to make Haifa the site of the International Chess Olympiad and of the conventions of the English section of the UJA and Israel Bonds. I also established, in collaboration with a private firm, an agency for the arrangement of conventions in the city, and already in my first year in office there had been more international conventions held there than in the five preceding years.

Because of its high level of industrialization, Haifa suffers from ecological problems. To deal with them, I invited Mr. I. Even, an engineer and Haifa resident who had served in that field with the UN, to work with us for a two-year period. I also tried to get greater cooperation between the Haifa municipality and the administrations of neighboring towns in fields such as fire and rescue services and sewage purification. To facilitate this, I helped found an association of regional cities and towns. Plans for the association and its operations were prepared by Yosef Ami, vice president of the Haifa Technion, and were well received both in the Ministry of Interior and by neighboring town governments.

Death of Pinhas Sapir

In August 1975 Pinhas Sapir died, a scroll of the Torah in his arms. His death left a gaping hole in the Labor party, the Alignment, and the labor movement as a whole. He had vast power and great influence in determining party choices for posts. Had he wished, he could himself have been prime minister, but he seemed to quail at the thought of supreme office. This was no pose: Sapir told me more than once that not even for a moment had he ever contemplated being prime minister, and I believed him. On the other hand, I do not doubt that Yitzhak Rabin would never have become Prime Minister had not Pinhas Sapir backed him massively.

Yet, for all of the work he did to make certain that Rabin and Katzir would be elected, he failed to look after his own interests when, toward the end of his life, he left the Ministry of Finance and took over the chairmanships of the Jewish Agency and Zionist Organization. The change of office weakened him greatly, and he was compared to Samson having his locks shorn. It seems to me that some of his close associates played, inadvertently perhaps, the role of Delilah. In any case, when he ceased being minister of finance he lost the source of his power, and in his last days he knew only disillusionment. Few had experienced so much disappointment and swallowed so many insults from their own party as had Pinhas Sapir. It was difficult to believe that, only a short time before, he had been exalted by everyone. Although few remained faithful to him near the end, all mourned the death of this man who had done so very much for the labor movement and the nation.

When Pinhas Sapir passed away, the search for a replacement for him in the posts he had left vacant in the Jewish Agency and the Zionist Organization began. I do not remember who first brought up my name in this connection, but when the possibility of my candidature was made public I began to give it my serious consideration and consulted with friends, among them Prime Minister Yitzhak Rabin, who wished me to take on the job. Abba Eban, too, thought I should do so; and when I asked him why he had not been proposed for the post, Eban replied that he thought it required someone better equipped than he to get things done. This was the reason, he said, that he had decided to help me in the contest against the Likud candidate, Arieh Dulzin. The choice would be decided in a secret ballot by the Zionist Executive Committee.

I had misgivings. I was not at all sure about the propriety of leaving my post as major of Haifa in mid-term; nor was I sure the position in prospect really suited me. My instincts were right: when I announced my decision to run, both fears proved justified. The first illusion to go was the belief that the people of Haifa would understand and accept the special circumstances making it necessary for me to leave municipal office—indeed, the reaction was quite the opposite. The steps I had taken aroused anger in the city, although the reason was not the same in all cases. Some were angered because of purely political considerations. There is no denying that I was the cause of distress for many honest citizens who wished in all sincerity for me to complete my term and finish the job I had begun. On their account I have great regrets.

Highly respected members of the public came on their own to warn me against taking the step I was contemplating, among them the poet Uri Zvi Grinberg; *Maariv*'s editor, Shalom Rosenfeld; Shlomo Shamgar from *Yedioth Ahronot;* and

Professor Binyamin Akzin. Among them were those who had supported me in my bid for municipal leaderships, but opposed my standing for leadership of the Zionist movement.

Nevertheless I did not believe that my chief rival, Arieh Dulzin, was more qualified for the post than I. Dulzin began the campaign by declaring that even people in the labor movement would vote for him, and that even were the Labor party to put up Abba Eban as its candidate he would still run. For the most part, the press supported neither of us and proposed a third candidate.

For the contest, the distribution of forces in the Zionist executive were as follows: Likud would vote for its own candidate, Arieh Dulzin; WIZO (the Women's International Zionist Organization) was reportedly going to split its vote, as was the National Religious Party; the Labor movement, I hoped, would stand behind me. The scales would be tipped in one direction or the other by the Zionist Confederation, led by the liberals and the women of Hadassah. The male members of the confederation, among them Kalman Sultanik; supported me; among the women, my strongest supporter was Rose Halprin, a long-standing and highly respected leader of the group. Above all there was my old friend Dr. Israel Goldstein. Important, too, was Prime Minister Yitzhak Rabin's backing and that of Abba Eban. I could look forward, as well, to the support of Yitzhak Koren, secretary of the International Labor movement; Yitzhak Navon, who was then chairman of the Zionist Executive Committee; and Mordecai Bar-On, chief of the Youth Department. The latter introduced me to Charlotte Jacobson, chairman of the American Section of the World Zionist Organization, a sage and energetic woman who was also influential in Hadassah.

Dulzin had the advantage of being treasurer of the Jewish Agency and acting chairman of the Zionist Executive, whereas I was hemmed in by disadvantage. A problem was my lack of acquaintanceship with most of the non-Zionists on the executive of the Jewish Agency.

My two-year term as mayor of Haifa had earned high marks among the public and in the press. In an article appearing in the October 8, 1975, edition of *Maariv*, Reuben Ben-Zvi reviewed my achievements in office:

> Despite his brief term of only two years, Yosef Almogi leaves Haifa a different place from the one he found when he arrived. Unfortunately for him, all of the things he succeeded in doing will be recognized and understood shortly, and others will reap what he hath sowed.

The late Arieh Nesher, chief of the Haifa branch of the editorial board of *Haaretz*, was a man of unquestionably antiestablishment views. Shortly before he died he wrote an article in which he assessed the work of the municipality during the period I served as mayor of Haifa. The following, in part, is what he had to say on October 6, 1975:

> Almogi had no wish to depend on the experience of others, and from the first day decided to make a fresh examination of the municipality's structure and the operation of its various departments. It was a breath of fresh air after so

many years of routine, when the calculation of new budgets was based on the addition of so-much-and-so-much percent to previous budgets. In this, Al-mogi's behavior contrasts with his predecessors'. He ordered surveys and tests from the Labor Productivity Institute and from efficiency experts. And on receiving their findings he set about carrying them out posthaste.

37

At the Helm of the Zionist Movement

I had been forced into a contest by Dulzin, who clung to the conviction he would win until the votes were counted. For me the contest was something of a nightmare: never before in all the decades of my public career had I ever had to stand for office in a personal election campaign. My opponent, with whom I was otherwise on the best of terms, believed that even the ballots of my colleagues in the Labor Alignment would be his; and he had every reason to believe that he enjoyed the confidence of the Zionist community abroad and of the representatives of the world Jewish community who sat on the executive of the Jewish Agency.

There were days when I was ready to give up just so I could stop having to drum up support. But all my life I had been used to keeping stubbornly to the goals I set myself, and now, too, I stayed in the contest even though it was not to my taste.

The deciding body was the Zionist Executive Committee, containing 120 members from all the Zionist parties in Israel and abroad, as well as well as from the Zionist federations in all the countries of the Free World. The federations are affiliated with no political party, but are nonpartisan associations of Hadassah and other groups; traditionally, they identify with the liberalism of Chaim Weizmann.

I had no choice but to meet with all these groups and their representatives to solicit their votes. Some of these sessions were very successful; others less so; still others not at all. Among the less successful ventures was my appearance at a gathering of the World Jewish Religious Movement. I was not wholly sympathetic to their outlook. I also regretted having given in to Yitzhak Koren's urgings to meet the president of WIZO, Mrs. Rayah Jaglom, at her home; as we spoke I sensed that Mrs. Jaglom and I had little, if anything, in common. On the other hand, I acquired a great respect for the World Confederation of General

Zionists, and enjoyed greatly appearing before its representatives at Mr. Sultanik's home in New York and at Beit Shalom in Jerusalem.

The Hadassah organization, with a membership of about 370,000 in the United States, is world renowned, and highly regarded in Israel because of the part it played in the establishment of the excellent hospital in Jerusalem. For some reason there is a general impression that it is primarily a philanthropic organization whose Zionism does not run very deep. That it is philanthropic is undeniably true, but the assertion that Hadassah lacks Zionist commitment is not: its commitment is very strong, indeed. In the matter of *aliyah* alone, Hadassah has done much more than other Zionist organizations. Over the years it has helped bring to Israel and rehabilitate more than 170,000 Jewish children from all over the world. Its work in the field of Zionist education is a marvel and of itself would be enough to give Hadassah a permanent place in the history of the Zionist movement.

The Zionist Executive Committee elects its own chairman, who is also the candidate for the chairmanship of the executive of the Jewish Agency and must be elected both in the executive and in the assembly, the Jewish agency's supreme body. It has 340 members, of whom 50 percent are appointed by the World Zionist Organization, 30 percent by the United Jewish Appeal, and 20 percent by organizations affiliated with the United Israel Appeal.

The election in the Agency is a matter of formality, but there can be problems. Once again I found myself having to meet Jewish leaders, this time from the Agency, for them to look me over. I met Max Fisher, an intelligent man with great affection for Israel, and an important Republican, but with a difference: Fisher's attitude toward social problems is a far cry from what is characteristic of his party. I also met some of the younger Zionist activists—intellectuals who treated their activities with high seriousness, among them: Jay Hoffberger, Frank Lautenberg, Irving Bernstein, and Irving Kessler of the United Israel Appeal.

An exceptional figure was the late Moshe Boukstein, who was legal adviser of the Jewish Agency for many years.

The results of the Agency elections were gratifying if for no other reason than because this time I was the only candidate. They laid the foundation for a period of fruitful work at the Jewish Agency.

Bad Advice

In my address to the Zionist Executive Committee, I outlined our main goals as I saw them: (1) to deepen Zionist consciousness among Zionists, (2) to strengthen the bonds between the Jewish people and the State of Israel, (3) to establish ties with those sectors of the the Jewish people with which existing organizations are out of touch (on the one hand, the community of intellectuals and and scientists, and on the other, the socially and economically deprived), and (4) to allocate more resources for the purpose of deepening and expanding Jewish education.

From the start I realized that Jewish Agency and Zionist Organization operations were in need of a change. Since the Zionist Congress was scheduled to convene at the end of the year, I decided to confine myself to planning the changes I had in mind and await the end of the congress before putting them into effect. I was not yet versed in the rules and regulations of the Zionist Congress and depended for guidance in these matters on senior people in the field. It was my first mistake in office, and as a result of it, we found ourselves, after a great deal of preparation for the congress, in an absurd fix: the court of the Zionist movement censured us and postponed the elections to the congress for a full year.

The source of the problem was the decision reached by the majority in the Zionist Executive Committee that if 90 percent of the representatives of political parties in the Zionist movement of a given country agreed to the distribution of their mandates in the congress, then no elections need be held in that country. The decision turned out to be in violation of the by-laws of the World Zionist Organization. That no one had set me right was bad enough. What was worse, though, was that the first I heard of the complaint lodged by Herut against the decision was during the court hearings, presided over by Justice Moshe Landau. The resulting reprimand to the Zionist Executive Committee and the postpone-ment of the congress was a poor way for me to have started my term of office. We had fallen into a trap, and the negative effects of our having done so would be felt in the Zionist movement for the next two years.

In my first months in office I faced an avalanche of invitations from private individuals and representatives of groups. My hosts all shared one purpose—to get financial assistance. Everyone took it for granted that I would follow in Pinhas Sapir's footsteps. What they seemed not to realize was that what Sapir could do I could not. Sapir was a financial wizard, and by sheer sorcery—so it seemed—he found money for the worthy out of the coffers of the government or the Jewish Agency—or from the pocket of someone he had in mind to ap-proach in the future. I observed that in his last period he gave a lot of help to religious institutions.

Unfortunately (or perhaps fortunately) I had no experience in money matters, and I would refer the people who were canvasing donations to our treasurer, Arieh Dulzin. Or I would gather together a few such requests and sit down to review them with the agency's treasurer, and then we would let our decision be known to the soliciting parties. I should note that my relations with Dulzin were for the most part untroubled; there were no strong bonds of sympathy between us, but neither was there friction. I suppose the proper word for our relations is "correct." From some of my younger associates, by contrast, I cannot say that I enjoyed an excess of the kind of treatment one would expect from colleagues.

A source of trouble I became familiar with early in my work were trips abroad, which were greatly in demand among Agency representatives and staff. I was aware that the problem of the large number of overseas trips would not easily be solved, since the Zionist movement is worldwide. Still, it seemed to me that the critics who had taken to calling the Jewish Agency the "Travel Agency" were not far off the mark. I decided to try to put an end to the abuse by reviewing every request for travel abroad on its merits. In my zeal I had committed a tactical error: I had gone after a sacred cow—perhaps the most sacred of all sacred cows—and I brought down on myself the wrath of many. There were cases in which I refused to approve a trip without even having to think twice about it, even though I was certain that my refusal would result in an unflattering item about me in one of the papers.

The scenarios of some of these requests were grotesque. One of my party colleagues would enter the office and without so much as a "hello" thrust a document out at me and say:

"Yosef, your signature, please."

"What for?" I would say.

"For a trip to a couple of South American countries."

"What for?" I would repeat, sticking to my guns.

Then he would lecture about how urgent the trip was, and how necessary. When it finally got through to him that I was unimpressed, he would say:

"Okay, forget South America. Just let me have a trip to Belgium and France."

There were complaints about the situation of the "receiving end," too. At every meeting I had with representatives from abroad, and with our agents stationed overseas, I would hear complaints about all the visitors they were getting from Israel. They were worse than useless—they were making a nuisance of themselves and wasting the time of our bona fide agents. The longer I stayed on the job, the more appalling the problem seemed to me. If the truth be told, I never found a solution for it, and neither has anyone else.

Meditations on Administration

The nerve center of the Zionist movement and the Jewish Agency had no first-rate man capable of commanding and focusing its activities: headquarters lacked a professional administrator, experienced and trained in management, who could act as its general director. Moshe Rivlin—erudite, a wonderful speaker and a man with many achievements to his credit—was not really the right man for the job. He was made for something more lofty than administration. At first I thought we ought to wait for the Zionist Congress to convene; there we might have had him elected to the executive. When the congress was postponed I was forced to abandon the plan, and it occurred to me that I could recommend him to head the JNF, to replace Yaacov Zur, who had resigned. After much exertion and numberless meetings, Rivlin was finally installed as head of the Board of Directors of the Jewish National Fund, and Adi Yaffe was elected director-general, pending approval of the executive of the Jewish Agency. To my great sorrow Yaffe died only a few months after taking office. Then Dulzin suggested Shmuel Lahis for the job, and I agreed. I had known Lahis in Haifa, and when I was labor minister, I had suggested to him that he submit his candidature for the post of judge in the Labor Court.

Scheduling the meetings of the executive of the Jewish Agency is an organizational problem of daunting complexity. Members of the executive come to its meetings from all over the world and demand—as indeed they should—to be brought up to date before making decisions on current issues. The executive convenes at least three times a year; once as the general assembly. A proposal to have it convene only once every two years, was defeated. Twice yearly the board of directors meets, and the executive is called into session two or three times a year. As if that were not enough, there are sessions of the Brussels Conference for Soviet Jews and the World Jewish Congress. In Israel, the Zionist Executive convenes every week, and there are also the sessions of the Zionist General Plenum. Add to the list the sessions of the Zionist Actions Committee and all the encounters, both formal and informal, that are unavoidable, and the picture is complete.

So I had my hands full. Much of my time was wasted in travel, since it was impossible to demand that all the meetings be held in Israel. But I did insist that most of them be, and I set as strict a limit as possible on the number of meetings abroad attended by Israeli representatives.

During my term in office, I managed to eliminate a number of problems that had troubled the work of the Jewish Agency for many years, particularly the financial burden placed on the Agency by the part it had in funding Zionist political parties in Israel. From the time it was founded, the Agency included among its activities the organization of fund drives for various causes and projects in Eretz Israel. In this connection, the Agency's leadership decided to do away with the collections undertaken separately by the different Zionist parties and movements, and instead set aside fixed sums for them out of its own budget. The practice had been seized on more than once by critics of the Zionist Organization and had served some of them as ammunition for demagogic attacks against what they claimed to be the organization's insatiable demands for money. In tackling the problem, I sought the aid of Max Fisher and Rabbi Kirschblum, and together we determined that money would be contributed to political parties only for constructive undertakings, and subject to review by the comptroller of the Zionist Organization.

Another matter I made it my business to attend to immediately on taking office was the mechanism of internal review and self-regulation in the Zionist movement and the Jewish Agency. After reviewing the problem, I decided that the comptroller of the Zionist Organization should function like the state comptroller in Israel. Material was to be submitted to the chairman, the responses of department heads were to be returned within a fixed period of time, and both the comptroller's report and the responses to his inquiries were to be published. In addition it was agreed that the objects of complaint would be reviewed to verify that the source of trouble had been corrected.

At the time, I began my work the dropout rate in immigration to Israel among Jews leaving the Soviet Union had reached 35 percent, and I expected it to go even higher. By putting its services at the disposal of the dropouts and rendering them assistance, HIAS bore at least some responsibility for the situation. I arranged for the heads of the Jewish Agency, a representative of the Zionist Confederation, and one from the Joint Distribution Committee to meet secretly with Prime Minister Rabin. At the meeting I demanded that HIAS be prevented from assisting the dropouts. As a result of our deliberations, a Commission of

Seven was appointed. It was to meet with the groups and representatives involed in the matter in the United States and reach a decision in keeping with my proposal. Max Fisher stuck by our decision for as long as he could. But the HIAS people raised a hue and cry and threatened to organize a separate fund if we insisted on pressing our point. Max Fisher gave in.

Meanwhile, the dropout rate increased. I decided to bring the problem up before the Presidium of the Brussels Conference, where it was debated heatedly. The representatives of the World Jewish Congress opposed taking any sort of action which could put an end to the practice of exploiting the benefits conferred by an Israeli visa for purposes other than immigrating to Israel. In Israel opinion on the subject was divided, even among Jews originating from Russia, and my advocacy of steps to alter the situation was fruitless.

The administrative structure of the Zionist movement was obsolete, and its operations were inefficient and costly. I appointed a committee of experts, with Raanan Weitz at its head, to study the matter and propose changes. The results of the committee's investigations were the subject of long deliberations in the Zionist Executive. We decided to bring the subject up for discussion at the Zionist Congress, and I proposed that until the new policies were adopted, we should establish in each country, or group of countries, a central, coordinating mechanism that would act as a liaison among all the organizations affiliated with the movement. I suggested that emissaries from Israel form the permanent link with the Executive Committee and that for each country or district there be appointed a chief emissary authorized by the executive committee to coordinate and supervise local operations. Despite the problems encountered by the first such chief emissary, in Argentina, I remained convinced that the system would eventually prove effective in making our work in the Diaspora more efficient.

Increasing Immigration

The problems created by the divisions of jurisdiction between the Jewish Agency and the Ministry of Absorption with regard to immigration and settlement occupied much of my attention. Before I took office, it had been decided that a committee would be formed by the government and the Jewish Agency to examine the matter and submit recommendations for new procedures in immigrant absorption. I met with the prime minister and proposed that Amos Horev, president of the Technion, be appointed chairman of such a committee. Rabin agreed, and the committee was formed and set to work. The Horev Committee recommended dismantling the Ministry of Absorption and transferring the responsibility for immigration and absorption entirely to the Jewish Agency. The recommendations of the Horev Committee were approved by the executive committee of the Jewish Agency. Only one of its members was opposed—the Herut representative, Yosef Klarman, an intelligent, fair-minded, and loyal man, who was one of my closest friends during my period of office in the Jewish Agency. Just then the "great upheaval" came: Labor was out of the government, and the Likud, with Menahem Begin at its head, was in. The recommendations of the Horev Committee got lost in the shuffle, and remain lost to this day.

In dealing with the subject of immigration, I came to the conclusion that a new tack had to be taken if we wished to increase immigration to Israel. From the many surveys made, I learned that there is no better stimulus to settlement in Israel that a visit to the country. A high percentage of tourists to Israel return for a second visit, and a respectable number of second-time visitors remain for extended stays. About a quarter of those staying in the country for a period of a year either remain to settle or return as immigrants. These statistics, it seemed to me, could be put to good use, and they formed the basis of an attempt to develop a program of regular visits to Israel arranged in collaboration with schools and universities in the Diaspora, and in coordination with Zionist federations and other Jewish organizations abroad, especially in the United States. Our experience with such projects has been good, and the results indicate that the program is well worth developing.

Another conclusion was that we were in need of a modern information center to serve both tourists and perspective settlers. It would be computer-based and make available up-to-date information on all aspects of the country. I discussed the subject in a series of meetings with Jewish community leaders and the administrators of Jewish community centers, where there are about forty Israeli representatives at work. I then asked Mordecai Bar-On to prepare a pilot program. Bar-On spent some months in the United States, where he visited a great many Jewish communities. He then submitted a very optimistic report. However, the sudden change in government was followed by replacement of those who had been responsible under the Labor government for tourism and settlement, and the project was suspended.

Immigrant associations in Israel make an important contribution to the work of attracting immigrants and helping them to settle. An outstanding job in this area is being done by the associations of English-speaking immigrants; the Association of British Immigrants deserves special mention for its work in the field.

Jewish settlers coming from the countries within the jurisdiction of this association represent a relatively higher ratio of immigration from the Jewish communities of their countries of origin and have a lower rate of return to their countries of origin than do settlers from other advanced countries.

I was so impressed with the work of the Association of British Immigrants that I proposed to the association of American immigrants that they, too, establish an office on the British model for the absorption of new settlers. To my regret, the person then responsible for administering the American association not only avoided meeting me to discuss the subject; he called a news conference in which he accused me of not helping immigrants from the United States. I was taken aback by his behavior. It was the only time that a head of any immigrant organization had ever used his position for partisan purposes: it appeared that the man was a member of the Herut (Likud) party and had used the occasion to make political capital. Fortunately, he was not reelected to office, but by then it was too late—I too had left office. I think it regrettable in the extreme that American settlers are still without services comparable to those enjoyed by English-speaking *olim* who have access to the office of the British Zionist Federation.

France has become the country with the largest Jewish population in Western Europe. It now contains half a million Jews. Although the Jewish community of France is not strongly Zionist in its inclinations, its ties to and sympathies with Israel can be strengthened. To this end, Melech Topiol, chairman of the Jewish Agency in France, advised me to meet with Guy de Rothschild, the leader of the Jewish community and head of the United Jewish Appeal in that country. My purpose was to persuade him to give Israeli youth counselors access to Jewish youth clubs in France as a way of encouraging the stronger affiliation of young French Jews with Israel and of furthering the cause of Jewish immigration to Israel from France. I met Guy de Rothschild in the offices of the Rothschild bank, and over a working lunch I unfolded my proposal for making Jewish schools and clubs in France centers for the expansion of Jewish education and instruments for deepening young Jews' consciousness of Israel. Rothschild's interest was awakened, and we concluded that he would come to Israel and formally put his name to an agreement about the subjects we had discussed. Rothschild kept his word, and during his visit to Israel, lasting a few days, the accord was signed at a formal ceremony attended by the representatives of the Jewish press.

I attached great importance to Zionist activities among intellectuals and members of the academic community abroad. For advice on ways in which activities in behalf of Zionism might be fostered among this highly influential group, I met with members of the academic community in Israel, among them Professors Dvortezky, Rotenstreich, and Davis. I also spoke with President Efraim Katzir, for whom the subject was of special interest.

The international movement of Reform Judaism joined the ranks of the Zionist movement at the same session of the Zionist General Council in which I was elected to office. In joining the Zionist movement, Reform Judaism added greatly to our strength, even though in doing so it left the choice of remaining outside the Zionist camp to its rabbis and their congregations.

On the day before the opening of the twenty-ninth Zionist Congress in Jerusalem in February 1978, the movement of Conservative Judaism was formally received into the Zionist fold by a decision of the Zionist Actions Committee. It was an important event, since most of the major movements in religious Judaism were now committed to the Zionist cause. Only some of the extreme Orthodox groups, such as the adherents of the Satmer Rabbi, remained anti-Zionist. Their absence from our ranks is to be greatly regretted.

The World Jewish Congress convenes at frequent intervals, and I thought it my duty to attend at least some of its sessions. At one of these, in Paris, I was able to prevent passage of a decision which might have been interpreted as recognition of the Palestine Liberation Organization. Debate over the item was heated, and the executive of the congress decided to discontinue the discussion. It should be recalled that the World Jewish Congress was being led at the time by Dr. Nahum Goldmann and Philip Klutznik, both of whom were strong "doves" on the issue of Israel's security. Among the leadership the only one who had kept himself out of the dovecote was Rabbi Arthur Hertzberg, one of the finest minds in the Jewish community, who was the leader of American Jewish Congress. I tried to maneuver gingerly between Klutznik, whom Goldmann had promised to install as president of the World Jewish Congress, and Hertzberg, who also had his eye on the office. Goldmann, however, was in no rush to make the change, and things dragged on until Klutznik threatened to withdraw his candidacy; he had no wish to remain forever a candidate for an office that did not look as though it would ever be vacated. He finally did make the presidency, but, unlike Goldmann, he understands the limitations of the organization he leads and rarely trumpets his opinions in the news and public relations media.

I tried to fulfill, to the best of my ability, my duties as head of the Zionist movement and the Jewish Agency. I had hoped that after the Twenty-ninth Zionist Congress I would be able to develop further the changes, projects, and policies I had initiated since taking office. I assumed that after the congress I would have four good years in which to bring my work to fruition. However, the congress was postponed until the end of February 1978, and before it met, Labor suffered a political reversal in Israel and lost seats in the Knesset, and in the Zionist Congress. It became a minority and had to bear the consequences of its defeat. I feel certain that had we not suffered electoral defeat, I would be at work now, trying to bring about the changes in the Zionist movement made necessary by our situation here at home and in the Diaspora.

I will not burden the reader with a detailed account of the changes I believe must be made if the movement is to be prodded out of its long sleep and freed from its demeaning dependence on the money of the Jewish Agency.

Much as I attach importance to organizational changes in the Zionist movement, I am aware that they alone cannot restore its vigor. For all the work done by the program committee chaired by Shlomo Derech, which after about two years of labor issued a comprehensive statement, neither the program it proposed nor the recommendations it made contain the least hope of getting the Zionist Congress moving or of rekindling its enthusiasm. The old debate over the commitment to *aliyah* and over the distinction between a Zionist and a supporter of Israel highlights the two main problems to be concentrated on. Unfortunately, we are still far from resolving them. Only when we do can we hope to breath new life into the Zionist movement.

There is a paradox in the fact that the closer Israel's friends approach the traditional concept of Zionism in their thinking, the more serious becomes the problem of the survival of the World Zionist Organization. The attitudes and activities of non-Zionists differ in no essential way from those recommended in the current Zionist program, which does no more than recognize the centrality of Israel in Jewish life. However, the Jewish Agency does more than simply recognize Israel's centrality in Jewish life: it is concerned with the problems of Jewish education in the Diaspora; it supports *aliyah* and seeks ways to resolve its problems; and it is filled with love for Israel and wholly devoted to its well-being.

The next Congress, the thirtieth should devote its time and thought to finding ways of committing Zionists to Zionism. It must plan fundamental reforms in the Zionism movement and in the Jewish Agency. It may well be that the time has come to carry out Ben-Gurion's basic idea—to merge the World Zionist Organization and the Jewish Agency into one and create a world Jewish organization on behalf of Israel whose members are committed to Zionist fulfillment and *aliyah*.

Epilogue

When I returned to Haifa in the summer of 1978, I was faced with an unexpected situation. For fifty years I had had more proposals for jobs than I could hope to take on, and more demands made on me than I could hope to fill. My problem had been finding hours to add to the day, days to add to the week, weeks to the month. Suddenly, I had all the time in the world, and I had to decide whether leisure was a curse or a blessing.

I took the optimistic view. My time was now entirely at my disposal, to do with as I pleased. It occurred to me to put the record of my fifty years of activity in Israel in writing, in three volumes. The first would be the story of my deeds. The second and third volumes would have to do with my thoughts and would include my speeches and articles. From time to time I publish articles, mainly in *Davar* and *Yedioth Ahronot,* and the editorial board of *Kol Haifa* ("Voice of Haifa") has been kind enough to offer me a permanent weekly column.

These activities take up a good deal of my time, but not all of it. I have enough time left to become familiar once more with a world whose existence I had forgotten and of which for many years I had caught only glimpses through the windows of a car. As for people, I saw them mostly in enclosed spaces, in offices and meeting halls. I now began to meet friends, neighbors, and just plain Haifaites in the street, on buses, sometimes even over a cup of coffee in a café.

I had stood godfather to hundreds of baby boys, taken part in family celebrations of friends and Haifa residents, and received thousands of letters filled with praises for my virtues. But I had always felt that these had come to me not because of any feeling for me personally, but because of my political status. Not a few of my "friends" were of the kind who cultivated me for the power I had to give or withhold favors. Now that everybody knows I have no political property to give away, I can permit myself to consider any show of friendship sincere. My personal life has become richer for that.

My colleagues and friends are waiting for me to finish writing and expect me to return to public life. I have yet to decide what turn my activities will take. So long as I continue to enjoy good health, I will go on planning projects, and I hope to be active for many years to come. Politics is only one of many possibilities

I have been asked whether, if I could choose to live my life over again, I would choose the same path. In the main, I would. I certainly would choose again to follow the path of socialist Zionism. Although in the course of a political career spanning five decades I made many errors, I do not think they were serious errors.

Have I had disappointments? I have and still do. My chief disappointment, and a bitter one it is, has to do with the failure of reality to match the vision we had of what kind of society we hoped to build. Fifty-two years ago, when I first arrived in Israel, I had no expectation of living to see the society I had come to build. All I hoped for was to be one of those who laid the foundations for a Jewish state, whose actual creation would be accomplished by my children or my grandchildren. Seen from this perspective, reality has overreached our wildest fantasies. But our conviction, our certainty, that we would be a "light unto the nations," a people whose moral character would be a model to the world, has yet to be vindicated.

None of us had dared hope that peace between ourselves and Egypt would come in our lifetime. If we believed that survival depended on maintaining and raising our moral level so that we could counter the quantity that our enemy could field against us, how much more important is it how now for us to look to our quality! In times of peace, moral and cultural values are the prerequisites for a people's preserving itself and preserving the peace.

Saturday night is when our sons, their wives, and our grandchildren visit. The children have the run of the house; the rest prefer to browse among the books. When the company leaves, and my wife and I are left to ourselves again, I allow myself to muse over my good fortune. In the public sphere, I lived to see the achievement of what I sought to build, and I had a share in building it in the company of the mighty. Privately, we have our joy in our progeny, our second and third generations.

I permit myself to indulge in imagining a time, perhaps a century or two hence, when my sons' sons will want to trace their roots, planted in the soil of Israel by a young couple from Poland and grown into a great and fruitful tree. I see them reaching for this book, here to read the story of an end to the wandering of the Jewish people, and the beginning of its renewal in its ancestral homeland.

Appendix: Missions Abroad

The Jewish National Fund

Throughout the fifty years of my involvement in the public life of Israel, I have never lost touch or interrupted my contact with my brethren abroad. I have been among the very few who felt no sentimental attachment to the scenes of their childhood, nor the least desire to visit the countries or towns of their birth. I did not love them and had no emotional ties with them

But to the Jewish people I am, and always have been, tied by bonds of love. It had been my fate to be in Nazi Germany and meet Jews, under death's shadow, from the extermination camps, but I have also met Jewish communities elsewhere in happier times. From the time of my return from my internment as a prisoner of war in Germany, I have been sent on countless missions to all the countries in the Free World in which Jews live, and I have witnessed firsthand the changes Jews have exprienced in their circumstances everywhere in the Diaspora. We Jews in Israel regard ourselves as emissaries in behalf of the whole Jewish people. Our lives in Israel are dedicated to building and securing a Jewish country for Jews who want to live as a free people in their own homeland; we are dedicated also to saving those Jews who face the threat of physical or cultural annihilation.

I was sent out among the Jews in the free countries of the world to advocate among them Zionist and pioneering values, and urge them to preserve their Jewish culture. Not a few of the institutions serving the people of Israel have been helped financially by the Jews of the world through the special funds maintained in Jewish communities abroad—institutions such as Hadassah, ORT, the universities, Magen David Adom, and the Soldiers' Welfare Committee. My own activities among Jewish communities abroad were on the behalf of the major funds for Israel: the Histadrut Campaign, the Jewish National Fund, the United Israel Appeal, the United Jewish Appeal, and the Independence Loan. My first such mission was in 1946, when I traveled on behalf of the Jewish National Fund.

Before the Jewish people's dispersal, they lived in a prosperous land flowing with milk and honey, but when they returned to their homeland, they found a desolate landscape filled with rock, sand, deserts, and malarial swamps. Foreign conquerors and occupiers had despoiled it. The Jews who returned to it in the modern period came not as conquerors, but as redeemers. One of the instruments of their redemption of the Land of Israel was the Zionist Organization's land and development fund called the Jewish National Fund (JNF), founded in 1901. The aim of the fund was to finance land purchase, forestation, swamp drainage, and the turning of arid deserts into fertile fields.

The land in Israel is owned in perpetuity by the whole Jewish people, not by Israeli citizens. The land is leased for settlement, to be lived on and farmed, for periods of forty-nine years at an annual rental fixed by the land management authority. In the 1960s the government of Israel transferred all public and government land to the Jewish National Fund to be cared for and developed. In the same period a joint authority, shared in by the government and the fund, was established for administering and developing all public lands—the *Minhal Karkaei Israel* (the "Israel Land Development Administration"), which has under its jurisdiction more than ninety percent of the land in the country.

Since the establishment of the State of Israel, the Jewish National Fund has reclaimed one million dunams of land and has thus made possible the establishment of some eight hundred agricultural settlements, from the Galilee in the North, where the problem is clearing boulders and huge quantities of stones from the land, to the Negev and Arava in the South, where the problem is leveling and stabilizing sand dunes.

The Jewish National Fund is the sole organization for forestation in Israel and has planted 150 million trees over an area of one million dunams. Through its policy of opening up the forests to the general public, the JNF has established hundreds of picnic and recreation areas as well as parks and summer camps for children.

A major JNF program is the development of an educational program for young people. Abroad, it works mainly within the framework of the Jewish schools to strengthen the ties between the children and Israel. In Israel, the emphasis is on the ties of the children with nature. The JNF network of summer camps enables children from Israel and abroad to meet and develop their shared ties to the Land of Israel.

The JNF is probably the most Zionist, educational, and popular of all movements that have arisen among the Jewish people. Contributions to the fund, collected in blue boxes in Jewish homes, institutions, and places of worship throughout the world, have become part of the national folklore. The registration of the name of a donor in the Golden Book of the JNF not only has educational value, but cultivates a feeling of personal involvement in developing the national homeland. Donations come to JNF not only in the form of contributions, but in bequests and legacies from all over the world.

The fund is headed by an international board of directors, whose present head is Moshe Rivlin. His predecessor, Yaacov Zur, retired in 1975. The president of the JNF in the United States is Mrs. Charlotte Jacobson.

Between 1947 and 1977 I was sent with great frequency, sometimes as often as twice a year, on missions to Jewish communities throughout South America. In Argentina, Brazil, and Uruguay I found, in addition to the large community of Sephardic Jews, a dynamic community of more recently arrived Jews of East European origin. In the beginning, when the Jews of Eastern Europe first arrived there, the two communities kept apart; in recent years, they have drawn closer together.

The only official recognition the Jewish community in Argentina enjoyed from government authorities was as a corporation for the purposes of burial. For this reason it had itself registered officially as the *Hevrah Kadisha,* or Jewish Burial Society, funded by the state budget set aside for cemeteries.

I visited the settlements of IKO *(Yiddishe Kolonizatorishe Organizatsie* or "Jewish Colonizing Organization"), founded on land purchased by Baron Maurice De Hirsch for the purpose of establishing agricultural communities in Argentina for European Jews. We Zionists knew that Jews could not be made a nation of workers and farmers anywhere but in Eretz Israel. When I first visited, I observed that the Jewish settlers were beginning to hire Gentile hands to do their work and were sending their children to the university rather than have them work the land. It didn't take long for the Jewish farmer to disappear and be replaced by the Jewish doctor, the Jewish lawyer, and the Jewish merchant. The younger generation is already experiencing difficulty in speaking Yiddish, and Yiddish culture is dying.

To this day, Jews in the Diaspora are struggling to provide their children with a Jewish education. But Jewish private schooling is very expensive, and not everyone can afford it. Years ago Jewish schools were qualitatively better than state-run schools, so that the added costs of sending one's children to Jewish institutions of education was worthwhile. Now, however, there is no difference in the educational levels of Jewish and state schools, save the price. These schools have now become a heavy financial burden on the ever-diminishing budgets of the Jewish communities.

Immigration from South America to Israel is slow in coming. Love for Israel among South American Jews is strong, but actually to come and settle requires great motivation based on strongly developed Zionist values—something which was never characteristic of the great mass of Jews, and even today is characteristic only of the few. Then, too, the standard of living of Jews in these countries is quite high. Such a living standard could not possibly be achieved by them in Israel.

Most South American Jews belong to the middle class. Immigration to Israel is easiest for those who are either very poor or very rich—a minority of the community. The majority, belonging to the middle income levels, stay put, and our hope is that the children of these middle-class families who come to Israel will draw their families after them.

Developments over the past thirty years have made Yiddish culture no longer the basis of communication in the Jewish communities of South America. At one time I could be confident that if I spoke to South Aemerican Jewish audiences in Yiddish I would be understood. This is no longer true. Sephardic Jews have drawn closer to Jews of Eastern European origin and are beginning to show signs of greater Jewish and Zionist activism. The Ashkenazim, for their part, have stopped learning Yiddish and have taken up English and Hebrew, instead. A new generation has grown up, active in the free professions and academic disciplines, and they represent a growing source of recruits to Zionist action and pioneering.

The Histadrut Campaign

In 1952 I was sent by the Israel General Federation of Labor, on behalf of the Histadrut Campaign, to the United States and Canada. The campaign was established in the United States in 1923 to asist the Histadrut in its work in the fields of education, construction, and mutual aid in Israel and to help it develop and maintain ties with labor unions in the United States and Canada. Already at the beginning of World War I, when David Ben-Gurion and Yitzhak Ben-Zvi were in the United States after having been exiled from Eretz Israel by the Turkish authorities, an effort had been made to solicit support for Israeli labor.

American Jews were very active in the creation of labor unions and in the struggle against the sweatshops. Yiddish was the spoken and written language among Jewish labor activists. The political conflicts within the Jewish community were between the anti-Zionist Bund and Poalei Zion, which sought a synthesis between Zionism and socialism. Among the enthusiastic supporters in American of the Labor movement in Eretz Israel were Joseph Shlossberg, secretary of the Carpenters' Union; Max Pine, head of the United Hebrew Trades in America, and important figures in the Poalei Zion movement.

The man at the head of the Histadrut Campaign in 1924 was Isaac Hamlin, a young and energetic workingman with extraordinary vision; under his leadership the Histadrut Campaign thrived and was able to secure financial assistance for Israel in every possible area of activity.

In Israel, it is hard to find a single leader of the labor movement who has not at one time or other been sent with delegations on behalf of the Histadrut Campaign to the United States. When I went I had the good fortune to be able to meet Joseph Shlossberg, who was then already ninety years old but still appeared daily in the offices of the Histadrut Campaign on East 67th Street and continued to take part in rallies and conferences. It was a pleasure to watch the late Yitzhak Hamlin energetically and resourcefully at work, as well as those still with us— Israel Stolarsky, Israel Feigenbaum, Dov Bigun, and the young Nahum Guttman. Other younger men who held important positions were Irving Kessler, now head of the United Israel Appeal, and Bernard Jacobson, now the very able and devoted general director of the Histadrut Campaign. At the time some well-known labor leaders were still active, among them David Dubinsky, Jacob Potofsky, Charles Zimmerman, and Meyer Miller.

During my three-month stay in North America I visited dozens of towns and cities from Los Angeles, California, to Winnipeg in Canada. I met many ordinary Jews, some of whom were already leaving manual work for trade. There were those among them who were in the process of becoming wealthy, but they all retained a nostalgia for socialism.

I was always impressed by the desire of American Jews to see Israel as not simply a country like any other, but one which was better and ethically more advanced—an attitude dramatized by Hamlin, who would always refer to Israel as a country of "social justice." Hamlin put his Zionist convictions into practice and settled in Israel, where a cultural centre has been built in his memory. Stolarsky, too, immigrated to Israel, and continues to work for the movement.

Up to the 1960s, I regularly visited the United States on behalf of the Histadrut and met the permanent representatives of the Histadrut in the United States, all of them excellent people: There was the remarkable Yosef Burstein, who was active in the Histadrut's cultural department; Ze'ev Barash; M. Bar-Tal; and my good friend Isaiah Avrech. The post is now held by Meir Gatt. Solomon Stein, an exceptionally gifted person, joined the Histadrut leadership. He established— and continues to administer—the important Legacy Fund, which has achieved impressive successes.

During my visits I participated in activities of the Farband and Poalei Zion, and formed a high opinion of their leaders, Louis Segal and Samuel Bonchek. I also took part in the activities of the Pioneer Women, one of the largest and most important Zionist labor organizations.

The State of Israel Bonds Campaign

In May 1951 the first prime minister of the State of Israel, David Ben-Gurion, announced at Madison Square Garden in New York the start of a development loan for Israel.

At that time, three years after independence, the economic situation in Israel could fairly be described as catastrophic. We lacked everything: housing, jobs, food, clothing. One hundred thousand destitute immigrants were living in tents. The financial aid we received from various organizations was insufficient to cover even a small part of the overwhelming needs of the new state. Immigration continued to flow into Israel and doubled the population, among whom the older settlers, too, were not well off. We began looking for new financial assistance, particularly investment in development and in the creation of jobs. The idea of adding a new channel of financial support for Israel outside the fund-raising campaigns was strongly resisted, especially by the United Jewish Appeal in Israel. Once the decision was taken, however, and the enterprise got under-way in 1951, the State of Israel Bonds Campaign was joined by an impressive team, including Henry Morgenthau, Henry Montor, Rudolf G. Sonneborn, and Sam Rothberg, who continues his good work to this day.

The undertaking succeeded beyond all expectations. In its first year alone, the total value of the bonds sold was more than $52 million. Annual sales of bonds gradually increased so that in 1967, the year of the Six-Day War, the total value of bonds sold reached more than $217 million. In 1973, the year of the Yom Kippur War, sales reached $502 million. The total sale of bonds from 1951 to 1980 has been more than $5.2 billion.

My primary activity in the United States, after the Histadrut Campaign, was for the Israel Bonds Independence Issue. I preferred appearing before audiences buying bonds than before those donating money. I especially enjoyed being able to give a balanced account of Israel's schievements and problems. I am of course aware that both forms of assistance are necessary. Still, I felt more comfortable explaining the economic and development needs of Israel. The response of the investors and the economic and social undertakings that resulted from their purchase of bonds gave me great pleasure. My success in the posts of minister of development and minister of housing had, in some degree, to do with the success of Israel Bonds.

The central administration of Israel Bonds established district and branch offices throughout North America and then in a great many other places throughout the free world. It also succeeded in drawing into its ranks people with excellent organizational skills, some of whom had never before been involved in any sort of work in Israel's behalf.

The campaign for the Independence Issue enlisted many new supporters and friends of Israel. In critical periods in Israel's existence, those of the Six-Day War and the Yom Kippur War, Israel received from the United Jewish Appeal and the Israel Bond drive about equal amounts—more than three times what it received on the average in any single year.

I found particularly exciting the appearances I made before non-Jewish groups, especially the labor unions, which purchased Israel Bonds with money from union funds. There were many cases, as well, of non-Jews purchasing bonds. An idea of the extensive activities of Israel Bonds emerges from looking at the kinds of enterprises that have purchased them: pension funds (9,500), banks (3,500), labor unions (1,500), and insurance firms (500).

In my meetings with labor union representatives, who included dozens of labor leaders we hosted at luncheons, I would speak about Israel and, particularly, about the Histadrut. I would compare Israel Bonds to a coin, one of whose sides represented the obligation of solidarity, the other good business and sound investment.

I also participated in official dinners given for labor leaders. Israel Bonds had a special department for work among labor unions in the United States; this department would send delegations of American labor unions to Israel. As minister of labor I was officially responsible for inviting the labor union representatives and for acting as host for the government. These tours had political importance as well.

Israel Bonds is a monumental undertaking which has made inestimable contributions to the development of Israel, and its leaders deserve our highest esteem. Sam Rothberg, who dedicates the whole of his time to this extraordinary enterprise, is permeated utterly by love of Israel and has done unforgettable service for the country.

United Jewish Appeal

Up until the early 1970s, I was active in behalf of all the fund drives for Israel except the United Jewish Appeal in America, which is the largest organization of its kind anywhere in the Diaspora. Money is collected in hundreds of Jewish communities and Jewish federations every year, and after a portion is distributed among local institutions, the remainder is handed over to UJA central headquarters. There the money is divided and set aside primarily for the Joint Distribution Committee (ORT, HIAS-Hebrew Immigrant Aid Society) and the UIA; the money given to the UIA is allocated to the Jewish Agency. The Jewish Agency then reapportions its allotment among various departments in Israel: land settlement, immigration and absorption, youth immigration, housing, education and higher education, social aid, and neighborhood rehabilitation.

In 1970, the Jewish Agency and the government of Israel decided to send delegations made up of one representative of the government and a senior officer in the Israel Defense Force who, together with a local UJA activist, would visit all of the Jewish communities in the United States to urge Jews to increase their contributions to Israel, even at the expense of local needs, if unavoidable. The chairman of the UJA at the time was Paul Zuckerman, and the general director was Rabbi Herbert Friedman.

During my many tours for the UJA campaigns, I often encountered problems arising from a conflict of interest: some community leaders were demanding that a larger allocation go for the needs of their communities at Israel's expense; others fought for the opposite course. There were some contributors to the UJA who specified just how much of the money they donated was to be set aside for Israel and how much for local needs.

The heads of Jewish communities also argued that in the absence of Jewish education, synagogues, and community centers, the Jewish people in the United States would lose their identity, and in such a case Israel could only be the loser. It was, therefore, necessary to be concerned, perhaps even primarily, with the needs of Jewish communities in the Diaspora. Some community leaders tended to view Israel as the center of the Jewish experience. I do not believe that the relation of Jews in the Diaspora to Israel is given expression only through their contributions to Israeli causes, but there is no doubt that these contributions are important indicators of their sense of affiliation with the Jewish people and the state.

The curve of Jewish contributions to Israel can be divided into three main periods: first, before the establishment of the state; second, from 1948 to 1967, the year of the Six-Day War; third, since the Six-Day War. From 1920 until 1947, the Jewish people contributed a total of $143 million; from 1948 until 1966, $265 million was contributed; and from 1967 to 1976—only nine years—$1,459 million was contributed. Other funds show a similar growth pattern. The period of the Six-Day War transformed the Jewish people, both in Israel and in the Diaspora.

At the beginning of 1967 all the military experts were agreed that it would take many years before our neighbors would venture to attack us. The prediction proved false. Quite suddenly we were confronted by the greatest danger we had faced since the War of Independence. Our enemies in the neighboring Arab countries were wildly enthusiastic for war. Their radio stations poured out torrents of threatening broadcasts proclaiming our imminent destruction. Nasser's and his army commanders' confidence and the wild popular demonstrations in all the Arab cities awakened memories of what had happened to the Jews of Europe less than a generation earlier. Memories of the recent Eichmann trial were still fresh in the minds of Israeli Jews. Schoolchildren in Israel were taught what had happened to the Jewish people in World War II, and there were plenty of adults who were reminded of the horrors they had experienced.

It is difficult to describe the atmosphere in Israel at the time: tension among the people was like a tightly coiled spring. They were ready for war to break out any moment; and some even wanted it. When war did break out, there was a total blackout on all news. All we heard were the Arab broadcasts proclaiming impressive victories. The hearts of Jews abroad beat in unison with those of their brethren in Israel, and Jews in the Diaspora began actually to experience in a very direct way the crisis being faced by Israel. The depth of feeling among Jewish people for Israel came as a surprise to everyone. Diaspora Jews themselves had not realized the strength of their ties to Israel.

Many thousands came as volunteers, and thousands more gave freely of their money. Among the contributors were many who had long before broken their ties with Judaism, and some who had even changed their faith and converted. This was the time when Jews renewed their ties with their homeland. When news of the extraordinary victory of the Israel Defense Force was published, the pride of all Jews was limitless. In every Jewish community I visited at the time I was told of the rise in Jewish self-esteem and in the respect Jews had won from their Gentile neighbors. This metamorphosis was particularly strong among the younger generation of Jews.

The war and its aftermath had an effect on the size of contributions to Israel— a fact which is clearly reflected by the statistics. Between the Six-Day War and the Yom Kippur War there was no sharp falling off in contributions, this despite the demands of some Jewish communities for an increase in funds for local community needs.

In all my public appearances, I never skirted the issue of the priority that must be given to settlement in Israel over contributions to fund-raising campaigns. I represented the state abroad in the 1950s, at a time when Jewish community leaders couldn't bear even hearing the mention of the word *aliyah*. But I also had the experience of individual Jews coming to me and boasting of the fact that their children or relations had come to Israel to settle; many would even say, not without pride, that they were about to buy an apartment in Israel and that one day they, too, would come to live in Israel.

A recent development is the claim that a certain apathy has developed among contributors. At the same time there are those in Israel who question the value of the campaign itself, since it produces only about 2 percent of Israel's gross national product.

I disagree with both of these views: the UJA campaign is not a substitute for Zionist and Jewish activity, but an ingredient of such activity. Nor do I think that there is any weakening or apathy on the part of the general public.

Keren Hayesod

Over a period of twenty years, I visited all of the countries in the Free World on missions for the Keren Hayesod (Foundation Fund). The KH was established in 1920 as a fund-raising instrument for the Zionist movement and the Jewish Agency to establish as laid down in the Balfour Declaration a national homeland for the Jewish people. When the Jewish Agency was established on a wider basis in 1929, the KH was made the chief financial instrument for the supply of its budget.

In 1956 the Knesset approved the Keren Hayesod Law, forming United Israel Company, Ltd., with a thirty-two-member board of directors, of whom eight are appointed by the Zionist Executive. They, in turn, select a board chairman from among themselves. Before the establishment of the State of Israel, the KH was responsible for collecting money to finance immigration activities, including the operations in which immigrants were smuggled past the British blockade after World War II. It also helped finance education, settlement, and arms purchases. After the establishment of the state, the KH helped in immigrant absorption, helping to provide housing, education, and social assistance to needy immigrants.

On some of my visits, I had the opportunity to participate in the opening of fund drives together with Dr. Israel Goldstein. I learned to appreciate his personal qualities, and I came to know him as one of the "beautiful Zionists" of the world movement.

During the Six-Day War, an emergency fund-raising headquarters was established in Israel, headed by Dr. Goldstein. The coordinator between the headquarters and the KH was the latter's general director, Shai Kreutner. Similar emergency headquarters were established in all countries having Jewish communities. In Australia, for example, Isidore Maggid, Max Freilich, Louis Klein, and Henry Krongold were very active. Maggid, a man totally committed to the affairs of Israel, is also a member of the Administrative Council of the Jewish Agency.

In Great Britain, participants were H. Morrison, Michael Sachar, and Trevor Chinn. It is interesting to note that Sachar and Chinn continue the traditions begun by their fathers: Michael is the son of the late Harry Sachar, who was a member of the Jewish Agency's executive when times were hard; Trevor's father was, and is, active in behalf of the JNF.

In my missions on behalf of the KH, I met a great many warm and loyal Jews. In Belgium, I met Leo Meirdorf and Mme. Halp, an exceptional woman who has worked tirelessly and indefatigably for the good of Zionism and the State of Israel; and in Canada, Phil Grenovsky, a member of the executive of the Jewish Agency and the head of board of governors of the KH. Phil's slight build would hardly lead one to suspect his enormous drive when it comes to matters concerning Israel.

During my visits to South Africa, I had the opportunity to observe firsthand the marvelous Jewish community there. It is a self-supporting community, maintaining an active Jewish existence. I developed a high respect for Judge Meizeis, a thoughtful and intelligent man, and for Julius Weinstein, who is a frequent visitor to Israel and who bears on his shoulders the whole burden of Zionist activity in South Africa.

At the beginning of 1978, there were personnel changes in the Zionist executive, in the wake of Labor's reversal in the Knesset elections. Party representation in the Zionist Congress is directly linked to the results of Knesset elections, since each party receives in the Congress double the number of seats it has in the Knesset. After the Knesset election, Avraham Avihai was elected chairman of the KH, the youngest chairman in its history, if I am not mistaken. Dr. Avihai immigrated to Israel from Canada and once served as advisor on Jewish affairs to Levi Eshkol. Because of his wide experience in the field, I would seek his advice on both the content and style of my fund-raising speeches abroad. He was very helpful to me.

During the same period the general director, Shai Kreutner, retired and was replaced by Yaacov Gilad, who had made a good name for himself in his work for the KH in France and the British Isles.

Another detail deserving mention is the amount contributed to the KH. During the period 1978–79, more than $100 million was raised; for 1979–80, the sum was $120 million.

Encounters

In my activities in the party, the Knesset, and the government, I had frequent occasion to meet persons who held important posts in the countries of the Free World. When I was still secretary of the Haifa Labor Council, I was given the task of playing host to two delegations whose reception was considered problematic. In the beginning of the 1950s, the first British delegation to Israel since the War of Independence arrived. Resentment against the British was still very strong, even against the British Labor party. We were afraid that there might be unpleasant incidents if the delegation were to encounter the Israeli public, but we managed to avoid any unpleasantness. I was able to keep up the friendly relations I had developed with personalities in England during my trip there, where I was helped by my friend Schneier Levenberg, a representative of the Jewish Agency in Great Britain and an important figure in the Zionist Labor movement there. On more than one occasion, I turned to him for his intelligent guidance.

Yugoslavia was at that time isolated in the Communist world and treated with suspicion even by the parties of the Left in the Free World. There were even those in Israel who took a dim view of our relations with Yugoslavia, which "rejected the enlightened socialism of Stalin." Needless to say, despite the great success with which we managed to welcome the Yugoslav delegation then, Yugoslavia is not among our friends today.

I had very strong ties with the labor unions in the United States. I met the late George Meany often and got to know him very well. Meany was an honest and courageous man, loyal to the workingman and an unswerving friend of Israel. He was also very strongly anticommunist, as was Lane Kirkland, head of the unions' political department.

I remember the time George Meany invited me, when I was minister of labor, to deliver the opening address at the big AFL-CIO convention in Miami in 1971. My speech was scheduled for 11:00 A.M. Two days before they convened, President Richard Nixon told Meany that he wanted to make his welcoming speech to the convention on the same day, at exactly the same time. I was, of course, ready to make way for the president, but Meany wouldn't have it: he told Nixon that the spot was reserved, and the president would have to appear after me.

I greatly enjoyed the marvelous reception I was accorded and listened proudly to Meany's warm words about Israel and its government.

I took special pleasure in talking with Lane Kirkland, who was union treasurer and was highly favored by the leadership of the AFL-CIO. Kirkland impressed me as a cultured man, well versed in issues that went far beyond purely labor union matters.

In 1972 I was asked to speak at a dinner arranged in honor of Kirkland, an invitation which I was happy to accept despite the technical problems involved in my appearance. In November 1979, Kirkland succeeded Meany as president of AFL-CIO. The strongest ties that exist between the State of Israel and any world organization are those it has with labor union movement in the United States.

In 1972, as minister of labor, I prepared the National Health Insurance Law in Israel, and the same year Senator Edward Kennedy paid me a visit. He was then chairman of the Senate Subcommittee on Health, and he came to discuss health service delivery problems with me. I was impressed by the senator's personality, and his sincere desire to find a solution for the problems of the public health services in the United States.

Index